Culinary Expressions

Chicken and Seafood Entrees
that take 20 minutes to bake.

by
Normand J. Leclair

Dome Publishing Co. Inc.

Cover Photography by
Ron Manville

Many illustrations by
Elizabeth Donovan

Library of Congress Cataloging-in-Publication Data
Leclair, Normand
Culinary Expressions
ISBN 1-880603-05-5

Published by
DOME PUBLISHING CO., INC.
Dome Building, Warwick, RI 02886

To
Alice Lussier Doak
Aunt, Friend and
Mentor

Always there for me

==========================ACKNOWLEDGEMENTS

The greatest joy of writing this cookbook is the memory of the 50-some years I worked in a restaurant kitchen. The customers, staff and friends I would like to thank for being part of my culinary world would cover all the pages in this cookbook. For very cookbook sold, twenty-five cents will be donated to the **Rhode Island Food Bank.**

THANK YOU

This cookbook, along with the frustrations and exhilarations of putting it together, has become a reality because of the help and support of many friends and colleagues. I wish to especially thank Donald Arel, Nancy Barr, Linda Beaulieu, Joseph Creedon, Elizabeth Cummiskey, Terry Desmarais, Elizabeth P. Donovan, Dome Publishing, Michael Dupre, Ruthe Eshleman, Gail Gregory, Rudi Hempe, Lois James, David Joachim, Rexford A. Kirkman, Peter Marx, Jeanette Rodrigues, Tom Sylvia, and Christopher D Czepyha
Special thanks to editor Pat LeVasseur
Cover Photography by Ron Manville

WORDS
Eating is one of the great pleasures of life, and for many, cooking is another. To enjoy the great satisfaction of cooking a great meal is beyond words.

Cooking can be creative and wild or soothing and mild. The kitchen is the heart of the home, it is a refuge, laboratory, artist studio, and gathering place for friends and family.

I hope this cookbook helps you make your cooking as good as it can be. Cooking is like choosing clothes to wear: you dress for yourself "first" then for others. You cook for yourself and then for your family and guests. You must please yourself before you can please anyone else.

"To dine is to enjoy many small experiences."

Normand J. Leclair

Other books by Normand J. Leclair
Chicken Expressions
Seafood Expressions

In the Spring of 1999, I attended the International Association of Culinary Professionals' annual conference in Phoenix. The conference was just great for me. I had never been to the Southwest, and I found the area quite amazing. I did some traveling in the area, visiting Flagstaff, Sedona, Hoover Dam and Las Vegas.

One evening during the conference, I was having dinner with David Joachim, a cookbook editor. I was reminiscing about my 45 years in the restaurant industry, the funny stories, great recipes, learning experiences. I talked about writing and self-publishing two cookbooks: *Chicken Expressions* and *Seafood Expressions.* As we enjoyed our wine and dinner, he suggested that I write another cookbook and include the little stories that everyone can tell if they own a restaurant or even work in one. When I returned home, I started thinking about my years in the restaurant business, and I began to write this book.

I started the cookbook with a biographical sketch, "An awareness of food." The piece begins when I was a child and explains how the changes in my life brought about an awareness of food that led to cooking in my own restaurant and traveling in search of new ideas for my restaurant menu.

In this cookbook, my goal is to set forth recipes that you can use for special occasions and for everyday dinners. I have also included many little stories about daily life in the restaurant industry.

I was in Montreal once for a visit. Traffic was in a mess, with construction everywhere. The taxi driver commented, "The road to success is always under construction."

That comment has stayed with me. I thought many times. "The road to culinary knowledge is always under construction, we can never learn enough." I hope some of these recipes will give you a little more knowledge for that ultimate goal: preparing a great meal for family, friends and mostly yourself.

This cookbook is a collection of many recipes that are designed to make home cooking interesting. I hope you enjoy these recipes and stories.

> *"We may live without poetry, music, and art;*
> *We may live without conscience and live without heart;*
> *We may live without friends; we may live without books;*
> *But civilized man cannot live without cooks."*
> *Owen Meredith*

===*FOOD CHAPTERS*

AN AWARENESS IN FOOD

I was born in Rhode Island in 1936 in a small mill town called Crompton. The mills were built next to large rivers in order to use the waterpower to run the looms. We lived in a mill house near the textile mill that had no hot water, no bathroom and no central heating. I remember the chamber pots under the bed when it was too cold to go outside to the little building with the crescent moon.

My maternal grandmother lived with us, and she had dietary restrictions. My mother cooked for her and for us, and thus we always had a variety of foods on the table.

When I was seven, my mother became ill and died, and this completely changed my life in so many ways. I became even more aware of food, because my father worked and we had relatives and neighbors who took care of us. Every day, my four-year-old sister, Terry, and I went to a different aunt or neighbor for dinner.

Eventually, my father remarried and we settled with a stepmother into her home (which had central heating, a bathroom and hot, running water). She had two children, Sylvia, 4, and Paul, 2. Her style of cooking was completely different from my mother's, so we had to adjust again to unfamiliar flavors. It's incredible how resilient children can be.

As time went on, we adjusted to our new home and family, and a new baby sister arrived who was named Lorraine. At that time in my life, I never dreamed that someday I would open a restaurant and have my sisters Terry and Lorraine come to work for me.

When I was twelve, I started working on a paper route, and around that time, cooking really started to interest me, especially baking. I was always baking pies and cakes, and I started selling them around the neighborhood. I also started making the Sunday dinner meal for my family; we always had a one-pan roast that included potatoes and carrots.

My first real job when I was 16 was at the Blinker Restaurant, a truck stop on Route 3 in West Warwick. I washed dishes six nights a week, and gradually I started learning to cook. Working in a restaurant gave me the opportunity to see and enjoy many different kinds of food than we had at home. I started to get hooked on food!

Cooking at the Blinker was indeed a challenge, particularly because the restaurant had a stove that used charcoal for fuel. We put steaks, chops, swordfish and burgers on racks that were placed sideways near the fire and gave the food a nice smoky flavor. The charcoal fire was in the middle of the stove, underneath a grate.

Cooking over this fire presented various problems, because the heat was always uneven. The charcoal heated up a flat grill for cooking eggs and toasting rolls, but sometimes it was red hot and sometimes, when the charcoal had burned way down, it was too cool. I almost had to be an engineer to cook on this stove.

When I graduated from high school, I took the morning shift at the Blinker, arriving at 5 a.m. to bake the muffins, start the charcoal fire and get ready to cook breakfast. The restaurant was located between Boston and New York, and we served many truck drivers, whose appetites staggered the imagination. This definitely taught me how to be a high-production cook.

The Warwick Musical Theater opened around the corner, and theater people were always concerned about their health, their diet and staying in shape. Since most of the actors and crew wanted lighter and healthier foods, we began to serve more salads. Our clientele of truckers, locals and theater people certainly made for an interesting time at the restaurant.

I worked at the Blinker for five years and then moved to a restaurant called Young's Steak House, cooking on the same kind of charcoal stove as the Blinker's. I cooked there for two years until I was drafted into the Army. When I went into the Army, John, the proprietor of Young's, promised to help me find a restaurant when I completed my military service.

Two years later, I purchased my first restaurant, named the Chick-n-Pick Restaurant. John was from the South, and he thought a fried chicken restaurant would work up North. And it turned out that it did.

The restaurant was located next to Quonset Point, a large Naval facility, so for the first five years of the Chick-n-Pick, we catered to Navy personnel and their families. When we were given an award as the best tourist restaurant on Post Road, all the locals started to come to us. Between breakfast, lunch, dinner, late meals and sandwiches, we served 1,000 people a day.

We cooked wonderful things like Virginia hams, using the whole hams with the bone, roasting them slowly, letting them cool to room temperature and placing them on a wire holder, ready to slice to order. We sold many hams, and with all the ham scraps, we made an outrageously good pea soup. My sister

Lorraine and Aunt Alice worked days and my sister Terry worked nights. Food was food. We never had to think of cooking in a healthy way.
We used beef fat for deep-frying; we used lots of butter; our steaks and hamburgers were fried. And our specialties were fried chicken and fish and chips. On a Friday night, we might cook over 300 pounds of fish. I worked seven days a week for those first five years, and then I closed the restaurant for one day a week.

It's funny how one event can change your life. I lived in Coventry, 45 minutes away from the restaurant, but I wanted to live closer. One morning, I was on the way to the bank to drop off a deposit, when lo and behold, I saw a for-sale sign on a house across the street from my restaurant! On a hunch, I pulled into the driveway, knocked on the door and asked the lady who answered how much she wanted for the house. The price sounded reasonable, so I gave her the money from my bank deposit as a retainer.

The sale went through, and I soon owned a house. When I first walked into the house, I mentioned to her that this would be my restaurant some day. In the meantime, I lived in the house and ran the Chick-n-Pick across the street. I was slowly getting all the legal preparations ready. Between financing, acquiring a liquor license, restaurant license, sewage permit, health permit and all the things it takes to build a restaurant, it took seven years to do all this!

The liquor license itself took quite a few years to get. I went before the Town Council in North Kingstown on the Chinese New Year of the Rooster, so that day I took a big ceramic red rooster from the Chick-n-Pick to the Chinese restaurant down the street and sat it near the Buddha for good luck. That night the council awarded me the liquor license and asked me what I was going to name the new restaurant. I thought of the rooster sitting on the mantle in the Chinese restaurant, and I said, "The restaurant will be called the **Red Rooster Tavern**."

Financing was very difficult to get. I tried several banks and they all turned me down. With restaurant mortality at a rate of 90% failure in the first five years, it is very difficult for a person to convince a bank to finance a restaurant. A short distance from our proposed restaurant, a new bank was being built. I made an appointment to speak with the president of this new bank, and he looked over my ideas and said he would get back to me.

A few days later, he called, and we met again. He said, "I will give you a mortgage for your proposed restaurant because I want your land for a new bank. The bank we are building is already obsolete because of the new drive-in banking and the ATMs that are coming to Rhode Island." I had enough land for cars to drive around the building.

I took on a partner, Frank Hennessey, who knew the liquor, wine and accounting part of the business, and we broke ground on September 5, 1969. Construction was going well. When the bank was supposed to give us our third installment on the mortgage and they required air conditioning, I thought to myself, "I need money to get me through the first winter–I do not need air conditioning in December." I went to an air conditioning company and asked if they had junk air conditioners. Sure enough, there was a big one behind the store. I took the cover off, brought it to the restaurant and placed it on the roof. We installed the entire ductwork and vents on the inside.

Thus, when the banker came to check on our air conditioning, I could point to the empty case on the roof, showing my new air conditioner. We got our third payment!

Opening night was December 9, 1969. We opened with a bang, because the first night a car crashed into our new sign. This turned into a positive thing, since we were on the front page of the local newspaper with the caption: "People are rushing to get into this new restaurant."

My Aunt Alice had worked for me at the Chick-n-Pick, and it was great to have her around because she was a link for me with my natural mother. She cooked breakfast and lunch, and when we were putting together the new restaurant, I wanted her to bake for us, just as she had done at home for her family. She made wonderful desserts. During the next ten years at the Red Rooster, she made the best homemade desserts a restaurant could serve. When she retired, a new baker, Phyllis, whom Aunt Alice had trained, took her place, and the quality of the desserts remained topnotch.

From the beginning, we found that hiring family members to work at the Red Rooster was a plus. Aunt Alice's three daughters, as well as their children, came aboard. My sister Terry and her children all worked for us. We never had to worry about employees not showing up because it was almost all family. Frank's daughter Susan also joined the team. We had a wonderful staff, and the customers kept coming.

Operating a first-class restaurant is a learning experience. We cooked lobsters, steaks, prime rib, shrimp and all the good things that come from New England. The restaurant was full to capacity every night. We opened with a 60-seat restaurant; within two years, we added two new rooms and an additional 40 seats. A short time later, we extended a dining room, adding 20 more seats. In 1980, we built a new cocktail lounge that could seat 100 people, and we could serve dinner in that room as well.

We were serving great wines, and we were awarded the prestigious Wine Spectator Magazine award. Things were going well for us. Frank and I worked long hours and rewarded ourselves with three weeks off every January. We closed the restaurant and traveled all over the world. In 1972, we flew to Paris to take a cruise on the *Ile de France*. We stayed in Paris a few days before the departure of the transatlantic cruise, and I remember dining at La Tour d'Argent, enjoying their famous pressed duck. The restaurant overlooks Notre Dame Cathedral, probably one of the most beautiful dining-room views in the world.

Dining on the *Ile de France*, known as one of the best restaurants in the world at that time, was indeed a treat: delicate onion soup; quenelles, a light dumpling made with fish, chicken or vegetables, so light it felt as if you were eating air. I had my first taste of morels, frog legs, sweetbreads, caviar, escargot, crepe suzettes, croissants and soufflés – they all excited my taste buds!

On the way to New York, the ship ran into quite a storm. One afternoon during the storm, as the ship was bouncing around, I went to the top deck to sit still and try not to get ill. A gentleman sitting opposite me engaged me in conversation, and as the time went on, I realized he was Salvadore Dali. We chatted for about three hours, an experience one could never anticipate.

The ship stopped in New York to pick up additional passengers and then sailed on to Haiti, where we terminated our part of the trip. What a shock from the *France* to Haiti! I remember the marketplace, the meat and fish stored with no refrigeration, the flies and the lack of cleanliness.

The next year we traveled to the Orient, where we enjoyed many different flavors. Trying to eat with chopsticks in Japan was a challenge, but the flavors and the decoration of the food were wonderful. Every dish was presented with color and style. The next part of the trip was Hong Kong, with its street restaurants with chickens, ducks and meat just hanging in the windows. That, along with the smells from the stir-frying, were complete culinary shocks for Westerners. We then went to Thailand and discovered the flavor of hot and spicy, a wonderful combination of foods that excited the palate but sometimes brought a tear to the eye.

One year we started a trip on the *Queen Elizabeth II* in London. I enjoyed a wonderful meal at the Savoy Restaurant, tasting for the first time a horseradish sauce that was served with roast beef and Yorkshire pudding. The ship also served great food: Beef Wellington, Chateaubriand, rack of lamb, potato and leek soup, rabbit and candied ginger, along with all came that wonderful British service and protocol.

Spain was another great awareness of flavors. At a restaurant in Madrid, we were served small eels (d'anguille) about the size of a nail. They were sautéed in olive oil and garlic and served with a wooden fork, to be eaten like spaghetti. This dish took a little daring to try, but after the first bite, it was great: a little crunch and wonderful. The garlic bread soup in Spain is also very special. This is where I experienced paella with sausage, unusual seafood and chicken dishes and the many varieties of *tapas,* those small appetizer-sized samples that are now making their way to the States.

Italy was a special vacation. Seeing the Coliseum and the Vatican was worth the whole trip. I would walk around Rome from morning till night, with no schedule and at every turn another wonder. I also enjoyed Naples, Venice, Tuscany and Capri. Each area of Italy has its own distinct personality in food: fresh mozzarella, polenta, risotto, fresh pasta, cappuccino, gelato, panna cotta, limone liqueur, Mascarpone, pine nuts, baby goat, rabbit and much, much more.

I brought back many of my culinary ideas from all over the world and shared them with my customers. From the U.S.: Bananas Foster, Eggs Benedict and New Orleans crawfish; chilies from Phoenix, sausages from Germany, blood sausage from Canada, flat bread from Morocco, pomme soufflé from France, my French-Canadian grandmother's meat pies.

In the early 1980's, at a time when we were looking to grow, a loyal employee, Bob, expressed an interest in running his own restaurant. With him, we purchased the Pump House Restaurant in South Kingstown. The building was the original water pumping station for the town. It is a beautiful structure, all stone with walls three feet thick in places. It sits next to a pond with ducks, a beautiful setting, and the building itself is on the National Historic Register.

The Rooster was as busy as a restaurant could be. We now had two restaurants, 60 employees at the Rooster and 30 at the Pump House, with each serving a great clientele. I had a very talented chef named Ronnie, and my sister Terry was the kitchen manager and night chef who kept everything and everyone in order. From the dishwashers to the line cooks, she helped keep our standards at a high level.

My job as Executive Chef consisted of working the line and planning and creating exciting foods from all over the world for both restaurants. I also enjoyed designing the kitchens and decorating the restaurant. I loved filling all the dining rooms with antiques and culinary artifacts. The customers would walk around and check out all the rooms, enjoying the decor as well as the food.

In the 1980's, we noticed a change in our customers' awareness about healthier dining and drinking. Clients were slowing down by skipping the Martini or Manhattan and settling for a glass of wine. Prime rib and steaks were no longer the big sellers. Instead, veal, chicken and seafood were our customers' choices. We added pasta and lighter meals, keeping the steaks for that person who still equated dining out with a steak and a baked potato.

Joe and Norma, a couple who often dined with us, chatted with me when I finished cooking. Joe, the president of a publishing company said to me one evening, "Why don't you write a cookbook, and I will publish it for you?" I just looked at him and said, "Sure, when do I have time to do this?"

Still, I took the question seriously. I started slowly by doing one recipe at a time. It takes a lot of time to put down on paper what you are thinking. I decided on a one-subject theme, all chicken, and all cooked in a special way, baked in the oven for 20 minutes. I had been doing that at the Rooster all along.

We did not have a sauté station at the restaurant during our early years, so I improvised recipes by breading skinless, boneless breasts of chicken and then adding different toppings. Testing these recipes was not too much of a problem, since we had cooked them in the restaurant many times. We knew that most homes did not have convection ovens, so we had to consider that for cooking times. I called the cookbook *Chicken Expressions* and the book has been very successful. Three years later, I wrote *Seafood Expressions.* Elizabeth Donovan did illustrations for both cookbooks.

In 1998, we sold the Rooster to an employee.

I now do promotions for the cookbooks, plus catering and teaching. I still spend some at the Pump House. After all those years in the restaurant kitchen, I now have a new life: writing, teaching, and cooking in homes. I enjoy this very much. I hope this book will share with you my love of food and entertaining, as I celebrate in 2002 fifty years in a restaurant kitchen.
Normand J. Leclair

> *"A book brings you on a journey that you did not know before."*
> *Jacqueline Kennedy Onassis*

===========CHEF'S TIPS AND SUGGESTIONS

RECIPES: Chicken and seafood recipes are for two servings, unless otherwise specified. Double or triple the ingredients for more servings.

PREPARING AHEAD: If you prepare a recipe ahead of time, take it out of the refrigerator 30 minutes before cooking time.

REMOVE SKIN FROM CHICKEN: To remove skin from fresh chicken, use a paper towel to hold the chicken skin, pull the skin while holding down the chicken and the skin should come right off.

FLATTEN CHICKEN: You can flatten trimmed chicken breasts between two pieces of wax paper or plastic wrap with the bottom of a sauté pan or a meat mallet, available in kitchen stores.

BREADING CRUMBS ON CHICKEN: If the boneless breasts of chicken are dry, moisten the chicken with a little milk and the crumbs will stick to the chicken.

ROLLED FISH OR CHICKEN: In all the recipes in the cookbook for rolled chicken, use a toothpick to secure the rolled chicken. A substitute for the toothpick is a piece of spaghetti. As the rolled chicken cooks, the spaghetti cooks and can be eaten. It saves you the trouble of removing the toothpicks. You can do this with rolled veal or fish.

INSULATED COOKIE SHEET: When baking puff pastry, often the bottom will burn before the top browns. Use an insulated cookie sheet. It has an air space between the layers.

BUTTER: You can substitute margarine for butter in any recipe.

SALT: Herbs and crumbs do the job, unless you need extra salt.

PANS: Use glass, Teflon coated, or aluminum; do not leave chicken or seafood overnight in or on aluminum. Pyrex glass is the best and safest cookware to use.

PASTRY SHELLS: In recipes using puff pastry, roll an extra shell. Decorating with the extra pastry allows you to create designs that compliment the dish.

OVEN: Since all entrees are baked, oven baked rice, roasted potatoes, and roasted vegetables can be baked at the same time. You must allow more oven time for some vegetables and potatoes.

HERBS AND SPICES: "Accentuate, don't overtake" is a good rule to follow, all recipes are lightly seasoned.

SAUTÉING: Heat a skillet first; add butter or oil, and then the vegetables; this keeps the vegetables from watering.

FRESH HERBS OR DRIED HERBS: When substituting dried herbs for fresh ones, use about one-third the amount called for in the recipe.

Chef's hints and suggestions continued-

FISH SIZE: In all the sole dishes, I suggest 3 to 4-ounce fillets, because I find this size is best to work with, but you may use whatever is available.

SKIN SIDE DOWN: The smoother side with a darker color is usually the skin side. If you have, any doubts about what side is the skin side ask the clerk when you purchase the fish.

SKINNING FISH: To skin fish, use a long sharp knife, grasp skin tightly, and move knife forward, keeping it tight against the skin to cut the fish away. (An easier way is to ask the clerk to do it for you.)

REMOVING BONES: Salmon have small needle-size bones; you can feel them with you fingers. Use needle-nose pliers or tweezers to remove bones.

SIZE OF SHRIMP: I use U-10 or U-12 shrimp in most recipes. The number is the amount of shrimp in each pound. Smaller shrimp are ok to use.

MINCING GARLIC: Garlic is easy to mince when the peeled clove is flattened with the flat side of a knife blade, then mince the garlic. (If you are using prepared minced garlic, refrigerate after opening container.)

JULIENNE (MATCHSTICK) STRIPS: Slice vegetable lengthwise to create a flat surface. Place the cut side down; slice the vegetable lengthwise into 1/4 or 1/8-inch strips. Cut strips again the same direction.

COOKING WITH WINE: When cooking with wine you should use a good wine, but it does not have to be expensive.

PARCHMENT PAPER: Parchment paper is available in any good cooking store. If you cannot find it, aluminum foil works as well.

READ THE RECIPE: Always read the recipe completely before you start, make sure you have all the ingredients and equipment that you need to prepare the dish.

PREPARATION: Prepare ingredients that require cutting, slicing and mincing ahead of time. Many of the recipes can be prepared earlier and assembled before dinner.

SANITATION: After cutting chicken, meat, or fish on a cutting board, wash the board with baking soda or lemon juice, rinse thoroughly. Wash knives in hot soapy water.

STORAGE: Store all chicken and fish in the coldest part of the refrigerator until ready to use. Store chicken or seafood in a glass container, stainless steel container, or plastic bag; in or on a bowl of ice. Do not store anything in aluminum.

Cook's hints and suggestions-

REMOVING COOKED FOOD FROM CASSEROLE:
Use a large spatula to remove cooked food from baking pans so that the
food does not break or fall apart.

SEEDING AND REMOVING SKINS FROM TOMATOES:
To remove skins from fresh tomatoes, bring a pot of water to a boil and drop
the tomatoes in hot boiling water for 20 seconds. Cool immediately in cold water.
Then peel the tomatoes from bottom to stem with a small knife. To remove the
seeds, cut the tomatoes in half crosswise, and scoop out the seedy pulp from
each half with your fingers. If you need to save the pulp and juice, seed the
tomato over a strainer that is on top a bowl and press what you collect through
the strainer. This will leave just the seeds in the strainer.

LEMON JUICE: To get more juice from a lemon, roll it on a counter with
your hands before cutting.

WASHING LEEKS: Trim off most of the green part. Cut off the root part,
cut the white part down to the stem in quarters. Wash thoroughly under cold
water; use your fingers to separate the leaves. Drain and drip-dry.

PEELING: When peeling pears and apples use a vegetable peeler, it takes less
time and saves more fruit.

CITRUS PEEL (zest): Peel is the outer skin layer of citrus found in oranges,
lemons, and limes. The peel can be removed with a citrus zester, grater, or
vegetable peeler. Use only the colored portion of the skin and not the white
part (pith). The aromatic oils in citrus peel are what add flavors to the food.

OVEN TEMPERATURE: Suggested oven temperatures, are selected for the
average home oven. I cook in many homes, use many ovens, and each oven
cooks a little different. Cooking times may vary a little depending on your oven.

BLENDING HOT LIQUID:
When blending hot soups or hot liquids, turn the blender on low speed then add
liquid slowly while blender is running. I find when adding the liquid, then starting
the blender, the steam and speed of the blender will make the liquid jump and the
cover come off.

BLANCHING PASTA: Cook dried pasta until 90% done. Drain the pasta and
cool it quickly in running cold water. When the pasta is cool, drain it, then
toss it with a little olive oil. The pasta will be ready to use for a couple of days,
store it in a plastic bag or covered container in the refrigerator. Reheat in hot
water or sauté with sauce.

Entertaining in your home is a challenge. We often rather be entertained than entertain, but when it's our turn, panic can set in.

The secret to a successful dinner party is to choose guests who can be fun and who complement each other. Sometimes you owe an invitation to someone who is not fun, and in those cases you just have to make the best of it.

In the restaurant business, we experience stress starting the week before Thanksgiving, and it didn't let up until the day after New Year's. Getting through all the Christmas parties and special dinners is a monumental task. We had group after group, all with special requests and needs. Keeping all of the details in order is very difficult and time-consuming, but also rewarding.

The same stress can be felt at home, between shopping and preparing all the special cooking that needs to be done, and keeping up with the special holiday traditions that most families consider very important. Getting as many things done ahead as you can is important.

Use the freezer; shop for all the non-perishables; have your linen and napkins ready. Make a list of all the things that must be done. This will help you to keep the stress out of entertaining during busy times. Remember: planning and organization are the key factors for stress-free entertaining. Keep the menu simple, go easy and be organized. You will be able to enjoy your own dinner parties and have time for your guests.

Many of the recipes in this cookbook can be prepared earlier in the day and cooked in the oven just before you need them.

"To dine," suggests the *art* of eating. Although dining may be considered a minor art, the hours devoted to it consume a good part of our lives. Both hosts and guests should derive pleasure from the efforts made for a dinner party.

Dinner parties that I really enjoy are small, between six and eight guests. It's important to choose a menu that will not consume you. I've been to dinner parties and felt sorry for the hosts. They opened cookbooks and tried to do the ultimate dinner. You can feel the tension as soon as you arrive

Choose a menu that is well-balanced, so that you can prepare most of the food before your guests arrive. Stress need not be a necessary ingredient. I've been to homes where the hosts are lost in the kitchen until dinnertime. If you do your homework with the menu, prepare food that you can do well. You can relax, enjoy your guests and give them the evening they came for.

Pages have been written about the possibilities of menus, variations of food, table arrangements. Before all is done, and after all is done, there is only one essential concern in entertaining, one enduring ingredient without which there is nothing: The guests.

A recipe is a communication tool. It is an abbreviated way of passing information from one person to another. It tells the cook what ingredients are needed for each recipe, and the procedure for preparing the recipe. One thing, a recipe does not communicate is how to become a good cook. Some people think that following a recipe is all there is to cooking. It's like learning English by reading a dictionary. It is important to learn how ingredients function together to make the dish work.

A good book to purchase is a food dictionary; such as the Food Lover's Companion or Brilliant Food Tips and Cooking Tricks. These books will explain how each food is grown, processed and used in cooking.

Cooking can be fun, and it can also be lots of work, but after the meal is eaten and the dishes are washed, the evening can warm your soul.

Company is coming and the menu you selected is a dish you have made many times. You follow the recipe to the letter and are confident of the outcome. But as you make the dish, somehow it feels different and comes out different. You say to yourself, "How can this happen?"

Well, that happens every time you cook. No one can duplicate a recipe exactly. The ingredients are different, the day is different or the stove may have a different heat. Recipes are a guide that can help you recreate a dish but nothing happens the same way twice. In the restaurant, we often made the same dish sometimes 50 times in one night, but each time it was a little different, no matter how careful we were.

The recipes in this cookbook have been tried and tested, hoping that your kitchen can duplicate mine. Brands of ingredients are always different, the strength of spices is always different, cooking is always an experiment. If you use the best ingredients you can find, your dish may be a little different, but it will always be good.

Cooking is always a good way to use all of your senses:

Touch: When cooking we must touch food to make it work.

Aroma: The aroma of food can be very stimulating, such as the smell of curry, garlic or peeling an orange.

Sight: When a plate of food is placed in front of you, first you eat with your eyes, looking at the color and presentation. When you walk around a grocery store, you purchase your choices first with your eyes, then your imagination takes over.

Hearing: The sauté of food, the boiling of potatoes, the comments about your cooking and the conversation at the dinner table are all part of the hearing in cooking.

Taste: This is the best part–the wonderful flavor of wine and food can stimulate all your emotions.

Enjoy your time in the kitchen; cooking is always an experiment no matter if you are the best cook in the world or just enjoy creating wonderful food.

APPETIZERS
STARTERS
HORS D'OEUVRES

EPD '90

=====APPETIZERS, STARTERS AND HORS D'OEUVRES

APPETIZER CHICKEN FINGERS

This recipe is also great as a main course for kids,
who love Chicken Fingers.
Serves 4

4 boneless chicken breasts, skinned, boned, flattened, with fat removed
2 eggs
1/4 cup milk
1 1/2 cups finely crushed cornflakes, potato chips, or tortilla
   chips (can be done in a food processor)
1 tablespoon olive oil

PREPARATION
1. Cut chicken into fingers, or nuggets. Beat the eggs and milk together
   in a medium bowl and add the chicken. Store in refrigerator
   until ready to use.
2. Place crushed corn flakes in a bowl.

ASSEMBLY
1. Oil an insulated cookie sheet, or cover it with parchment paper.
2. Remove chicken pieces from egg mixture and cover chicken
   pieces completely with crushed cornflakes. Place breaded chicken on
   cookie sheet as you do them.
3. Bake in a preheated 400° oven for about 15 minutes.
4. Remove cookie sheet from oven and serve chicken pieces as
   appetizers with a dipping sauce, or as children's meals.

Dipping sauces: Ketchup, honey mustard, oriental barbeque
sauce.

<u>Helpful Hint</u>
When you are serving buffet style stack the dinner plates at the
start of the buffet table and silverware and napkins at the end.
This way hands are free to fill up plates.

=====ASPARAGUS AND TWO CHEESE CUSTARD

Serve these custards as a first course or for lunch with a salad.

Serves 6

1 1/2 pounds asparagus, trimmed, tips removed (1-inch)
2 tablespoons butter
1/2 cup chopped onions
1/2 cup whole milk ricotta cheese
1 cup freshly grated Parmesan cheese
1/4 cup flour
4 large eggs
1 cup milk
1/2 cup fresh or dried bread crumbs

PREPARATION
1. Cook asparagus tips in boiling water in a saucepan until crisp tender. (About 4 minutes.) Drain and save 1 cup of cooking liquid. Plunge tips in cold water to stop cooking. Save for later.
2. Melt one tablespoon butter in a skillet. Add onion; sauté until tender. Add reserved asparagus water and asparagus to skillet and simmer until stalks are tender. Drain liquid and cool onions and asparagus.
3. Transfer cooked asparagus (not the tips) to a food processor and puree. Add ricotta, Parmesan, and flour. Pulse until blended.
4. Whisk eggs and milk in a bowl to blend. Stir in asparagus puree. Coarsely chop all but 12 of the asparagus tips and stir into the custard. (These steps can be done earlier in the day and stored in refrigerator.)

ASSEMBLY
1. Butter six 3/4 cup custard cups; coat them with bread crumbs, shake out excess.
2. Select an ovenproof pan large enough to contain the six custard cups. Place cups in pan; divide the custard among cups. Pour hot water into pan to 1-inch of tops of custard cups.
3. Bake in a preheated 350° oven for 35 minutes or until custard is set.
4. Remove pan from oven, be careful of the hot water. Allow custards to rest in the hot water for 10 minutes. Remove custards from hot water.
5. To serve run a knife around custard. Take your serving plate and place on top of custard dish up side down and turn over. In a moment, the custard should drop to the plate.
Garnish with reserved asparagus tips.
Can be served at room temperature.

===========================ASPARAGUS AU GRATIN

This wonderful asparagus appetizer or side dish is so easy to prepare.
Serves 4

1 pound asparagus (about 24 spears) trimmed
1 cup grated Parmesan cheese
1/2 cup fresh or dried bread crumbs
1 clove garlic, finely chopped
1/4 cup olive oil

PREPARATION
1. Mix Parmesan cheese, bread crumbs, garlic, and half the olive oil in a mixing bowl.

ASSEMBLY
1. Oil an ovenproof casserole dish large enough to contain the asparagus spears flat in four portions.
2. Spoon Parmesan cheese mixture evenly on asparagus.
3. Bake in a 400° oven for about 12 minutes or until crumbs and cheese are golden and the asparagus are cooked.
4. Remove asparagus from casserole dish with a spatula to individual serving plates.

To make fresh bread crumbs: Take 4 slices of day old Italian or sourdough bread, cut off the crusts, break up and process in a food processor.

<u>Helpful Hint</u>
When you want to chill Champagne or white wine in a hurry, forget the freezer. Instead, place the bottle in a bucket of ice water; the cold water will envelop the bottle better than ice alone. You should have nice chilled bubbly or white wine in a short time.

==================BRUSCHETTA FROM TUSCANY

In Italy, they used a creamed Gorgonzola; I found this blend in good cheese shops. I blended the two cheeses because creamed Gorgonzola is hard to find. This bruschetta was served to us in Italy with grilled half of fresh fig. The flavor was just wonderful. When fresh figs are available, use them with this appetizer. I use dried dates because dates are always available.

Serves 6 to 8

Loaf of good quality Italian bread or French bread
Olive oil
1 1/2 cups Gorgonzola cheese
1/2 cup Mascarpone cheese
Dried dates or fresh grilled figs

PREPARATION
1. Slice bread in 1 inch slices. With a pastry brush or fingers spread a little olive oil on one side of sliced bread.
2. Place bread slices oil side up on a cookie sheet and bake in a preheated 400° for about 5 minutes or until slightly toasted. Remove from oven and cool.
3. Cream Gorgonzola cheese and Mascarpone cheese in a mixing bowl until completely blended.

ASSEMBLY
1. Spread each slice of toasted bread on oiled side with 1 tablespoon of the cheese blend, slice dates in half and place on top of cheese or grilled figs. Place on serving platter and serve.

In October of 2000, I visited Tuscany with some culinary colleagues. That area of Italy is full of history with beautiful walled medieval towns on top of mountains. I found the food to be simple but made of the freshest ingredients and flavors. We took a day tour of the Chianti area of Tuscany. Rows of grape vines lined the hills and each turn was another place to take a picture. One thing I will always remember, do not eat the olives off the trees.

This is a great easy pass around treat when entertaining.
Serves 8 to 10

Thin white bread slices, or dark bread
1 cup whole egg mayonnaise (such as Hellmann's)
1 cup grated Parmesan cheese
1 tablespoon finely chopped green onions (scallions)

PREPARATION

1. Stamp out as many bread rounds, as you need, with a cookie cutter about 1 1/4 to 1 1/2 inches round. Place bread rounds on a cookie sheet and bake in a preheated 400° oven for about 10 minutes. Bread should be dry but not brown.
2. Mix mayonnaise, Parmesan cheese, and green onions in a mixing bowl.

ASSEMBLY

1. Spoon and spread cheese mixture on each toast round. Place rounds on a cookie sheet (I like to use an insulated cookie sheet).
2. Bake in a preheated 400° oven until bubbly and a little brown. Remove toast rounds from cookie sheet to a serving plate with a spatula (cheese will be very hot).

Variations are many; you can add one of the following, drained chopped crabmeat, finely chopped sun dried tomatoes, minced ham, finely chopped red bell pepper, finely chopped smoked salmon, finely chopped shrimp, or whatever your imagination comes up with.

"Flowers bring more true smiles, hugs and kisses than any other gift."
Unknown

COQUILLE ST. JACQUES

This recipe will make six appetizer portions, or two dinner portions, if you have scallop shells use them for the appetizer portions. This dish can be prepared earlier in the day, wrapped in plastic wrap and stored in the refrigerator. Take out 1/2 hour before cooking.

Serves 6 as appetizers or 2 as main course
1 pound scallops (if small, leave whole, if large, cut each one in half)
3 tablespoons butter
1/4 cup chopped onion
1 cup sliced fresh mushrooms
1 cup white wine
Pinch thyme
Dash nutmeg
1 tablespoon lemon juice
1/4 cup chopped green onions (scallions)
1 bay leaf
1/2 cup half-and-half cream or evaporated milk
1/4 cup all purpose flour
1/4 cup seafood crumbs, page 257
2 tablespoons grated fresh Parmesan cheese

PREPARATION
1. Melt 1 1/2 tablespoons of butter over medium heat in a saucepan; sauté chopped onion and mushrooms until mushrooms are wilted, stirring often. Stir in wine, thyme, nutmeg, lemon juice, green onion, bay leaf, cream, and scallops. Cook for about 2 minutes or until scallops are turning white. Remove from heat and drain, saving 1 1/2 cups of the broth.
2. Melt 1 1/2 tablespoons butter in a saucepan, add flour and mix while cooking on low heat to form a smooth paste. Gradually add broth while stirring until thickened. Remove from heat and stir in scallops and mushroom mixture. Remove bay leaf.

ASSEMBLY
1. Spoon mixture into 6 lightly buttered scallop shells or 2 individual casserole dishes. Sprinkle with crumbs and Parmesan cheese.
2. Preheat oven to 400°. Place scallop shells on cookie sheet and bake until browned, about 10 minutes. Place on serving plates.

==========INDIVIDUAL CHILLED CRAB MOUSSE

A wonderful first course or a perfect lunch dish served with a salad.
Serves 6

1 can (6 1/2-ounce) crabmeat, drained, save juice
1 envelope (1 tablespoon) unflavored gelatin
1/2 cup cold water
1 can (10 1/2-ounce) cream of mushroom soup
1 (8-ounces) package cream cheese, softened
1/2 cup finely chopped celery
1/4 cup finely chopped onion
1 teaspoon dried dill
1/2 cup mayonnaise
1/2 cup sour cream
Vegetable oil or cooking spray

PREPARATION
1. Sprinkle gelatin over 1/2 cup cold water in small bowl, let soften for at least ten minutes.
2. Add mushroom soup and crab juice to a saucepan. Heat to almost boiling while stirring. Add softened gelatin and mix until gelatin dissolves.
3. Place softened cream cheese in a bowl, mix until creamy, then add soup mixture, Mix smooth with a whisk. Allow mixture to cool to tepid temperature. (I like to place the bowl of cream cheese mixture in a bowl of ice water to speed cooling.)

ASSEMBLY
1. Lightly oil six individual cups or molds (5 to 6-ounces).
2. Add celery, onion, dill, mayonnaise, and sour cream to the bowl of mushroom soup mixture. Mix until completely blended; stir in crabmeat.
3. Spoon into prepared cups. Top with plastic wrap and store in refrigerator for at least 12 hours.
4. When ready to serve follow the inside of the cup with a table knife to loosen. Place serving plate on top of cup, turn plate over; the mousse should drop on plate. Do this with each serving. Serve as a first course, or use it as a nice lunch dish.

===========CRUMBED SHRIMP WITH SHERRY

A wonderful first course or a great lunch item served with a salad.
Serves 4

12 jumbo shrimp (U 11-15), shelled, deveined, tails removed
1/2 cup butter, softened
2 cloves garlic, finely minced
2 tablespoons dry sherry
1/2 cup dry or fresh bread crumbs
1/4 cup finely chopped fresh parsley
1/4 cup sliced almonds
1/4 cup water
Lemon wedges

PREPARATION
1. Mix butter, garlic, sherry, bread crumbs, and parsley until blended in a mixing bowl.

ASSEMBLY
1. Select 4 individual casserole dishes that will contain the three shrimp in 1 layer. Place shrimp in casserole and spoon crumb mixture evenly on shrimp. Top with almonds. Add a little water to each casserole.
2. Bake casseroles in a preheated 400° oven on a cookie sheet for about 15-20 minutes, until the shrimp are cooked and the topping is golden.
3. Remove casserole dishes from oven and place them on individual dinner plate. Serve with lemon wedges.

I like to use doilies or lettuce on the dinner plate to keep the casseroles from sliding around.
U plus number is the amount of shrimp to a pound.
Shrimp can be prepared ahead and stored in refrigerator until ready to cook.

"If we did all we were capable of doing,
we would literally astonish ourselves."
Thomas Edison

CURRIED CREAM CHEESE MOLD

A delicately flavored cold mousse that can be served as a first course.
I enjoy surrounding the mold with greens and a light dressing.
Serve it as a hors d'oeuvres dip with crackers for dipping.
Serves 6

1 envelope (1 tablespoon) unflavored gelatin
1/4 cup cold water
1 package (8-ounce) cream cheese
1 garlic clove, minced
1 (10 1/2-ounce) can beef consommé
1 teaspoon curry powder
2 tablespoons finely chopped green onions (scallions)
1/4 cup finely chopped red bell pepper
Cooking spray or olive oil

PREPARATION

1. Sprinkle gelatin over cold water in a small saucepan; allow to soften for at least 10 minutes. Stir over low heat until gelatin completely dissolves, about 2 minutes. Remove from heat; let stand for about 5 minutes. (You can also heat in microwave.)
2. Blend cream cheese, minced garlic, beef consommé, and curry powder in a blender until smooth. Pour cream cheese mixture in a mixing bowl.

ASSEMBLY

1. Spray 6 (5-ounce) ramekins or small soufflé cups with cooking spray.
2. Stir green onions, peppers, and gelatin into the cream cheese mixture, combining completely.
3. Spoon mousse into prepared ramekins; top with plastic wrap. Chill until set, about 6 hours.
4. To serve, run a knife around mold and invert on a plate; cream cheese mousse should drop onto the plate. If it is a little stubborn, dip the ramekin in hot water for a minute, then invert it.

ESCARGOT UNDER PUFF PASTRY

Canned escargot are available in gourmet markets and many supermarkets.

Serves 4

4 tablespoons butter
1/4 cup minced onion
3 cloves garlic, minced
16 mushrooms, cleaned, chopped
1 tablespoon soy sauce
1/4 teaspoon sesame oil
Dash ground red pepper (cayenne)
20 canned escargot, rinsed and drained
1 sheet frozen puff pastry, thawed
1 egg, plus 1 tablespoon milk

PREPARATION

1. Melt the butter in a medium skillet; sauté onion and garlic until onion is soft. Stir in the mushrooms and sauté over medium heat, stirring occasionally, until mushrooms are tender and their liquid has evaporated, about ten minutes. Stir in soy sauce, sesame oil, and tabasco. Cool.

ASSEMBLY

1. Spoon mushroom mixture evenly into four 4 1/2 ounce ramekins or soufflé dishes. Top mushrooms with five escargots.
2. Place puff pastry on flat surface. Cut out four circles of puff pastry, 1/2-inch larger than the diameter of the ramekins. Beat the egg and milk together in a small bowl. Brush the rims of the ramekins and edges of the pastry round with egg wash.
3. Cover each ramekin with pastry round; press the edges against sides of the ramekins. Brush top of pastry round with egg wash. Cut a small hole in the center of each pastry. Store in refrigerator until ready to use.
4. Bake in a preheated 400° oven on a cookie sheet for 20 minutes or until pastry is golden and puffed.
5. Remove ramekin from cookie sheet with a spatula to serving plate. Serve in ramekin. Enjoy the wonderful aroma.

============GRUYÈRE CHEESE GOUGÈRES

Do not let the French words in this recipe scare you. It is actually the same basic recipe for crème puffs. It makes a great pass around hors-d'euvre. Every time I make these they fly off the plate.
Makes about 35 to 40

1 cup water
7 tablespoons butter (1 tablespoon less than one stick) cut into
  small pieces
1/2 teaspoon salt
1/4 teaspoon white pepper
3/4 cup all-purpose flour
1 tablespoon Dijon-style mustard
5 large eggs
1 cup (packed) shredded Gruyere or Swiss cheese
Butter and flour for preparing cookie sheet

PREPARATION
1. Combine water, butter, salt and pepper in a medium
    saucepan; bring to a boil over medium heat, make sure
    all the butter is melted.
2. Add flour all at once and stir vigorously with a wooden spoon
    until mixture forms a smooth ball. Make sure that all the flour
    has left the side of the pan. Remove pan from heat and beat
    in the mustard. Beat in eggs completely 1 at a time.
    Stir in cheese and mix thoroughly.

ASSEMBLY
1. Butter and flour two cookie sheets. (Insulated cookie sheet if
    you have one.)
2. Drop batter by heaping teaspoonfuls on floured cookie sheets,
    spacing about 1 1/2 inches apart.
3. Bake in a preheated 400° oven for about 15 minutes. Reverse
    position of cookie sheets and cook for another 5 minutes or until
    puffs are golden brown. Remove puffs from cookie sheet with a
    spatula. Serve warm.

=========INDIVIDUAL FOUR-CHEESE GALETTE

Great for a first course and wonderful served for lunch with a salad.

Serves 6

1 1/2 cups all purpose flour
Dash salt
1/2 cup (1-stick) cold butter
1/3 cup cold water
1/3 cup feta cheese
1/2 cup ricotta cheese
1/3 cup grated mozzarella cheese
2 tablespoons grated Parmesan cheese
1/4 cup sour cream
1/4 cup finely chopped green onions (scallions)
Cooking spray or olive oil
Milk for pastry

PREPARATION

1. Add flour and salt to a mixing bowl. Cut butter into flour until mixture resembles small peas. Add water and mix until a ball is formed. Store in refrigerator for at least one hour. Separate dough into six even portions. Roll dough into six 5-inch rounds. Store on individual wax paper in refrigerator until ready to use.
2. Mix feta cheese, ricotta cheese, mozzarella cheese, grated Parmesan, sour cream, and green onions in a mixing bowl.

ASSEMBLY

1. Spray a cookie sheet with cooking spray or wipe with olive oil.
2. Place rolled pastry dough on cookie sheet. In the center of each pastry round spoon cheese mixture evenly, leaving at least a one inch border. Lift the edges of the dough and fold them in over the filling. Work around the tart folding the dough into itself in spaced pleats leaving opening in center. Use a pastry brush or your fingers to brush the milk on the pastry.
3. Bake in a preheated 400° oven for about 30 minutes or until pastry is nice and brown.
4. Remove to serving plates with a spatula. Serve with greens with a light dressing.

INDIVIDUAL SHRIMP MOUSSE

A combination of shrimp and tomato makes this appetizer light and flavorful. A great lunch item served with a salad.

Serves 6

1/2 pound raw shrimp, peeled, deveined, tails removed
Water for cooking shrimp
1 envelope (1 tablespoon) unflavored gelatin
1/2 cup cold water
1 can (10 1/2-ounce) tomato soup
1 (8-ounce) package cream cheese, softened
1/2 cup finely chopped celery
1/4 cup finely chopped onion
1/2 teaspoon Cajun seasoning or cayenne powder
1/2 cup mayonnaise
Vegetable oil or cooking spray
1/2 cup sour cream

PREPARATION
1. Place shrimp in a small sauce pan, cover shrimp with water and cook until shrimp is done (takes just a minute after the boil). Drain, reserving 1/2 cup of cooking liquid. Cool shrimp and chop coarsely.
2. Sprinkle gelatin over 1/2 cup cold water in a small bowl to soften for at least 10 minutes.
3. Place tomato soup and shrimp water in a saucepan. Heat until almost boiling while stirring. Add softened gelatin and mix until gelatin is dissolved.
4. Place softened cream cheese in a bowl, mix until creamy, and then add soup mixture. Mix until smooth with a whisk. Allow mixture to cool to tepid temperature. (I like to place tomato mixture in a bowl of ice to speed cooling.)

ASSEMBLY
1. Lightly oil six individual cups or molds (5 to 6-ounces).
2. Add celery, onion, Cajun seasoning, mayonnaise, and sour cream to the bowl of tomato soup mixture and mix completely, and then stir in shrimp.
3. Spoon shrimp mixture evenly into prepared cups. Top each cup with plastic wrap and store in refrigerator for at least 12 hours before serving.
4. When ready to serve run a table knife around the inside of the cup to loosen. Place serving plate on top of cup; turn plate over, the mousse should drop to plate. Do this with each serving. Garnish with a little sour cream.

So easy to make, and great for pass around appetizer.

1 package (8-ounce) cream cheese, softened
1/4 cup chopped green olives, with or without pimento
1/4 cup canned chopped green chilies
1/4 cup finely chopped green onion (scallions)
1/4 teaspoon chili powder
1/4 cup sweet red bell pepper, finely chopped
3 or 4 roll-up square flat bread such as Lavash

ASSEMBLY

1. Mix cream cheese, olives, chilies, green onion, chili powder, and peppers in a bowl. Spread mixture on flat bread evenly. Roll up tightly like a jellyroll. Store in plastic wrap in the refrigerator until ready to use.
2. Slice and place on serving plate, serve with dot of salsa, picante sauce, or just as it is.

Helpful Hint

If you have an oven or stove top fire, shut off the heat source, sprinkle baking soda on the fire. Do not try to put out the fire with water.

MUSHROOM SAUTÉ

A wonderful appetizer that is easy to make for the mushroom lover.
Serves 6

1/4 cup butter
1/4 cup minced onion
2 cloves garlic, minced
1 1/2 pounds mushrooms (you can use a variety of mushrooms)
   sliced 1/4 inch thick (including the stems)
1/4 cup chopped fresh parsley
1 tablespoon soy sauce
1 cup sour cream
3 English muffins cut in half, toasted

ASSEMBLY

1. Melt butter in a medium skillet or wok, and sauté onion and garlic
   until onion is soft. Stir in mushrooms and sauté over medium heat stirring
   occasionally until mushrooms are tender and their liquid has evaporated,
   about ten minutes. Stir in parsley, soy sauce, and sour cream; mix completely.
   Remove from heat; do not overcook the sour cream or it turns to liquid.
   If it does, add a little flour to thicken.
2. Place half of toasted English muffin on each plate and spoon mushroom
   mixture evenly over each muffin using all the sauce. Serve immediately.

For a variation, serve over puff pastry, toast points, or small biscuits.

*"The greatest compliment for the home cook is, while you are serving
a dinner course, you get a nod of appreciation from your guests as they
are stimulated by your presentation. Then, with the first taste, there is
a silence, and then with the second taste you see a smile of appreciation
and compliments for your effort."*
Author

===OVEN BAKED SPINACH POLENTA SQUARES

Polenta can be prepared ahead. To reheat polenta squares, sauté in a skillet with olive oil or reheat in the oven in an ovenproof casserole with a little olive oil. Refrigerate extras for later.
Serves 8-10

4 tablespoons olive oil
1 tablespoon butter
1/2 cup chopped green onions (scallions)
1 teaspoon ground fennel or fennel seeds, slightly crushed
1/2 pound fresh spinach, stems removed and finely chopped
2 cups ricotta cheese
2 cups whole milk
1 1/4 cup grated Parmesan cheese
1 1/2 cups yellow cornmeal
1/2 teaspoon ground black pepper
1/2 teaspoon salt
Marinara sauce (optional)

PREPARATION
1. Heat 2 tablespoons olive oil and 1 tablespoon butter in a skillet over medium heat; stir in green onions and fennel and cook until scallions soften, about 2 minutes. Stir in spinach and cook, stirring, until spinach is wilted. Remove from heat and set aside.
2. Mix ricotta and milk in a large mixing bowl; stir in Parmesan, corn meal, pepper, salt, and spinach mixture.

ASSEMBLY
1. Oil with 1 tablespoons olive oil a 13x9x2-inch glass-baking dish
2. Transfer spinach mixture to glass baking dish. Brush or spread 1 tablespoon olive oil over top of polenta.
3. Bake in a preheated 375° oven for about 35 minutes, or until a little brown on edges and firm in center.
4. Remove from oven, allow to rest for about 10 minutes and cut into squares. Remove with a spatula.
5. Spoon a little warm marinara sauce on a plate and with a spatula place a polenta square on sauce. Garnish with fresh basil or a spinach leaf. Polenta is great as a first course or a side dish.

============PORTOBELLO MUSHROOM PIZZA

Mushrooms can be prepared ahead and stored in refrigerator before baking.

Serves 4

4 portobello mushrooms about 3 1/2 to 4 inches across, stems
   removed, wiped clean
1 tablespoon olive oil
1/4 cup finely chopped onion
2 sweet Italian sausages, casings removed
Cooking spray or olive oil for brushing mushrooms with oil
3/4 cup marinara sauce
1/2 teaspoon dried basil or 2 tablespoons chopped fresh basil
1/4 cup grated fresh Parmesan cheese
4 slices provolone cheese

PREPARATION

1. Add oil to a medium skillet; over medium heat, sauté onion until
   translucent. Stir in sausage; sauté until it is brown and cooked through,
   breaking up sausage with back of a spoon. Drain fat and cool.

ASSEMBLY

1. Spray bottom of mushrooms with cooking spray or brush
   with olive oil. Place mushroom rounded side down in an
   ovenproof casserole dish or cookie sheet.
2. Divide sausage evenly among mushrooms. Spoon marinara
   sauce evenly on top of sausage, sprinkle with basil, Parmesan
   cheese, and top with provolone cheese.
3. Bake in a preheated 400° oven for 20 minutes.
4. Remove from casserole with a spatula to individual serving
   plates.

For variation, add chopped pepperoni and chopped bell peppers.
To make a completely different version of Portobello make
Mexican Portobello: Instead of the marinara sauce, add salsa and
shredded Monterey Jack cheese on top of sausage.

=============PROSCIUTTO WRAPPED PEARS WITH GORGONZOLA

Serve for lunch with greens, also perfect as a first course.

Serves 4

4 ripe Bosc pears or any firm pear
Water
1/2 lemon
12 thin slices Prosciutto (Italian cured ham)
Olive oil
1 1/2 tablespoons butter
1 1/2 tablespoons flour
1 cup milk
1/4 cup crumbled Gorgonzola cheese

PREPARATION

1. Peel pears, cut each pear in three pieces lengthwise, remove core and stem.
   Place pear pieces in a bowl, cover with water, squeeze
   lemon juice in water. This will keep pears from discoloring.
   Pears can be prepared ahead until ready to assemble.

ASSEMBLY

1. Lightly oil a cookie sheet. Place 1 slice of Prosciutto on a flat
   plate. Place a pear piece on Prosciutto and wrap pear with
   Prosciutto. Place wrapped pear on cookie sheet, core side down.
   Do this with all the pears. Drizzle wrapped pears with a little
   olive oil. Pears can be prepared ahead and stored in refrigerator.
2. Bake wrapped pears in a 375°oven for about 20 minutes or
   until pears are hot to the touch.
3. In medium saucepan over medium heat, melt butter, stir
   in flour and cook for about one minute. Gradually whisk in milk
   and heat, stirring often, until milk thickens. On low heat stir in
   Gorgonzola, stirring constantly, until cheese melts and sauce is
   smooth. Sauce can be made ahead of time and kept warm.
4. Remove cooked pears from cookie sheet with a spatula and
   place three pieces on each plate. Spoon sauce around and on
   pears. Garnish with red bell pepper or mixed greens.

Enjoy the delicate flavors of salmon with a touch of horseradish, cream cheese and dill.

Serves 6 to 8

1 (16-ounce) can red salmon, drained, bones removed, skinned
   (or one pound cooked fresh salmon)
1 (8-ounce) package cream cheese, softened
1 tablespoon lemon juice
1 tablespoon grated horseradish
2 teaspoons dried dill
2 tablespoons minced onions
1/4 cup chopped fresh parsley
1/4 teaspoon liquid smoke (optional)
1 teaspoon Worcestershire sauce
Dash hot-pepper sauce (Tabasco)

ASSEMBLY

1. Add all ingredients to a food processor. Pulse process until all ingredients are mixed smooth. Place salmon mixture in a mold lined with plastic wrap, or individual molds lined with plastic wrap. Refrigerate for several hours. Place upside down on a plate then remove mold from salmon and remove plastic wrap.

   Use as hors-d'oeuvres or as a first course. Serve with toast, crackers or raw vegetables.

   Garnish with chopped pecans, sliced olives, chopped green onions, or whatever your imagination comes up with.

> *"Burgundy makes you think of silly things,*
> *Bordeaux makes you talk of them and*
> *Champagne makes you do them."*
> *Brillat-Savarin*

Helpful Hint
I like to run my sponges and scrubbers in the dishwasher on occasion. It keeps them fresh and clean.

=SEVEN VARIATIONS OF STUFFED MUSHROOMS

Stuffed mushrooms are always on the top of the list for appetizers or for a fist course when entertaining. All recipes can be prepared ahead and stored in the refrigerator until ready to cook.

Serves 6

=====================CRABMEAT STUFFED MUSHROOMS

24 larger mushrooms, stems removed, wiped clean
1 1/2 cups seafood crumbs, page 257
1/4 pound plus 1 tablespoon butter, melted
1 (10-ounce) can crab meat, drained, check for bones
1/8 cup white wine
1 teaspoon lemon juice
2 tablespoons finely chopped green onions (scallions)
1 tablespoon mayonnaise

PREPARATION
1. Mix crumbs, 1 tablespoon melted butter, crabmeat, white wine, lemon juice, green onions, and mayonnaise in a mixing bowl.

ASSEMBLY
1. Fill mushroom caps with stuffing. Stick a toothpick in the stuffed mushroom cap and dip into melted butter. Place stuffed mushroom on a cookie sheet of ovenproof casserole.
2. Bake in a preheated 400° oven for about 10 minutes.
3. Serve four mushrooms on individual plates when used as an appetizer. If stuffed mushrooms are served as hors-d'oeuvres, place mushrooms on a serving plate.

Mushroom stems can be used in a salad, sauce, or any other use.

"Laughter is the best seasoning there is."
Barbara Kafka

==========SAUSAGE-GORGONZOLA STUFFED MUSHROOMS

24 larger mushrooms, wiped clean, stems removed and chopped,
1 teaspoon olive oil
1/4 cup chopped onions
2 cloves garlic, chopped
1/4 pound mild or hot Italian sausage, casings removed
1/4 cup Gorgonzola cheese, (any of the blue cheeses can be used)
2 tablespoons grated Parmesan cheese
1/2 cup seasoned bread crumbs
1/2 teaspoon oregano
1/4 pound melted butter

PREPARATION

1. Heat olive oil in a medium skillet, then sauté onions and garlic until onion is soft. Stir in sausage meat and cook until sausage looses its pink color Add chopped mushroom stems and cook for a couple of minutes. Drain.
2. Spoon sausage mixture into a food processor. Process sausage mixture until smooth. Add Gorgonzola and pulse food processor until cheese is mixed in.
3. Mix sausage mixture, Parmesan cheese, bread crumbs, and oregano in a mixing bowl.

ASSEMBLY

1. Fill mushroom cap with stuffing. Stick a toothpick in the stuffed mushroom cap and dip into melted butter. Place mushroom cap on a cookie sheet or ovenproof casserole.
2. Bake in a preheated 400° oven for about 10 minutes.
3. Serve four mushrooms on individual plates when used as an appetizer. If stuffed mushrooms are served as hors-d'oeuvres, place mushrooms on serving plate.

=====SAUSAGE WALNUT STUFFED MUSHROOMS

24 larger mushrooms, stems removed, wiped clean,
   stems chopped
1 tablespoon butter
1/4 cup chopped onion
2 cloves garlic, chopped
1 pound bulk pork sausage
1/4 cup finely chopped walnuts
2 tablespoons chopped fresh parsley
1/2 cup shredded sharp cheddar cheese
1/4 cup sour cream
1/2 cup seasoned bread crumbs
1/4 pound melted butter

PREPARATION
1. Melt the butter in a medium skillet; sauté onion and garlic until onion is soft. Stir in sausage meat and cook until sausage looses its pink color. Add chopped mushroom stems and cook for a couple of minutes. Drain.
2. Spoon sausage mixture into food processor and pulse process until mixture is smooth.
3. Mix sausage mixture, walnuts, parsley, cheddar, sour cream, and bread crumbs in a mixing bowl.

ASSEMBLY
1. Fill caps with stuffing. Stick a toothpick in the stuffed mushroom cap and dip into melted butter. Place mushroom cap on cookie sheet or ovenproof casserole.
2. Bake in a preheated 400° oven for 10 minutes.
3. Serve four mushrooms on individual plates when used as an appetizer. If stuffed mushrooms are served as hors-d'oeuvres, place mushrooms on serving plate.

=============BACON-STUFFED MUSHROOMS

Bacon can be cooked between paper towels in a microwave.

24 larger mushrooms, wiped clean, stems removed and finely chopped
8 slices hickory smoked bacon
1/2 cup finely chopped onion
2 tablespoons finely chopped parsley
1 (8-ounce) package cream cheese softened
1/2 cup seasoned bread crumbs
1 tablespoon grated Parmesan cheese
1/4 cup melted butter

PREPARATION
1. Cook bacon in a skillet until crisp. Drain on paper towels. Save one tablespoon of bacon drippings in same sauté pan. Sauté onions for about a minute. Add finely chopped mushroom stems. Cook until soft, about 3 minutes.
2. Finely chop bacon on a cutting board.
3. Mix bacon, onion mixture, parsley, softened cream cheese, bread crumbs, and Parmesan cheese.

ASSEMBLY
1. Fill mushroom caps with stuffing. Stick a toothpick in the stuffed mushroom cap and dip into melted butter. Place on cookie sheet or ovenproof casserole.
2. Bake in a preheated 400° oven for 10 minutes.
3. Serve four mushrooms on individual plates when used as an appetizer. If stuffed mushrooms are served as hors-d'oeuvres, place mushrooms on a serving plate.

"If a man has a talent and doesn't use it, he has failed. If he has a talent and uses only half of it, he has partly failed. If he has a talent and learns somehow to use the whole of it, he has gloriously succeeded and won a satisfaction and a triumph few men ever know."
Thomas Wolf

=============SHRIMP STUFFED MUSHROOMS

24 larger mushrooms, stems removed, wiped clean
1 (8-ounce) package cream cheese, softened
1 cup finely chopped cooked shrimp
2 tablespoons finely chopped onion
1 tablespoon grated horseradish
Dash Worcestershire sauce
1/2 cup seasoned bread crumbs
2 tablespoons chopped fresh parsley
1 beaten egg
1/4 cup melted butter

PREPARATION
1. Mix cream cheese, shrimp, onion, horseradish,
   Worcestershire sauce, bread crumbs, parsley, and beaten egg.

ASSEMBLY
1. Fill mushroom caps with shrimp mixture. Stick a toothpick in stuffed
   mushroom cap and dip into melted butter. Place on a cookie sheet or
   ovenproof casserole.
2. Bake in a preheated 400° oven for 10 minutes.
3. Serve four mushrooms on individual plates or when used as hors-d'oeuvres,
   place mushrooms on serving plate.

The mushroom stems can be used in salad, or many other recipes

Helpful Hint
*Many of the saute pans and cookie sheets are nonstick. Never use metal
utensils on them, metal will scratch the surface. Use wood
or plastic utensils.*

=========ESCARGOT STUFFED MUSHROOMS

The best escargots come from France. I like using the canned variety for this dish.

24 larger mushrooms, stems removed, wiped clean
24 escargots (canned escargots are available in most supermarkets
   and specialty markets)
2 tablespoons butter
2 tablespoons flour
1 1/2 cups milk, warm
2 tablespoons finely chopped green onions (scallions)
3 cloves garlic, minced
2 tablespoons chopped fresh parsley
6 slices provolone cheese

PREPARATION
1. Melt the butter in a saucepan on medium heat. Stir in flour and make a roux. Cook roux, while stirring, for about 3 minutes; add half of warm milk and stir with a whisk until milk is a thick paste. Add remainder of milk and whisk until you have a smooth sauce. If the sauce is too thick, add a little more milk. Cool.

ASSEMBLY
1. Place four mushrooms in six individual casserole dishes. Place one escargot in each mushroom cap.
2. Mix green onion, minced garlic, and parsley into the white sauce. Spoon sauce evenly on escargot. Top with provolone cheese.
3. Bake in a preheated 400° oven for 15 minutes or until sauce is bubbly and cheese is melted.
4. Serve casserole on plates. Be careful they will be hot. I like to put the casseroles on a cookie sheet to prevent a spillover in the oven.

"You know you've reached middle age when your weightlifting consists of merely standing up."
Bob Hope

=========SCALLOPS STUFFED MUSHROOMS

A wonderful way of enjoying succulent scallops.

24 larger mushrooms, stems removed, wiped clean,
    stems minced
24 medium scallops, small muscle removed
3 tablespoons butter
1/4 cup finely chopped onion
2 large cloves garlic, minced
1/2 cup seasoned bread crumbs
1 egg, beaten
2 tablespoons white wine
2 tablespoons chopped fresh parsley
1/4 pound melted butter
6 slices provolone cheese

PREPARATION
1. Melt the butter in a medium skillet, then sauté onions
   and garlic; stir in mushroom stems and sauté until mushrooms
   wilt a little. Cool.
2. Mix mushroom mixture, bread crumbs, egg, white wine, and parsley
   in a mixing bowl.

ASSEMBLY
1. Place four mushrooms in six individual casserole dishes.
   Spoon stuffing mixture evenly into each mushroom. Top stuffing
   with a scallop, pressing down a little. Stick a toothpick in the stuffed
   mushroom cap and dip into melted butter.
   Top mushrooms with a slice of provolone cheese.
2. Bake in a preheated 400° oven for 15 minutes.
3. Serve casserole on plates. Be careful they will be hot. I like to put the
   casseroles on a cookie sheet to prevent a spillover in the oven and
   it makes them easier to take out of the oven.

*"In the last analysis, a pickle is nothing more than a
cucumber with experience."*
                    Irena Chalmers

SHRIMP LORRAINE

This is a wonderful tasty appetizer or entrée. I have served samples of this shrimp at a cooking demonstration for the Rhode Island Food Bank. Serve two shrimp as an appetizer, four as dinner. Smaller shrimp are ok to use.

8 uncooked U-10 shrimp, shelled, deveined, tails removed
1 tablespoon butter
1/2 chopped green onions (scallions)
6 mushrooms, cleaned and sliced
1 teaspoon soy sauce
1/4 cup sour cream
1/4 teaspoon paprika
1 tablespoon grated Parmesan cheese

ASSEMBLY

1. Heat a large skillet and melt butter until it foams. Stir in green onions, mushrooms, and cook for just a minute; add shrimp and sauté until shrimp are cooked.
   Stir in soy sauce and cook for a minute; stir in sour cream and paprika until sour cream is dissolved; stir in Parmesan cheese and remove from the stove.
2. Spoon shrimp on serving plates; spoon sauce on and around shrimp.

"There is really nothing new in (cooking). I have four thousand cookbooks dating back to 1503 and everything that is in "nouvelle cuisine" was there two hundred years ago."
Anton Mosimann

======= *SMOKED SALMON-ASPARAGUS MOUSSE*

A wonderful combination of salmon and asparagus, served as an appetizer or a luncheon with a salad.

Serves 6

24 asparagus spears, trimmed, blanched firm, cooled,
    reserve 1/2 cup of blanching water
1 envelope (1 tablespoon) unflavored gelatin
1/2 cup cold water
1 cup mayonnaise
1 cup sour cream
1/2 cup finely chopped celery
1/2 cup finely chopped onion
Dash ground red pepper (cayenne)
1/2 pound smoked salmon, sliced thin
Vegetable oil or cooking spray

PREPARATION

1. Sprinkle gelatin over 1/2 cup cold water to soften in a small saucepan; allow to sit at least 10 minutes. Add asparagus water; heat over low heat, to almost a boil, stirring constantly. Cool.
2. Remove tips (1-inch) from asparagus, save to use later as garnish.
3. Place asparagus in a food processor, process until smooth. Place asparagus in a mixing bowl; and thoroughly mix gelatin mixture, mayonnaise, sour cream, celery, onion, and cayenne.

ASSEMBLY

1. Lightly oil six individual cups or molds (6 to 8-ounce).
2. Thinly line the cups with smoked salmon. Spoon asparagus mousse evenly into the cups on top of smoked salmon. Top with a piece of smoked salmon. Wrap in plastic wrap and store in refrigerator for at least 12 hours.
3. When ready to serve, use a table knife along the inside of the cup to loosen. Place a serving plate on top of cup, turn plate over; the mousse should drop onto plate. Do this with each serving.
4. Garnish with asparagus tips, and a little dollop of sour cream on top of mousse.

=STUFFED PORTOBELLO MUSHROOMS ROBERT

I love to serve this appetizer because the presentation is beautiful.
Serves 4

4 portobello mushrooms about 3 ½ to 4 inches across, wiped clean, stems
   removed and chopped
1 tablespoon butter
2 cups red onions, chopped or thinly sliced
1 tablespoon soy sauce
1 tablespoon balsamic vinegar
Olive oil or cooking spray
2 tablespoons Gorgonzola cheese
4 slices dilled Havarti cheese or cheddar
2 tablespoons hoisin sauce (available in all markets)
2 ripe peaches

PREPARATION

1. Melt butter in a medium skillet on medium heat and sauté onions,
   stirring occasionally, until onions are light golden. Stir in chopped
   mushroom stems and continue cooking until mushrooms are completely
   cooked. Stir in soy sauce and balsamic vinegar. Cool.

ASSEMBLY

1. Brush oil on the bottom of the mushrooms and place in an ovenproof
   casserole or cookie sheet large enough to hold the mushrooms. Spoon
   onion mixture evenly into each mushroom. Top onions with Gorgonzola
   cheese and Havarti cheese.
2. Bake in a preheated 400° oven for about 20 minutes.
3. Select four plates and spread hoisin sauce evenly in the middle of each
   plate. Peel peachs, cut in half, remove pit. Slice peaches into 12 slices.
4. Remove cooked mushroom from casserole to prepared plates.
   Place mushroom in center of hoisin sauce; garnish plate with
   sliced peaches.

"Once we sowed wild oats, now we cook them in the microwave."
Irena Chalmers

THREE CHEESE TORTE

The green peppercorns add a little zip to this crus less torte.
Serves 6 or 8

1/2 pound Mascarpone cheese
1/2 pound Gorgonzola cheese
1/2 pound Stracchino cheese (if not available use cream cheese)
1/2 cup walnut pieces
1 tablespoon canned green peppercorns or 1/4 teaspoon ground
   green peppercorns

ASSEMBLY
1. Process all the ingredients in a food processor until smooth.
2. Select a 3 cup mold or 6 1/2 cup molds. Line with plastic
   wrap. Fill mold or molds with cheese mixture.
3. Place molds in refrigerator for a few hours or overnight.
4. To remove the torte, turn over on a plate and allow cheese to
   drop from mold, then remove plastic wrap. Serve with greens,
   sliced pears, crackers, or as a dip for vegetables. It is also wonderful
   with cold shrimp.

*Green peppercorns are available in small cans or jars packed
in water in specialty stores.*

*"It is good to be spontaneous, it is good to be thorough,
it is good to have something that inspires you."*
Paul McCartney

=====================================VEGETABLE PIZZA

Fresh pizza dough is available in most grocery stores.
Serves 4 to 6

1 pound pizza dough
1 sweet red bell pepper, cored, seeded, and sliced thin
1 green bell pepper, cored, seeded, and sliced thin
1 small red onion, peeled, cut in half and sliced thin
1/4 teaspoon fennel seeds
1/4 teaspoon dried basil or 1/4 cup chopped fresh basil
2 tablespoons olive oil
1/2 cup shredded mozzarella or prepared pizza cheese

PREPARATION
1. Mix peppers, onions, fennel seeds, basil, and 1 tablespoon olive
   oil in a mixing bowl.

ASSEMBLY
1. Oil a cookie sheet. Spread pizza dough on cookie sheet with
   your fingers, pressing towards the edges until dough is flat and
   the desired size and thickness is reached.(as you spread the dough it
   pulls back, but keep spreading) I like to put a little oil on
   top of the dough; it keeps your fingers from sticking to it If
   you wish smaller pizzas spread half of dough on two sheets.
2. Spoon and spread vegetable mixture evenly on dough. Sprinkle cheese
   on top of vegetables
3. Bake in a preheated 425° oven on middle shelf for 20 minutes
   or until pizza is cooked.
4. Cut into portions and enjoy. I cut the pizza with kitchen scissors.
   A knife can be used also.

Helpful Hint
If you run out of silver cleaner to clean silverware, try
using toothpaste to polish silverware or small silver objects.
It works great.

Dinner should be a bonding time for the family, a time to celebrate the day's events and share them at the table. The conversation should be about all of the things that happened in the course of the day or week. Happy and caring conversation is what I like at the dinner table. Forget the stress conversation.

I have a friend who shuts off the phone and turns off the television during the dinner hour. She puts on soothing music and makes sure there are flowers on the table, trying to make each dinner special. Each dinner starts with a prayer, said every evening by someone different at the table. A normal evening dinner can be special if you make it that way. Don't be afraid to use the dining room.

In many young families, dinner is often done on the run, sandwiched among sports activities, work schedules and meetings. Try to keep a few nights a week to have that special dinner. When you start, everyone may think you need a shrink, but they'll get accustomed to it, especially if you do it on a regular basis.

I know people who eat in front of the television every evening. Shut off the television, eat at the table and talk to each other. You will be surprised at how much conversation can be enjoyed.

We should be thankful for the abundance of food we have and for our family and friends. Some of our best times can and should be at the dinner table.

I have worked most of my professional life making dinners special. I believe elegance is a state of mind, and can created with just a little creativity. Dining experiences can become elegant with a few extra ingredients – flowers, candles, lighting, music, great food, and good conversation. You can turn your family dining room into something special with just a little imagination.

SOUPS
CHOWDERS

EPD '90

========*Hints and Suggestions*

CHOWDER: The word "chowder" comes from the French word Chaudiere, a large caldron in which communal fish stews were made in fishing villages. Each fisherman contributed something of his catch to the pot. The difference between a chowder and fish stew is not always clear, but generally the classic chowder base is salt pork, onions, potatoes, and milk. My parents always made clam chowder with tomato. Staunch New Englanders always used milk. (In 1939 a bill was introduced into the Maine legislature to make tomatoes in chowder illegal; it did not get passed.)

BLENDING HOT LIQUID: When blending hot soups or hot liquids, turn the blender on low speed then add liquid slowly while blender is running. I find when adding the liquid, then starting the blender, the steam and speed of the blender will make the liquid jump and the cover come off.

WASHING LEEKS: Trim off most of the green part. Cut off the root part, cut the white part down to the stem in quarters. Wash thoroughly under cold water; use your fingers to separate the leaves. Drain and drip-dry.

BUTTERNUT SQUASH SOUP

I love living in South County, Rhode Island, there is so much history here. It is the home of the Narraganset Indian Tribe. They taught the early Colonist how to survive, grow, and store food for the winter; one such food was askatasquash. It was too difficult for the Colonist to pronounce, so they nicknamed it squash.

Serves 6-8

1 or 2 butternut squash (4 pounds) halved, peeled, seeded cut into
   1 inch chunks
2 tablespoons butter
1 cup chopped onions
1 cup sliced leeks, white part only, washed thoroughly
2 cloves garlic, chopped
1 tablespoon fresh ginger, peeled and finely chopped
2 tablespoons honey
2 tablespoons soy sauce
1/2 cup flour
6 cups chicken broth (fresh or canned)
1/3 cup applejack liquor or bourbon liquor (optional)
1/4 cup sherry wine
1/4 teaspoon nutmeg
1 cup half-and-half cream or evaporated skim milk

PREPARATION

1. Melt butter in a large, heavy saucepan. Add onion; sauté
   until onion is yellow. Add leeks and garlic; sauté
   until leeks are soft. Stir in ginger, honey, and soy sauce; bring
   to a slight boil. Stir in flour, blending completely. Add chicken
   stock and mix thoroughly. Add diced butternut squash. Cook
   over medium low heat until squash is tender, about 40 minutes.
   (Soup can be refrigerated at this point, and finished later.)

ASSEMBLY

1. Working in batches, carefully puree soup in a blender or use an
   immersion blender. Return soup to the saucepan. Add
   applejack, sherry wine, nutmeg, and cream. Heat on
   low heat, stirring, until hot; do not bring to a boil.
2. Ladle into soup bowls and garnish with croutons.

================================CLAM CHOWDER

In Rhode Island four varieties of chowder are enjoyed. In South County, the chowder is served natural without the cream. In my family the cream and dill were omitted and chopped tomato was added. In Manhattan, the cream is omitted and diced vegetables and tomato are added. In Boston, chowder is served with milk or cream. This recipe is made with cream.
Serves 6 to 8

1 teaspoon olive oil
4 ounces salt pork, cut in slices
2 cups chopped onions
2 tablespoons flour
3 (8-ounce) bottles clam juice
1 pound potatoes, peeled, cut into 1/2-inch dice
1 bay leaf
4 (6-1/2 ounce) cans of chopped clams
1 teaspoon dried dill or 2 teaspoons chopped fresh dill
1 cup half-and-half cream, or evaporated milk

PREPARATION
1. Heat olive oil in a large saucepan over medium heat. Add salt pork and cook until salt pork starts to brown and render. Stir in onion and sauté, while stirring, until onions are light brown and tender. Stir in flour and cook for about two minutes. Gradually add clam juice, potato, and bay leaf; bring to a light boil over medium heat for about 20 minutes or until potatoes are cooked. Add clams to cooked potatoes and just bring to a boil. Lower heat and add dill and cream. Remove salt pork slices and bay leaf.
2. Ladle chowder into soup bowls. Serve with oyster crackers.

If you can get fresh clams (quahogs) use them instead of the canned clams.
Quahog is the American Indian name for the East Coast hard-shell clam.

COLD AVOCADO SOUP

Florida was the site of the first U.S. avocado trees. Most of today's crop comes from California. The avocado is native of the tropics and sub tropics. This cold soup is wonderful on a hot night.
Serves 6 to 8

4 large very ripe avocados
1 cup chopped onions
Juice from one lemon
1 cup sour cream
4 cups milk
1/2 teaspoon hot-pepper sauce (Tabasco)
1 teaspoon salt

PREPARATION

1. Cut avocados in half; remove seed and scoop the flesh into a blender or food processor. Add onions, lemon juice, and sour cream. Blend until smooth. Spoon avocado mixture into a mixing bowl and stir in milk, Tabasco, and salt. Store in refrigerator until ready to serve.

ASSEMBLY

1. Ladle chilled soup into soup bowls. Serve with crackers or crusty French bread.

===================COLD STRAWBERRY SOUP

Cold fruit soups are always refreshing on a warm day.
Serves 6 to 8

1 quart ripe strawberries, hulled, washed (frozen can be used)
1 cup sour cream or yogurt
1/2 teaspoon cinnamon
1 quart half-and half-cream (for a lighter soup, use milk)
2 tablespoons sherry wine
Mint leaves for garnish (optional)

PREPARATION
1. Place strawberries and sour cream in a food processor, blend
   until smooth. Transfer strawberry mixture to a mixing bowl. Stir
   in cinnamon, cream, and sherry wine. Store in refrigerator until
   ready to use.

ASSEMBLY
1. Ladle chilled soup in soup bowl and garnish with mint leaves.

VARIATIONS

RASPBERRY
Place raspberries and sour cream in food processor, blend until
smooth. Sieve the mixture by pressing down with back of spoon
and pushing raspberries thru the sieve to remove the seeds. Then
add cinnamon, cream, and sherry wine.

PEACH
Peel and pit peaches; process in the same way as strawberries.
Then add cinnamon, cream, and sherry wine.

MELON
Cut melon in quarters; remove seeds, and skin. Process the same
way as strawberries. Then add cinnamon, cream, and sherry wine.

=====================COLD ZUCCHINI SOUP

Summer time and the zucchini is abundant. Instead of making zucchini bread, make this soup. This soup can be served warm as well.

Serves 6 to 8

3 large zucchini, stems removed, washed and sliced
1 cup chopped onion
1 green bell pepper, cored, seeded and rough cut
2 cups chicken broth, canned or fresh
1/4 teaspoon dried rosemary or 3/4 teaspoon fresh rosemary
1/2 teaspoon dried basil or 2 tablespoons chopped fresh basil
1/4 cup chopped green onions (scallions)
2 cups milk
1 cup sour cream or yogurt
1/2 teaspoon salt
Pepper to taste
1 lime, sliced thin, seeds removed for garnish

PREPARATION
1. Place zucchini, onion, pepper, and chicken broth in a saucepan
    over medium heat. Bring to a boil and cook until squash is tender.
    Cool slightly and puree in a food processor or blender. Return squash
    to saucepan and thoroughly stir in rosemary, basil, green onions, milk,
    sour cream, salt, and pepper. Cool; store in refrigerator until ready to use.

ASSEMBLY
1. Ladle soup into soup bowls and garnish with a slice of lime.
    Serve with nice crusty bread.

"A good cook is like a sorceress who dispenses happiness."
Elsa Schiapirelli

A hearty, wonderful chowder that is always better on the second day.
Serves 6 to 8

1 teaspoon olive oil
4 ounces salt pork, sliced (bacon can also be used)
2 cups chopped onions
4 cups chicken broth(canned or fresh)
1 pound potatoes, peeled and cut into 1/2-inch dice
1 bay leaf
1 (15-ounce) can cream of corn
2 cups corn kernels, canned, frozen, or fresh
1 cup evaporated milk or half-and-half cream

PREPERATION

1. Heat olive oil over medium heat in a large saucepan. Add salt pork
    slices; cook until salt pork starts to brown and render. Stir in
    chopped onions; sauté, while stirring, until onions are light
    brown and tender. Add chicken stock, potatoes, and bay leaf.
    Bring to a light boil and cook for about 20 minutes or until
    potatoes are cooked. Remove salt pork and bay leaf. Add cream
    of corn and corn kernels. Bring to a light boil for about ten
    minutes. Add evaporated milk or cream. Keep on very low
    heat until ready to use.
2. Ladle soup into soup bowls. Serve with oyster crackers or a
    nice crusty bread.

Chowder can be prepared ahead and refrigerated.
For variation, add some diced ham to the corn chowder.

Helpful Hint
When I remove cooked or raw corn kernels from a cob, I invert a large
glass in a mixing bowl; Place the corn on the glass upright, use a sharp
knife and cut straight down, slicing the kernels from the cob.
Cut a few rows of corn at a time on the cob; don't cut to close to the cob.

"You cannot control getting older, but being and thinking old is up to you."
Author

CREAM OF CARROT SOUP

This tasty soup can be either hot or chilled.

Carrots have been renowned for over 2,000 years for their health-giving properties and high vitamin A content. They are a member of the parsley family.

Serves 6 or 8

2 tablespoons butter
1 cup chopped onions
2 1/2 pounds carrots, peeled, and sliced
1/2 cup chopped celery
6 cups chicken broth canned or fresh
1/3 cup chopped fresh dill or 2 teaspoons dried dill
Dash ground red pepper (cayenne)
2 cups evaporated milk or half-and-half cream
Salt and pepper to taste
Sour cream or yogurt for garnish
Dill sprigs for garnish

PREPARATION

1. Melt butter in a large saucepan over medium heat. Add onions; cook until yellow. Add carrots, celery, and chicken broth. Bring to a boil, reduce heat and simmer for about 30 minutes or until carrots are tender. Allow soup to cool a little.
2. Puree the soup in batches, in a blender or food processor. Return soup to saucepan over medium low heat. Stir in dill, milk, cayenne, salt, and pepper. Keep on low heat until ready to serve.

ASSEMBLY

1. Ladle soup into soup bowls. Spoon a dollop of sour cream on soup and garnish with dill sprig.

For variation, use curry instead of dill

*"A crust eaten in peace is better
than a banquet partaken in anxiety."*
Aesop

=========CREAM OF POTATO AND LEEK SOUP

A classic soup (vichyssoise) that is wonderful served either hot or cold.
Serves 6 to 8

2 tablespoons butter
1 cup chopped onions
6 leeks, green part removed, split lengthwise and rinsed well to
    remove sand, cut in thin slices
6 large potatoes, peeled and diced or sliced
5 cups chicken broth, canned or fresh
1 teaspoon salt
1/4 teaspoon ground red pepper (cayenne)
1/8 teaspoon nutmeg
1 cup evaporated milk or half-and-half cream
Fresh green onions, (scallions) finely sliced for garnish

PREPARATION
1. Melt butter over medium heat in a large saucepan. Stir in onions;
   sauté until soft and yellow. Stir in leeks; sauté until tender. Add
   potatoes, chicken broth, salt, cayenne, and nutmeg. Bring to a low
   boil and cook for about 25 minutes or until potatoes are tender.
2. Working in batches, purec the soup in a blender or with an immersion
   blender until smooth. (If you wish, leave the soup chunky,
   without blending.) Return soup to the saucepan on low heat.
   Add milk and keep warm on low heat until ready to use.

ASSEMBLY
1. Ladle the soup into soup bowls and garnish with green onions.
   If soup is too thick, add a little more milk or cream.

> *"To teach through example*
> *is a language anyone can understand."*
> *Author*

===========CURRIED SWEET POTATO BISQUE

We think of sweet potatoes usually during the holiday season.
This is a great soup anytime of the year.
Serves 6 to 8

2 tablespoons butter
1 cup chopped onions
1 cup sliced leeks, white part only, washed
2 teaspoons curry powder
1/4 teaspoon allspice
5 cups chicken broth, canned or fresh
4 pounds sweet potatoes, peeled and cubed
1 cup evaporated skim milk or half-and-half cream
Sour cream or yogurt for garnish
Sliced green onions (scallions) for garnish

PREPARATION
1. Melt butter over medium heat in a large saucepan. Stir in onions;
   sauté until soft and yellow. Stir in leeks; sauté until tender. Stir
   in curry powder and allspice; cook for about one minute. Add
   chicken broth and diced sweet potato. Bring to a low boil and
   cook for about 25 minutes or until potatoes are tender.
2. Working in batches, puree the soup in a blender or with an immersion
   blender until smooth. Return the soup to the saucepan on low
   heat. Add milk and keep warm on low heat until ready to use.

ASSEMBLY
1. Ladle the soup into soup bowls and spoon a dollop of sour
   cream on soup. Garnish with sliced green onions.

For variation, use butternut squash instead of sweet potato.

"Cooking is like love it should be
entered with abandon or not at all."
Harriot Van Horne

=========FENNEL BISQUE WITH CRABMEAT

Fennel is a wonderful aromatic plant. Fennel eaten raw or cooked, has a light, licorice flavor. Italians eat fennel after dinner for digestion.
Serves 6 or 8

2 tablespoons butter
1 cup chopped onions
1 cup sliced leeks (white part only washed thoroughly)
2 fennel bulbs halved lengthwise, cored and cut into
   1/2 inch pieces, fronds (tops) saved for garnish
4 cups chicken broth, canned or fresh
1 large Yukon Gold potato, peeled, and sliced
1 cup evaporated milk or half-and-half cream
1/2 pound fresh, frozen, or canned crabmeat (check for bones)

PREPARATION
1. Melt butter over medium heat in a large saucepan. Stir in
   onions; cook until soft and yellow. Stir in leeks and fennel;
   sauté on low heat, while stirring, until vegetables are tender,
   about 12 minutes. Add chicken stock and potato. Bring to a low
   boil and simmer until vegetables are cooked.
2. Working in batches, puree the soup in a blender or with an immersion
   blender until smooth. Return the soup to the saucepan on low
   heat. Add cream and keep on low heat until ready to use.
   Just before serving, add crabmeat.

ASSEMBLY
1. Ladle the soup into soup bowls. Garnish with sprig of fennel fronds (tops).

*"Food can be art, entertainment, glamour, fashion,
relaxation, love, sustenance."*
            Bruce Seidel
            Food Network

=================================MUSHROOM-LEEK SOUP

Hearty delicate flavors that make the kitchen smell so good.

Serves 6

2 tablespoons butter
1 cup chopped onions
2 cups thinly sliced leeks (white parts only washed thoroughly)
1 pound mushrooms, cleaned and sliced
2 tablespoons flour
4 cups chicken broth, canned or fresh
2 tablespoons dry sherry
1 cup half-and-half cream
1/4 cup chopped green onions (scallions)

PREPARATION
1. Melt butter over medium heat in a large saucepan. Add onions; cook until yellow. Stir in leeks and mushrooms; sauté, while stirring, until leeks and mushrooms are wilted.
2. Stir in flour; cook for about 1 minute. Gradually stir in chicken stock. Bring to a low boil, stirring frequently. Reduce heat to low and simmer for about 10 minutes.

ASSEMBLY
1. Add sherry, cream, and green onions; simmer for about 5 minutes. Keep soup on very low heat until ready to use. I like to put a little water in a larger pan than the one I cooked the soup in (like a double-boiler). It keeps the soup hot without scorching.
2. Ladle soup into soup bowls and garnish with croutons.

"Of all the items on the menu, soup is that which exacts the most delicate perfection and the strictest attention."
-Auguste Escoffier

We served many bowls of this onion soup at the restaurant.
I made the soup ahead and allowed it to age in the refrigerator for a few
days before serving it. It gave the soup time to come to its peak.
Serves 6 or 8

2 tablespoons butter
1 tablespoon olive oil
9 cups onion, peeled and thinly sliced
1 tablespoon brown sugar
2 tablespoons flour
1 quart chicken broth (home made or canned)
1 quart beef broth (home made or canned)
1 (10 1/2-ounce) can of beef consommé
1/3 cup brandy
1/3 cup sherry wine
Slices of French bread
Parmesan cheese

PREPARATION

1. Add butter and olive oil in a deep saucepan over medium heat.
   When butter is melted; stir in onions, sauté until onions yellow.
   Add brown sugar and sauté, stirring until onions are a dark
   golden color. Stir in the flour and cook, while stirring, for about
   2 minutes. In the meantime, heat the chicken broth and whisk
   chicken stock in the onions. Add beef broth, consommé, brandy,
   and sherry wine. Simmer for about 2 hours.
   Onion soup can be cooled and refrigerated at this point and reheated later.

ASSEMBLY

1. Ladle hot onion soup into a soup bowl top with slice of French
   bread and grated Parmesan cheese.

> *"As the days grow short, some faces grow long. But not mine.*
> *Every autumn, when the wind turns cold and darkness comes early,*
> *I am suddenly happy. It's time to start making soup again."*
> *Leslie Newman*

==============*BAKED ONION SOUP GRATINEE*

*We buttered the bread on one side then toasted the slices of French
bread in the oven before using them in the soup.*
We also used these croutons under filet mignon to absorb the juice.

Onion soup, page 65
Sliced French bread
Parmesan cheese
Swiss cheese or Gruyere cheese

Ladle onion soup into an ovenproof soup bowl. Top soup with
slice of French bread; top bread with spoon of Parmesan cheese.
Top Parmesan cheese with a slice of Swiss or Gruyere cheese.
Bake in a 400° oven until bubbly, about 10-15 minutes. Be
careful taking bowls out of the oven. I like to bake the soup on a
cookie sheet. The cookie sheet keeps
the soup from bubbling
over in the oven and makes it easier
to take soup out of the oven.

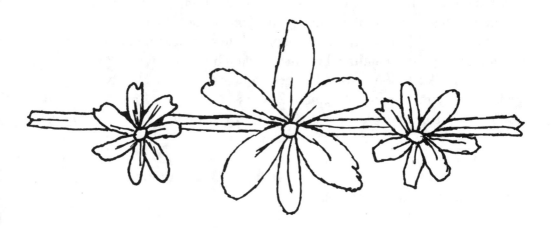

=================ROASTED VEGETABLE SOUP

Roasted vegetables make this a hearty cold weather soup.
Serves 6 to 8

2 large beets, peeled, halved, and sliced 1/2-inch thick
2 large carrots, peeled, and sliced in 1 inch pieces
1 medium turnip, peeled, halved and sliced 1/2-inch pieces
1 medium parsnip, peeled and sliced in 1 inch pieces
1 leek, white part only, stem removed, sliced in half and washed
1 large onion, peeled and sliced in 1/2-inch slices
1 large potato, peeled and sliced in 1/2-inch slices
2 tablespoons olive oil
5 cups chicken broth, canned or fresh
Salt and pepper to taste
Sour cream for garnish
Chopped fresh dill for garnish (dried dill can be used)

PREPARATION
1. Add all the vegetables to a large bowl. Stir in olive oil and
   coat vegetables with olive oil. Select a large rimmed baking
   sheet. Spread the oiled vegetables evenly on the sheet. Bake in a
   preheated 475° oven for about 25 minutes. Stir on occasion.
   Bake until vegetables brown a little.
2. Place the roasted vegetables and chicken broth in a large
   saucepan over medium heat. Add salt and pepper; bring to a
   low boil for about 15 minutes or until vegetables are tender.
3. Working in batches, puree the soup in a blender or with an immersion
   blender until smooth. (If you wish, leave the soup chunky
   without blending.) Return the soup to the saucepan on low heat.
   If the soup is too thick, add a little more chicken broth.

ASSEMBLY
1. Ladle the soup into soup bowls and garnish with a dollop of sour
   cream and dill. Serve with some nice crusty bread.

"Worries go down better with soup."
Yiddish proverb

SPLIT PEA SOUP

A fireplace and a bowl of pea soup with great bread is all you need on a winter night. Mix cream of tomato soup and a little milk or cream with left over pea soup for a different treat.
Serves 6 to 8

1 (16-ounce) package dried split peas, rinsed
1 hambone, 2 meaty ham hocks, or 2 cups diced ham
1 cup chopped onions
3 carrots, peeled, diced or grated
1 cup chopped celery
2 garlic cloves, minced
1 bay leaf
1 1/2 quarts of hot water

PREPARATION
1. Place all ingredients in a large saucepan over medium heat. Bring to a low boil. Use low heat and simmer for about two to three hours, stirring frequently to prevent sticking as soup thickens. Add a little more water if soup becomes too thick.

ASSEMBLY
1. Remove ham, the hambone or ham hocks from soup as well as the bay leaf. Cut ham off bone or ham hocks. Chop ham and return to the soup.
2. Ladle soup into a soup bowl and serve with nice crusty bread.

   Puree soup for a creamier soup.

   With good friends...and good food on board, and good wine in the pitcher, we may well ask: "When shall we live if not now?"
   M.F.K. Fisher

============SWEET RED BELL PEPPER BISQUE

*Red has always been my favorite color; this soup looks beautiful
and is full of flavor. Sweet and hot peppers are native of the Western
Hemisphere and were brought back to Spain by Christopher Columbus.
Peppers quickly found their place in Spanish cooking.*
Serves 6

2 tablespoons butter
1 cup chopped onions
1 cup sliced leeks, washed white part only
4 large sweet red bell peppers, core and seeds removed, cut into 1 inch pieces
2 jalapenos, seeded and coarsely chopped (optional)
4 cups chicken broth (fresh or canned)
1 large Yukon Gold potato, peeled and cut into slices
2 tablespoons soy sauce
1/4 cup chopped fresh parsley
1/4 cup sherry wine
1 cup evaporated milk or half-and-half cream
Sour cream for garnish

PREPARATION
1. Melt butter over medium heat in a large saucepan. Stir in the
   chopped onion; sauté until soft. Stir in leeks, peppers, and
   jalapenos. Sauté, stirring occasionally, until vegetables start to
   soften. Add chicken broth, potato, soy sauce, and parsley. Bring
   to a low boil and simmer on low heat until vegetables are
   cooked, about 25 minutes.
2. Working in batches, puree the soup in a blender or in an immersion
   blender until smooth. Return the soup to sauce pan and reheat
   over low heat; add sherry wine and evaporated milk or cream.
     (If soup is too thick, add a little more milk or cream)

ASSEMBLY
1. Ladle soup into soup bowls and spoon a little sour cream
   on top of the soup.

===============================TOMATO BISQUE

Tomato soup has such a beautiful color. The light red soup garnished with the green fresh basil, can made ahead and served hot or cold.
Serves 6 or 8

2 tablespoons butter
1 1/2 cups onion, chopped
2 large cloves garlic, chopped
1 (28-ounce) can whole tomatoes
1 (46-ounce) can tomato juice
2 bay leaves
1 (8-ounce) package cream cheese
2 cups half-and-half cream
1 teaspoon fresh lemon juice
Chopped fresh basil for garnish

PREPARATION
1. Melt butter over medium heat in a large saucepan. Stir in onions and garlic; sauté until onions turn yellow. Add the tomatoes, tomato juice, and bay leaves. Simmer for 20 minutes. Remove from heat allow to cool a bit. Drain the tomatoes, reserving the juice; (remove bay leaf) process the tomatoes and cream cheese in a food processor or blender. Mix the puree with reserved juice. Add half-and-half and lemon juice. Re-heat or serve cold, according to the season.

ASSEMBLY
1. Ladle soup into soup bowls and garnish with chopped basil.

Serve with crusty bread or drop croutons in the soup.

This soup is great for lunch with a beautiful salad. The word salad comes from the Romans; they ate green leafy vegetables seasoned only with salt, and it is from their word salt that we get the word "salad."

WHITE BEAN SOUP WITH CHICKEN AND SPINACH

Beans are among the worlds oldest foods, dating back at least 4000 years.
Serves 6 to 8

1 tablespoon butter
1 tablespoon olive oil
1 cup chopped onion
4 garlic cloves, minced
4 cups chicken broth, canned or fresh
1 (19-ounce) can of white beans, drained (cannellini or
  Great Northern)
1/2 pound boneless, skinless chicken breast, sliced thin crosswise
1 pound fresh spinach, stems removed, washed, coarsely chopped
Dash ground red pepper (cayenne)
Salt and pepper to taste

PREPARATION

1. Melt butter and olive oil over medium heat in a large saucepan.
    Stir in onions and garlic; sauté until onions turn yellow. Add
    chicken broth, beans, and chicken. Bring to a low boil.
    Stir in spinach, cayenne, salt, and pepper to taste. Lower heat
    and simmer until ready to serve.

ASSEMBLY

1. Ladle soup into soup bowls
    and serve with nice crusty bread.

WINE SOMETIMES IS NOT WONDERFUL

After Quonset Naval Air Station closed and the Navy left, we suddenly enjoyed a boom time at the restaurant. Offshore oil exploration firms wanted to drive oil wells into our best fishing area called Georges Banks. The political atmosphere in Rhode Island was oil versus fish. We hosted many lunches at the restaurant that were part of the many meetings among oil people, politicians and environmental people.

One day my niece, Donna, was the waitress serving a party of eight businessmen for lunch. They were all very nicely dressed. She was serving eight glasses of red wine. The host was conversing with his guests when he raised his arm suddenly and knocked the tray out of her hand. Wine glasses dropped on the table and wine went everywhere.

Everyone was momentarily startled as the wine splashed all over the table and their suits. Donna stood there in shock for a second, looking at the startled men. Then she said, "If it would make you all feel better, I could cry." The men started to laugh as she gave everyone napkins to brush the wine off their suits. She cleaned up the table and started all over again.

The off-shore oil exploration never produced any wells and the fishing area off New England is still producing wonderful seafood.

==========================WALKING FISH

I was having some electrical and construction work done in the restaurant, on a day the restaurant was closed. My brother-in-law, Raymond, was doing the electrical work and he brought his four-year-old son, Raymond Jr., with him. While he was working on wiring, his son was quietly watching my fish swimming in the fish tank. Raymond kept asking his son, "Are you OK?"

Young Raymond spotted a pile of sawdust on the floor near the tank and proceeded to fill the tank with sawdust with his little shovel.

I walked in the restaurant the next morning; looked at the fish tank and saw the fish were just about walking on the sawdust! I was able to remove most of the sawdust with a strainer and tried to clean the water. It took a while but I finally got the tank clean. None of the fish died. Raymond Jr. eventually came to work for me in the kitchen and as a bus person. He is now married and has two sons.

CHICKEN

========== *BREADING CRUMBS FOR CHICKEN*

In Rhode Island in the 1970's and early 1980's, all that was needed on restaurant menus were steaks, prime rib, baked stuffed shrimp, and roast stuffed, boneless, chicken breast. In the middle 1980's changes in eating habits were beginning to happen. Cookbooks and television started to educate people about the benefits of cutting down on fats and red meat.

We started to change our menus, adding more chicken, veal, and seafood; keeping red meat and the dishes that were popular in a first class restaurant.

We did not have a sauté station in our restaurant; we cooked on the grill and in the oven. We came up with a special breading for boneless skinless breast of chicken that we could bake in the oven with different toppings and stuffings. After trial and error, we came up with this breading. We used the cornmeal for a little crunch, the seasoned bread crumbs for flavor, and the paprika for color.

3/4 cup seasoned bread crumbs
1/4 cup yellow cornmeal
1/2 teaspoon paprika

ASSEMBLY
1. Mix bread crumbs, cornmeal, and paprika in a mixing bowl.

Breading can be stored in covered container. Place enough crumbs in a flat dish to bread chicken. Any remaining crumbs in flat plate that have been used to bread chicken must be discarded.
Covered left over crumb mixture will have a shelf life
of a few weeks.

=====*PREPARING CHICKEN FOR COOKING*

Purchase the boneless, skinless, chicken breasts. If you have a whole chicken breast with the bone in, fillet the chicken breast, remove skin, and remove tenderloin (save tenderloin to use later).

Flatten the chicken breast by putting it between two sheets of waxed paper or plastic wrap and flatten evenly with a poultry or meat flattener. (You can also use the bottom of a sauté pan.)

"Poultry is for the cook what canvas is for the painter."
Brillat-Savarin

NOW SHE'S COOKING WITH CLASS

*I teach quite a few classes a year. I teach at many different levels from cooking with little kids to adult classes. I taught a cooking class for the North Kingstown Adult Education Fall session. A reporter from the **Standard Times** was scheduled to review my class. I wish to share with you this newspaper article.*

By: Megan Speenburgh   November 29, 2001

NORTH KINGSTOWN-

When I told my roommate that I would be cooking dinner last weekend, she didn't come home until way past dinnertime. Maybe it was because of my reputation as a bad cook.

Which isn't really true. I can make a killer taco and unbelievable baked macaroni and cheese. This is basically as far as my cooking goes.

Hey, I just graduated college. It's a step above Ramen Noodles or pasta for seven nights a week.

What Vikki, my roommate, didn't know was that I had just gone to a cooking demonstration by Chef Normand Leclair as part of the North Kingstown Adult Education classes. This is where I got the brilliant idea to have a small dinner party for my family, who would be visiting for the weekend.

During the demonstration, Leclair effortlessly showed 47 of us how to make about 15 different entrees including Chicken Indienne, Cashew Chicken, Pesto Chicken, Shrimp Lorraine, and Chicken in a Crust with Asparagus and Red Peppers. And we got to taste each one.

As I am watching Leclair prepare these wonderful dishes, my mouth is watering and I start thinking "I can do this." It doesn't look too difficult, plus Leclair is selling his cookbooks at the end. As long as I follow the directions, how hard could it be? So, I buy both of his cookbooks, Chicken Expressions and Seafood Expressions.

By the time the class is over, I have myself believing that I can really impress my family and friends with my new knowledge.

I go home and look through the cookbooks and decide that I will make the Chicken in a Crust with Asparagus and Sweet Red Peppers. Nothing too fancy for my first dinner.

Friday night comes and so do my parents. They go to their hotel to check in and I tell them dinner will be around 7:30. That gives me an hour and a half to go to the store, buy everything I need, and cook the dinner.

I figured Leclair made 15 entrees in about two hours, I'm only making one, so an hour and a half is plenty of time to have it in the oven by the time my guests arrive.

This way we can sit down, have an appetizer and a glass of wine, before eating dinner.

I get everything I need and I'm ready to cook. A crab dip out of Seafood Expressions cookbook. Not too difficult and it looks good too.

Okay not the entrée. I rinse and bread the chicken and sauté lightly. My parents arrive, and they are late. I, however, have only just begun the entrée. At least I have the appetizer.

I steam the asparagus for one minute, but I forget about it, so it's actually for about 3 minutes, which makes it a little soft. Oh, well, it will have to do.

I take out the frozen pastry shells, but I am not sure what to do with them. They did not look like this in Leclair's class at all. I read the recipe again because I'm afraid I bought the wrong thing. I call my dad into the kitchen for help. My dad is a great cook, so I figure he will know.

He tells me the pastries have to thaw a little and then I have to roll them out. So I roll them out, but they still don't look like Leclair's. They look a little smaller. I assemble the first entrée by putting a half of the breaded chicken breast on the rolled out pastry, four asparagus spears on top of that, the other half of chicken breast, and a quarter of a sweet red pepper on top of that. Then I fold up the pastry around the small pile I have, so it is completely covered. They turn out not to be too small.

The first entrée is finished. Oh, no! I forgot the American cheese and the basil! So, I try to open it back up, which doesn't really work, and sneak the cheese and basil into the entrée and cover it back up again. No one will notice, I do the the same for four people. I put them in the oven for 20 minutes, just enough time to make some rice for a side.

And dinner is served. It even looks like Normand Leclair's (Almost.) I wait for everyone to take a bite and see their reaction. And they smile and say it's wonderful. Which Normand Leclair said, "There is nothing better than when you set down a plate in front of the person and everyone at the table gets quiet. The first person takes a bite and then you see a smile."

And so it was a success about an hour later than I anticipated, but hopefully my reputation is changed and the next time my roommate won't want to miss dinner when I say I'm cooking.

CHICKEN BREAST BAKED WITH TOPPINGS

====*CHICKEN BREAST BAKED WITH TOPPINGS*

All recipes are for two in this chapter.

Chicken Breast Baked with Toppings Continued-

Chicken Breast Baked with Toppings Continued-

===========*Hints and Suggestions*

RECIPES: Chicken and seafood recipes are for two servings, unless otherwise specified. Double or triple the ingredients for more servings.

PREPARING AHEAD: If you prepare recipes ahead of time, take them out of the refrigerator 30 minutes before cooking time.

REMOVE SKIN FROM CHICKEN: To remove skin from fresh chicken, use a paper towel to hold the chicken skin, pull the skin while holding down the chicken and the skin should come right off.

FLATTEN CHICKEN: You can flatten trimmed chicken breasts between two pieces of wax paper or plastic wrap with the bottom of a sauté pan or a meat mallet, available in kitchen stores.

BREADING CRUMBS ON CHICKEN: If the boneless breasts of chicken are dry, moisten the chicken with a little milk and the crumbs will stick to the chicken.

ALMOND-ORANGE CHICKEN

Almond-chicken topped with a tasty colorful orange sauce.

2 whole chicken breasts, skinned, boned, halved, flattened,
  with fat removed
1 egg beaten with 1 teaspoon milk in a small bowl
3/4 cup ground almonds (can be done in a food processor)
1/4 cup cornflake crumbs (can be done in a food processor)
3 tablespoons butter
1/4 cup finely chopped onion
1/4 cup chopped green onions (scallions)
1 tablespoon flour
1/8 teaspoon poultry seasoning
1/2 cup milk
1 tablespoon orange marmalade
1/4 teaspoon grated orange peel (zest)
2 tablespoons orange juice

PREPARATION
1. Mix ground almonds and cornflake crumbs in a mixing bowl.
2. To make the sauce, melt 1 tablespoon of butter in a saucepan over
   medium heat; sauté onions and green onions for a couple of minutes.
   Stir in flour and poultry seasoning to make a smooth paste. Gradually
   whisk in milk and heat to a smooth sauce. Stir in orange marmalade,
   grated orange peel, and orange juice. Keep warm.

ASSEMBLY
1. Butter with 1 tablespoon of butter an ovenproof casserole dish that is
   just large enough to contain the chicken. Dip chicken in egg wash,
   allowing the excess to drip off; press chicken into almond breading,
   coating completely. Place breaded chicken in buttered casserole dish.
   Dot with butter.
2. Bake in a preheated 400° oven for 20 minutes.
3. Remove cooked chicken from casserole to heated plates with a spatula.
   Spoon the orange sauce on and around chicken.

APPLE GOAT CHEESE CHICKEN

Substitute the goat cheese with cream cheese if you wish.

2 whole chicken breasts, skinned, boned, halved, flattened,
  with fat removed
3 tablespoons goat cheese
1 large baking apple, peeled, quartered, cored, and grated
1/2 teaspoon grated lemon peel (zest)
1/4 cup chopped fresh parsley
1/2 cup breading crumbs, page 75
1 tablespoon grated Parmesan cheese
1 tablespoon olive oil
4 slices provolone cheese

PREPARATION
1. Put goat cheese in mixing bowl; crumble it with a fork;
   stir in grated apple, grated lemon peel, and chopped parsley.
2. Mix crumbs and Parmesan cheese in a mixing bowl.

ASSEMBLY
1. Oil an ovenproof casserole dish that is large enough to contain the
   four chicken breasts.
2. Press chicken breasts into crumbs, coating completely.
3. Place breaded chicken in casserole. Spoon and spread apple mixture
   evenly on each chicken breast. Top with provolone cheese.
4. Bake in a preheated 400° oven for 20 minutes.
5. Remove cooked chicken from casserole to heated plates with a spatula.
   Spoon remaining stuffing and juices around chicken.

"It is good to be spontaneous, it is good to be thorough,
it is good to have something that inspires you."
Paul McCartney

==============ASIAGO-ALMOND CHICKEN

Asiago cheese is a semi firm Italian cheese.

2 whole chicken breasts, skinned, boned, halved, flattened,
   with fat removed
1 1/2 cups ranch style salad dressing
2 garlic cloves, minced
1 teaspoon lemon juice
1 cup sliced almonds
2 ounces Asiago cheese, cut into small pieces
1/4 cup seasoned dry bread crumbs
1 tablespoon olive oil
1 tablespoon butter

PREPARATION
1. Mix ranch dressing, minced garlic, and lemon juice in a mixing bowl.
   Add chicken breasts to mixture, coating completely, turning occasionally.
   Marinate for at least one hour in the refrigerator.
2. Process the almonds, cheese, and crumbs in a food processor
   fitted with a metal blade; process to a coarse meal. Place in a shallow bowl.

ASSEMBLY
1. Oil an ovenproof casserole dish large enough to contain the four
   chicken breasts.
2. Remove the chicken breasts from the ranch mixture one at a time with
   a fork, allowing excess mixture to drip off; press in almond-cheese mixture,
   coating completely. Place breaded chicken breast in oiled casserole dish.
   Dot with butter.
3. Bake in a preheated 400° oven for 20 minutes.
4. Remove cooked chicken from casserole to heated plates with a spatula.

Helpful Hint
*I like to use parchment paper when I'm baking the chicken breast
with toppings or puff pastry. Parchment paper is strong enough be
able to bake without the paper burning. I love it because you discard
the paper after baking and clean up is easy. Parchment is coated with a
silicone that helps make it non-stick. (Great for baking cookies.)*

==============ASPARAGUS-SHRIMP CHICKEN

Shrimp is the most popular shellfish eaten in the world.

1 whole chicken breast, skinned, boned, halved, flattened,
  with fat removed   (2 individual chicken breasts)
1 tablespoon olive oil
1/2 cup breading crumbs, page 75
4 (U-12) large shrimp shelled, cleaned, with tail removed
6 asparagus spears, blanched firm
Dash nutmeg
1 teaspoon butter
2 slices Monterey Jack cheese
1/4 cup chopped fresh parsley

ASSEMBLY
1. Oil an ovenproof casserole dish that is just large enough to contain the two chicken breasts.
2. Place special crumbs in a flat dish and press chicken into crumbs, coating completely.
3. Place breaded chicken breasts in oiled casserole dish. Place shrimp on each end of chicken; cut and arrange asparagus to fit in the middle. Sprinkle with a little nutmeg. Dot with butter; top with Monterey Jack cheese and chopped parsley.
4. Bake in a preheated 400° oven for 20 minutes.
5. Remove cooked chicken from casserole to heated plates with a spatula.

If shrimp are extra large, extend cooking time a few minutes. U-12 means 12 shrimp to the pound.

Helpful Hint
Toothpaste can remove stubborn smells from the hands when handling shellfish, fish, garlic, and onions. Toothpaste can also remove crayon marks from painted walls. It can also clean chrome and silver.

AVOCADO CHICKEN

Many supermarket avocados are hard and under-ripe;
to speed ripening, place avocados in a paper bag with an apple.
Store at room temperature.

2 whole chicken breasts, skinned, boned, halved, flattened,
   with fat removed
1 firm ripe avocado, peeled and sliced
1/2 cup sour cream
1 teaspoon ground cumin
1/4 cup chopped green onions (scallions)
1/2 sweet red bell pepper, cored and small diced
1/4 cup chopped fresh parsley
1/2 cup breading crumbs, page 75
1 tablespoon olive oil
4 slices Monterey Jack cheese

PREPARATION
1. Place sliced avocado in a mixing bowl; stir in sour cream,
    ground cumin, chopped green onions, diced red pepper, and parsley.
    Mix very carefully trying not to break avocado.

ASSEMBLY
1. Oil an ovenproof casserole dish that is just large enough to contain
    the four chicken breasts.
2. Place crumbs in a flat dish and press chicken into crumbs
    coating chicken completely. Place breaded chicken in oiled
    casserole dish.
3. Spoon the avocado slices and sauce evenly on the breaded chicken.
    Top with slice of Monterey Jack cheese.
4. Bake in a preheated 400° oven for 20 minutes.
5. Remove cooked chicken from casserole to heated plates with a
    spatula. Spoon any remaining juices from casserole on and
    around chicken.

Helpful Hint
To dice an avocado, cut an avocado in half and remove the pit
With a paring knife, make long slits the length of the avocado, being
careful not to cut thru the skin. Turn the avocado and make small
slits crosswise making a cube pattern. Bend the avocado in half and push
out the cubes or scoop them out with a spoon.

=============BARBEQUE-ONION CHICKEN

Bottled barbecue sauce is made with tomatoes, mustard, onion, brown sugar, garlic, and vinegar. To customize your sauce, add beer, wine, green bell pepper, chili peppers, herbs, minced ginger, horseradish, or spicy mustard

2 whole chicken breasts, skinned, boned, halved, flattened,
   with fat removed
2 tablespoons olive oil
1/2 cup breading crumbs, page 75
1/2 cup hickory smoked barbecue sauce
4 slices Monterey Jack cheese
1/4 cup chopped fresh parsley
1 medium onion, peeled, halved and sliced thin
1/2 teaspoon brown sugar

ASSEMBLY

1. With 1 tablespoon oil, oil an ovenproof casserole dish large enough to contain the four chicken breasts, plus extra room for the onions.
2. Place crumbs in a flat dish and press chicken into crumbs, coating completely.
3. Place breaded chicken breasts in oiled casserole dish. Spoon barbecue sauce evenly on chicken. Top with Monterey Jack cheese and chopped parsley.
4. Mix sliced onion, brown sugar, and remaining olive oil in a mixing bowl; stir to coat onions with brown sugar and oil.
5. Place prepared onions into casserole dish around chicken. Do not place onions on chicken.
6. Bake in a preheated 400° oven for 20 minutes.
7. Remove chicken from casserole to heated plates with a spatula.

Spoon roasted onions and juices around the chicken.

Helpful Hint
Add a little vinegar to water in a tea kettle and boil, to remove lime deposit.

BROCCOLI CHICKEN

Broccoli can be cooked or eaten raw. The name comes from the Italian word meaning "cabbage sprout." The deep green vegetables should have tight clusters of tiny bulbs.

2 whole chicken breasts, skinned, boned, halved, flattened,
  with fat removed
1 small bunch broccoli, cut into small florets, cooked al dente.
  (Drop broccoli in boiling water for 3 minutes, drain and
  plunge in ice water, drain)
1 tablespoon butter
1 small onion, minced
2 cloves garlic, minced
1/4 cup sweet red bell pepper, cored, small diced
6 medium mushrooms, sliced
1/4 cup chopped green onions (scallions)
1 tablespoon olive oil
1/2 cup breading crumbs, page 75
4 slices Swiss cheese
1/4 cup chopped fresh parsley

PREPARATION
1. Melt butter in a medium skillet, then sauté onions until soft. Stir in garlic, peppers, and mushrooms; sauté for about 2 minutes. Stir in green onions and cooked broccoli. Cool.

ASSEMBLY
1. Oil an ovenproof casserole dish that is just large enough to contain the four chicken breasts.
2. Place crumbs in a flat dish and press chicken into crumbs, coating completely.
3. Place breaded chicken in oiled casserole dish. Spoon and spread broccoli mixture on chicken evenly. Top with Swiss cheese and parsley.
4. Bake in a preheated 400° oven for 20 minutes.
5. Remove cooked chicken from casserole to heated plates with a spatula. Spoon remaining topping around chicken.

Every February and March the Spring Hill Sugar House in Exeter, Rhode Island is making daily truck runs into the woods to collect the sap from the maple trees; staying up until well past midnight boiling it down to make maple syrup. It takes about 20 gallons of sap to make one gallon of syrup. It is quite a sight to see the sugarhouse; built from rough-hewn wood planks with a hole in the roof that lets out the steam from the boiling syrup and the smoke from the wood fueled stove.

2 whole chicken breasts, skinned, boned, halved, flattened,
   with fat removed
1 tablespoon butter
1/2 cup breading crumbs, page 75
4 slices Canadian bacon (ham can be used as well)
1 1/2 tablespoons whole grain mustard
1/4 cup chopped fresh parsley
4 slices provolone cheese
1 1/2 tablespoons maple syrup

ASSEMBLY

1. Butter an ovenproof casserole dish that is just large enough to contain the four chicken breasts.
2. Place crumbs in a flat dish and press chicken into crumbs, coating completely.
3. Place breaded chicken in buttered casserole dish; top with Canadian bacon. Spoon mustard evenly on each slice of Canadian bacon; add chopped parsley and top with provolone cheese.
4. Bake in a preheated 400° oven for 20 minutes.
5. Remove casserole from oven, spoon maple syrup on chicken. Remove cooked chicken from casserole to heated plates with a spatula. Spoon any remaining juices from casserole around chicken.

Helpful Hint

Never place good wooden handled knives in the dishwasher; wash them carefully in hot soapy water then rinse completely and dry.

=================CAPE COD CHICKEN

Dried cranberries available in most supermarkets, are dried like raisins.

2 whole chicken breasts, skinned, boned, halved, flattened,
   with fat removed
2 bacon slices, diced
1/4 cup chopped onions
1/2 cup peeled, cored, diced baking apple
1/4 cup chopped dried cranberries
1/4 teaspoon poultry seasoning
1/4 teaspoon ground cinnamon
1 tablespoon seasoned bread crumbs
1 tablespoon olive oil
1/2 cup breading crumbs, page 75
4 slices Monterey Jack cheese
1/4 cup chopped pecans

PREPARATION
1. Sauté bacon in a skillet over medium heat until crisp. Remove bacon and drain on paper towels. Save 1 tablespoon of bacon fat and sauté chopped onions until they are yellow. Stir in diced apple and cranberries; cook while stirring for about 3 minutes. Do not allow apples to get mushy. Remove skillet from heat and stir in cooked bacon, poultry seasoning, cinnamon, and bread crumbs. Mix well. Cool.

ASSEMBLY
1. Oil an ovenproof casserole dish that is just large enough to contain the four chicken breasts.
2. Place crumbs in a flat dish and press chicken into crumbs, coating completely.
3. Place breaded chicken in casserole. Spoon and spread cranberry-apple mixture evenly on each chicken breast. Top with Monterey Jack cheese and chopped pecans.
4. Bake in a preheated 400° oven for 20 minutes.
5. Remove cooked chicken from casserole to heated plates with a spatula. Spoon remaining stuffing and juices around chicken.

=============CARAMELIZED ONION CHICKEN

If you like caramelized onions, this dish will be special for you.
The sweetness of the onions and the melting Monterey Jack cheese will
surprise the palate.

2 whole chicken breasts, skinned, boned, halved, flattened,
    with fat removed
1 tablespoon butter
2 cups onions, peeled, cut in half, and sliced thin
1/2 teaspoon brown sugar
1/4 cup chopped fresh parsley
1 teaspoon Medeira wine
1 tablespoon olive oil
1/2 cup breading crumbs, page 75
4 slices Monterey Jack cheese

PREPARATION
1. In a sauté pan heat 1 tablespoon of butter. Add sliced onion
    and sauté slowly for 10 minutes; stir in brown sugar, and continue
    cooking until onions are light brown. Stir in half of chopped parsley
    and Madeira wine. Cool.

ASSEMBLY
1. Oil and ovenproof casserole dish large enough to contain the four
    chicken breasts.
2. Place special crumbs in a flat dish and press chicken into crumbs,
    coating completely.
3. Place chicken breasts in oiled casserole dish. Spoon onions evenly on
    each chicken breast. Top with Monterey Jack cheese and remaining
    chopped parsley.
4. Bake in a preheated 400° oven for 20 minutes.
5. Remove cooked chicken from casserole to heated plates with a spatula.

Helpful Hint
Store extra garbage liners inside the bottom of the kitchen
trash can. Remove the filled bag and you just slip in a new liner.

CASINO STYLE CHICKEN

Clam casino topping was the inspiration for this dish.
The color and aroma will excite all the senses.

2 whole chicken breasts, skinned, boned, halved, flattened,
   with fat removed
1 small red bell pepper, cored, sliced in thin strips
1 small green bell pepper, cored, sliced in thin strips
1 small red onion, peeled, halved, sliced thin
1 teaspoon dried basil or 1/4 cup chopped fresh basil
1/8 teaspoon fennel seeds
1/4 cup chopped fresh parsley
1/4 cup olive oil
1 tablespoon butter
1/2 cup breading crumbs, page 75
2 slices bacon, cut in half

PREPARATION
1. Mix sliced red pepper, sliced green pepper, sliced red onion, basil,
   fennel, parsley, and olive oil in a mixing bowl, coating vegetables
   with oil.

ASSEMBLY
1. Butter an ovenproof casserole dish that is just large enough to contain
   the four chicken breasts.
2. Place crumbs in a flat dish and press chicken into
   crumbs, coating completely.
3. Place breaded chicken breasts in buttered casserole dish. Spoon
   and spread pepper topping evenly on each chicken breast.
   Place a slice of bacon on top of pepper mixture.
4. Bake in a preheated 400° oven for 20 minutes.
5. Remove cooked chicken from casserole to heated plates with a
   spatula. Spoon any topping that may have fallen off the chicken
   on and around chicken.

"There cannot be a crisis next week. My schedule is already full."
Henry Kissinger

=================CHEESE-CRUSTED CHICKEN

Sesame seeds came from Africa to America on slave ships.
Crackers can be crushed in a food processor.

2 whole chicken breasts, skinned, boned, halved, flattened,
   with fat removed
1 cup finely crushed cheese crackers (such as Cheez-its)
1/4 cup sesame seeds
1/4 cup chopped fresh parsley
Dash ground red pepper (cayenne)
2 tablespoons grated Parmesan cheese
2 eggs, plus 1 tablespoon milk
1 tablespoon olive oil
1 tablespoon butter

PREPARATION
1. Mix crushed cheese crackers, sesame seeds, chopped parsley,
   cayenne pepper, and Parmesan cheese in a mixing bowl.
2. Whisk eggs and milk in a small bowl.

ASSEMBLY
1. Oil an ovenproof casserole dish that is just large enough to contain
   the four chicken breasts.
2. Place chicken breasts, one at a time, in egg wash,
   allowing excess egg mixture drip off; press in cheese crumb
   breading, coating completely. Place breaded chicken in oiled
   casserole dish. Dot each breaded breast with butter.
3. Bake in preheated 400° oven for 20 minutes.
4. Remove cooked chicken from casserole to heated plates with a
   spatula.

HELPFUL HINT
Before grating or shredding cheese, brush vegetable oil or
cooking spray on the grater and it cleans easier.

93

CHESTNUT-APPLE CHICKEN

To cook fresh chestnuts: Cover chestnuts with water and bring to a boil. Reduce heat and simmer for ten minutes. Drain and place chestnuts on cutting board; cut in half and spoon out meat. Skin should stay in the shell.

2 whole chicken breasts, skinned, boned, halved, flattened,
   with fat removed
1 tablespoon butter
1 small onion, chopped
1 celery stalk, chopped
1/2 cup apple, peeled, cored, and chopped
1/4 cup chopped roasted chestnuts (canned or you can prepare fresh chestnuts)
1/2 teaspoon poultry seasoning
1/4 cup plain fresh or dried bread crumbs
1 tablespoon olive oil
1/2 cup breading crumbs, page 75
4 slices Monterey Jack cheese

PREPARATION

1. Melt butter in a medium skillet; sauté onion and celery
   until onion is soft. Stir in apples, chestnuts, poultry seasoning, and sauté
   while stirring until apples are warm. Stir in bread crumbs and mix
   thoroughly. Cool.

ASSEMBLY

1. Oil an ovenproof casserole dish that is just large enough to contain the
   four chicken breasts.
2. Place crumbs in a flat dish and press chicken into crumbs,
   coating completely.
3. Place breaded chicken in casserole. Spoon and spread apple
   topping evenly on chicken. Top with Monterey Jack cheese.
4. Bake in a preheated 400° oven for 20 minutes.
5. Remove cooked chicken from casserole to heated plates with
   a spatula. Spoon remaining topping and juices around chicken.

CHESTNUT-FIG CHICKEN

If you cannot find dried figs, you can use dried dates.

2 whole chicken breasts, skinned, boned, halved, flattened,
   with fat removed
2 tablespoons olive oil
1/4 cup chopped onion
2 mild Italian sausages, casings removed
1/4 cup chopped fresh parsley
1/4 cup chopped dried figs
1/4 cup chopped, peeled, roasted or boiled chestnuts (or jarred chestnuts)
2 tablespoons seasoned bread crumbs
1/2 teaspoon dried thyme
1 1/2 tablespoons brandy (optional)
1/2 cup breading crumbs, page 75
4 slices provolone cheese

PREPARATION
1. Heat 1 tablespoon olive oil in a medium size skillet; sauté onion until
   yellow. Stir in sausage and sauté over medium heat until sausage loses
   its pink color. Drain.
2. Spoon sausage mixture into a food processor. Process sausage until
   smooth.
3. Mix sausage mixture, parsley, figs, chestnuts, bread crumbs, thyme,
   and brandy in mixing bowl. Cool.

ASSEMBLY
1. Oil an ovenproof casserole dish that is just large enough to contain the
   four chicken breasts.
2. Place crumbs in a flat dish and press chicken into crumbs,
   coating completely.
3. Place breaded chicken in casserole. Spoon and spread
   fig topping evenly on chicken. Top with provolone cheese.
4. Bake in a preheated 400° oven for 20 minutes.
5. Remove cooked chicken from casserole to heated plates with
   a spatula. Spoon remaining stuffing and juices around chicken.

About half of the world's raisins come from California. It is
incredible how many grapes are grown; think of the grapes that
we eat, the wine we drink, and the raisins we cook and eat in cereal.

2 whole chicken breasts, skinned, boned, halved, flattened,
   with fat removed
2 tablespoons butter
1 small onion, chopped
1 clove garlic, minced
1/2 cup cooked rice
1/4 cup white raisins, chopped
1/4 cup chopped fresh parsley
1/2 teaspoon curry powder
1/4 teaspoon poultry seasoning
1/2 teaspoon brown sugar
1/2 cup breading crumbs, page 75
4 slices Monterey Jack cheese

PREPARATION

1. Melt 1 tablespoon butter in a medium skillet; sauté onion and garlic
   until yellow. Cool.
2. Mix cooled onion and garlic, cooked rice, white raisins, chopped parsley,
   curry powder, poultry seasoning, and brown sugar in a mixing bowl.

ASSEMBLY

1. Butter an ovenproof casserole dish that is just large enough to contain
   the four chicken breasts.
2. Place crumbs in a flat dish and press chicken into
   crumbs, coating completely.
3. Place breaded chicken breasts in buttered casserole dish. Spoon
   and spread topping evenly on each chicken breast.
   Top with Monterey Jack cheese.
4. Bake in a preheated 400° oven for 20 minutes.
5. Remove cooked chicken from casserole to heated plates with a
   spatula. Spoon remaining topping and juices around chicken.

Try to find firm, bright green thinner asparagus for this dish.
Store asparagus in the refrigerator in water until ready to use.

2 whole chicken breasts, skinned, boned, halved, flattened,
   with fat removed
1 can (10 1/2-ounce) condensed cream of chicken soup
1 teaspoon lemon juice
2 tablespoons softened butter
1/2 cup breading crumbs, page 75
12 fresh asparagus blanched for 2 minutes and then cooled;
   cut spears to the same size as the chicken breasts (long way)
4 slices cheddar cheese
1/2 cup sliced almonds

PREPARATION
1. Mix cream of chicken soup and lemon juice in a mixing bowl.

ASSEMBLY
1. With 1 tablespoon of butter, butter an ovenproof casserole dish
   that is just large enough to contain the chicken breasts.
2. Place crumbs in a flat dish and press chicken into crumbs,
   coating completely.
3. Place breaded chicken breasts in buttered casserole dish. Spoon
   chicken soup mixture evenly on chicken breasts. Top each
   breast with 3 asparagus spears, top with a slice of cheddar, then
   sprinkle almonds on top of cheese. Dot with butter.
4. Bake in a preheated 400° oven for 20 minutes.
5. Remove cooked chicken from casserole to heated plates with
   a spatula. Spoon any remaining sauce around chicken.

"Visits always give pleasure—if not the arrival, the departure."
Portuguese proverb

=======================CHICKEN LORRAINE

Every time I visit my sister Lorraine, she sends me home with a container of her sauce with meatballs and sausage. One day I tried her sauce and sausage with chicken. It was different and good. Use leftover sliced meatballs instead of sausage if you wish.

2 whole chicken breasts, skinned, boned, halved, flattened,
   with fat removed
1 tablespoon olive oil
1/2 cup breading crumbs, page 75
4 cooked Italian sausages, cooled, remove skin, cut in half lengthwise
1 cup tomato sauce (marinara sauce)
4 slices provolone cheese
1/4 cup chopped fresh parsley

ASSEMBLY
1. Oil an ovenproof casserole dish that is just large enough to contain the four chicken breasts.
2. Place crumbs in a flat dish and press chicken into crumbs, coating completely.
3. Place breaded chicken breasts in oiled casserole dish. Top with 2 pieces of the sausage on each chicken breast. Spoon tomato sauce on sausage and chicken. Top with provolone cheese and parsley.
4. Bake in a preheated 400° oven for 20 minutes.
5. Remove cooked chicken from casserole to heated plates with a spatula. Spoon any remaining sauce on and around chicken.

Helpful Hint
If you spill red wine on a carpet, especially a white or light carpet, immediately pour white wine on the spill. The white wine will neutralize the red wine. Blot the wine on the carpet with paper towels or cloth towels.

"Strange to see how a good dinner and feasting reconciles everybody."
Samuel Pepps

===========================CHICKEN MICHAEL

The light taste of mustard and tarragon accents the chicken.

2 whole chicken breasts, skinned, boned, halved, flattened,
　with fat removed
2 eggs
1 tablespoon Dijon-style mustard
1 teaspoon dried tarragon
1/4 cup finely chopped fresh parsley
1 cup breading crumbs, page 75
2 teaspoons butter

PREPARATION
1. Whisk eggs, mustard, tarragon, and parsley in a mixing bowl.
    Add chicken breasts covering chicken completely with egg
    mixture. Marinate chicken in egg mixture in refrigerator for
    about 15 minutes.

ASSEMBLY
1. With 1 teaspoon of butter, butter an ovenproof casserole that is
    just large enough to contain the four chicken breasts.
2. Place crumbs in a flat dish. Remove chicken breast from
    egg mixture with a fork, then press into crumbs one at a time
    (use more crumbs if you need them). Place breaded chicken in
    buttered casserole dish. Dot with butter.
3. Bake in a preheated 400° oven for 20 minutes.
4. Remove cooked chicken from casserole to heated plates with a
    spatula.

"We are shaped and fashioned by what we love."
Goethe

CHICKEN NORMANDE

Calvados is a dry, apple brandy made in the Normandy region of France. Dishes in France that use apples and Calvados in cooking are usually named Normande.

2 whole chicken breasts, skinned, boned, halved, flattened,
   with fat removed
2 tart apples, peeled, cored, and diced
1 teaspoon lemon juice
1 small onion, minced
1 garlic clove, minced
1/4 cup chopped green onions (scallions)
1/4 teaspoon dried thyme
1 tablespoon Calvados or Apple Jack liquor (optional)
1 cup shredded Swiss cheese or Gruyere
1/4 cup plain bread crumbs
1 tablespoon butter
1/2 cup breading crumbs, page 75
Dash paprika

PREPARATION
1. Mix diced apple, lemon juice, minced onion, minced garlic, chopped green onions, thyme, Calvados, shredded Swiss cheese, and plain bread crumbs in a mixing bowl.

ASSEMBLY
1. Butter an ovenproof casserole dish that is just large enough to contain the four chicken breasts.
2. Place crumbs in a flat dish and press chicken into crumbs, coating completely.
3. Place breaded chicken in buttered casserole dish. Spoon and spread apple topping on chicken evenly. Sprinkle with paprika.
4. Bake in a preheated 400° oven for 20 minutes.
5. Remove cooked chicken from casserole to heated plates with a spatula. Spoon any remaining apple mixture on and around chicken.

CHICKEN THOMAS

A combination of olives, feta, and pine nuts is luscious.

2 whole chicken breasts, skinned, boned, halved, flattened,
   with fat removed
1/4 cup crumbled feta cheese (any blue cheese can be used instead)
1 small red bell pepper, roasted, peeled, seeded, and finely chopped or
   (you can use 1/4 cup chopped jarrcd roasted red peppers)
5 kalamata olives, pitted and chopped (black brined olives)
2 garlic cloves, minced
1 1/2 tablespoons toasted pine nuts
1/4 cup chopped green onions (scallions)
1/4 cup chopped fresh parsley
1 tablespoon olive oil
1/2 cup breading crumbs, page 75
4 slices provolone cheese

PREPARATION
1. Mix feta cheese, chopped peppers, chopped olives, minced garlic,
    pine nuts, chopped green onions, and parsley in a mixing bowl.

ASSEMBLY
1. Oil an ovenproof casserole dish that is just large enough to
    contain the four chicken breasts.
2. Place crumbs in a flat dish and press chicken into crumbs,
    coating completely.
3. Place breaded chicken in casserole. Spoon and spread feta,
    topping evenly on chicken. Top with provolone cheese.
4. Bake in a preheated 400° oven for 20 minutes.
5. Remove cooked chicken from casserole to heated plates with
    a spatula. Spoon remaining stuffing and juices around chicken.

"To teach is to learn twice."
Joseph Joubert

=========CHICKEN WITH A MEAT STUFFING

A meat stuffing made with three cheeses. Ricotta is actually a by-product from making provolone and mozzarella, called "whey".

2 whole chicken breasts, skinned, boned, halved, flattened,
   with fat removed
2 tablespoons olive oil
2 garlic cloves, minced
1/2 pound ground veal (beef or pork can be used as well)
1 cup ricotta cheese
1/4 cup grated Parmesan cheese
1 egg, beaten
1/4 cup minced fresh basil leaves or 1 teaspoon dried
1/4 cup chopped fresh parsley
1/2 cup breading crumbs, page 75
4 slices provolone cheese

PREPARATION
1. Heat 1 tablespoon olive oil in a medium skillet, then quickly sauté minced garlic. Stir in ground meat and cook until meat loses its pink color. Drain off fat and cool.
2. Thoroughly mix cooled meat mixture, ricotta cheese, Parmesan cheese, beaten egg, basil, and parsley in a mixing bowl.

ASSEMBLY
1. Oil an ovenproof casserole dish that is just large enough to contain the four chicken breasts.
2. Place crumbs in a flat dish and press chicken into crumbs, coating completely.
3. Place breaded chicken breasts in oiled casserole dish. Spoon and spread stuffing evenly on each chicken breast. Top with provolone cheese.
4. Bake in a preheated 400° oven for 20 minutes
5. Remove cooked chicken from casserole to heated plates with a spatula. Spoon any remaining stuffing around chicken.

This dish is a little thicker, cook a bit longer if needed.

===============CHICKEN WITH A PECAN CRUST

Pecans are available in any specialty or grocery store.

2 whole chicken breasts, skinned, boned, halved, flattened,
 with fat removed
3/4 cup seasoned dried bread crumbs
3/4 cup chopped pecans
2 eggs
1/2 teaspoon ground red pepper (cayenne)
1 clove garlic, minced
1 teaspoon lemon juice
1/4 cup chopped fresh parsley
1 tablespoon olive oil
1 tablespoon of butter

PREPARATION
1. Process bread crumbs and pecans in a food processor until pecans are finely ground. Transfer to a flat plate.
2. Whisk eggs, cayenne, minced garlic, lemon juice, and chopped parsley in a mixing bowl.

ASSEMBLY
1. Add chicken to egg mixture for about 15 minutes.
2. Oil an ovenproof casserole dish that is just large enough to contain the four chicken breasts.
3. Remove each chicken breast from the egg mixture with a fork, allowing excess egg mixture drip off; press chicken in the pecan crumb mixture, coating completely. Place breaded chicken in oiled casserole dish. Dot with butter.
4. Bake in a preheated 400° oven for 20 minutes.
5. Remove chicken from casserole to heated plates with a spatula.

"Clear you mind of can't."
Dr. Samuel Johnson

=======CHICKEN WITH A SHRIMP STUFFING

Americans developed cream cheese in the late 1800's as a spreadable cheese. It's mild flavor blends well with shrimp. Where would the cheesecake be without cream cheese?

2 whole chicken breasts, skinned, boned, halved, flattened,
   with fat removed
1 tablespoon butter, room temperature
1/2 cup cream cheese, room temperature
1 cup cooked shrimp, chopped
1/4 cup chopped fresh parsley
1/4 cup chopped green onions (scallions)
1 small onion, minced
Dash hot-pepper sauce such as Tabasco
Dash Worcestershire sauce
1/4 cup plain bread crumbs, dry or fresh
1 tablespoon olive oil
1/2 cup breading crumbs, page 75
4 slices provolone cheese
1 tablespoon butter
1 cup sliced fresh mushrooms

PREPARATION

1. Thoroughly mix softened butter and cream cheese in a mixing bowl. Stir in cooked shrimp, chopped parsley, chopped green onions, chopped onion, hot-pepper sauce, Worcestershire sauce, and bread crumbs.

ASSEMBLY

1. Oil an ovenproof casserole dish that is just large enough to contain the four chicken breasts.
2. Place crumbs in a flat dish and press chicken into crumbs, coating completely.
3. Place breaded chicken breasts in oiled casserole dish. Spoon and spread shrimp topping evenly on each chicken breast. Top with slice of provolone cheese.
4. Bake in a preheated 400° oven for 20 minutes.
5. While chicken is cooking, melt butter in skillet over medium heat. Stir in mushrooms; sauté until wilted. Keep warm.
6. Remove cooked chicken from casserole to heated plates with a spatula. Spoon sautéed mushrooms on and around chicken.

=CHICKEN WITH A WALNUT PARMESAN CRUST

Walnuts, Parmesan cheese, sage, and onions make this chicken dish distinct.

2 whole chicken breasts, skinned, boned, halved, flattened,
  with fat removed
2 tablespoons olive oil
1 medium onion, minced
1/4 cup chopped fresh parsley
1/2 cup walnut halves or pieces (pecans can be used as well)
1/2 cup plain dry bread crumbs
1/4 cup grated Parmesan cheese
1/2 teaspoon ground thyme or 1 1/2 teaspoons chopped fresh thyme
2 eggs
1 tablespoon butter

PREPARATION
1. Heat 1 tablespoon of olive oil in a medium skillet; sauté onion until golden; stir in parsley, remove from heat and cool.
2. Finely chop walnuts or pulse process in a food processor until grainy. Mix walnuts, bread crumbs, Parmesan cheese, and thyme in a mixing bowl.
3. Whisk eggs and cooled onions in a mixing bowl.

ASSEMBLY
1. Oil an ovenproof casserole dish large enough to contain the four chicken breasts.
2. Dip chicken breast into egg mixture taking up some of the onion, then press into walnut crumb breading, coating completely on both sides. Place breaded chicken in oiled casserole dish. (You can use a fork for this procedure or you can use your fingers.) Dot each chicken breast with butter.
3. Bake in a preheated 400° oven for 20 minutes.
4. Remove cooked chicken from casserole to heated plates with a spatula.

CHICKEN WITH OYSTERS

It takes a lot of courage to try an oyster for the first time.

2 whole chicken breasts, skinned, boned, halved, flattened,
   with fat removed
1 tablespoon butter
1/4 cup minced onion
4 mushrooms, sliced
1 cup frozen spinach, thawed, drained, and squeezed
   dry, or chopped fresh spinach (10-ounce bag)
1 cup (8-ounces) rough chopped shucked fresh oysters
1/4 cup sour cream
1/4 cup chopped fresh parsley
1 teaspoon Pernod, optional (a licorice-flavored liquor)
1 tablespoon grated Parmesan cheese
1/4 cup plain dried or fresh bread crumbs
1/2 cup breading crumbs page 75
1 tablespoon olive oil
4 slices cheddar cheese

PREPARATION
1. Melt butter in a medium skillet; sauté onions until they turn yellow.
    Stir in sliced mushrooms; cook until mushrooms wilt and loose
    some liquid. Cool.
2. Gently mix cooled onions and mushrooms, spinach, oysters, sour cream,
    parsley, Pernod, grated Parmesan, and plain bread crumbs in a mixing
    bowl. Be careful not to crush the oysters.

ASSEMBLY
1. Oil an ovenproof casserole dish that is just large enough to contain
    the four chicken breasts.
2. Place crumbs in a flat dish and press chicken into crumbs coating
    chicken completely.
3. Place breaded chicken in oiled casserole dish. Spoon and spread
    oyster stuffing evenly on each chicken breast. Top with cheddar cheese.
4. Bake in a preheated 400° oven for 20 minutes.
5. Remove cooked chicken from casserole to heated plates with
    a spatula.

==CHICKEN WITH VEGETABLES EN PAPILLOTE

En papillote means "in paper", referring to the parchment packets in which the French cooked. Often in the States, we use aluminum foil. Parchment paper is available in grocery stores or specialty markets.

2 whole chicken breasts, skinned, boned, halved, flattened
  with fat removed
1/2 cup flour
Dash ground red pepper (cayenne)
Heavy-duty aluminum foil or parchment paper
8 pieces of asparagus, cut into 2 inch lengths
1 small onion, sliced
1 small red bell pepper, cored and sliced thin
1 medium carrot, peeled and cut into julienne strips
2 mushrooms, sliced thin
1 teaspoon lemon juice
1/2 teaspoon dried tarragon
1/4 cup chopped fresh parsley
1 tablespoon butter (optional)

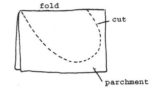

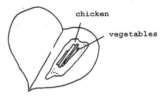

PREPARATION
1. Mix flour and cayenne in a small bowl.

ASSEMBLY
1. Tear off two lengths of aluminum foil or parchment paper large enough to permit adequate wrapping and to allow for heat circulation and expansion. (8x8 pieces)
2. Flour chicken breast, shaking off extra flour.
3. Place floured chicken breasts in center of lower half of each length of foil or parchment; you will have two breasts side by side on foil. Top each breast with an even amount of asparagus, onion, pepper, carrots, and mushrooms. Top with lemon juice, tarragon, chopped parsley, and butter.
4. Fold upper half of foil or parchment over ingredients making a series of locked folds; repeat folds for ends. Press tight to seal. Place on a cookie sheet.
5. Bake in a 400° oven for 20 minutes.
6. To serve, cut an X in the top of foil packet; fold back foil and serve in foil or parchment on a heated plate.

=CHICKEN WITH WHITE BEANS AND TOMATOES

The tomato is native to South America; it made its way up to Central America and Mexico. The Spanish carried tomato plants back to Spain. Tomato plants were used for decoration in gardens because they were thought to be poisonous. Later on, the French used the tomato for aphrodisiac powers. The tomato started to gain some popularity in the States in the early 1900's. Today the tomato is one of the world's most popular foods.

2 whole chicken breasts, skinned, boned, halved, flattened
   with fat removed
2 teaspoons olive oil
1/4 cup chopped onion
2 cloves garlic minced
1 can (16-ounce) cannellini beans
1 sprig fresh thyme leaves or 1/2 teaspoon dried
1/4 cup chopped fresh parsley
1/2 cup breading crumbs, page 75
8 slices fresh tomato
1/4 cup chopped fresh basil or 1 teaspoon dried basil
4 slices provolone cheese

PREPARATION
1. Heat 1 teaspoon oil in a skillet over medium heat; sauté onion and chopped garlic until onion is soft. Stir in beans, thyme, and chopped parsley. Heat to almost a boil and keep warm.

ASSEMBLY
1. With 1 teaspoon oil, oil and ovenproof casserole dish that is large enough to contain the four chicken breasts.
2. Place crumbs in a flat dish and press chicken into crumbs, coating completely
3. Place breaded chicken in oiled casserole dish; top with sliced tomatoes, basil, and provolone cheese.
4. Bake in a preheated 400° oven for 20 minutes.
5. Remove cooked chicken from casserole to heated plates with a spatula; spoon warm beans around chicken.

CHORIZO STUFFED CHICKEN

Chorizo is a highly seasoned, coarsely ground pork sausage, used in Mexican, Spanish, and Portuguese cooking.

2 whole chicken breasts, skinned, boned, halved, flattened,
  with fat removed
1/2 cup peeled, finely diced, green apple
1/2 cup finely chopped chorizo (peel off skin)
1/2 cup fresh bread crumbs
1 small jalapeno, cored, seeded, and minced
1/4 cup chopped green onions (scallions)
1/4 cup shredded cheddar cheese
1/4 cup chopped fresh parsley
2 tablespoons sour cream
1 tablespoon olive oil
1/2 cup breading crumbs, page 75

PREPARATION
1. Mix apples, chorizo, bread crumbs, jalapeno, green onions, cheddar, sour cream, and parsley in a mixing bowl.

ASSEMBLY
1. Oil an ovenproof casserole dish that is just large enough to contain the four chicken breasts.
2. Place crumbs in a flat dish and press chicken into crumbs, coating completely.
3. Place breaded chicken in casserole. Spoon and spread chorizo topping evenly on chicken.
4. Bake in a preheated 400° oven for 20 minutes.
5. Remove cooked chicken from casserole to heated plates with a spatula. Spoon remaining stuffing and juices around chicken.

Helpful Hint
Use ketchup to clean copper bottom pans. Spread the ketchup on the copper bottom, rub in the ketchup. Rinse with warm water and wipe dry.

CHUTNEY-COCONUT CHICKEN

The coconut palm grows in the very warm areas of the world.

2 whole chicken breasts, skinned, boned, halved, flattened,
   with fat removed
3 tablespoons apricot jam
3 tablespoons chunky peanut butter
1/2 cup packaged cornflake crumbs (or crushed cornflakes)
1 cup shredded, unsweetened coconut
1 teaspoon curry powder
1/2 teaspoon grated fresh ginger or 1/4 teaspoon dried
Dash ground red pepper (cayenne)
1 tablespoon olive oil
1 tablespoon butter
1/2 cup prepared chutney, chopped fine
1/4 cup orange juice

PREPARATION
1. Heat and stir peanut butter and apricot jam in a skillet over low heat until melted and mixed. Cool to room temperature.
2. Mix cornflake crumbs, shredded coconut, curry, ginger, and cayenne in a mixing bowl.

ASSEMBLY
1. Oil an ovenproof casserole dish that is just large enough to contain the four chicken breasts.
2. Dip the chicken breasts in the apricot peanut butter mixture, allowing excess to drip off. Press chicken into the coconut breading, coating the chicken completely. Place breaded chicken in oiled casserole dish. Dot with butter.
3. Bake in a preheated 400° oven for 20 minutes.
4. While chicken is baking, heat and stir chutney and orange juice in a small saucepan. Keep warm.
5. Remove cooked chicken from casserole to heated plates with a spatula. Spoon the chutney sauce on and around chicken.
   Coconut is usually available in cans or plastic bags.

Crabs, enjoyed for their sweet, succulent meat, are second to shrimp for enjoyment in dining. Crabmeat should be checked for tiny broken shells sometimes left in the meat.

2 whole chicken breasts, skinned, boned, halved, flattened,
   with fat removed
4 (1/2-cup) ounces crabmeat, small shells removed, drained
1/2 cup sour cream
1/2 teaspoon dried dill or fresh dill chopped fine (stems removed)
1/4 cup chopped fresh parsley
1/4 cup plain dried or fresh bread crumbs
1 tablespoon butter
1/2 cup breading crumbs, page 75
4 mushroom caps, without stems, wiped cleaned
4 slices Monterey Jack cheese

PREPARATION
1. Gently mix crabmeat, sour cream, dill, chopped parsley, and bread crumbs in a mixing bowl.

ASSEMBLY
1. Butter an ovenproof casserole dish that is just large enough to contain the four chicken breasts.
2. Place crumbs in a flat dish and press chicken into crumbs, coating completely.
3. Place breaded chicken breasts in buttered casserole dish. Spoon and spread crab stuffing evenly on each chicken breast; top crab stuffing with a mushroom cap, and Monterey Jack cheese.
4. Bake in a preheated 400° oven for 20 minutes.
5. Remove cooked chicken from casserole to heated plates with a spatula. Spoon any remaining stuffing and juices around chicken.

"The supreme happiness of life is the conviction that we are loved."
Victor Hugo

CRISPY CHICKEN TERRY

Crispy cornflake chicken is great to feed the kids. It is crispy and oven-baked. For a variation, cut the chicken like fingers and you will have a hit. My sister Terry serves this dish to her grandchildren all the time. It is also great for adults.

2 whole chicken breasts, skinned, boned, halved, flattened,
   with fat removed
2 eggs
1 tablespoon milk
1/8 teaspoon thyme
1/4 cup chopped fresh parsley
1 tablespoon olive oil
1 cup finely crushed cornflakes or prepared cornflake crumbs
1 tablespoon butter

PREPARATION
1. Whisk eggs, milk, thyme, and chopped parsley in a mixing bowl.

ASSEMBLY
1. Oil an ovenproof casserole dish large enough to contain the four chicken breasts.
2. Place cornflake crumbs in a flat dish.
3. Dip chicken breasts in egg mixture, allowing excess to drip off. Press chicken into cornflake crumbs, coating completely. Place coated chicken in oiled casserole dish. Dot with butter.
4. Bake in a preheated 400° oven for 20 minutes.
5. Remove cooked chicken from casserole to heated plates with a spatula.

"The table
Attracts more friends
Than the mind."
Publilius Syrus

═══════════════════CUCUMBER CHICKEN

Cucumber seeds can be bitter. To seed a cucumber, cut it lengthwise in half, then use a teaspoon to scrape out the seeds.

2 whole chicken breasts, skinned, boned, halved, flattened,
  with fat removed
1 tablespoon butter or olive oil
1 small onion, chopped
1 cucumber, peeled, seeded, and cut into 1/4-inch slices
1/2 teaspoon dried dill weed or 1 teaspoon fresh chopped dill
1 tablespoon olive oil
1/2 cup breading crumbs, page 75
4 slices cheddar cheese

PREPARATION
1. Melt butter in a medium skillet; sauté onion until it turns yellow. Stir in cucumber and dill; sauté until cucumber is slightly softened. Cool.

ASSEMBLY
1. Oil an ovenproof casserole dish that is just large enough to contain the four chicken breasts.
2. Place crumbs in a flat dish and press chicken into crumbs, coating chicken completely. Place breaded chicken breasts in oiled casserole dish. Spoon cooled cucumber mixture evenly on each breaded chicken breast. Top with cheddar cheese.
3. Bake in a preheated 400° oven for 20 minutes.
4. Remove cooked chicken from casserole to heated plates with a spatula.

Helpful Hint
This cleanup trick works. Lay barbecue grill rack and oven racks on the lawn overnight. The dew will combine with the enzymes in the grass should loosen any burned on grease.

"The more things change, the more they remain the same."
Alphonse Karr

===============CURRIED PEANUT CHICKEN

Peanut butter was first made in 1890 and promoted as a health food in 1904 at the St. Louis World's Fair.

2 whole chicken breasts, skinned, boned, halved, flattened,
   with fat removed
1 cup whole egg mayonnaise
1 1/2 tablespoon mango chutney, any big pieces chopped
1 tablespoon dry sherry
1 tablespoon curry powder
1/4 teaspoon turmeric
1 cup finely chopped unsalted peanuts (you can use salted)
1/4 cup chopped fresh parsley
1 tablespoon butter
1/2 cup breading crumbs, page 75

PREPARATION
1. Mix mayonnaise, chutney, sherry, curry powder, turmeric, chopped peanuts, and chopped parsley in a mixing bowl.

ASSEMBLY
1. Butter an ovenproof casserole dish that is just large enough to contain the four chicken breasts.
2. Place crumbs in a flat dish and press chicken into crumbs, coating chicken completely. Place breaded chicken in buttered casserole dish.
3. Spread the peanut mixture evenly on the four chicken breasts.
4. Bake in a preheated 400° oven for 20 minutes.
5. Remove cooked chicken from casserole to heated plates with a spatula.

Chopped pecans, walnuts, or pistachios can be used instead of peanuts.

"The way to a man's heart is through his stomach."
Willis Parton

DILL-ALMOND CHICKEN

This recipe sounds like it came from the health-food store.
Except for the butter, it helps give the dish a nice flavor.

2 whole chicken breasts, skinned, boned, halved, flattened,
   with fat removed
1 cup regular wheat germ
1 teaspoon dried dill weed
1/2 cup almonds, chopped fine
1 tablespoon olive oil
1 cup yogurt
1 tablespoon butter

PREPARATION
1. Mix wheat germ, dill weed, and chopped almonds in a mixing bowl.

ASSEMBLY
1. Oil an ovenproof casserole dish just large enough to contain the
    four chicken breasts.
2. Put yogurt in a mixing bowl. Place chicken breasts in yogurt,
    coating chicken.
3. Take chicken out of yogurt one at a time; press chicken into wheat
    germ breading, coating completely. Place breaded chicken in oiled
    casserole dish. Dot with butter.
4. Bake in a preheated 400° oven for 20 minutes.
5. Remove cooked chicken from casserole to heated plates with
    a spatula.
    Yogurt is a dairy product that has fermented and coagulated
    because friendly bacteria have invaded it.

Helpful Hint
To keep my mixing bowl from sliding around the counter top,
I place the bowl on a wet dishcloth. The cloth holds the bowl steady.

"I had three chairs in my house: one for solitude,
two for friendship, three for society."
Henry David Thoreau

DILL-LEMON CHICKEN

Dill was thought by the Romans to be a good luck symbol. This annual herb grows up to a height of about three feet. I love the delicate flavor dill can bring to food.

2 whole chicken breasts, skinned, boned, halved, flattened,
  with fat removed
3/4 cup whole egg mayonnaise (such as Hellmann's)
2 tablespoons chopped fresh dill or 1 teaspoon dried dill
1 teaspoon grated lemon peel (zest)
1 small onion, minced
1 teaspoon lemon juice
1 tablespoon butter
1/2 cup breading crumbs, page 75

PREPARATION

1. Mix mayonnaise, dill, lemon peel, minced onion, and lemon juice in a mixing bowl.

ASSEMBLY

1. Butter an ovenproof casserole dish that is just large enough to contain the four chicken breasts.
2. Place crumbs in a flat dish and press chicken into crumbs, coating completely.
3. Place breaded chicken in buttered casserole dish. Spoon and spread lemon topping evenly on chicken.
4. Bake in a preheated 400° oven for 20 minutes.
5. Remove cooked chicken from casserole to heated plates with a spatula.

Helpful Hint

Use a generously salted lemon half to clean stainless steel sinks. After cleaning the sink run the disposal with the lemon half and it will freshen and make it smell good.

"This world is but canvas to our imaginations."
Henry David Thoreau

================FLORENTINE STYLE CHICKEN

Spinach originated in the Middle East and was grown and eaten in Spain during the 8th century. The Spanish brought spinach plants to the Americas. Spinach should be washed thoroughly to remove sand and should be stored in the refrigerator.

2 whole chicken breasts, skinned, boned, halved, flattened,
   with fat removed
1 tablespoon butter
1 small onion, chopped
1 (10-ounce) package of fresh spinach, trimmed, cleaned,
   and roughly chopped
1/8 teaspoon nutmeg
1 tablespoon olive oil
1/2 cup breading crumbs, page 75
4 slices of cheddar cheese
1/4 cup chopped fresh parsley

PREPARATION
1. Melt butter in a large skillet over medium heat; sauté onions until they turn yellow. Stir in spinach and nutmeg; stir on heat until spinach is wilted. Cool.

ASSEMBLY
1. Oil an ovenproof casserole dish that is just large enough to contain the four chicken breasts.
2. Place crumbs in a flat dish and press chicken into crumbs, coating completely.
3. Place breaded chicken breasts in oiled casserole dish. Spoon and spread cooled spinach mixture evenly on each chicken breast. Top with cheddar cheese and chopped parsley.
4. Bake in a preheated 400° oven for 20 minutes.
5. Remove cooked chicken from casserole to heated plates with a spatula.

"No man can climb out beyond the limitations of his own character."
John,Morley

==**GARLIC CHICKEN**

Garlic is a member of the lily family, along with leeks, chives, onions, and shallots. For centuries, its medicinal claims have boasted many cures. Garlic is credited with providing strength for the workers building the pyramids in Egypt.

2 whole chicken breasts, skinned, boned, halved, flattened,
   with fat removed
1/2 cup breading crumbs, page 75
1/4 cup grated Parmesan cheese
1/4 cup chopped fresh parsley
4 tablespoons butter
2 garlic cloves, minced
1/4 cup chopped green onions (scallions)
1 tablespoon olive oil

PREPARATION
1. Mix crumbs, grated Parmesan cheese, and chopped parsley in a mixing bowl.
2. Melt butter in a skillet; sauté minced garlic and green onions for just a minute. Cool, but keep butter liquid.

ASSEMBLY
1. Oil an ovenproof casserole dish that is just large enough to contain the four chicken breasts.
2. Place crumbs in a flat dish.
3. Brush both sides of the chicken breasts with garlic butter and press chicken into crumbs, coating completely. Place breaded chicken in oiled casserole dish. If there is any garlic butter left, spoon on top of chicken.
4. Bake in a preheated 400° oven for 20 minutes.
5. Remove cooked chicken from casserole to heated plates with a spatula.

"To look up and not look down, To look forward and not back,
To look out and not in, and To lend a hand."
Edward Everett Hale

GEORGIA-PECAN CHICKEN

Pecans are native to America, a member of the hickory family.

2 whole chicken breasts, skinned, boned, halved, flattened,
   with fat removed
2 eggs
1 tablespoon finely chopped green onions (scallions)
3/4 cup finely chopped pecans (can be done in food processor)
1/4 cup plain dried bread crumbs
2 tablespoons butter

PREPARATION
1. Beat eggs in a small mixing bowl; stir in chopped green onions.
2. Mix chopped pecans and bread crumbs in a bowl.

ASSEMBLY
1. Butter with 1 tablespoon butter an ovenproof casserole dish that
    is large enough to contain the four chicken breasts.
2. Dip each chicken breast in egg mixture allowing excess to drip
    off, then press chicken into pecan crumbs, coating completely.
    Place breaded chicken in casserole dish; dot with remaining
    butter.
3. Bake in a preheated 400° oven for 20 minutes.
4. Remove cooked chicken from casserole with a spatula to
    heated plates.

Helpful Hint
*Instead of chopping green onions (scallions) cut them with
kitchen shears.*

"Nothing can bring you peace but yourself."
Ralph Waldo Emerson

119

GINGER-SESAME CHICKEN

Ginger and sesame are the flavors found in most Oriental cooking.

2 whole chicken breasts, skinned, boned, halved, flattened,
  with fat removed
2 eggs
1 tablespoon peeled, finely chopped, fresh ginger
1 cup finely crushed sesame crackers (use rolling pin or
  food processor)
1 tablespoon sesame seeds
1 tablespoon butter
1 tablespoon soy sauce
1/8 teaspoon sesame oil

PREPARATION
1. Beat eggs in a small mixing bowl, stir in chopped ginger.
2. Mix crushed sesame crackers and sesame seeds in a bowl.

ASSEMBLY
1. Butter with 1 teaspoon of butter an ovenproof casserole dish that
   is large enough to contain the four chicken breasts.
2. Dip chicken breasts in egg mixture, then press chicken into
   crumbs, coating completely. Place breaded chicken breasts in
   buttered casserole dish; dot with remaining butter.
3. Bake in a preheated 400° oven for 20 minutes.
4. Mix soy sauce and sesame oil in a small bowl.
5. Remove cooked chicken from casserole with a spatula to heated
   plates; spoon soy mixture around chicken.

Helpful Hint
*For extra-shiny, streakless glasses, add a little vinegar to
final rinse water.*

"Nature and books belong to the eyes that see them."
Ralph Waldo Emerson

=*GORGONZOLA CHICKEN WITH ONION SPAGHETTI*

If you like the flavor of onions, this dish zips in the flavors. When slicing onions, use a mandoline, if you have one, a compact, hand operated machine with adjustable blades for thin to thick slicing. It is great for slicing onions and vegetables.

2 whole chicken breasts, skinned, boned, halved, flattened,
   with fat removed
1 medium red onion, sliced very thin
2 tablespoons olive oil
1/2 cup breading crumbs, page 75
2 tablespoons prepared barbeque sauce
2 ounces Gorgonzola cheese
4 slices provolone cheese

PREPARATION
1. Mix onions and 1 tablespoon of olive oil in a small bowl.

ASSEMBLY
1. Oil an ovenproof casserole dish that is just large enough to contain the four chicken breasts.
2. Place crumbs in a flat dish and press chicken into crumbs, coating completely. Place breaded chicken in oiled casserole dish.
3. Spread barbeque sauce evenly on breaded chicken. Crumble Gorgonzola cheese on top barbeque sauce evenly; top with provolone cheese. Spread onions evenly on top of provolone.
4. Bake in a preheated 400° oven for 20 minutes.
5. Remove cooked chicken from casserole to heated plates with a spatula. Spoon any remaining onions and juices around chicken.

For variation instead of barbeque sauce whole grain mustard can be substituted.

"The reward of a thing well done, is to have done it."
Ralph Waldo Emerson

==========GREEN PEPPERCORN AND BLUE CHEESE CHICKEN

Blue cheese is treated with molds that form blue or green veins throughout the cheese, it gives the cheese its interesting flavor. Any of the blues, including Gorgonzola, Roquefort, and Stilton can be used in this recipe.

2 whole chicken breasts, skinned, boned, halved, flattened,
   with fat removed
1/2 pound blue cheese, crumbled
1 tablespoon green peppercorns (available in small cans,
   packed in water)
1/4 cup plain dried or fresh bread crumbs,
1/4 cup chopped fresh parsley
1/4 cup chopped green onions (scallions)
1 tablespoon olive oil
1/2 cup breading crumbs, page 75
Dash paprika

PREPARATION
1. Mix crumbled blue cheese, peppercorns, plain bread crumbs, parsley, and green onions in a mixing bowl.

ASSEMBLY
1. Oil an ovenproof casserole dish that is just large enough to contain the four chicken breasts.
2. Place crumbs in a flat dish and press chicken into crumbs, coating completely.
3. Place breaded chicken in oiled casserole dish. Spoon and spread blue cheese topping on chicken evenly. Sprinkle with paprika.
4. Bake in a preheated 400° oven for 20 minutes.
5. Remove cooked chicken from casserole to heated plates with a spatula. Spoon any remaining sauce around chicken.

Green peppercorns can be found packed in water in specialty shops.

GRIST MILL CHICKEN

The earliest American settlers were taught by the Indians how to grow, grind, and cook corn. In southern Rhode Island we have two gristmills, Kenyon's and Carpenter's. These mills are powered by water that turns the stone that grinds the dried corn. It is interesting to see this large stone turning without the use of electricity.

2 whole chicken breasts, skinned, boned, halved, flattened,
   with fat removed
2 eggs
1 tablespoon Dijon-style mustard
1/4 cup finely chopped parsley
1 tablespoon finely chopped fresh thyme or 1/4 teaspoon dried
3/4 cup yellow cornmeal
1/2 cup fresh or dried bread crumbs
2 tablespoons butter

PREPARATION
1. Whisk eggs, mustard, parsley, and thyme in a mixing bowl.
2. Stir in chicken breasts, covering chicken completely with egg mixture.
3. Marinate chicken in egg mixture in refrigerator for about 15 minutes.
4. Mix cornmeal and bread crumbs in a small bowl.

ASSEMBLY
1. With 1 tablespoon butter, butter an ovenproof casserole large enough to contain the four chicken breasts.
2. Remove chicken breast from egg mixture, one at a time, with a fork, allowing excess to drip off, and press chicken into crumbs evenly. Place breaded chicken in casserole dish. Dot with butter.
3. Bake in a preheated 400° oven for 20 minutes.
4. Remove cooked chicken from casserole dish to heated plates with a spatula.

"Beauty is the eye of the beholder."
Margaret Wolfe Hungerford

Butternut squash is the surprise in this recipe.

2 whole chicken breasts, skinned, boned, halved, flattened,
   with fat removed
1 tablespoon butter
1 small onion, (1/4-cup) chopped
2 cloves garlic, minced
1/2 ounce dried porcini mushrooms, soaked for 30 minutes
    in warm water. (After soaking, drain and chop)
1 cup chopped fresh cultivated button mushrooms
1 cup butternut squash, peeled, seeded, and diced small
1 teaspoon minced fresh sage or 1/2 teaspoon dried
2 tablespoons seasoned bread crumbs
1 tablespoon olive oil
1/2 cup breading crumbs, page 75
4 slices Monterey Jack cheese

PREPARATION

1. Melt butter in a medium skillet over medium heat; sauté onion and garlic until onion turns yellow. Stir in mushrooms, squash, and sage. Sauté, stirring over medium heat until, squash is firm cooked, about 5-6 minutes. Stir in bread crumbs. Cool.

ASSEMBLY

1. Oil an ovenproof casserole dish just large enough to contain the four chicken breasts.
2. Place crumbs in a flat dish and press chicken into crumbs, coating completely.
3. Place breaded chicken in casserole. Spoon and spread cooled butternut-mushroom topping evenly on chicken. Top with Monterey Jack cheese.
4. Bake in a preheated 400° oven for 20 minutes.
5. Remove cooked chicken from casserole to heated plates with a spatula. Spoon remaining topping and juices around chicken.

There are hundreds of different honeys throughout the world. .

2 whole chicken breasts, skinned, boned, halved, flattened,
   with fat removed
1 cup regular oats, uncooked (such as Quaker)
2 tablespoons grated Parmesan cheese
1/4 teaspoon paprika
2 garlic cloves, minced
2 tablespoons honey
1/4 cup chopped fresh parsley
1 tablespoon olive oil
1 tablespoon butter

PREPARATION
1. Blend the oats, grated Parmesan cheese, and paprika in a food processor until breading resembles coarse meal; place in a medium bowl.
2. Mix honey, minced garlic, and chopped parsley in a small bowl.

ASSEMBLY
1. Oil an ovenproof casserole dish large enough to contain the four chicken breasts.
2. Dip each chicken breast in honey mixture with a fork allowing excess to drip off. Press into oat breading, coating completely. Place breaded chicken in the oiled casserole dish. Dot the chicken with butter.
3. Bake in a preheated 400° oven for 20 minutes.
4. Remove cooked chicken from casserole to heated plates with a spatula.

Helpful Hint
When a recipe calls for honey, molasses, corn syrup, or maple syrup, spray the measuring cup or spoon with nonstick cooking spray. The sticky liquid slides out of the cup or spoon with ease.

"What we anticipate seldom occurs;
what we least expected generally happens."
Henrietta Temple

================ITALIAN EGGPLANT CHICKEN

The eggplant is thought to be a vegetable; it is actually in the fruit family.

2 whole chicken breasts, skinned, boned, halved, flattened,
    with fat removed
1 small eggplant, peeled, cut into 1/2-inch slices
1 teaspoon salt
1/4 cup flour
2 tablespoons olive oil
1/2 cup breading crumbs, page 75
1/4 cup grated Parmesan cheese
3/4 cup tomato sauce (marinara)
4 slices provolone cheese
1/4 cup chopped fresh parsley

PREPARATION
1. Salt the slices of eggplant; let them sit for one hour. Rinse and dry with paper towel.
2. Dredge eggplant in flour; shake off excess.
3. Heat 1 tablespoon olive oil in a skillet over medium heat; sauté eggplant on both sides. Drain on paper towels. Cool.

ASSEMBLY
1. Oil an ovenproof casserole dish large enough to contain the four chicken breasts.
2. Place crumbs in a flat dish and press chicken into crumbs, coating completely.
3. Place breaded chicken breasts in oiled casserole dish. Top each breast with sautéed eggplant, Parmesan cheese, tomato sauce, provolone cheese and chopped parsley.
4. Bake in a preheated 400° oven for 20 minutes. (If chicken is thick, cook a little longer.)
5. Remove cooked chicken from casserole to heated plates with a spatula.

================JOE AND NORMA'S CHICKEN

Joseph and Norma Martella from Dome Publishing helped me publish my first two cookbooks. I will be eternally grateful to them for giving me a chance to share recipes, ideas, and my feelings about food.

2 whole chicken breasts, skinned, boned, halved, flattened,
   with fat removed
4 ounces blue cheese
1 cup sour cream
1/2 teaspoon Worcestershire sauce
2 cloves garlic, minced
1/4 cup chopped green onions
1/4 cup chopped fresh parsley
2 tablespoons plain, (dried or fresh) bread crumbs
1 tablespoon butter
1/2 cup breading crumbs, page 75
Dash paprika

PREPARATION
1. Crumble blue cheese with a fork in a mixing bowl. Mix in sour cream, Worcestershire sauce, minced garlic, chopped green onions, chopped parsley, and plain crumbs.

ASSEMBLY
1. Butter an ovenproof casserole dish that is just large enough to contain the four chicken breasts.
2. Place special crumbs in a flat dish and press chicken into crumbs, coating completely.
3. Place breaded chicken breasts in buttered casserole dish. Spoon and spread blue cheese topping evenly on each chicken breast. Sprinkle with paprika.
4. Bake in a preheated 400° oven for 20 minutes.
5. Remove cooked chicken from casserole to heated plates with a spatula. Spoon any blue cheese sauce remaining in casserole on and around chicken.

LEMON-PARMESAN CHICKEN

This dish is wonderful with cooked rice.

2 whole chicken breasts, skinned, boned, halved, flattened,
   with fat removed
1/2 cup breading crumbs, page 75
1/4 cup grated Parmesan cheese
1 tablespoon grated lemon peel (zest)
1 tablespoon olive oil
1 tablespoon butter
1 (10-1/2 ounce) can of cream of chicken soup
1/2 cup milk
1 teaspoon lemon juice
1/4 cup chopped fresh parsley
1/4 cup chopped green onions (scallions)

PREPARATION
1. Mix crumbs, Parmesan cheese, and half of the grated lemon peel in
    a mixing bowl.

ASSEMBLY
1. Oil an ovenproof casserole dish that is just large enough to contain the
    four chicken breasts.
2. Press breading into chicken, coating chicken completely. Place breaded
    chicken in oiled casserole dish. Dot with butter.
3. Bake in a preheated 400° oven for 20 minutes.
4. While chicken is cooking. Heat cream of chicken soup, milk,
    remaining lemon peel, lemon juice, chopped parsley, and chopped
    green onion in a saucepan, over medium heat, stirring occasionally.
    Keep warm.
5. Remove cooked chicken from casserole to heated plates with a
    spatula. Spoon the sauce on and around chicken. If sauce is too thick,
    add a little more milk.

"A poet can survive everything but a misprint."
Oscar Wilde

==========LEMON-PEPPER CHEESE CHICKEN

Enjoy the zesty exciting lemon-pepper and cheese flavor.

2 whole chicken breasts, skinned, boned, halved, flattened,
  with fat removed
2 eggs
1/2 teaspoon grated lemon peel (zest)
1 teaspoon lemon juice
1/2 cup breading crumbs, page 75
1/2 cup grated Parmesan cheese
1 tablespoon lemon-pepper seasoning (in spice section of markets)
1 tablespoon olive oil
1 tablespoon butter

PREPARATION
1. Mix eggs, lemon peel, and lemon juice in a mixing bowl.
2. Mix crumbs, Parmesan cheese, and lemon-pepper
    seasoning in a mixing bowl.

ASSEMBLY
1. Oil an ovenproof casserole dish just large enough to contain
    the four chicken breasts.
2. Dip chicken in egg mixture, then press chicken into crumbs,
    coating completely.
3. Place breaded chicken in oiled casserole. Dot chicken evenly
    with butter.
4. Bake in a preheated 400° oven for 20 minutes.
5. Remove cooked chicken from casserole to heated plates with
    a spatula.

"All glory comes from daring to begin."
Eugene F. Ware

==========LEMON YOGURT-GINGER CHICKEN

Flavored yogurt has sugar and fruit added. Some flavored yogurts contain gelatin or stabilizers for a thicker texture. This dish is perfect served with rice.

2 whole chicken breasts, skinned, boned, halved, flattened,
   with fat removed
1 tablespoon lemon juice
3/4 cup lemon yogurt
1/4 cup whole egg mayonnaise
1 garlic clove, minced
1/2 teaspoon minced fresh ginger (peeled)
1/2 teaspoon grated lemon peel, (zest)
1/4 cup chopped fresh parsley
1/2 cup breading crumbs, page 75
1 teaspoon olive oil

PREPARATION
1. Mix lemon juice, yogurt, mayonnaise, minced garlic, minced ginger, lemon peel, and chopped parsley in a mixing bowl.

ASSEMBLY
1. Oil an ovenproof casserole just large enough to contain the four chicken breasts.
2. Place crumbs in a flat dish and press chicken into crumbs, coating completely.
3. Place breaded chicken in oiled casserole. Spoon and spread yogurt topping evenly on chicken.
4. Bake in a preheated 400° oven for 20 minutes.
5. Remove cooked chicken from casserole to heated plates with a spatula. Spoon any topping left in casserole around chicken.

Helpful Hint
Room temperature foods cook and bake faster than foods taken out of the refrigerator. (Keep food safety in mind.)

LIME YOGURT CHICKEN

The flavor of lime with the spices adds a peppy flavor to chicken.

2 whole chicken breasts, skinned, boned, halved, flattened,
  with fat removed
1/2 cup breading crumbs, page 75
1/2 teaspoon ground curry powder
1/2 teaspoon ground cinnamon
1/2 teaspoon ground ginger
1/4 teaspoon garlic powder (not garlic salt)
1 tablespoon olive oil
1 tablespoon butter
1/2 cup plain yogurt
1 teaspoon grated lime peel (zest)
1 teaspoon lime juice

PREPARATION
1. Mix crumbs, curry powder, ground cinnamon, ground ginger, and garlic powder in a mixing bowl.

ASSEMBLY
1. Oil an ovenproof casserole dish large enough to contain the four chicken breasts.
2. Place crumbs in a flat dish and press chicken into crumbs, coating completely. Place breaded chicken in oiled casserole dish. Dot with butter.
3. Bake in a preheated 400° oven for 20 minutes.
4. While chicken is cooking, mix yogurt, lime peel, and lime juice in a mixing bowl.
5. Remove cooked chicken from casserole to heated plates with a spatula. Serve yogurt sauce on side. Garnish with lime wedges.

The word "zest" refers to the outer colored portion of the citrus. The white pith is bitter and should not be used.

"The painter should not paint what he sees,
  but what will be seen."
    Paul Valéry

MANGO CHUTNEY CHICKEN

This dish was a favorite at the "Taste of the Nations", the annual world hunger bash at the Convention Center in Rhode Island. Chutney is an Indian spicy condiment that contains fruit, vinegar, sugar, and spices. My favorite is the mango chutney.

2 whole chicken breasts, skinned, boned, halved, flattened,
  with fat removed
2 tablespoons butter
1/2 cup breading crumbs, page 75
1 cup mango chutney, big pieces chopped
1/4 teaspoon curry powder
1/2 cup sliced almonds
!/4 cup chopped fresh parsley

PREPARATION
1. Combine chutney and curry in a small bowl.

ASSEMBLY
1. Using half the butter, butter an ovenproof casserole dish.
    large enough to contain the four chicken breasts.
2. Place crumbs in a flat dish and press chicken into
    crumbs, coating completely.
3. Place breaded chicken breasts in buttered casserole dish. Spoon
    chutney topping evenly on each chicken breast. Top with almonds,
    parsley, and dot with butter.
4. Bake in a preheated 400° oven for 20 minutes.
5. Remove cooked chicken from casserole to heated plates with
    a spatula.

"People ask you for criticism, but they only want praise."
William Somerset Maugham

==============================MEXICAN CHICKEN

Salsa is the Mexican word for "sauce." Salsas can be cooked or uncooked. Supermarkets have a large selection of salsas, fresh, canned, or in jars.

The Tortilla is Mexico's every day bread. It resembles a very thin pancake; when fried it becomes a tortilla chip.

2 whole chicken breasts, skinned, boned, halved, flattened,
  with fat removed
1 egg, plus 1 teaspoon of milk
Tortilla chips for breading (Corn chips can be used)
Prepared salsa, mild, medium or hot depending on your taste
1 tablespoon olive oil
4 slices Monterey Jack cheese
1/4 cup chopped fresh cilantro or chopped fresh parsley

PREPARATION
1. Crush tortilla chips by hand to break up large pieces;
  process in a food processor until chips resemble bread crumbs.

ASSEMBLY
1. Oil an ovenproof casserole dish large enough to contain the
  four chicken breasts.
2. Whisk egg and milk in a mixing bowl.
3. Place tortilla crumbs in a flat dish.
4. Place chicken in the egg wash with a fork allowing excess to drip off.
  Press chicken into crumbs coating completely. Place coated
  chicken in oiled casserole dish. Spoon the salsa evenly on coated chicken.
  Top with Monterey Jack cheese and chopped cilantro or parsley.
5. Bake in a preheated 400° oven for 20 minutes.
6. Remove cooked chicken from casserole to heated plates
  with a spatula. Garnish with whole tortilla chips.
    Garnish with guacamole or sour cream or both.

"A promise made is a debt unpaid."
Robert William Service

MONTEREY CHICKEN

This dish will surprise you with its unbelievable flavors.

2 whole chicken breasts, skinned, boned, halved, flattened,
   with fat removed
2 tablespoons olive oil
1 teaspoon butter
1 1/2 cups thinly sliced onions
1 garlic clove, minced
1 sweet red bell pepper, cut in half, seeded, cored, and sliced thin
4 large mushrooms, sliced thin
1 teaspoon soy sauce
1/2 cup breading crumbs, page 75
4 slices Monterey Jack cheese
1/4 cup chopped fresh parsley

PREPARATION
1. Heat 1 tablespoon olive oil, and 1 teaspoon butter in a skillet;
   sauté onion and garlic for one minute. Stir in sliced pepper and
   mushrooms; sauté while stirring for about 2 minutes until vegetables
   are soft. Stir in soy sauce. Cool.

ASSEMBLY
1. Oil an ovenproof casserole large enough to contain the
   four chicken breasts.
2. Place crumbs in a flat dish and press chicken into crumbs,
   coating completely.
3. Place breaded chicken in oiled casserole dish. Spoon and spread
   cooled vegetable topping evenly on each chicken breast; top with
   Monterey Jack cheese and chopped parsley.
4. Bake in a preheated 400° oven for 20 minutes.
5. Remove cooked chicken from casserole to heated plates with a spatula.
   Spoon any vegetables that may have fallen off chicken
   on and around chicken.

*This chicken dish is a little thick, if the chicken is thick allow a
little more time for cooking.*

PARMIGIANA STYLE CHICKEN

Chicken Parmigiana is a dish we always kept on the menu at the restaurant. When younger clients came in with their parents and grandparents, it gave them something they could relate to and order for dinner. Often, first class restaurants forget menu items for young people.

2 whole chicken breasts, skinned, boned, halved, flattened,
  with fat removed
1 tablespoon olive oil
1/2 cup breading crumbs, page 75
1 cup tomato sauce (marinara sauce)
1/2 teaspoon dried basil or 2 tablespoons chopped fresh basil
1 tablespoon grated Parmesan cheese
4 slices provolone cheese
1/4 cup chopped fresh parsley

ASSEMBLY

1. Oil an ovenproof casserole dish large enough to contain
   the four chicken breasts.
2. Place crumbs in a flat dish and press chicken into
   crumbs, coating completely.
3. Place breaded chicken breasts in oiled casserole dish. Spoon
   tomato sauce evenly on each chicken breast. Sprinkle with basil and
   Parmesan cheese. Top with provolone cheese and chopped parsley.
4. Bake in a preheated 400° oven for 20 minutes.
5. Remove cooked chicken from casserole to heated plates with a spatula.
   Spoon any remaining sauce around chicken.

"Much that I sought, I could not find;
Much that found, I could not bind;
Much that I bound, I could not free;
Much that I freed returned to me."
Lee Wilson Dodd

=================PECAN-MUSTARD CHICKEN

It is important to use whole egg mayonnaise in this dish;
low fat or diet mayonnaise will not work as well.
Whole grain mustard is also stone ground mustard.

2 whole chicken breasts, skinned, boned, halved, flattened,
   with fat removed
1 cup whole egg mayonnaise
1 tablespoon whole grain mustard
Sprig of parsley, chopped
1 tablespoon freeze-dried chives or fresh chopped chives
1 tablespoon olive oil
1/2 cup breading crumbs, page 75
1/2 cup chopped pecans

PREPARATION
1. Combine mayonnaise, mustard, parsley, and chives in a mixing bowl.

ASSEMBLY
1. Oil an ovenproof casserole dish large enough to contain the four
   chicken breasts.
2. Place crumbs in a flat dish and press chicken into
   crumbs, coating completely.
3. Place breaded chicken breasts in oiled casserole dish. Spoon
   and spread mayonnaise topping evenly on each chicken breast.
   Top with chopped pecans.
4. Bake in a preheated 400° oven for 20 minutes.
5. Remove cooked chicken from casserole to heated plates with
   a spatula.

"Everything is funny as long as it is happening to somebody else."
Will Rogers

PESTO PROVOLONE CHICKEN

Pesto is an uncooked sauce made with fresh basil, garlic, Parmesan cheese, olive oil, and pine nuts. The classic way to make pesto is in a mortar and pestle. You can also use a food processor. Once presto is made, it should be kept in the refrigerator in a covered container. Prepared pesto is available in supermarkets.

2 whole chicken breasts, skinned, boned, halved, flattened,
   with fat removed
1 tablespoon olive oil
1/2 cup breading crumbs, page 75
1/2 cup pesto
4 slices provolone cheese
1/4 cup chopped fresh parsley

ASSEMBLY

1. Oil an ovenproof casserole dish large enough to contain the four chicken breasts.
2. Place crumbs in a flat dish and press chicken into crumbs, coating completely.
3. Place breaded chicken in oiled casserole dish. Spoon pesto evenly on each chicken breast. Top with provolone cheese and chopped parsley.
4. Bake in a preheated 400° oven for 20 minutes.
5. Remove cooked chicken from casserole to heated plates with a spatula.

Helpful Hint

If a bee stings you, apply a slice of onion to the spot and hold it there for a minute or two. Unless you have an allergy, this should help the sting.

"There is no such thing as a great talent without great will-power."
Honoré de Balzac

PROVOLONE CHEESE CHICKEN

Provolone cheese comes from southern Italy where the cows graze in lush, abundant fields. It has a firm texture and a mild smoky flavor. It is a wonderful cheese to cook with because it melts firm and does not string when baked. Provolone cheese is also made here in the United States.

2 whole chicken breasts, skinned, boned, halved, flattened,
   with fat removed
1 tablespoon olive oil
1/2 cup breading crumbs, page 75
1/2 teaspoon dried oregano or basil
4 slices provolone cheese
1/4 cup chopped fresh parsley

ASSEMBLY

1. Oil an ovenproof casserole dish large enough to contain the four chicken breasts.
2. Place crumbs in a flat dish and press chicken into crumbs, coating completely.
3. Place breaded chicken in oiled casserole dish. Sprinkle oregano on each chicken breast. Top with provolone cheese and chopped parsley.
4. Bake in a preheated 400° oven for 20 minutes.
5. Remove cooked chicken from casserole to heated plates with with a spatula.

Helpful Hint

A great cleaning solution for washing windows and mirrors is 1/2 cup rubbing alcohol to one quart of warm water. Use in a pail or a spray bottle. Then wipe with a clean towel or paper towel.

"There is no great genius without some touch of madness."
Lucius Annaeus Seneca

One day I was having a sandwich in a deli; you guessed it, a Reuben. I said to myself, "I can use this combination in a chicken dish." Sauerkraut is made with shredded cabbage, spices and salt; the mixture is then fermented.

2 whole chicken breasts, skinned, boned, halved, flattened,
   with fat removed
1 cup sauerkraut, drained
1/2 cup Thousand Island dressing
1/8 teaspoon ground fennel
1 tablespoon olive oil
1/2 cup breading crumbs, page 75
4 slices of ham
4 slices Swiss cheese
1/4 cup chopped fresh parsley

PREPARATION
1. Combine drained sauerkraut, Thousand Island dressing, and ground fennel in a mixing bowl.

ASSEMBLY
1. Oil an ovenproof casserole dish large enough to contain the four chicken breasts.
2. Place crumbs in a flat dish and press chicken into crumbs, coating completely.
3. Place breaded chicken breast in oiled casserole dish. Top with slice of ham about the same size as chicken breast. Spoon and spread the sauerkraut topping on ham; top with Swiss cheese and chopped parsley.
4. Bake in a preheated 400° oven for 20 minutes.
5. Remove cooked chicken from casserole to heated plates with a spatula.
   This chicken dish is a little thick, add more cooking time if necessary.

"I never worry about diets. The only carrots that interest me are the number you get in a diamond."
Mae West

RICOTTA-PEPPERONI CHICKEN

Pepperoni is Italian salami made with beef and pork and seasoned with red and black pepper. Air-dried, it can be eaten without being cooked. It can add flavor to many cooked dishes. One of the most popular dishes in this county is pepperoni pizza. Instead of pizza, we use chicken.

2 whole chicken breasts, skinned, boned, halved, flattened,
   with fat removed
20 thin slices pepperoni, coarsely chopped
1/2 cup ricotta cheese
1/2 cup tomato sauce (marinara sauce)
1 tablespoon Parmesan cheese
1 tablespoon olive oil
1/2 cup breading crumbs, page 75
4 slices provolone cheese
1/4 cup chopped fresh parsley

PREPARATION
1. Combine pepperoni, ricotta cheese, tomato sauce, and Parmesan cheese in a mixing bowl.

ASSEMBLY
1. Oil an ovenproof casserole dish large enough to contain the four chicken breasts.
2. Place crumbs in a flat dish and press chicken into crumbs, coating completely.
3. Place breaded chicken breasts in oiled casserole dish. Spoon and spread ricotta-pepperoni topping evenly on each chicken breast. Top with provolone cheese and chopped parsley.
4. Bake in a preheated 400° oven for 20 minutes.
5. Remove cooked chicken from casserole to heated plates with a spatula. Spoon any remaining topping around chicken.

This dish is a little thicker; add more time for cooking if needed

===================RICOTTA-TOMATO CHICKEN

Taking a walk through the vegetable garden in late summer is a real pleasure. The aroma of a just picked native tomato can remain in your mind for the winter.

2 whole chicken breasts, skinned, boned, halved, flattened,
   with fat removed
2 tablespoons butter
2 garlic cloves, minced
1 small onion, chopped
1/4 cup chopped green onions (scallions)
1/8 teaspoon dried thyme
1 cup ricotta cheese
1 egg, beaten in a small cup
1/4 cup chopped fresh parsley
1/2 cup breading crumbs, page 75
4 (1/4-inch) thick fresh tomato slices
4 slices provolone cheese

PREPARATION
1. Melt 1 tablespoon butter in a medium skillet; sauté minced garlic, chopped onion and chopped green onions until onion is soft. Cool.
2. Combine cooled onion mixture, thyme, ricotta cheese, beaten egg, and chopped parsley in a mixing bowl.

ASSEMBLY
1. Butter an ovenproof casserole dish large enough to contain the four chicken breasts.
2. Place crumbs in a flat dish and press chicken into crumbs, coating completely.
3. Place breaded chicken in buttered casserole dish. Spoon and spread ricotta cheese mixture evenly on each chicken breast. Top with tomato slice, then provolone cheese.
4. Bake in a preheated 400° oven for 20 minutes.
5. Remove cooked chicken from casserole to heated plates with a spatula. Spoon any remaining topping around chicken.
     This dish is thicker; add more time for cooking if needed.

ROCKEFELLER STYLE CHICKEN

Rockefeller style uses Pernod, a yellow licorice-flavored liquor. Pernod is a very popular drink in France. This recipe is usually prepared with oysters, but I like the variation with chicken.

2 whole chicken breasts, skinned, boned, halved, flattened,
  with fat removed
1 tablespoon butter
1 small onion, chopped
1 (10-ounce) package of fresh spinach, trimmed, cleaned and roughly chopped
1 teaspoon Pernod liquor (anisette liquor can be used)
1 teaspoon Parmesan cheese
1 tablespoon plain bread crumbs, dried or fresh
1 tablespoon olive oil
1/2 cup breading crumbs, page 75
4 slices cheddar cheese
1/4 cup chopped fresh parsley

PREPARATION
1. Melt butter in a large skillet; sauté onion until soft. Stir in spinach, continuously stirring, until spinach is wilted. Remove from heat, stir in Pernod, Parmesan cheese, and bread crumbs. Cool.

ASSEMBLY
1. Oil an ovenproof casserole dish large enough to contain the four chicken breasts.
2. Place crumbs in a flat dish and press chicken into crumbs, coating completely.
3. Place breaded chicken breasts in oiled casserole dish. Spoon and spread cooled spinach topping evenly on each chicken breast. Top with cheddar cheese and chopped parsley.
4. Bake in a preheated 400° oven for 20 minutes.
5. Remove cooked chicken from casserole to heated plates with a spatula.

"Come quickly I am tasting the stars!"
        Dom Pérignon, the moment he discovered Champagne

══════════════ROQUEFORT-LEMON CHICKEN

*Roquefort cheese made from sheep's milk, exposed to a mold
known as Penicillium roquiforti and aged for three months in
limestone caverns near the village of Roquefort, France.*

2 whole chicken breasts, skinned, boned, halved, flattened,
   with fat removed
2 tablespoons sour cream
1/4 cup crumbled Roquefort cheese
1/4 cup fresh bread crumbs
1 teaspoon fresh lemon juice
1 teaspoon grated lemon peel (zest)
2 tablespoons thinly sliced green onions (scallions)
1 tablespoon butter
1/2 cup breading crumbs, page 75

PREPARATION
1. Mix sour cream, Roquefort cheese, bread crumbs, lemon juice,
   lemon peel, and sliced green onions in a mixing bowl.

ASSEMBLY
1. Butter an ovenproof casserole dish large enough to contain the
   four chicken breasts.
2. Place crumbs in a flat dish and press crumbs into chicken,
   coating chicken completely. Place breaded chicken in buttered
   casserole dish.
3. Spoon and spread Roquefort cheese topping evenly on each chicken breast.
4. Bake in a preheated 400° oven for 20 minutes.
5. Remove cooked chicken to heated plates with a spatula.
   Spoon any remaining topping around chicken.

*Gorgonzola or blue cheese can be substituted for Roquefort.
This dish is rich; serve with plain starch and vegetables.*

*"Every morning one must start from scratch,
with nothing on the stoves. That is cuisine."*
Fernand Point

SAVORY APPLE CHICKEN

The tartness of an apple is derived from the balance of malic acid and the fruit's natural sugar.

2 whole chicken breasts, skinned, boned, halved, flattened,
  with fat removed
1/2 cup apple juice
1/2 cup plain fresh or dried bread crumbs
1 apple, peeled, cored and chopped
1/4 cup raisins
1 small onion, chopped fine
1 teaspoon brown sugar
1/2 teaspoon curry powder
1/2 teaspoon poultry seasoning
1 clove garlic, minced
1/2 cup breading crumbs, page 75
1 tablespoon butter
4 slices cheddar cheese

PREPARATION
1. Combine apple juice, bread crumbs, chopped apple, raisins, chopped onion, brown sugar, curry powder, poultry seasoning, and minced garlic in a mixing bowl.

ASSEMBLY
1. Butter an ovenproof casserole dish large enough to contain the four chicken breasts.
2. Place crumbs in a flat dish and press chicken into crumbs, coating completely. Place breaded chicken in buttered casserole dish. Spoon and spread stuffing evenly on each breaded chicken breast. Top with slice of cheddar.
3. Bake in a preheated 400° oven for 20 minutes.
4. Remove cooked chicken from casserole to heated plates with a spatula. Spoon any remaining stuffing around chicken.

This dish is thicker; allow more time for cooking if needed.

SAVORY STUFFED CHICKEN

*Freeze any extra stuffing for another meal. This stuffing can
also be used for stuffed mushrooms.*

2 whole chicken breasts, skinned, boned, halved, flattened,
   with fat removed
2 tablespoons butter
1 small onion, minced
1 stalk of celery, minced
1 package of prepared chicken stuffing mix (Stove top, Pepperidge
   Farm for example)
1/2 cup breading crumbs, page 75
4 slices Swiss cheese
1 (10-1/2 ounce) cream of chicken soup
1/2 cup milk
1/4 cup chopped fresh parsley

PREPARATION

1. Melt 1 tablespoon butter in a medium saucepan; sauté minced onion for
   one minute. Add minced celery; and cook for one minute until soft.
2. Add stuffing mix to onion in saucepan, add liquid according to package
   directions, and add seasoning package in box. Mix well and cool.

ASSEMBLY

1. Butter an ovenproof casserole dish large enough to contain the
   four chicken breasts.
2. Place crumbs in a flat dish and press crumbs into chicken,
   coating completely. Place breaded chicken in oiled casserole dish.
3. Spoon and spread a layer of stuffing evenly on the chicken breasts.
   Top with slice of Swiss cheese. Dot with butter.
4. Bake in a preheated 400° oven for twenty minutes.
5. Heat the cream of chicken soup and milk in a small saucepan over
   medium-low heat, stirring well until it resembles a smooth sauce. If sauce
   is too thick, add a little more milk. Keep warm until ready to use.
6. Remove cooked chicken from casserole to heated plates with a spatula.
   Spoon the sauce on and around chicken. Garnish with chopped parsley.
   Add a teaspoon of dry sherry, Madeira or Marsala wine to the sauce if you wish.

SHRIMP AND BASIL CHICKEN

Shrimp is America's favorite shellfish. Combining it with ricotta cheese, sun-dried tomatoes, and provolone cheese is rewarding.

2 whole chicken breasts, skinned, boned, halved, flattened,
   with fat removed
1 teaspoon butter
2 cloves garlic, minced
1/4 cup chopped raw shrimp (shelled, deveined, tails off)
6 fresh basil leaves, rough chopped
1/4 cup ricotta cheese
1 tablespoon minced sun-dried tomatoes
1 tablespoon olive oil
1/2 cup breading crumbs, page 75
4 slices provolone cheese

PREPARATION

1. Melt butter in a medium skillet; sauté garlic just a minute. Stir in chopped shrimp; cook while stirring until shrimp firms up. Remove from heat; stir in chopped basil. Cool in skillet.
2. When shrimp mixture is cool, stir in ricotta cheese and sun-dried tomato.

ASSEMBLY

1. Oil an ovenproof casserole dish large enough to contain the four chicken breasts.
2. Place crumbs in a flat dish and press chicken into crumbs, coating completely.
3. Place breaded chicken breasts in oiled casserole dish. Spoon and spread cooled shrimp topping evenly on each chicken breast. Top with provolone cheese.
4. Bake in a preheated 400° oven for 20 minutes.
5. Remove cooked chicken from casserole with a spatula. Spoon any remaining topping around chicken.

Helpful Hint

Always chop, measure and prepare all the ingredients for a recipe before beginning to cook.

=====================SOUR CREAM CHICKEN

A mild taste with green onions, Parmesan cheese, and sour cream.

2 whole chicken breasts, skinned, boned, halved, flattened,
  with fat removed
Dash red pepper sauce (Tabasco)
1/4 teaspoon dried paprika
2 tablespoons grated Parmesan cheese
1/4 cup chopped fresh parsley
1/4 cup chopped green onion (scallion)
3/4 cup sour cream or yogurt
1 tablespoon whole egg mayonnaise
1/4 cup dried or fresh plain bread crumbs
1 tablespoon olive oil
1/2 cup breading crumbs, page 75

PREPARATION
1. Combine red pepper sauce, paprika, grated Parmesan cheese, chopped
   parsley, chopped green onions, sour cream, mayonnaise, and plain bread
   crumbs in a mixing bowl.

ASSEMBLY
1. Oil an ovenproof casserole dish large enough to contain the
   four chicken breasts.
2. Place crumbs in a flat dish and press chicken into
   crumbs, coating completely.
3. Place breaded chicken in oiled casserole dish. Spoon and spread
   sour cream topping evenly on each chicken breast.
4. Bake in a preheated 400° oven for 20 minutes.
5. Remove cooked chicken from casserole to heated plates with
   a spatula. Spoon any remaining sauce on and around chicken.

*"Non-cooks think it's silly to invest two hours' work in two
two minutes' enjoyment; but if cooking is evanescent, well,
so is the ballet."*
            Julia Child

SOUTH WESTERN CHICKEN

Monterey Jack Cheese originated in Monterey, California. I love cooking with this cheese because it melts so well in baked dishes. Its mild flavor accents other flavors.

2 whole chicken breasts, skinned, boned, halved, flattened,
   with fat removed
1 tablespoon olive oil
1/2 cup breading crumbs, page 75
1/2 cup hickory smoked barbecue sauce
4 sliced smoked bacon, cut in half, cooked until crispy
4 center cut slices of ripe tomato
4 slices Monterey Jack cheese
1/4 cup chopped fresh parsley

ASSEMBLY

1. Oil an ovenproof casserole large enough to contain the four chicken breasts.
2. Place special crumbs in a flat dish and press crumbs into chicken, coating completely.
3. Lay breaded chicken breast in oiled casserole dish. Spoon and spread barbeque sauce evenly on each chicken breast; place two cooked bacon halves on top of sauce. Top bacon with sliced tomato, Monterey Jack cheese, and chopped parsley.
4. Bake in a preheated 400° oven for 20 minutes.
5. Remove cooked chicken from casserole to heated plates with a spatula.

Helpful Hint

Next time a plastic wrapper melts onto the toaster or the coffeepot, rub some petroleum jelly on the spot, reheat the appliance, and use a paper towel to rub off the plastic and the printing.

"Great wine is a work of art. It....sharpens the wit, gladdens the heart, and stimulates all that is most generous in human nature."
H. Warner Allen

=========SPINACH AND RICOTTA CHICKEN

The flavors of fennel seeds, pine nuts, tomato, spinach, and cheese sends the taste buds flying.

2 whole chicken breasts, skinned, boned, halved, flattened,
  with fat removed
3 tablespoons olive oil
1 small onion, chopped
1/2 teaspoon dried fennel seeds
1 tablespoon pine nuts, chopped
1/4 cup ricotta cheese
2/3 cup finely chopped, cooked spinach, drained (frozen spinach optional)
1/2 cup breading crumbs, page 75
4 slices provolone cheese
1 clove garlic, minced
1 can (14-ounces) chopped tomatoes
1 teaspoon tomato paste
1/4 cup chopped fresh basil or 1/2 teaspoon dried basil
1/4 cup chopped fresh parsley

PREPARATION

1. Heat 1 tablespoon olive oil in a medium skillet; sauté
   onion until it turns yellow. Stir in fennel seeds and pine nuts; sauté
   for a minute. Remove from heat; stir in spinach and ricotta cheese. Cool.

ASSEMBLY

1. Oil an ovenproof casserole dish large enough to contain the four
   chicken breasts.
2. Place crumbs in a flat dish and press chicken into
   crumbs, coating completely.
3. Place breaded chicken in oiled casserole dish. Spoon and spread
   spinach topping evenly on each chicken breast. Top with provolone cheese.
4. Bake in a preheated 400° oven for 20 minutes.
5. While chicken is cooking, heat 1 tablespoon olive oil in a skillet; sauté
   garlic for a minute. Stir in chopped tomatoes and tomato paste. Bring
   to a boil and simmer for 15 minutes. Stir in chopped basil (sauce can
   be made in advance).
6. Remove cooked chicken from casserole to heated plates with a spatula.
   Spoon the tomato sauce on and around chicken. Garnish with chopped parsley.

===*SPINACH, PINE NUT, PROVOLONE CHICKEN*

Pine nuts come from several varieties of pine trees. The nut is in the pinecone; most of the time the pinecones are heated to help remove the nut. Pine nuts should be stored in an airtight container in the refrigerator or freezer.

2 whole chicken breasts, skinned, boned, halved, flattened,
  with fat removed
2 tablespoons olive oil
1 small onion, chopped
1 clove of garlic, minced
1 tablespoon pine nuts
1 (10-ounces) package of fresh spinach, trimmed, washed and roughly chopped
1 tablespoon grated Parmesan cheese
1/2 cup breading crumbs, page 75
4 slices provolone cheese
1/4 cup chopped fresh parsley

PREPARATION
1. Heat 1 tablespoon olive oil in a large skillet; sauté chopped
   onion for a minute. Stir in garlic and pine nuts, cook for just one minute.
   Stir in spinach, continuously stirring, until spinach is wilted. Remove
   from heat and stir in Parmesan cheese. Cool.

ASSEMBLY
1. Oil an ovenproof casserole dish large enough to contain
   the four chicken breasts.
2. Place crumbs in a flat dish and press chicken into
   crumbs, coating completely.
3. Place breaded chicken breasts in oiled casserole dish. Spoon and
   spread cooled spinach evenly on each chicken breast. Top with provolone
   cheese and chopped parsley.
4. Bake in a preheated 400° oven for 20 minutes.
5. Remove cooked chicken from casserole to heated plates with a
   spatula. Spoon any remaining stuffing around chicken.

Helpful Hint
*Squeezing all the water out of frozen spinach can be a problem.
If you have a potato ricer, put thawed spinach in the ricer. With one or
two presses of the handle, much of the water is removed.*

===========SQUASH-PROSCIUTTO CHICKEN

Prosciutto is an Italian ham that is cured in salt and air-dried. The meat is pressed, which produces a firm dense texture. Most of the hams produced in the United States are smoked.

2 whole chicken breasts, skinned, boned, halved, flattened,
  with fat removed
1 acorn squash halved, seeded and cooked, see page 429
1/8 pound proscuitto, minced fine, (ham can be used as well)
1 egg, beaten in a small cup
1/4 cup Parmesan cheese
2 tablespoons plain bread crumbs, (fresh or dried)
1 tablespoon minced fresh sage leaves or 1/2 teaspoon dried sage
Dash nutmeg
1 tablespoon olive oil
1/2 cup breading crumbs, page 75
4 slices provolone cheese

PREPARATION
1. Combine squash, prosciutto, beaten egg, Parmesan cheese, bread crumbs, sage, and nutmeg in a mixing bowl.

ASSEMBLY
1. Oil an ovenproof casserole dish large enough to contain the four chicken breasts.
2. Place crumbs in a flat dish and press chicken into crumbs, coating completely.
3. Place breaded chicken breasts in oiled casserole dish. Spoon and spread squash topping evenly on each chicken breast. Top with provolone cheese.
4. Bake in a preheated 400° oven for 20 minutes.
5. Remove cooked chicken from casserole to heated plates with a spatula. Spoon any remaining topping around chicken.

"Life is too short for cuisine minceur and for diets.
Dietetic meals are like an opera without the orchestra."
Paul Bocuse

SUMMER TOMATO CHICKEN

This dish is at its best with summer native tomatoes.

2 whole chicken breasts, skinned, boned, halved, flattened,
with fat removed
1 tablespoon olive oil
1/2 cup breading crumbs, page 75
8 slices ripe fresh tomatoes
1/4 teaspoon dried basil or 1/4 cup chopped fresh basil
4 slices provolone cheese
1/4 cup chopped fresh parsley

ASSEMBLY

1. Oil an ovenproof casserole dish large enough to contain the
   four chicken breasts.
2. Place crumbs in a flat dish and press chicken into crumbs,
   coating completely.
3. Place breaded chicken breasts in oiled casserole. Top with sliced
   tomato, basil, provolone cheese and chopped parsley.
4. Bake in a preheated 400° oven for 20 minutes.
5. Remove cooked chicken from casserole dish to heated plates with
   a spatula.

<u>Helpful Hint</u>

*Tape a note pad to the inside of one of your kitchen cabinet doors
to create a running grocery list by jotting down items as you think of
them or run out.*

*"Because of the media hype and woefully inadequate information,
too many people nowadays are deathly afraid of their food, and what
does fear of food do to the digestive system? I am sure that an unhappy
or suspicious stomach, constricted and uneasy with worry, cannot
digest properly. And if digestion is poor, the whole body politic suffers."*
Julia Child

SUN-DRIED TOMATO MUSTARD, ALMOND CHICKEN

Any style of specialty mustards can be used for this dish, such as honey mustard, ginger mustard or tarragon mustard. There are so many variations of mustards available; your choices are unlimited.

2 whole chicken breasts, skinned, boned, halved, flattened,
   with fat removed
2 tablespoons butter
1/2 cup breading crumbs, page 75
Sun-dried tomato mustard (available in specialty stores)
1/2 cup sliced almonds
1/4 cup chopped fresh parsley

ASSEMBLY
1. Using half the butter, butter an ovenproof casserole dish large enough to contain the four chicken breasts.
2. Place crumbs in a flat dish and press chicken into crumbs, coating completely.
3. Place breaded chicken breasts in buttered casserole dish. Spoon a thin layer of sun-dried tomato mustard on each chicken breast. Top with almonds, parsley and dot with butter.
4. Bake in a preheated 400° oven for 20 minutes.
5. Remove cooked chicken from casserole to heated plates with a spatula.

If you cannot find sun-dried tomato mustard, make your own by chopping sun-dried tomatoes and mixing with Dijon-style mustard.

"I've discovered that people who are not interested in food always seem rather dry and unloving and don't have a real gusto for life."
Julia Child

=================TERIYAKI- SESAME CHICKEN

Teriyaki sauce comes from the kitchens of Japan. It is a mixture of soy sauce, Sake, ginger, seasonings, and sugar. The sugar gives the food a slight glaze. Teriyaki sauce is available in grocery stores.

2 whole chicken breasts, skinned, boned, halved, flattened,
  with fat removed
1 tablespoon olive oil
1/2 cup teriyaki sauce
1 cup sesame seeds
1 teaspoon butter
1/4 cup chopped fresh parsley

ASSEMBLY
1. Oil an ovenproof casserole dish large enough to contain the four chicken breasts.
2. Place sesame seeds in a shallow dish.
3. With a pastry brush or a spoon, coat the chicken breasts with teriyaki sauce. Place chicken in sesame seeds, coating completely. You may need extra sesame seeds. Place sesame coated chicken on oiled casserole dish. Sprinkle with chopped parsley. Dot with butter.
5. Bake in a preheated 400° oven for 20 minutes
6. Remove cooked chicken from casserole to heated plates with a spatula.

Helpful Hint
Use your salad spinner to dry shredded potatoes when making potato pancakes.

"Tis not the meat, but 'tis the appetite makes eating a delight."
Sir John Suckling

=============*WILD MUSHROOM CHICKEN*

Store fresh mushrooms, unwashed, in the refrigerator. Never store fresh mushrooms in a plastic bag. Dried mushrooms should be stored in a cool dark place. Clean mushrooms with a damp cloth or paper towel.

2 whole chicken breasts, skinned, boned, halved, flattened,
   with fat removed
1 ounce dried porcini mushrooms
2 tablespoons olive oil
1 teaspoon butter
2 garlic cloves, minced
1/2 pound domestic mushrooms, cleaned and minced
1/4 cup chopped fresh parsley
3/4 cup ricotta cheese
1/4 cup grated Parmesan cheese
1 egg, beaten in a small cup
1/4 cup green onions (scallions)
1/2 cup breading crumbs, page 75
4 slices provolone cheese

PREPARATION
1. Cover porcini with boiling water and soak for 30 minutes.
   Drain, cool, and mince.
2. Heat 1 tablespoon olive oil and 1 teaspoon butter in a medium skillet;
   sauté minced garlic for one minute. Stir in both chopped mushrooms
   and cook until wilted. Cool.
3. Thoroughly mix cooled mushrooms, chopped parsley, ricotta cheese,
   Parmesan cheese, beaten egg, and green onions.

ASSEMBLY
1. Oil an ovenproof casserole dish large enough to contain the
   four chicken breasts.
2. Place crumbs in a flat dish and press chicken into
   crumbs, coating completely.
3. Place breaded chicken breasts in oiled, casserole dish. Spoon
   and spread mushroom topping evenly on each chicken breast.
   Top with provolone cheese.
4. Bake in a preheated 400° oven for 20 minutes.
5. Remove cooked chicken from casserole to heated plates with a
   spatula. Spoon remaining topping around chicken.

Catering is always interesting. You bring the restaurant to a home, with everything you need for a dinner party, but working in a strange kitchen is always a challenge.

A woman I work for in Rhode Island asked me to do a Christmas party in her New York City apartment. The day of the party, three staff and I left for the big city. For country folks, it turned out to be quite an experience.

Once we finally found the building, we realized that the front entrance was for guests, not for caterers. We had to bring everything up in the service elevator, which was quite a haul from the street. We finally got everything to the seventh floor and then didn't know what to do with our car. I asked the doorman to watch it, and luckily, he agreed to do so.

The menu was chicken, salmon, roasted potatoes and stir-fried julienne vegetables. This December evening was unusually warm, and the hostess had all of the air conditioners on. I had the chicken, salmon, and roasted potatoes in double stack ovens. Everything went smoothly until I turned on my electric wok to stir-fry vegetables. A circuit breaker tripped and the apartment, party guests and all, was in darkness. While we were looking for candles, someone brushed against a mirror, and it smashed to the floor. Picking up glass in the dark was an adventure. We finally found the breaker box and were able to get lights on except in the kitchen.

"If we turn off the air-conditioners, we probably could get the power back in the kitchen," I said to the hostess. "Normand," she replied, "I would rather be cool than eat– by the way what time is dinner?"

She called the apartment next door and asked if we could use their oven. "Okay," the woman said, "but what are you cooking?" We told her and she said, "You can cook the salmon but not the chicken, because this is a kosher kitchen."

We ended up cooking the salmon in their oven, and I was able to get one oven working and finished the chicken. I also found sauté pans and finished the vegetables.

We finally got everyone fed and left the city about 1 a.m. The hostess had put us up in a hotel in Old Greenwich, Connecticut, but we hit a traffic jam on the freeway and didn't arrive there until 4 a.m. It took us three hours to go 50 miles. We finally got to bed, only to get up three hours later to drive the rest of the way home. This was just another day in the life of a caterer.

1.Take one day at a time. Do not allow yourself to become angry and stressed. Give yourself a positive self-talk every day. Make yourself say, "I am going to have a good day today."

2. Practice deep breathing for at least 10 minutes each day, sit in a comfortable place and breath from your stomach, close your eyes and think of a relaxed place in your mind that will sooth you.

3. Eat slowly and savor each bite without distractions such as the television or reading material and try to eat healthier. Read cookbooks, healthy-cooking magazines and cooking web sites. Get your mind going and try to cook a new recipe at least once a week.

4. Take stairs when you can instead of the elevator. Park your car in a further spot in parking lots to get the extra walk. Walk everyday. I do water aerobics three mornings a week; 150 seniors are doing this in my class. Do what you can at your pace.

5. Lie on the floor and stretch that body. Reach forward as far as you can toward your toes, pushing your abdominal muscles in. Lift your legs and stretch your body while breathing.

6. Turn off the television and read a book or magazine; do a puzzle, write a poem or story about something that may interest you.

7. Watch a beautiful sunset; go for a walk at dusk. That time of the evening is usually so peaceful.

8. Eliminate the junk food in your diet, eat more healthy and you will find with the extra exercise and healthier food the pounds will come off.

9. Locate "exit signs" when you are in a public building. During restaurant staff meetings, we did an emergency drill on how we would help clients out of the building in the case of an emergency. I always check for a way out in a hotel, restaurant, and public buildings.

10. Take someone to lunch or dinner that could use your company. It always makes you feel better when you surprise someone who does not expect it.

The road to a healthier life begins with small simple steps and you can be in charge of your own life and happiness.

CHICKEN BREAST
BAKED
WITH SAUCES

=======CHICKEN BREAST BAKED WITH SAUCES

All recipes are for two in this chapter.

Chicken Baked with Sauces Continued-

===========*Hints and suggestions*

RECIPES: Chicken and seafood recipes are for two servings, unless otherwise specified. Double or triple the ingredients for more servings.
PREPARING AHEAD: If you prepare recipes ahead of time, take them out of the refrigerator 30 minutes before cooking time.
REMOVE SKIN FROM CHICKEN: To remove skin from fresh chicken, use a paper towel to hold the chicken skin, pull the skin while holding down the chicken and the skin should come right off.
FLATTEN CHICKEN: You can flatten trimmed chicken breasts between two pieces of wax paper or plastic wrap with the bottom of a sauté pan or a meat mallet, available in kitchen stores.
BREADING CRUMBS ON CHICKEN: If the boneless breasts of chicken are dry, moisten the chicken with a little milk and the crumbs will stick to the chicken.

============================ALMOND PRUNE CHICKEN

Prunes (dried plum), traced back to the Romans, are a great winter fruit because they can be stored without a problem.

2 whole chicken breasts, skinned boned, halved, flattened,
  with fat removed
1/4 cup chopped green onions (scallions)
1/4 cup pitted prunes, chopped
1/4 cup sliced almonds
1 teaspoon brown sugar
1 cup chicken broth
1/4 cup chopped fresh parsley
1/2 cup breading crumbs, page 75
1 teaspoon butter

PREPARATION
1. Mix green onions, prunes, almonds, brown sugar, chicken broth, and parsley in a mixing bowl.

ASSEMBLY
1. Select an ovenproof casserole dish large enough to contain the four chicken breasts.
2. Place crumbs in a flat dish and press chicken into crumbs, coating completely.
3. Place breaded chicken in casserole; spoon prune mixture on and around chicken. Dot with butter.
4. Bake in a preheated 400° oven for 20 minutes.
5. Remove cooked chicken from casserole to heated plates with a spatula. Spoon the prune mixture on and around chicken.

This dish is perfect with rice. Place the rice on the plate with the chicken, and spoon the sauce on rice and chicken.

"I have always felt that one of the most important things in life was to give my acquired knowledge to the next generation."
Chef Louis Szathmary
(Chef Louis left his vast collection to the Johnson & Wales University.)

============================APRICOT CHICKEN

Apricot jelly, for some reason, is hard to find in the supermarket; it is usually found in baking or specialty shops. The jelly is melted and used as a glaze in baking.

2 whole chicken breasts, skinned, boned, halved, flattened,
   with fat removed
1/2 cup apricot jelly (or jam)
2 garlic cloves, minced
1/8 teaspoon dried ginger or 1/4 teaspoon fresh grated ginger
Pinch ground red pepper (cayenne)
1 tablespoon white vinegar
1 tablespoon soy sauce
1/2 cup breading crumbs, page 75
4 large mushrooms caps, stems removed
2 tablespoons butter
1/4 cup chopped fresh parsley

PREPARATION
1. Whisk apricot jelly, minced garlic, ginger, cayenne powder, vinegar, and soy sauce in a mixing bowl until completely blended.

ASSEMBLY
1. Using half the butter, butter an ovenproof casserole dish large enough to contain the four chicken breasts.
2. Place crumbs in a flat dish and press chicken into crumbs, coating completely.
3. Place breaded chicken breasts in buttered casserole dish. Top with mushroom caps; spoon apricot glaze on and around chicken. Top with parsley. Dot with remaining butter.
4. Bake in a preheated 400° oven for 20 minutes.
5. Remove cooked chicken from casserole to heated plates with a spatula. Spoon the remaining glaze on and around chicken.

"Sharing food with another human being is an intimate act that should not be indulged in lightly."
M.F.K. Fisher

===============ARTICHOKE CHEESE CHICKEN

This dish is wonderful on a bed of noodles. The juice from the baking dish ends up as the sauce.

2 whole chicken breasts, skinned, boned, halved, flattened,
   with fat removed
3/4 cup chicken broth
1 teaspoon honey
1 tablespoon balsamic vinegar
1/2 teaspoon soy sauce
1 tablespoon butter
1/2 cup breading crumbs, page 75
4 artichoke hearts, fresh, canned, or frozen, drained, cut in half
1/4 teaspoon sage
4 slices Monterey Jack cheese
1/4 cup chopped fresh parsley

PREPARATION
1. Mix chicken broth, honey, balsamic vinegar, and soy sauce in a
   small mixing bowl.

ASSEMBLY
1. Butter an ovenproof casserole dish large enough to contain
   the four chicken breasts.
2. Place crumbs in a flat dish and press chicken into
   crumbs, coating completely.
3. Place breaded chicken breasts in buttered casserole dish. Top with
   eight artichoke halves. Dust with sage and top with Monterey Jack cheese
   and chopped parsley. Spoon chicken broth mixture around chicken.
4. Bake in a preheated 400° oven for 20 minutes.
5. Remove cooked chicken from casserole to heated plates with a spatula.
   Spoon remaining juices on and around chicken.

   If artichokes are large, add a little more cooking time.
   (If you are using frozen artichokes, make sure they are thawed.)

=========================ASIAN-STYLE CHICKEN

Oriental flavors are so popular today. I do not know one city or town in the country that does not have at least three oriental restaurants. Enjoy these lively flavors from the Far East.

2 whole chicken breasts, skinned, boned, halved, flattened,
   with fat removed
1/3 cup hoisin sauce
1 tablespoon fresh lime juice
1/2 teaspoon sesame oil
1 teaspoon Asian chili paste
1 tablespoon soy sauce
1 teaspoon rice-wine vinegar
1/2 teaspoon finely chopped fresh ginger
1/4 cup chopped green onions (scallions)
1/4 cup finely chopped red bell peppers
1 tablespoon water
1/4 cup sliced water chestnuts (available in small cans)
1/2 cup breading crumbs, page 75

PREPARATION
1. Mix hoisin sauce, lime juice, sesame oil, chili paste, soy sauce, wine vinegar, chopped ginger, scallions, chopped red peppers, water, and water chestnuts in a mixing bowl.

ASSEMBLY
1. Select an ovenproof casserole dish large enough to contain the four chicken breasts.
2. Place crumbs in a flat dish and press chicken into crumbs, coating completely.
3. Place breaded chicken in casserole dish. Spoon hoisin mixture on and around chicken.
4. Bake in a preheated 400° oven for 20 minutes.
5. Remove cooked chicken from casserole to heated plates with a spatula. Spoon remaining sauce on and around chicken.
      This dish is great with rice.

      You can substitute non-salted cashews for water chestnuts.

============BALSAMIC CHICKEN WITH PEARS

Balsamic vinegar is made from white Trebbeano grape juice; it gets its dark color and sweetness from aging in wooden barrels.

2 whole chicken breasts, skinned, boned, halved, flattened,
   with fat removed
2/3 cup chicken broth
1 1/2 tablespoons balsamic vinegar
Pinch rosemary
2 Bosc pears, peeled, cut in half, cored and stem removed
1/2 cup breading crumbs, page 75
4 slices Monterey Jack cheese
1 tablespoon butter

PREPARATION
1. Mix chicken broth, balsamic vinegar, and rosemary in a mixing bowl.

ASSEMBLY
1. Select an ovenproof casserole dish that is just large enough to contain the four chicken breasts, plus the pears.
2. Place special crumbs in a flat dish and press chicken into crumbs, coating completely.
3. Place breaded chicken breasts and pears core side down in casserole dish. Top each chicken breast with a slice of Monterey Jack cheese. Spoon balsamic sauce on and around chicken and pears. Dot with butter.
4. Bake in a preheated 400° oven for 20 minutes.
5. Remove cooked chicken and pears from casserole to heated plates with a spatula. Spoon remaining juices on and around chicken.

This dish is wonderful with rice or noodles.

*"Think of cooking as an outlet for your ideas,
a release for the artist in you."*
Wolfgang Puck

==============*BANANA-GRAPEFRUIT CHICKEN*

*Bananas are grown in the warm humid tropics and picked green;
the flavor is better when ripened off the bush. Banana bushes mature in
15 months and can produce one 50-pound bunch of bananas per bush.*

2 whole chicken breasts, skinned, boned, halved, flattened,
   with fat removed
1 cup unsweetened grapefruit juice
1/4 teaspoon ground curry powder
1/4 cup chopped fresh parsley
1/4 cup chopped green onions (scallions)
2 ripe bananas, peeled and cut in 2-inch rounds
2 tablespoons butter
1/2 cup breading crumbs, page 75
1/2 cup sliced almonds

PREPARATION
1. Mix grapefruit juice, curry powder, chopped parsley, and chopped green
    onions in a mixing bowl. Stir in cut bananas; mix until bananas are
    coated with liquid.

ASSEMBLY
1. Using half the butter, butter an ovenproof casserole dish large
    enough to contain the four chicken breasts, plus room for the
    bananas.
2. Place crumbs in a flat dish and press chicken into crumbs,
    coating completely.
3. Place breaded chicken breasts in buttered casserole dish. Spoon banana
    mixture around chicken, and spoon remaining sauce on the chicken.
    Top with almonds. Dot with butter.
4. Bake in a preheated 400° oven for 20 minutes.
5. Remove cooked chicken from casserole to heated plates with a spatula.
    Spoon bananas and sauce on and around chicken.

Add shredded coconut to this dish before baking for a different flavor.

The flavor of blue cheese and light beer surprises the taste buds.

2 whole chicken breasts, skinned, boned, halved, flattened,
  with fat removed
1/2 cup blue cheese dressing (refrigerated fresh type)
1/2 cup light beer
1/2 teaspoon hot pepper sauce (Tabasco)
1/4 teaspoon chopped fresh parsley
1 teaspoon white wine vinegar
1 tablespoon butter
1/2 cup breading crumbs, page 75

PREPARATION

1. Thoroughly mix blue cheese dressing, beer, hot sauce, chopped parsley, and vinegar in a mixing bowl.

ASSEMBLY

1. Butter an ovenproof casserole dish large enough to contain the four chicken breasts.
2. Place crumbs in a flat dish and press chicken into crumbs, coating completely. Place chicken in casserole dish.
3. Spoon blue cheese sauce on and around chicken.
4. Bake in a preheated 400° oven for 20 minutes.
5. Remove cooked chicken from casserole to heated plates with a spatula. Spoon remaining juices on and around the chicken.

This dish goes well with orzo, pasta that looks like rice.

Helpful Hint

*Spilled wax on carpet can be a problem. It happened so many times at the restaurant. We placed a brown paper bag or newspaper on the wax, gently running a **warm** iron over the bag. The wax melted and the bag absorbed it. A **hot** iron can hurt your carpet*

"If you can't stand the heat, get out of the kitchen."
Harry S. Truman

==============*BOSC PEARS WITH CHICKEN*

Purchase pears that are free of blemishes, firm, but not hard.
When you core the pear, be sure to get all the gritty flesh around the core.

2 whole chicken breasts, skinned, boned, halved, flattened,
   with fat removed
1 cup chicken broth
1 tablespoon balsamic vinegar
1 teaspoon soy sauce
1/8 teaspoon grated fresh ginger
1/4 cup white seedless raisins
2 Bosc pears peeled, cored and each cut into 6 wedges
1/2 cup breading crumbs, page 75
1 teaspoon butter

PREPARATION
1. Mix chicken broth, balsamic vinegar, soy sauce, ginger, raisins,
   and pears in a mixing bowl.

ASSEMBLY
1. Select an ovenproof casserole dish large enough to contain the
   four chicken breasts plus a little more room.
2. Place special crumbs in a flat dish and press chicken into
   crumbs, coating completely.
3. Place breaded chicken in casserole dish, spoon pear mixture on and
   around chicken using all the liquid. Dot with butter.
4. Bake in a preheated 400° oven for 20 minutes.
5. Remove cooked chicken from casserole to heated plates with
   a spatula. Spoon pears and sauce on and around chicken.

"If a man be sensible and one fine morning, while he is lying in
bed, count at the tips of his fingers how many things in this life truly
will give him enjoyment, invariable he will find food is the first one."
Lin Yutang

====*BOURBON AND PEACH GLAZED CHICKEN*

Bourbon is named for Bourbon County, Kentucky; the liquor is distilled from fermented grain.

2 whole chicken breasts, skinned, boned, halved, flattened,
   with fat removed
1/2 cup peach preserves (jam)
1 teaspoon grated orange peel (zest)
1/4 cup orange juice
2 garlic cloves, minced
1/2 teaspoon chopped fresh rosemary or 1/4 teaspoon dried
1 teaspoon chopped fresh ginger
1/4 cup bourbon whiskey
1/4 teaspoon crushed red pepper
1/4 cup chopped green onions (scallions)
1/2 cup breading crumbs, page 75
1 teaspoon butter

PREPARATION
1. Mix peach preserves, orange zest, orange juice, minced garlic, rosemary, ginger, bourbon whiskey, crushed red pepper, and green onions in a mixing bowl.

ASSEMBLY
1. Select and ovenproof casserole dish large enough to contain the four chicken breasts.
2. Place crumbs in a flat dish and press chicken into crumbs, coating completely.
3. Place chicken breasts in casserole. Spoon peach-bourbon sauce on and around chicken breasts.
4. Bake in a 400° oven for 20 minutes.
5. Remove cooked chicken from casserole to heated plates with a spatula, spoon sauce on and around chicken.

"Good food keeps the body and soul together."
Austrian proverb

BURGUNDY CHICKEN

The Burgundy area in eastern France produces superb red and white wines. It's a beautiful part of France, with outstanding countryside.

2 whole chicken breasts, skinned, boned, halved, flattened,
 with fat removed
1 small onion, minced
1 garlic clove, minced
1 tablespoon tomato paste or catsup
1/2 cup red burgundy wine (or any red wine)
1/2 cup chicken broth
1/4 teaspoon dried tarragon
1/2 cup breading crumbs, page 75
4 slices cheddar cheese
1/4 cup chopped fresh parsley

PREPARATION
1. Mix minced onion, minced garlic, tomato paste,
 burgundy wine, chicken broth, and tarragon in a mixing bowl.

ASSEMBLY
1. Choose an ovenproof casserole dish large enough to contain the
 four chicken breasts.
2. Place crumbs in a flat dish and press chicken into crumbs,
 coating chicken completely. Place breaded chicken in
 casserole dish.
3. Top each chicken breast with slice of cheddar. Spoon wine
 sauce on and around chicken. Top with chopped parsley.
4. Bake in a preheated 400° oven for 20 minutes.
5. Remove cooked chicken from casserole to heated plates with a
 spatula. Spoon some remaining sauce on and around chicken.

<u>Helpful Hint</u>
Houseplant food: To supplement an extra dose of nitrogen, add a little gelatin to the water once a month. Just empty an envelope of unflavored gelatin into 1 cup of boiling water, stir until the gelatin dissolves, and mix with 3 cups of cool water. Apply immediately; discard any leftover liquid.

==========BUTTER-RUM CHEDDAR CHICKEN

Rum is liquor distilled from fermented sugarcane or molasses. Most of the world's rum comes from the Caribbean.

2 whole chicken breasts, skinned, boned, halved, flattened,
  with fat removed
1/4 cup packed dark brown sugar
1 tablespoon water
1/4 cup dark rum
1 tablespoon Dijon-style mustard
1 tablespoon cider vinegar
1/4 teaspoon black pepper
1/2 cup breading crumbs, page 75
4 thin slices of cheddar cheese
1/4 cup (1/2-stick) softened butter

PREPARATION
1. Mix brown sugar, water, rum, mustard, vinegar, and
   black pepper in a mixing bowl.

ASSEMBLY
1. Using half the butter, butter an ovenproof casserole dish just
   large enough to contain the four chicken breasts.
2. Place crumbs in a flat dish and press chicken into crumbs,
   coating completely.
3. Place breaded chicken in buttered casserole dish. Top with
   cheddar cheese; spoon sauce around chicken and dot with
   remaining butter.
4. Bake in a preheated 400° oven for 20 minutes.
5. Remove cooked chicken from casserole dish to heated plates
   with a spatula. Spoon remaining sauce on and around chicken.

Napkins, traced to early Rome, when guests brought their own wiping cloths to a friends feast. It is believed during this era finer napkins were made for dining and wiping. Noblemen wore large collars, so the napkins were tied around their necks to shield the ruffles. This was quite a difficult maneuver, hence, we get the expression "to make both ends meet.

CALIFORNIA FIG CHICKEN

Figs, thought to be sacred by the ancient civilizations. A symbol of peace and prosperity, brought to California by the Spanish Franciscan missionaries, who started the popular Mission fig.

2 whole chicken breasts, skinned, boned, halved, flattened,
   with fat removed
1/4 cup chopped dried figs
1/4 cup chopped dried apricots
2 cloves garlic, minced
1/4 cup chopped green onions (scallions)
1/4 cup chopped pecans
1/4 teaspoon dried thyme
1/4 teaspoon ground ginger or fresh grated ginger
1/4 teaspoon ground cumin
1/4 cup chopped fresh parsley
2 tablespoons balsamic vinegar
2 tablespoons Madeira wine
1/2 cup chicken broth
1 tablespoon butter
1/2 cup breading crumbs, page 75

PREPARATION
1. Thoroughly mix chopped figs, chopped apricots, minced garlic, chopped green onions, chopped pecans, thyme, ginger, cumin, parsley, balsamic vinegar, Madeira wine, and chicken broth in a mixing bowl.

ASSEMBLY
1. Butter an ovenproof casserole large enough to contain the four chicken breasts.
2. Place crumbs in a flat dish and press chicken into crumbs, coating completely.
3. Place breaded chicken in buttered casserole dish. Spoon fig mixture on and around chicken.
4. Bake in a preheated 400° oven for 20 minutes.
5. Remove cooked chicken from casserole to heated plates with a spatula. Spoon the sauce on and around chicken.

The color and aroma from this dish will fill the table with nothing but smiles. This dish can also be prepared with chopped pecans, or unsalted chopped peanuts in place of cashews.

2 whole chicken breasts, skinned, boned, halved, flattened,
  with fat removed
1/2 cup chicken broth
1 tablespoon soy sauce
1 tablespoon balsamic vinegar
1/4 cup diced red bell pepper, cored and seeded
1/4 cup diced green bell pepper, cored and seeded
1/4 cup chopped green onions (scallions)
1/4 cup coarsely chopped unsalted cashews
1/2 cup breading crumbs, page 75
1 tablespoon butter

ASSEMBLY
1. Mix chicken broth, soy sauce, balsamic vinegar, red pepper, green pepper, green onions, and cashews in a mixing bowl.

PREPARATION
1. Select an ovenproof casserole dish large enough to contain the four chicken breasts.
2. Place crumbs in a flat dish and press chicken into crumbs, coating completely.
3. Place breaded chicken in casserole. Spoon cashew sauce on and around chicken. Dot with butter.
4. Bake in a preheated 400° oven for 20 minutes.
5. Remove cooked chicken from casserole to heated plates with a spatula. Spoon cashews and sauce on and around chicken.

If you cannot find unsalted cashews, place them in a sieve and run them under cold water to remove salt.

"Cuisine is when things taste like themselves."
Maurice Edmond Sailland

CHEESY APPLE CHICKEN

This is a wonderful fall dish when apples and fresh cider are everywhere.

2 whole chicken breasts, skinned, boned, halved, flattened,
  with fat removed
1 tablespoon butter
1/2 cup breading crumbs, page 75
2 tart apples, peeled, cut in half, cored and sliced
Dash nutmeg
1/4 cup chopped fresh parsley
4 slices Monterey Jack cheese
Dash paprika
1 cup cider or apple juice

ASSEMBLY

1. Butter an ovenproof casserole dish large enough to contain
   the four chicken breasts.
2. Place special crumbs in a flat dish and press chicken into
   crumbs, coating completely.
3. Place breaded chicken breasts in buttered casserole dish. Top with
   sliced apple; sprinkle with nutmeg, parsley, Monterey Jack cheese,
   and paprika. Pour cider around chicken.
4. Bake in a preheated 400° oven for 20 minutes.
5. Remove cooked chicken from casserole to heated plates with a
   spatula. Spoon the sauce on and around chicken.

*To keep sliced apples from browning after peeling and slicing,
toss them with a little citrus juice*

*"The fact is that it takes more than ingredients and techniques to
cook a good meal. A good cook puts something of himself into the
preparation–he cooks with enjoyment, anticipation, spontaneity,
and he is willing to experiment."*
    Pearl Bailey

CHICKEN CASA BELLA

My version of a wonderful meal I had in Florida.
Serve with pasta or orzo, spoon some of the sauce on the pasta.

2 whole chicken breast, skinned, boned, halved, flattened,
    with fat removed
1/4 cup chopped fresh basil or 1 teaspoon dried
1/4 teaspoon dried oregano
1/4 teaspoon crushed rosemary
2 cloves garlic, minced
1/2 cup chicken broth
1/2 cup white wine
1 teaspoon balsamic vinegar
1/4 teaspoon red pepper sauce (Tabasco)
1 cup sliced mushrooms
1 tablespoon butter
1/2 cup breading crumbs, page 75
4 slices provolone cheese

PREPARATION
1. Mix basil, oregano, rosemary, garlic, chicken broth, wine,
   balsamic vinegar, red pepper sauce, and sliced mushrooms in a mixing
   bowl.

ASSEMBLY
1. Butter an ovenproof casserole dish large enough to contain the
   four chicken breasts plus the sauce.
2. Place special crumbs in a flat dish and press chicken into
   crumbs, coating completely.
3. Place breaded chicken breasts in buttered casserole dish. Top
   with provolone cheese. Spoon sauce and mushrooms on and
   around chicken.
4. Bake in a preheated 400° oven for 20 minutes.
5. Remove cooked chicken from casserole to heated plates
   with a spatula. Spoon sauce and mushrooms on and around
   chicken.

==========================CHICKEN CHEF RON

*This dish, is named after Ron, a wonderful chef and friend
who worked for us at the Red Rooster for many years.*

2 whole chicken breasts, skinned, boned, halved, flattened,
   with fat removed
1/2 cup ginger ale
1 teaspoon brown sugar
1 teaspoon soy sauce
1/8 teaspoon ground ginger or 1/4 teaspoon fresh grated ginger
1/2 cup coarsely chopped pecans
1/4 cup chopped fresh parsley
1/4 cup chopped green onions (scallions)
1 tablespoon butter
1/2 cup breading crumbs, page 75
2 ripe pears, peeled, cored and quartered
4 slices Monterey Jack cheese

PREPARATION
1. Mix ginger ale, brown sugar, soy sauce, ginger, pecans, chopped parsley,
   and chopped green onions in a mixing bowl.

ASSEMBLY
1. Butter an ovenproof casserole dish large enough to contain
   the four chicken breasts.
2. Place special crumbs in a flat dish and press chicken into
   crumbs, coating completely.
3. Place breaded chicken breasts in buttered casserole dish. Top
   each breast with half of pear, and Monterey Jack cheese. Spoon the
   ginger ale sauce around chicken.
4. Bake in a preheated 400° oven for 20 minutes. (If pear is large,
   adjust cooking time 5 to 10 minutes longer.)
5. Remove cooked chicken from casserole to heated plates. Spoon
   sauce on and around chicken.

"Repetition is the Mother of Skill."
Chef Benjamin Savelo

CHICKEN CORDON BLEU

Chicken cordon bleu is a dish that is a staple on many of the menus in Rhode Island. It translates to "blue ribbon", given to chefs for culinary excellence.

2 whole chicken breasts, skinned, boned, halved flattened,
   with fat removed
1 tablespoon olive oil
1/2 cup breading crumbs, page 75
4 slices of ham (same size as chicken breast)
4 slices Swiss cheese
1/4 cup chopped fresh parsley
1 small jar of prepared chicken gravy, (available in grocery store)
1 teaspoon Marsala wine or dry sherry wine

ASSEMBLY

1. Oil an ovenproof casserole dish large enough to contain
   the four chicken breasts.
2. Place special crumbs in a flat dish and press chicken into
   crumbs, coating completely.
3. Place breaded chicken breasts in oiled casserole dish. Top with
   ham, Swiss cheese, and chopped parsley.
4. Bake in a preheated 400° oven for 20 minutes.
5. While chicken is cooking heat chicken gravy (using directions on
   container); add wine.
6. Remove cooked chicken from casserole to heated plates with a
   spatula. Spoon the gravy on and around chicken.

"It is not the critic who counts, not the man who points out how the strong man stumbled, or where the doer of deeds could have done them better. The credit belongs to the man who is actually in the arena; whose face is marred by dust and sweat and blood; who strives valiantly; who errs and comes short again and again; who knows the great enthusiasms, the great devotions, and spends himself in a worthy cause; who, at the best, knows in the end the triumph of high achievement; and who at the worst, if he fails while daring greatly, so that his place shall never be with those cold and timid souls who know neither victory nor defeat."
                    Brother Theodore Roosevelt

CHICKEN MARGARITA

My greatest pleasure when dinning in a Mexican restaurant is enjoying a Margarita. I have taken this drink and turned it into a sauce for a spirited tasty chicken dish, its great served with rice.

2 whole chicken breasts, skinned, boned, halved, flattened,
   with fat removed
1/2 cup chicken broth
1 1/2 tablespoons (either) Cointreau, Grand Marnier or Triple Sec
1 tablespoon tequila
1/4 teaspoon grated lime peel (zest)
1 tablespoon fresh lime juice
1/2 cup breading crumbs, page 75
4 slices Monterey Jack cheese or 1/2 cup shredded Monterey Jack
1/4 cup chopped fresh cilantro or chopped fresh parsley

PREPARATION
1. Mix chicken broth, Cointreau, tequila, grated lime peel, and lime juice in a small bowl.

ASSEMBLY
1. Select an ovenproof casserole just large enough to contain the four chicken breasts.
2. Place chicken crumbs in a flat dish and press chicken into crumbs, coating completely
3. Place breaded chicken in casserole dish. Top with Monterey Jack cheese and cilantro. Spoon the tequila sauce around chicken.
4. Bake in a preheated 400° oven for 20 minutes.
5. Remove cooked chicken from casserole to heated plates with a spatula. Spoon remaining sauce on and around chicken.

   Garnish with Tortilla chips.

Helpful Hint
To remove a small amount of fat on the surface of a hot stock, place two sheets of paper towel on the top of the stock and remove immediately. This should remove most of the fat. Do it again if needed.

=====CHICKEN PANCETTA WITH MUSHROOMS

Pancetta is Italian bacon that is cured with salt and spices but not smoked.

2 whole chicken breasts, skinned, boned, halved, flattened,
   with fat removed
1 tablespoon olive oil
2 ounces pancetta cut in small dice (or bacon)
1/2 cup chopped onions
1 cup sliced mushrooms
1/4 cup chopped green onions (scallions)
1 teaspoon butter
1/2 cup Marsala wine
1/2 cup breading crumbs, page 75
4 slices provolone cheese
Chopped parsley for garnish

PREPARATION

1. Heat olive oil in a medium skillet over medium heat. Add diced
   pancetta, cook and stir until crisp and lightly brown. Drain all but
   1 teaspoon of remaining fat. Stir in onions; sauté until slightly yellow.
   Stir in mushrooms and green onions; sauté until mushrooms are wilted.
   Stir in Marsala wine and cool.

ASSEMBLY

1. Butter an ovenproof casserole dish large enough to contain the
   four chicken breasts.
2. Place special crumbs in a flat dish and press chicken into
   crumbs, coating completely.
3. Place breaded chicken breasts in buttered casserole dish. Top
   breaded chicken with provolone cheese; spoon mushroom
   sauce on and around chicken.
4. Bake in a preheated 400° oven for 20 minutes.
5. Remove cooked chicken from casserole to heated plates
   with a spatula. Spoon mushrooms and sauce on and around
   chicken.

=CHICKEN WITH A MUSTARD-BOURBON SAUCE

Bourbon, mustard and cheese make this dish full-flavored.

2 whole chicken breasts, skinned, boned, halved, flattened,
  with fat removed
1/4 cup chopped green onions (scallions)
2 tablespoons Dijon-style mustard
1/4 cup bourbon liquor
1/4 cup chicken broth
2 tablespoons dark brown sugar
1/2 teaspoon Worcestershire sauce
1/2 cup breading crumbs, page 75
1 tablespoon butter
4 slices Havarti or Monterey Jack cheese

PREPARATION

1. Mix green onions, mustard, bourbon, chicken broth, brown sugar,
   and Worcestershire sauce in a mixing bowl.

ASSEMBLY

1. Butter an ovenproof casserole dish large enough to contain the
   four chicken breasts.
2. Place special crumbs in a flat dish and press chicken into
   crumbs, coating completely.
3. Place breaded chicken breasts in butter casserole dish. Top
   with Havarti cheese. Spoon bourbon sauce on and around
   chicken.
4. Bake in a 400° oven for 20 minutes.
5. Remove cooked chicken from casserole with a spatula.
   Spoon the bourbon sauce on and around chicken.

*"What I love about cooking is that after a hard day, there is
something comforting about the fact that if you melt butter and
add flour, then hot stock, it will get thick! It's a sure thing. It's
a sure thing in a world where nothing is sure!"*
Nora Ephron

=======CHICKEN WITH HORSERADISH CREAM

Enjoy this bold, but surprisingly mild variation for chicken.
Horseradish, one of the five bitter herbs of the Jewish Passover festival,
is an ancient herb from Eastern Europe.

2 whole chicken breasts, skinned, boned, halved, flattened,
   with fat removed
1 (11-ounce) can cream of chicken soup
1/2 cup milk
2 tablespoons sour cream
1 tablespoon prepared white horseradish
1/2 teaspoon Dijon-style mustard
1/4 cup chopped fresh parsley
1/4 cup chopped green onions (scallions)
1 tablespoon butter
1/2 cup breading crumbs, page 75
1 tablespoon Parmesan cheese

PREPARATION
1. Whisk cream of chicken soup, milk, sour cream, horseradish, mustard, parsley, and green onions in a mixing bowl.

ASSEMBLY
1. Butter an ovenproof casserole dish large enough to contain the four chicken breasts.
2. Place crumbs in a flat dish and press chicken into crumbs, coating completely.
3. Spoon horseradish sauce on and around chicken. Sprinkle with Parmesan cheese.
4. Bake in a preheated 400° oven for 20 minutes.
5. Remove cooked chicken from casserole dish to heated plates with a spatula. Spoon sauce on and around chicken. If sauce is a little thick, thin it with a little milk.

"The hostess must be like the duck—calm and unruffled on the surface, and paddling like hell underneath."
Anonymous

=======CHICKEN WITH MUSTARD AND HONEY

'Whole grain mustards are usually spicier and smoother tasting than the usual hotdog mustard.

2 whole chicken breasts, skinned, boned, halved, flattened,
  with fat removed
2 teaspoons honey
3 teaspoons whole grain mustard (stone ground)
1/2 cup of chicken broth
2 garlic cloves, minced
1/4 cup chopped green onions (scallions)
1/4 cup chopped fresh parsley
1 1/2 tablespoons butter
1/2 cup breading crumbs, page 75

PREPARATION
1. Whisk honey, mustard, chicken broth, minced garlic, green onions, and chopped parsley in a mixing bowl.

ASSEMBLY
1. With half the butter, butter a casserole dish large enough to contain the four chicken breasts.
2. Place special crumbs in a flat dish and press chicken into crumbs, coating completely.
3. Place breaded chicken breasts in casserole dish. Spoon honey mustard sauce on each chicken breast. Dot with butter.
4. Bake in a preheated 400° oven for 20 minutes.
5. Remove cooked chicken from casserole to heated plates with a spatula. Spoon any remaining sauce on and around chicken.

"Blessed are those who help clean up after dinner!"
Anonymous

============= *CHICKEN WITH VEGETABLES*

*This is a wonderful one-dish meal. A great favorite in France; it is usually made with chicken pieces or beef and called a **bouilli**.*

2 whole chicken breasts, skinned, boned, halved, flattened,
   with fat removed
1/2 cup flour
1 medium carrot, peeled, cut like match sticks
2 small onions, peeled, cut in quarters
1 small zucchini, ends trimmed, cut in eighths lengthways
4 cleaned mushroom caps, without stems
4 cherry tomatoes
1/2 teaspoon dried tarragon
1 cup white wine or chicken broth

PREPARATION
1. This dish needs a casserole with a cover that can contain the four chicken breasts and the vegetables.

ASSEMBLY
1. Place flour in a flat dish and press chicken into flour, coating completely.
2. Place floured chicken breasts in the casserole dish; around chicken add all the prepared vegetables; (carrots, onions, zucchini, mushrooms, and tomatoes). Sprinkle with tarragon. Add wine or chicken broth.
3. Cover the casserole dish and bake in a preheated 400° oven for 20 minutes. If the casserole dish is thick, check after 20 minutes to make sure chicken is cooked. It may take a few minutes longer.
3. Remove casserole from oven. With a large spoon, remove chicken to heated plates. Spoon vegetables and wine sauce on and around chicken.
   The sauce will thicken a little because of the flour on the chicken.

"Stock to a cook is voice to a singer."
Anonymous

CHINESE SESAME CHICKEN

Biting flavors that will excite your the taste buds.

2 whole chicken breasts, skinned, boned, halved, flattened,
   with fat removed
1/4 cup chopped red bell peppers, cored and seeded
1/4 cup chopped green onions (scallions)
1 tablespoon soy sauce
1 tablespoon maple syrup
1 tablespoon dry sherry
1 teaspoon finely chopped fresh ginger
1/2 teaspoon Chinese five-spice powder
1 cup chicken broth
1 or 2 drops of sesame oil
2 tablespoons sesame seeds
3/4 cup plain fresh or dry bread crumbs
1 teaspoon peanut oil or any vegetable oil
1/2 head of shredded iceberg lettuce (like cole slaw)

PREPARATION

1. Mix peppers, green onions, soy sauce, maple syrup, sherry,
   ginger, five-spice powder, chicken broth, and sesame oil in a
   mixing bowl. Add chicken and marinate in refrigerator for about
   20 minutes.
2. Mix sesame seeds and bread crumbs in a mixing bowl.

ASSEMBLY

1. Oil an ovenproof casserole dish large enough to contain
   the four chicken breasts.
2. Remove chicken from marinade with a fork, allowing excess
   to drip off, then press chicken into sesame seed crumbs, coating
   completely.
3. Place breaded chicken in oiled casserole dish. Spoon marinade
   around chicken.
4. Bake in a preheated 400° oven for 20 minutes.
5. Place shredded lettuce on individual dinner plates. Remove
   cooked chicken from casserole and place on lettuce with
   a spatula. Spoon remaining sauce on and around chicken.

=============CINNAMON GLAZED CHICKEN

Cinnamon, once used as perfume for wealthy Romans, was also was used as a love potion. Cinnamon is the inner bark of a tropical tree. The bark is harvested during the rainy season when it's more pliable. It dries into long quills and is either ground or used as cinnamon sticks.

2 whole chicken breasts, skinned, boned, halved, flattened,
   with fat removed
1 teaspoon cinnamon
1/2 cup honey
1/2 cup dry sherry
1 tablespoon fresh lime juice
1/4 cup chopped fresh parsley
1 garlic clove, minced
1 tablespoon butter
1/2 cup breading crumbs, page 75
4 slices provolone cheese

PREPARATION
1. Mix cinnamon, honey, sherry, lime juice, chopped parsley, and minced garlic in a mixing bowl.

ASSEMBLY
1. Butter an ovenproof casserole dish large enough to contain the four chicken breasts.
2. Place crumbs in a flat dish and press chicken into crumbs, coating completely.
3. Place breaded chicken in buttered casserole dish. Spoon cinnamon honey sauce over chicken. Top chicken with provolone cheese.
3. Bake in a preheated 400° oven for 20 minutes
4. Remove cooked chicken from casserole dish to heated plates with a spatula. Spoon remaining sauce on and around chicken.

*"Summer cooking implies a sense of immediacy,
a capacity to capture the fleeting moment."*
Elizabeth David

=========CITRUS-APRICOT GLAZED CHICKEN

*China has been growing and cultivating apricots for 4000 years;
enjoy the apricot and citrus combination.*

2 whole chicken breasts, skinned, boned, halved, flattened,
   with fat removed
1 each, orange, lime, lemon, cut in half, remove and save juice
1 can (12-ounce) apricot halves
1 tablespoon brown sugar
1/4 teaspoon ground dried ginger
Dash ground nutmeg
1/4 cup chopped fresh parsley
1/2 cup breading crumbs, page 75
1 tablespoon butter

PREPARATION
1. Mix in a blender juice from orange, lime, lemon, the apricots including
   liquid, brown sugar, ginger, and nutmeg.

ASSEMBLY
1. Select an ovenproof casserole dish large enough to contain the
   four chicken breasts.
2. Place crumbs in a flat dish and press chicken into crumbs,
   coating completely. Place breaded chicken in casserole dish.
3. Add chopped parsley to apricot mixture and spoon over chicken.
   Dot with butter.
4. Bake in a preheated 400° oven for 20 minutes.
5. Remove cooked chicken from casserole to heated plates with
   a spatula. Spoon remaining juices on and around the chicken.

Rice is great with this dish.

*"Friends are like melons.
Shall I tell you why?
To find one good you must a hundred try."*
Claude Mermet

================COCONUT RUM CHICKEN

The alcohol from the Rum and Pernod will evaporate during cooking. The good flavor will remain. Pernod and anisette are licorice-flavored liqueur.

2 whole chicken breasts, skinned, boned, flattened,
  with fat removed
3/4 cup coconut milk (available canned in supermarkets)
2 tablespoons dark rum
1 tablespoon Pernod or anisette liquor
1/4 cup chopped green onions (scallions)
1/4 cup chopped fresh parsley
1/2 cup breading crumbs, page 75
4 slices of Monterey Jack cheese

PREPARATION
1. Mix together coconut milk, rum, Pernod, chopped green onions, and chopped parsley in a mixing bowl.

ASSEMBLY
1. Select an ovenproof casserole dish large enough to contain the four chicken breasts.
2. Place crumbs in a flat dish and press chicken into crumbs, coating completely. Place breaded chicken in casserole dish. Spoon the coconut sauce on and around chicken. Top chicken with Monterey Jack cheese.
3. Bake in a preheated 400° oven for 20 minutes.
4. Remove cooked chicken from casserole to heated plates with a spatula. Spoon the sauce from casserole on and around chicken.

"You can't use up creativity.
The more you use, the more you have."
Maya Angelou
(Especially in the kitchen.)

==============FAR EAST ORANGE CHICKEN

Oranges originated in Southeast Asia. This fragrant fruit has always been associated with fertility; this lush evergreen tree can simultaneously produce flowers, fruit, and foliage. It thrives around the world in warm-climate areas.

2 whole chicken breasts, skinned, boned, halved, flattened,
  with fat removed
1 small can sliced water chestnuts, drained
1 small onion, minced
1/2 teaspoon grated orange peel (zest)
1 cup orange juice
1 teaspoon soy sauce
1 teaspoon brown sugar
1/4 teaspoon dried ginger or 1/2 teaspoon fresh grated ginger
1/2 cup breading crumbs, page 75
2 oranges peeled, sliced with seeds removed
1/2 cup sliced almonds
1/4 cup chopped fresh parsley
1 teaspoon butter

PREPARATION
1. Mix water chestnuts, minced onion, orange peel, orange juice,
   soy sauce, brown sugar, and ginger in a mixing bowl.

ASSEMBLY
1. Choose an ovenproof casserole dish large enough to contain the
   four chicken breasts.
2. Place special crumbs in a flat dish and press chicken into
   crumbs, coating completely.
3. Place breaded chicken breasts in casserole dish. Top with orange slices
   fitting them on chicken breast, sliced almonds, and chopped parsley.
   Spoon the orange sauce around chicken. Dot with butter.
4. Bake in a preheated 400° oven for 20 minutes.
5. Remove cooked chicken from casserole to heated plates with a
   spatula. Spoon the sauce on and around chicken.

GINGER-ORANGE CHICKEN

The flavor of dried ground ginger is quite different from fresh ginger, and cannot be substituted for fresh ginger in this dish. Fresh ginger is available in most markets. Store ginger in refrigerator or freezer.

2 whole chicken breasts, skinned, boned, halved, flattened,
   with fat removed
2 teaspoons minced, peeled, fresh ginger
1/2 teaspoon dry mustard
1 tablespoon brown sugar
1 teaspoon grated orange peel (zest)
1/2 cup thinly sliced green onions (scallions)
1 cup orange juice
1 tablespoon butter
1/2 cup breading crumbs, page 75
1/2 cup sliced almonds

PREPARATION
1   Thoroughly mix minced ginger, dry mustard, brown sugar,
    grated orange peel, green onions, and orange juice in a mixing bowl.

ASSEMBLY
1. Butter an ovenproof casserole dish large enough to contain the
   four chicken breasts.
2. Place crumbs in a flat plate and press chicken into crumbs,
   coating completely.
3. Place breaded chicken in casserole. Spoon sauce on and around
   chicken. Sprinkle almonds on chicken.
4. Bake in a preheated 400° oven for 20 minutes.
5. Remove cooked chicken from casserole to heated plates with
   a spatula. Spoon the sauce on and around chicken.

*"Eating is not merely a material pleasure. Eating well gives
a spectacular joy to life and contributes immensely to goodwill and
happy companionship. It is of great importance to the morale."*
Elsa Schiaparelli

==========GORGONZOLA-TARRAGON CHICKEN

Roquefort, Stilton or blue cheese can be substituted for the Gorgonzola cheese.

2 whole chicken breasts, skinned, boned, halved, flattened,
  with fat removed
1/4 cup crumbled Gorgonzola cheese
1/4 cup chicken broth
1/4 cup evaporated milk
1/2 cup sliced mushrooms
1 teaspoon minced fresh tarragon or 1/2 teaspoon dried tarragon
1 teaspoon softened butter
1/2 cup breading crumbs, page 75

PREPARATION
1. Mix Gorgonzola cheese, chicken broth, evaporated milk,
   sliced mushrooms, and tarragon in a mixing bowl.

ASSEMBLY
1. Butter an ovenproof casserole dish
   large enough to contain the four chicken breasts.
2. Place crumbs in a flat dish and press chicken into crumbs,
   coating completely.
3. Place breaded chicken in buttered casserole dish. Spoon the
   Gorgonzola sauce on and around chicken.
4. Bake in a preheated 400° oven for 20 minutes.
5. Remove cooked chicken from casserole dish to heated plates
   with a spatula. Spoon the sauce on and around chicken.
     Someone E-mailed this to me recently; I thought I would share it.

HOME RULES
If you sleep on it	*make it up*
If you wear it	*hang it up*
If you drop it	*pick it up*
If you step on it	*wipe it off*
If you open it	*close it*
If you empty it	*fill it up*
If it rings	*answer it*
If it howls	*feed it*
If it cries	*love it*

=============GRAND MARNIER CHICKEN

Grand Marnier is a clear, golden, brandy-based French liquor flavored with orange peel. It brings to mind the famous Crêpe Suzette, served tableside in great restaurants.

2 whole chicken breasts, skinned, boned, halved, flattened,
   with fat removed
1/4 cup Grand Marnier
2 tablespoons lemon juice
1/4 cup honey
1 teaspoon grated orange peel (zest)
1 tablespoon soy sauce
1/4 cup chopped green onions (scallions)
1/4 cup chopped fresh parsley
1/2 cup breading crumbs, page 75
1 tablespoon butter
4 slices cheddar cheese

PREPARATION
1. Whisk Grand Marnier, lemon juice, honey, grated orange peel, soy sauce, green onions, and parsley in a mixing bowl.

ASSEMBLY
1. Butter an ovenproof casserole dish large enough to contain the four chicken breasts.
2. Place crumbs in a flat dish and press chicken into crumbs, coating completely. Place breaded chicken in buttered casserole dish. Spoon Grand Marnier sauce on and around chicken; top chicken with cheddar cheese.
3. Bake in a preheated 400° oven for 20 minutes.
4. Remove cooked chicken from casserole to heated plates with a spatula. Spoon the remaining sauce on and around chicken.

"One of the most wonderful things about life is that we must regularly stop what we are doing and devote our attention to eating."
Anon

=======HOISIN-STYLE MUSHROOM CHICKEN

Hoisin sauce is a thick reddish-brown sauce that is sweet and spicy; it is available in most supermarkets and Asian markets.

2 whole chicken breasts, skinned, boned, halved, flattened,
  with skin removed
1 tablespoon olive oil
1/2 cup chopped onion
1 clove garlic, minced
1/4 cup chopped green onions (scallions)
1 cup sliced mushrooms
2 tablespoons ketchup
1 tablespoon hoisin sauce
1/4 cup rice-wine vinegar
1 teaspoon chili sauce
1 tablespoon soy sauce
1/4 cup sliced water chestnuts (drained)
1/4 cup chopped fresh parsley
1/2 cup breading crumbs, page 75

PREPARATION
1. Heat olive oil over medium heat in a large skillet; sauté chopped onion
   for a minute, stir in garlic, green onions, and mushrooms; cook until
   mushrooms are wilted. Off heat stir in ketchup, hoisin sauce, rice-wine
   vinegar, chili sauce, soy sauce, water chestnuts, and chopped parsley. Cool.

ASSEMBLY
1. Select an ovenproof casserole dish large enough to contain the
   four chicken breasts.
2. Place crumbs in a flat plate and press chicken into crumbs,
   coating completely.
3. Place breaded chicken in casserole. Spoon the sauce on and
   around chicken.
4. Bake in a 400° oven for 20 minutes.
5. Remove cooked chicken to casserole to heated plates with
   a spatula. Spoon the mushroom sauce on and around chicken.

Rice is perfect with this dish

======HONEY, ORANGE, CHEDDAR CHICKEN

This chicken dish is fragrant, mouth-watering, fruity, slightly sweet and refreshing.

2 whole chicken breasts, skinned, boned, halved, flattened,
   with fat removed
1/4 cup honey
1/4 cup Dijon-style mustard
1 clove garlic, minced
1/4 cup white wine
1/2 cup orange juice
1 teaspoon grated orange peel (zest)
1/4 cup finely chopped parsley
1/2 cup breading crumbs, page 75
4 slices cheddar cheese

PREPARATION
1. Mix honey, mustard, garlic, wine, orange juice, orange peel, and
   parsley in a mixing bowl.

ASSEMBLY
1. Select an ovenproof casserole dish that is large enough to
   contain the four chicken breasts.
2. Place breading crumbs in a flat dish and press chicken into
   crumbs, coating completely.
3. Place breaded chicken in casserole dish. Spoon sauce on
   chicken, and top chicken with cheddar cheese.
4. Bake in a preheated 400° oven for 20 minutes.
5. Remove chicken from casserole dish and spoon remaining
   sauce on and around chicken.

Serve with rice and steamed vegetables.

Helpful Hint
To freshen your garbage disposal, toss in some baking soda and sliced orange or lemon peels, grind with water running.

===================================*JAMAICAN CHICKEN*

This spirited chicken dish is for the banana lover. If you want to ripen bananas more quickly, wrap them in a damp paper towel and place them in a brown paper bag.

2 whole chicken breasts, skinned, boned, halved, flattened,
   with fat removed
1 small onion, minced
1 clove garlic, minced
1 teaspoon soy sauce
1 tablespoon of Myers rum
1 teaspoon grated orange peel (zest)
3/4 cup coconut milk
1/4 cup chopped fresh parsley
2 bananas, cut in 2 inch slices (keep round)
1 tablespoon butter
1/2 cup breading crumbs, page 75

PREPARATION
1. Mix minced onion, minced garlic, soy sauce, rum, orange peel, coconut milk, and parsley in a mixing bowl. Stir in bananas.

ASSEMBLY
1. Butter an ovenproof casserole dish large enough to contain the four chicken breasts, plus extra room for bananas.
2. Place crumbs in a flat dish and press chicken into crumbs, coating completely.
3. Place breaded chicken in buttered casserole dish. Spoon bananas and sauce around and in between chicken.
4. Bake in a preheated 400° oven for 20 minutes.
5. Remove cooked chicken and bananas from casserole to heated plates with a spatula. Spoon the sauce on and around chicken.

Rice will go well with this dish.

"A good meal ought to begin with hunger."
French Proverb

=MANGO-MUSTARD-CHEDDAR GLAZED CHICKEN

Mangoes, one of the world's favorite fruit, originated in India and are widely cultivated in sub-tropical countries. Apart from being eaten fresh as a fruit, mangoes, are a favorite for making chutneys. To prepare a mango, first cut off both sides of the fruit, on either side of the stone, then scoop the flesh out of the skin with a spoon. After that, strip the skin off the remaining central part and trim around the stone.

2 whole chicken breasts, skinned, boned, halved, flattened,
   with fat removed
1 cup chopped peeled mango
1 cup pineapple juice
1 tablespoon stone-ground mustard
1/4 cup apricot jam (peach jam can be substituted)
1 teaspoon butter
1/2 cup breading crumbs, page 75
4 slices cheddar cheese

PREPARATION
1. Mix chopped mango, pineapple juice, mustard, and apricot jam in a mixing bowl.

ASSEMBLY
1. Butter an ovenproof casserole large enough to contain the four chicken breasts.
2. Place crumbs in a flat dish and press chicken into crumbs, coating completely.
3. Place breaded chicken breasts in buttered casserole dish. Top each with a slice of cheddar cheese. Spoon and spread mango sauce around chicken.
4. Bake in a preheated 400° oven for 20 minutes.
5. Remove cooked chicken from casserole to heated plates with a spatula. Spoon mango and sauce on and around chicken.

Rice is a prefect starch for this dish

MAPLE-CHICKEN WITH PEARS

New England is full of maple trees. I have had the pleasure of watching a "sugarhouse" in action. The "sugar makers" insert spouts into maple trees, then hang buckets from them to catch the sap. They boil the sap in a large metal container. The fuel used is wood; the "sugarhouse" has a hole in the roof to allow the smoke and steam to escape. It takes between 20 and 30 gallons of sap to make one gallon of maple syrup.

2 whole chicken breasts, skinned, boned, halved, flattened,
  with skin removed
1/3 cup maple syrup
1/4 cup melted butter
1/4 teaspoon crushed rosemary
1/4 water
1 teaspoon softened butter
1/2 cup breading crumbs, page 75
2 Bosc pears, peeled, cut in half, core and stem removed
4 slices Monterey Jack cheese

PREPARATION
1. Mix maple syrup, melted butter, rosemary, and water in a small bowl.

ASSEMBLY
1. Butter an ovenproof casserole dish large enough to contain the four chicken breasts plus the pears.
2. Place crumbs in a flat dish and press chicken into crumbs, coating completely.
3. Place breaded chicken breasts and pears, core side down, in casserole dish. Top each chicken breast with a slice of Monterey Jack cheese. Use a pastry brush or spoon and spread maple syrup mixture on the pears and chicken breast. Use all the maple syrup.
4. Bake in a preheated 400° oven for 20 minutes
5. Remove cooked chicken and pears from casserole to heated plates with a spatula. Spoon the remaining juices on and around chicken.

MAPLE GLAZED CHICKEN

Colonists were taught by the Native Americans, how to tap the maple trees for their sap and how to boil it down and make maple syrup.

2 whole chicken breasts, skinned, boned, halved, flattened,
   with fat removed
2 slices Hickory Smoked bacon, cooked, and chopped
1/4 cup ketchup
1/4 cup maple syrup
1 teaspoon cider vinegar
1/2 teaspoon Dijon-style mustard
1/4 cup chopped fresh parsley
1 tablespoon butter
1 large onion, peeled and sliced thin
1/2 cup breading crumbs, page 75
4 slices Monterey Jack cheese

PREPARATION
1. Mix chopped bacon, ketchup, maple syrup, vinegar, mustard, and parsley in a mixing bowl.

ASSEMBLY
1. Butter an ovenproof casserole dish large enough to contain the four chicken breasts.
2. Place crumbs in a flat dish and press chicken into crumbs, coating completely.
3. Place onion slices in buttered casserole dish, spreading evenly. Top with breaded chicken breasts.
4. Spoon maple syrup sauce on and around breaded chicken breasts. Top breaded chicken with Monterey Jack cheese.
5. Bake in a preheated 400° oven for 20 minutes.
6. Remove cooked chicken from casserole dish to heated plates with a spatula. Spoon onions and remaining juices around chicken.

*"Shake and shake The catsup bottle,
None will come out, And then a lot'll."
Ogden Nash*

==============MOLASSES GLAZED CHICKEN

During the refining of sugar cane and sugar beets, the juice squeezed from these plants is boiled to a syrupy mixture from which sugar crystals are extracted. The remaining brownish black liquid is molasses. In 1733 the English Parliament passed the Molasses Act to regulate trade and levy tariffs on imported molasses. Some historians say it was the tax on molasses that helped spur the Revolutionary War.

2 whole chicken breasts, skinned, boned, halved, flattened,
  with fat removed
1/4 cup dry sherry
1/4 cup pineapple juice
1 tablespoon soy sauce
2 tablespoons molasses
1/2 teaspoon brown sugar
1/4 teaspoon ground cinnamon
1/4 teaspoon ground ginger
1/4 cup red bell pepper, seeded and diced
1/4 cup chopped green onions (scallions)
1 clove garlic, minced
1/4 cup chopped fresh parsley
1 tablespoon butter
1/2 cup breading crumbs, page 75

PREPARATION
1. Mix pineapple juice, soy sauce, molasses, brown sugar, cinnamon, ginger, pepper, green onions, minced garlic, and chopped parsley in a mixing bowl.

ASSEMBLY
1. Butter an ovenproof casserole dish large enough to contain the four chicken breasts.
2. Place special crumbs in a flat dish and press chicken into crumbs, coating completely.
3. Place breaded chicken in casserole dish. Spoon molasses mixture on and around chicken.
4. Bake in a preheated 400° oven for 20 minutes.
5. Remove cooked chicken from casserole to heated plates with a spatula. Spoon the sauce on and around chicken.

MUSTARD SESAME CHICKEN

The crunch of sesame seeds with the pungent flavor of mustard and apricot is delightful.

2 whole chicken breasts, skinned, boned, halved, flattened,
  with fat removed
1 teaspoon lemon juice
1/2 teaspoon Worcestershire sauce
1 teaspoon soy sauce
2 garlic cloves, minced
1/4 teaspoon dried oregano
2 eggs
1/4 cup finely chopped fresh parsley
3/4 cup breading crumbs, page 75
1/4 cup sesame seeds
1 tablespoon olive oil
1 tablespoon butter
2 tablespoons Dijon-style mustard
2 tablespoons apricot jam
1/2 cup half-and-half cream, or milk

PREPARATION
1. Whisk lemon juice, Worcestershire sauce, soy sauce, minced garlic, oregano, eggs, and chopped parsley. Place chicken breasts in mixture for about 15 minutes, coating the chicken.
2. Mix crumbs and sesame seeds in a mixing bowl.

ASSEMBLY
1. Oil an ovenproof casserole dish large enough to contain the four chicken breasts.
2. Remove the chicken breasts from the egg mixture with a fork, one at a time, allowing excess egg mixture to drip off; place in the sesame-crumb mixture, coating completely. Place breaded chicken in oiled casserole dish. Dot each breaded breast with butter.
3. Bake in a preheated 400° oven for 20 minutes
4. While chicken is baking, heat and stir mustard, apricot jam, and cream in a small saucepan. Keep warm.
5. Remove cooked chicken from casserole to heated plates with a spatula. Spoon the sauce on and around chicken.

MUSTARD-CAPER CHICKEN

A distinct flavor from the capers, mustard, honey, and cheddar will have your guest asking for more.

2 whole chicken breasts, skinned, boned, halved, flattened,
   with fat removed
1 cup chicken broth
1/4 cup drained capers
2 tablespoons Dijon-style mustard
1 tablespoon honey
1/4 teaspoon dried thyme
1/2 teaspoon dried crumbled rosemary
1 tablespoon softened butter
1/2 cup breading crumbs, page 75
4 slices cheddar cheese or 1/2 cup shredded cheddar

PREPARATION
1. Mix chicken broth, capers, honey, thyme, and rosemary
   in a mixing bowl.

ASSEMBLY
1. Butter an ovenproof casserole dish large enough to contain the
   four chicken breasts.
2. Place crumbs in a flat dish and press chicken into crumbs,
   coating completely.
3. Place breaded chicken in casserole dish. Spoon caper mixture
   on and around chicken; top chicken with cheddar cheese.
4. Bake in a 400° oven for 20 minutes.
5. Remove cooked chicken from casserole to heated plates with
   a spatula. Spoon remaining juices on and around chicken.

Serve with couscous, rice or noodles.

"The height of cleverness is to be able to conceal it."
François, Duc de La Rochefoucauld

================================ORANGE GLAZED CHICKEN

If oranges are extra large just use one orange.
*Soy sauce is a dark salty sauce made by fermenting boiled
soybeans, roasted wheat or barley.*

2 whole chicken breasts, skinned, boned, halved, flattened,
   with fat removed
1 cup orange juice
1 teaspoon soy sauce
1/4 teaspoon dried ginger, 1/2 teaspoon fresh grated ginger
1/4 teaspoon five spice powder or allspice
1 teaspoon brown sugar
1/4 cup chopped fresh parsley
2 tablespoons butter
1/2 cup breading crumbs, page 75
2 oranges, peeled, sliced with seeds removed
1/4 cup sliced almonds

PREPARATION
1. Mix orange juice, soy sauce, five spice powder, brown sugar,
    and chopped parsley in a mixing bowl.

ASSEMBLY
1. With 1 tablespoon of the butter, butter a casserole dish large
    enough to contain the four chicken breasts.
2. Place crumbs in a flat dish and press chicken into crumbs,
    coating completely.
3. Place breaded chicken breasts in buttered casserole dish. Top with
    orange slices and almonds. Spoon the orange sauce on and around
    chicken. Dot with remaining butter.
4. Bake in a preheated 400° oven for 20 minutes.
5. Remove cooked chicken from casserole to heated plates with a
    spatula. Spoon remaining orange sauce on and around chicken.

Helpful Hint
*I like to keep a 1/2-cup measuring cup in my flour and sugar bin.
It saves time measuring*

ORANGE RUM CHICKEN

Cumin is an ancient spice that dates back to the Old Testament. It looks like a caraway seed and comes from the parsley family.

Rum is liquor distilled from sugarcane or molasses. Most of the world's rum comes from the Caribbean area.

2 whole chicken breasts, skinned, boned, halved, flattened,
  with fat removed
1 teaspoon grated orange peel (zest)
1/2 teaspoon of dried ground cumin
1/4 teaspoon ground dry ginger or fresh minced ginger
1/4 cup Myers rum or any dark rum
1/4 cup orange juice
1/4 cup chopped fresh parsley
1 tablespoon butter
1/2 cup breading crumbs, page 75
4 slices Monterey Jack cheese

PREPARATION

1. Mix grated orange peel, cumin, ginger, rum, orange juice, and parsley in a mixing bowl.

ASSEMBLY

1. Butter an oven proof casserole dish large enough to contain the four chicken breasts.
2. Place crumbs in a flat dish and press chicken into crumbs coating completely.
3. Place breaded chicken in buttered casserole dish. Spoon rum mixture on and around chicken. Top chicken with Monterey Jack cheese.
4. Bake in a preheated 400° oven for 20 minutes.
5. Remove cooked chicken from casserole dish to heated plates with a spatula. Spoon the sauce on and around chicken.

"Cuisine is only about making foods taste the way they are supposed to taste."
Charlie Trotter

============ORANGE-CURRY-PECAN CHICKEN

This full-flavored colorful dish is full of surprises.

2 whole chicken breasts, skinned, boned, halved, flattened,
  with fat removed
1/2 teaspoon grated orange peel (zest)
2 tablespoons orange marmalade
1/4 cup orange juice
1 teaspoon curry powder
1 tablespoon soy sauce
1/2 cup chopped red bell pepper, cored and seeded
1/4 cup pecan pieces
1/4 cup chopped green onions (scallions)
1 teaspoon butter
1/2 cup breading crumbs, page 75
4 slices provolone cheese

PREPARATION

1. Mix orange peel, orange marmalade, orange juice, curry powder,
   soy sauce, chopped red pepper, pecans, and green onions in a mixing
   bowl.

ASSEMBLY

1. Butter an ovenproof casserole dish large enough to contain
   the four chicken breasts.
2. Place crumbs in a flat dish and press chicken into crumbs,
   coating completely.
3. Place breaded chicken breasts in buttered casserole dish. Top
   with provolone cheese and spoon orange sauce around chicken.
4. Bake in a preheated 400° oven for 20 minutes.
5. Remove cooked chicken from casserole to heated plates with
   a spatula. Spoon the orange sauce on and around chicken.

This dish is great with rice and steamed broccoli.

*"I would much rather be a chef who remembers I am a cook
than a cook that thinks I am a chef."*

Richard (Ric) Peterson

PEACHY CHICKEN

Peaches are native to China, brought to Europe, then to the Americas. Use a ripe peach for this dish. To ripen, place peaches in a paper bag with an apple at room temperature.

2 whole chicken breasts, skinned, boned, halved, flattened,
   with fat removed
1 small onion, chopped
1/2 cup diced green bell pepper, cored and seeded
1/2 cup diced red bell pepper, cored and seeded
1/4 cup chopped fresh parsley
1/2 cup ketchup
1 teaspoon honey
1 tablespoon soy sauce
1 cup diced peach, peeled and cored
1/2 cup breading crumbs, page 75
1 tablespoon butter

PREPARATION
1. Mix chopped onion, diced green pepper, diced red pepper, parsley, ketchup, honey, and soy sauce in a mixing bowl. Stir in peaches.

ASSEMBLY
1. Butter an ovenproof casserole dish large enough to contain the four chicken breasts.
2. Place crumbs in a flat dish and press chicken into crumbs, coating completely.
3. Place breaded chicken in buttered casserole dish. Spoon peach mixture on and around chicken.
4. Bake in a preheated 400° oven for 20 minutes.
5. Remove cooked chicken from casserole to heated plates with a spatula. Spoon the peach mixture on and around chicken.

"A restaurant is a fantasy-a kind of living fantasy in which dinners are the most important members of the cast."
Warner LeRoy

PINEAPPLE CHICKEN

Pineapple was first found in South America. Hawaii is now the leading producer of pineapples. For centuries the pineapple has been revered to symbolize hospitality.

2 whole chicken breasts, skinned, boned, halved, flattened,
   with fat removed
1 (14-1/2 ounce) can crushed pineapple or 2 cups chopped fresh pineapple
1/2 cup sliced almonds
1 small onion, minced
1/2 cup chicken broth
1 (5-ounce) can water chestnuts, drained and sliced
1 teaspoon soy sauce
1/8 teaspoon sesame oil (use very little)
1/4 teaspoon five-spice powder
1/2 cup chopped green onions (scallions)
1/4 cup chopped fresh parsley
1/2 cup breading crumbs, page 75
4 slices Monterey Jack cheese

PREPARATION
1. Mix crushed pineapple, almonds, minced onion, chicken broth, sliced water chestnuts, soy sauce, sesame oil, five-spice powder, green onions, and chopped parsley in a mixing bowl.

ASSEMBLY
1. Choose an ovenproof casserole dish large enough to contain the four chicken breasts.
2. Place crumbs in a flat dish and press chicken into crumbs, coating completely. Place breaded chicken in casserole dish.
3. Top each chicken breast with a slice of Monterey Jack cheese, spoon pineapple mixture around chicken.
4. Bake in a preheated 400° oven for 20 minutes.
5. Remove cooked chicken from casserole to heated plates with a spatula. Spoon the sauce on and around chicken.

"A gourmet who thinks of calories is like a tart who looks at her watch."
James Beard

Plums are grown all over the world. The combination of these flavors with the beautiful plum color is pleasing to the eye and the palate.

2 whole chicken breasts, skinned, boned, halved, flattened,
  with fat removed
1/2 cup plum preserves (jam)
1/2 cup orange juice
1 teaspoon soy sauce
1/2 teaspoon ground ginger, or 1 teaspoon grated fresh ginger
1/4 teaspoon dry mustard
Dash hot-pepper sauce (Tabasco)
1/4 cup chopped green onions (scallions)
1/4 cup chopped fresh parsley
1 tablespoon butter
1/2 cup breading crumbs, page 75
4 slices cheddar cheese

PREPARATION
1. Mix plum preserves, orange juice, soy sauce, ginger, dry mustard, hot-pepper, green onions, and parsley in a mixing bowl.

ASSEMBLY
1. Butter an ovenproof casserole dish large enough to contain the four chicken breasts.
2. Place crumbs in a flat dish and press chicken into crumbs, coating completely.
3. Place breaded chicken in buttered casserole dish. Top chicken with cheddar cheese. Spoon plum sauce on and around chicken.
4. Bake in a preheated 400° oven for 20 minutes.
5. Removed cooked chicken from casserole to heated plates with a spatula. Spoon the remaining sauce on and around chicken.

Garnish with fresh plum quarters if available.

"Only dull people are brilliant at breakfast."
Oscar Wilde

==PROVOLONE CHICKEN MARSALA WITH FIGS AND WALNUTS

This dish is great when fresh figs are available.

2 whole chicken breasts, skinned, boned, halved, flattened,
  with fat removed
1/2 cup fresh figs cut in half lengthwise (dried dates can be used)
1/4 cup chopped green onions (scallions)
1/2 cup Marsala wine
1/2 cup chicken broth
1/4 cup chopped walnut pieces
1 tablespoon chopped fresh basil or 1/2 teaspoon dried basil
1 teaspoon butter
1/2 cup breading crumbs, page 75
4 slices provolone cheese

PREPARATION
1. Mix figs, green onions, Marsala wine, chicken broth, walnut pieces, and basil in a mixing bowl.

ASSEMBLY
1. Butter an ovenproof casserole dish large enough to contain the four chicken breasts plus the fig mixture.
2. Place crumbs in a flat dish and press chicken into crumbs, coating completely.
3. Place breaded chicken breasts in buttered casserole dish. Top each chicken breast with a slice of provolone cheese. Spoon fig mixture around chicken.
4. Bake in a preheated 400° oven for 20 minutes.
5. Remove cooked chicken from casserole with a spatula. Spoon figs and sauce around chicken.

Great with rice or buttered noodles.

"Man does not live by words alone,
despite the fact that sometimes he has to eat them."
Adlai E. Stevenson

=============ROSEMARY ALMOND CHICKEN

I love to touch Rosemary then smell the wonderful aroma on my fingers. Enjoy this full-flavored chicken.

2 whole chicken breasts, skinned, boned, halved, flattened,
  with fat removed
1 small onion, chopped
1 teaspoon dried or fresh rosemary
1/2 teaspoon dried poultry seasoning
1 (10-1/2 ounce) can condensed cream of celery soup
1/2 cup milk
1/4 cup chopped fresh parsley
1 tablespoon butter
1/2 cup breading crumbs, page 75
1/4 cup sliced almonds

PREPARATION
1. Mix chopped onion, rosemary, poultry seasoning, cream
   of celery soup, milk, and chopped parsley in a mixing bowl.

ASSEMBLY
1. Butter an ovenproof casserole dish large enough to contain
   the four chicken breasts.
2. Place crumbs in a flat dish and press chicken into crumbs,
   coating completely.
3. Place breaded chicken breasts in buttered casserole dish. Spoon
   sauce on and around chicken. Top with almonds.
4. Bake in a preheated 400° oven for 20 minutes.
5. Remove cooked chicken from casserole to heated plates with a
   spatula. Spoon the sauce on and around chicken.
   (If the sauce is thick, add a little milk.)

"As for rosemary, I let it run all over my garden walls, not only because my bees love it but because it is the herb sacred to remembrance, and to friendship, whence a sprig of it hath a dumb language."
           Sir Thomas More

=SAKONNET VINEYARD CHICKEN WITH GRAPES

Located on a peninsula in Rhode Island with the ocean all around, Sakonnet Vineyard, a former potato farm is a wonderful place to grow grapes and to visit; its 125 acres are always beautiful and change with each season. Founded in 1975 and winning many awards, Sakonnet vineyard produces a variety of beautiful wines.

2 whole chicken breasts, skinned, boned, halved, flattened,
  with fat removed
2 tablespoons butter
1/2 cup breading crumbs, page 75
1 cup seedless white grapes, stems removed
1/2 cup white wine or chicken broth
1/2 cup evaporated milk
1/4 cup chopped fresh parsley

ASSEMBLY

1. Using half the butter, butter an ovenproof casserole dish large
    enough to contain the four chicken breasts.
2. Place crumbs in a flat dish and press chicken into crumbs,
    coating completely.
3. Place breaded chicken in buttered casserole dish. Spread grapes
    around chicken; add wine, milk, and parsley. Dot with remaining butter.
4. Bake in a preheated 400° oven for 20 minutes.
5. Remove cooked chicken from casserole to heated plates with a spatula.
    Spoon grapes and sauce on and around chicken.

Evaporated milk is unsweetened milk, homogenized with 60 percent of the water removed. It comes in whole, low fat and skim forms. It can be substituted for fresh milk in most recipes.

"Reminds me of my safari in Africa. Somebody forgot the corkscrew and for several days we had to live on nothing but food and water."
WC Fields

SANTA FE CHICKEN

I attended the International Association of Culinary Professionals Conference in Phoenix, and enjoyed the wonderful cuisine of the Southwest. Living in New England all my life, these flavors were new and very enjoyable to me.

2 whole chicken breasts, skinned, boned, halved, flattened,
  with fat removed
1 (10-ounce) can (mild, medium or hot) enchilada sauce
1 small onion, minced,
2 cloves garlic, minced
1/4 cup diced green chilies (fresh or canned)
1/4 cup chopped green onions (scallions)
1/4 cup diced green bell pepper, cored and seeded
1/4 cup chopped fresh cilantro or parsley
1/2 cup breading crumbs, page 75
4 slices Monterey Jack cheese

PREPARATION
1. Mix enchilada sauce, minced onion, minced garlic, diced green chilies, green onions, green pepper, and cilantro in a mixing bowl.

ASSEMBLY
1. Choose an ovenproof casserole dish large enough to contain the four chicken breasts.
2. Place crumbs in a flat dish and press chicken into crumbs, coating completely.
3. Place breaded chicken in casserole dish. Spoon sauce on and around chicken. Top chicken with Monterey Jack cheese.
4. Bake in a preheated 400° oven for 20 minutes.
5. Remove cooked chicken from casserole to heated plates and spoon sauce and vegetables on and around chicken.

This dish goes well with rice.

"Strange to see how a good dinner and feasting reconciles everyone."
Samuel Pepys

SOUTH OF THE BORDER CHICKEN

A little influence from our Mexican neighbors.

2 whole chicken breasts, skinned, boned, halved, flattened,
  with fat removed
1/4 cup orange juice
1/4 cup cranberry juice
2 tablespoons lime juice
1 teaspoon dried oregano
1/2 teaspoon ground dried cumin
1/2 teaspoon dried chili powder
1 garlic clove, minced
1/4 cup chopped green onions (scallions)
2 dashes hot-pepper sauce, such as Tabasco
1 cup ground tortilla chips (can be ground in a food-processor)
4 slices Monterey Jack cheese

PREPARATION
1. Mix orange juice, cranberry juice, lime juice, oregano, cumin,
   chili powder, minced garlic, green onions and, hot sauce in
   a mixing bowl.

ASSEMBLY
1. Select an ovenproof casserole dish large enough to contain
   the four chicken breasts.
2. Place ground tortilla chips in a flat dish and press chicken into
   crumbs, coating completely.
3. Place breaded chicken in buttered casserole dish. Top with
   Montcrey Jack cheese. Spoon the sauce on and around chicken.
4. Bake in a preheated 400° oven for 20 minutes.
5. Remove cooked chicken from casserole to heated plates with
   a spatula. Spoon the sauce on and around chicken.

    This dish is great served with rice.
    Before processing the tortilla chips, crush them a bit.

SWEET AND SOUR CHICKEN

These pungent flavors excite all the taste buds.

2 whole chicken breasts, skinned, boned, halved, flattened,
   with fat removed
1/2 teaspoon dry mustard
1 clove garlic, minced
1/4 cup honey
1 tablespoon sugar
1/4 cup wine vinegar
1/4 cup soy sauce
1/2 cup ketchup
1/4 cup chopped green onions (scallions)
1/4 cup chopped fresh parsley
1/2 cup breading crumbs, page 75
1 tablespoon butter

PREPARATION

1. Thoroughly mix dry mustard, minced garlic, honey, sugar, vinegar, soy sauce, ketchup, green onions, and parsley in a mixing bowl.

ASSEMBLY

1. Butter an oven proof casserole dish large enough to contain the four chicken breasts.
2. Place crumbs in a flat dish and press chicken into crumbs, coating completely.
3. Place breaded chicken in buttered casserole dish. Spoon sweet and sour sauce on and around chicken.
4. Bake in a preheated 400° oven for 20 minutes.
5. Remove cooked chicken from casserole dish to heated plates with a spatula. Spoon remaining sauce on and around chicken.

Rice is perfect with this dish.

"Sour, Sweet, Bitter, Pungent, all must be tasted."
–Chinese proverb

TOMATO-PEPPER CHICKEN

Tomatoes and basil are the perfect marriage.

2 whole chicken breasts, skinned, boned, halved, flattened,
  with fat removed
1 small onion, chopped
1/2 cup diced green bell pepper, cored and seeded
1/2 cup diced red bell pepper, cored and seeded
1/4 cup chopped fresh basil or 1 teaspoon dried basil
1/4 cup chopped fresh parsley
1 cup chopped canned tomatoes with juice
1/2 cup evaporated milk
1 tablespoon butter
1/2 cup breading crumbs, page 75
4 slices provolone cheese

PREPARATION
1. Mix chopped onion, diced green pepper, diced red pepper, basil,
   parsley, canned tomatoes, and evaporated milk in a mixing bowl.

ASSEMBLY
1. Butter an ovenproof casserole dish large enough to contain the
   four chicken breasts.
2. Place crumbs in a flat dish and press chicken into crumbs,
   coating completely.
3. Place breaded chicken in buttered casserole dish. Top chicken
   with provolone cheese. Spoon sauce around chicken.
4. Bake in a preheated 400° oven for 20 minutes.
5. Remove cooked chicken from casserole to heated plates with
   a spatula. Spoon the sauce and vegetables on and around chicken.

*Instead of canned chopped tomatoes, peel, seed and dice
fresh tomatoes.*

Helpful Hint
*If you sprinkle salt into the water when you are washing
vegetables and greens, it will help draw out insects and sand.*

========WATER CHESTNUT GLAZED CHICKEN

Water chestnut is an edible tuber that comes from Southeast Asia. This spicy chicken dish is energetic and mouth-watering.

2 whole chicken breasts, skinned, boned, halved, flattened,
  with fat removed
1 tablespoon hoisin sauce
1 teaspoon rice vinegar
1/2 teaspoon red chili sauce
1 teaspoon soy sauce
1 garlic clove, minced
1/4 cup chopped green onions (scallions)
1/2 cup diced red bell pepper, cored and seeded
1/4 cup sliced water chestnuts, drained (available in small cans)
1/4 cup chicken broth
1/2 cup breading crumbs, page 75

PREPARATION

1. Mix hoisin sauce, rice vinegar, chili sauce, soy sauce, garlic, green onions, red pepper, water chestnuts, and chicken broth in a mixing bowl.

ASSEMBLY

1. Select an ovenproof casserole dish just large enough to contain the four chicken breasts.
2. Place crumbs in a flat dish and press chicken into crumbs, coating completely.
3. Place breaded chicken in casserole dish. Spoon sauce mixture on and around chicken.
4. Bake in a preheated 400° oven for 20 minutes.
5. Remove cooked chicken from casserole to heated plates with a spatula. Spoon the sauce on and around chicken.

    This dish is great served with rice or oriental noodles.

*"A man seldom thinks with more earnestness of
anything than he does of dinner."*
    Samuel Johnson

There is no such thing as a bad customer! These are words I have said many times while operating the Red Rooster. We are professional and can handle any situation. But sometimes situations can test your endurance.

My cousin, Dennis, was working in a Providence restaurant, a wonderful bistro-type place. One Sunday afternoon in the spring of 1999, he was at work getting ready for a busy day. It was Brown University's graduation day.

The host told him he had a party of six but they were seated at two different tables in two different rooms. This confused him for a minute, but in the restaurant business normal is not always the rule. He approached the first table of two ladies and one gentleman. He gave them the menus and asked about drinks. He then went to the second table where the three gentlemen were seated and each one was talking on a cell phone and speaking a strange language. (He found out afterwards that they were bodyguards.) They just wanted coffee. Dennis thought to himself, "Oh well, we get them all." He proceeded to take the first table's order, and they just wanted light appetizers. Later, one of the three men asked for the check and tipped him very well. Dennis said to himself, "Well, you just can't judge people."

The next morning, he picked up the *Providence Journal*, and there on the front cover was the picture of a lady, Queen Noor from Jordan. "That's the lady I waited on yesterday," he said.

She was here in Providence to speak at the Brown University graduation. And it goes to show that in the restaurant business you sometimes never know who the customer is.

ROLLED BAKED
CHICKEN BREAST

========== *ROLLED BAKED CHICKEN BREAST*

All recipes are for two in this chapter.

==========*Hints and suggestions*

RECIPES: Chicken and seafood recipes are for two servings, unless otherwise specified. Double or triple the ingredients for more servings.

PREPARING AHEAD: If you prepare recipes ahead of time, take them out of the refrigerator 30 minutes before cooking time.

REMOVE SKIN FROM CHICKEN: To remove skin from fresh chicken, use a paper towel to hold the chicken skin, pull the skin while holding down the chicken and the skin should come right off.

FLATTEN CHICKEN: You can flatten trimmed chicken breasts between two pieces of wax paper or plastic wrap with the bottom of a sauté pan or a meat mallet, available in kitchen stores.

BREADING CRUMBS ON CHICKEN: If the boneless breasts of chicken are dry, moisten the chicken with a little milk and the crumbs will stick to the chicken.

ROLLED CHICKEN: In all the recipes in the cookbook for rolled chicken, use a toothpick to secure the rolled chicken. A substitute for the toothpick is a piece of spaghetti. As the rolled chicken cooks, the spaghetti cooks and can be eaten. It saves you the trouble of removing the toothpicks. You can do this with rolled veal and fish.

ROLLED CHICKEN

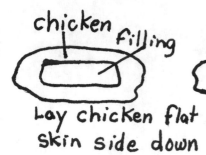

chicken — filling
Lay chicken flat
skin side down

chicken
filling
Start to
roll around
filling

rolled chicken
toothpicks

"The difference between a rather average cook and a chef is that the chef is never really satisfied with what he is serving. He is constantly trying to achieve the high expectation he has set for himself. He is seeking to develop his palate and to enhance the skills of his palate through cooking, travel, and just being open. By keeping yourself open to what's new or who's doing something a little bit better, you strive for perfection. I'm always looking to improve on what I do."

Bradley Ogden

Saltimbocca in Italian means, "jump in your mouth." This classic dish is usually made with veal, my version is made with chicken. (You can make it with veal if you wish.)

2 whole chicken breasts, skinned, boned, halved, flattened,
   with fat removed
1 teaspoon dried sage or fresh sage leaves, chopped
1 tablespoon grated Parmesan cheese
4 thin slices proscuitto or thinly sliced ham
Toothpicks, wooden
1 tablespoon olive oil
1/2 cup of flour for dredging
2 eggs beaten with 1 tablespoon milk, in a small bowl
1 cup breading crumbs, page 75
4 slices provolone cheese
1/4 cup chopped fresh parsley

PREPARATION
1. On a flat surface, lay out chicken skin side up. On each chicken breast, sprinkle sage, Parmesan cheese, and slice of prosciutto. Roll up jellyroll style and secure with wooden toothpicks. Keep cold in refrigerator.

ASSEMBLY
1. Oil an ovenproof casserole dish large enough to contain the four rolled chicken breasts.
2. Place flour in a dish. Place crumbs in a dish.
3. Dredge rolled chicken in flour, shaking off excess, then in egg wash, allowing excess to drip off. Roll in crumbs, coating completely.
4. Place chicken, seam side down, in oiled casserole dish. Top with provolone cheese and chopped parsley.
5. Bake in a preheated 400° oven for 20 minutes. (If chicken is thick, allow a few extra minutes.)
6. Remove casserole from oven. Use needle-nosed pliers and a fork to hold chicken, remove the toothpicks. Remove cooked chicken to heated plates with a spatula.

==============CHICKEN WRAPPED SAUSAGE

A full-flavored variation for chicken and Italian sausage that
is accented with a wonderful sauce. That is great with pasta.

2 whole chicken breasts, skinned, boned, halved, flattened thin,
   with fat removed
4 hot or mild Italian sausages, cooked, (roasted or sautéed)
   cooled, skin removed
1 tablespoon butter
1 small onion, minced
2 cloves garlic, minced
1/2 cup sliced fresh mushrooms
1/2 cup chopped green bell pepper, cored and seeded
1/2 cup chopped red bell pepper, cored and seeded
1/2 cup chopped green onions (scallions)
1/4 cup chopped fresh parsley
1 cup tomato puree
1/4 cup chopped fresh basil or 1 teaspoon dried basil
Toothpicks, wooden
1 tablespoon olive oil
1/2 cup flour for dredging
2 eggs, beaten with 1 tablespoon milk, in a small bowl
1 cup breading crumbs, page 75
4 slices provolone cheese

PREPARATION
1. Heat a medium skillet, add butter, onion, and garlic; sauté for
    one minute until yellow. Add sliced mushrooms, green pepper,
    and red pepper. Sauté for a couple of minutes until vegetables are soft.
    Stir in green onions, parsley, tomato puree, and basil. Bring to a low
    boil for just a minute. Cool.

ASSEMBLY
1. On a flat surface lay out chicken, skin side up. Place cooked
    peeled sausage in the middle of each chicken breast. Roll chicken
    like a jellyroll and secure with a toothpick.

Chicken wrapped sausage continued-

2. Oil an ovenproof casserole dish large enough to contain the four chicken breasts.
3. Place flour in a dish. Place crumbs in a dish.
4. Dredge rolled chicken in flour, shaking off excess, then in egg wash, allowing excess to drip off. Roll in crumbs, coating completely.
5. Place rolled breaded chicken in casserole dish, seam side down. Spoon tomato sauce on and around chicken; top chicken with provolone cheese.
6. Bake in a preheated 400° oven for 20 minutes or until cooked.
7. Remove casserole from oven, using needle-nosed pliers and a fork to hold chicken, remove the toothpicks. Remove cooked chicken to heated plates with a spatula. Spoon the sauce and vegetables on and around chicken.

This dish is a little thick; check chicken with a meat thermometer, it should read 170 to 180.

Helpful Hint
I live in an area with many pine trees. I often get tree sap on my car. I tried so many things to remove that sticky sap that did not work. A friend suggested using nail polish remover on a cotton ball. I used the non-acetone type. I could not believe how the sap just dissolved. After removing sap, wash and rinse area. Dry and wax area to reseal paint.

"My mothers menu consisted of two choices:
Take is or leave it."
Buddy Hackett

==ROLLED BACON AND MOZZARELLA CHICKEN

The term "rolled" in cooking means a thin slice of meat, chicken, or fish rolled around a filling. In French cooking, it is called "roulade" or "paupiettes". In Italian cooking, it is called "rollatini".

2 whole chicken breasts, skinned, boned, halved, flattened thin,
  with fat removed
1/2 cup (2-ounces) shredded mozzarella cheese
4 slices bacon, cooked and chopped
2 tablespoons chopped fresh basil or 1/4 teaspoon dried basil
2 tablespoons plain dried or fresh bread crumbs,
1/4 cup chopped fresh parsley
Toothpicks, wooden
1 tablespoon olive oil
1/2 cup flour for dredging
1 egg beaten with 1 tablespoon milk, in a small bowl
1 cup breading crumbs, page 75
1 tablespoon butter

PREPARATION
1. Mix shredded mozzarella, chopped cooked bacon, basil, plain bread crumbs, and chopped parsley in a mixing bowl.

ASSEMBLY
1. On a flat surface place chicken breast skin side up, spoon cheese stuffing equally on each chicken breast. Roll up jellyroll style and secure with a toothpick.
2. Oil an ovenproof casserole dish large enough to contain the the four rolled chicken breasts.
3. Place flour in a dish. Place breading crumbs in a dish.
4. Dredge rolled chicken in flour, shaking off excess, then in egg wash, allowing excess to drip off. Roll in breading crumbs, coating completely.

Rolled bacon and mozzarella chicken continued-

5. Place breaded chicken, seam side down, in oiled casserole dish.
   Dot with butter.
6. Bake in a preheated 400° oven for 20 minutes.
7. Remove casserole from oven. Using needle nosed pliers and a fork
   to hold chicken, remove toothpicks. Remove cooked chicken
   from casserole to heated plates with a spatula.

Instead of bacon in this recipe, you can use finely chopped ham.

Helpful Hint
Wrap a clear plastic bag over an open cookbook. It will keep the cookbook clean and keep the book open to your recipe.

" I received this wonderful Hallmark birthday card from a friend while I was working on this recipe and decided to share the words with you."

"The beauty of friendship is like the beauty of flowers...there are many kinds, and yet each has unique beauty to offer. There are friends who share our paths during certain stages of our lives, while others stay close to us year after year. Some are vibrant, admired for their strength, while others are delicate whispers of color whose gentleness has a special place in our hearts."

===ROLLED CHICKEN WITH A CRAB STUFFING

This dish looks like more work than it really is. It can be prepared earlier in the day and baked just before dinner.

2 whole chicken breasts, skinned, boned, halved, flattened thin,
   with fat removed
1 tablespoon butter
1 1/4 cup onion, minced
1/4 cup minced red bell pepper, cored and seeded
6 mushrooms, cleaned and chopped
1 (10 1/2-ounce) can cream of shrimp soup
1/3 cup crushed saltines (about 8 crackers)
1 (6-ounce) can of crabmeat, drained, flaked (check for small bones)
1/2 cup (2-ounces) shredded Swiss cheese
1/4 cup chopped fresh parsley
Toothpicks, wooden
1 tablespoon olive oil
1/2 cup flour for dredging
2 eggs beaten with 1 tablespoon milk, in a small bowl
1 cup breading crumbs, page 75
1/2 cup milk
1 teaspoon sherry wine

PREPARATION

1. Heat butter in a skillet over medium heat; sauté onions until yellow. Stir in minced pepper and mushrooms; sauté until mushrooms are wilted. Cool.
2. Mix cooled mushrooms, 1/3 cup of cream of shrimp soup (save remaining soup for later), crushed saltines, crabmeat, shredded Swiss cheese, and chopped parsley in a mixing bowl.

Rolled chicken with a crab stuffing continued-

ASSEMBLY
1. Oil an ovenproof casserole dish large enough to contain the four chicken breasts.
2. On a flat surface lay flattened chicken breast skin side up.
   Spoon and spread crab stuffing evenly on each chicken breast.
   Roll up like a jellyroll and secure with a toothpick.
3. Place flour in a dish. Place crumbs in a dish.
4. Dredge rolled chicken in flour, shaking off excess, then in egg wash allowing excess to drip off. Roll in crumbs, coating completely. Place rolled chicken seam side down in oiled casserole dish. Dot with butter.
5. Bake in a preheated 400° oven for 20 minutes.
6. While chicken is cooking heat a small saucepan over medium heat. Add remaining shrimp soup, 1/4 cup of milk and sherry. Stir and heat until smooth. Keep warm.
7. Remove casserole from oven, with needle-nosed pliers and a fork to hold chicken, remove toothpicks.
   Place chicken rolls on heated plates, spoon sauce on and around chicken.

Helpful Hint
An empty Worcestershire sauce bottle is a great oil dispenser.
Wash the bottle thoroughly before using. Use a funnel to fill and use the drip less cap.

"Cheese: milk's leap towards immortality."
Clifton Fadiman

========ROLLED CHICKEN WITH GOAT CHEESE AND SUN-DRIED TOMATOES

Sun-dried tomatoes are usually dried in the sun, resulting in a chewy, sweet, flavorful, dark red tomato. They are dry packed, packed in oil, or other liquids.

2 whole chicken breasts, skinned, boned, halved, flattened,
   with fat removed
4 ounces goat cheese, room temperature
1/4 cup chopped sun-dried tomatoes, drained of liquid
1/4 cup chopped fresh basil, or 1 teaspoon dried basil
1/4 cup chopped fresh parsley
Toothpicks, wooden
1 tablespoon olive oil
1/2 cup flour for dredging
2 eggs beaten with 1 tablespoon milk in a mixing bowl
1 cup breading crumbs, page 75
1 tablespoon butter.

PREPARATION
1 Mash goat cheese with a fork in a mixing bowl. Thoroughly mix in chopped sun-dried tomatoes, chopped basil, and chopped parsley.

ASSEMBLY
1. Oil an ovenproof casserole dish large enough to contain the chicken breasts.
2. On a flat surface lay flattened chicken breast skin side up. Spoon and spread cheese tomato mixture evenly on each chicken breast. Roll up and secure with a toothpick.
3. Place flour in a dish. Place crumbs in a dish.
4. Dredge rolled chicken in flour, shaking off excess then in egg wash, allowing excess egg to drip off. Roll in crumbs, coating completely. Place chicken in oiled casserole dish, seam side down. Dot with butter.
5. Bake in a preheated 400° oven for 20 minutes.
6. Remove casserole from oven. With needle-nosed pliers and a fork to hold chicken, remove toothpicks.
7. Remove chicken rolls from casserole with to heated plates with a spatula.

=ROLLED CHICKEN WITH PEACH AND COCONUT

Peaches and coconut almost sounds like dessert, but it is a refreshing chicken dish.

2 whole chicken breasts, skinned, boned, halved, flattened,
  with fat removed
1/2 cup flour
1/2 teaspoon thyme
1/2 teaspoon curry
2 tablespoon butter
1/2 cup unsweetened, grated coconut
1/2 cup breading crumbs, page 75
4 slices prosciutto or thinly sliced ham
1 ripe peach, peeled, pit removed, cut in quarters
Toothpicks, wooden
2 eggs beaten with 1 tablespoon milk, in a mixing bowl

PREPARATION
1. Mix flour, thyme, and curry in a mixing bowl.
2. Mix grated coconut and crumbs in a mixing bowl.

ASSEMBLY
1. On a flat surface place chicken breasts skin side up, top with prosciutto and peach quarter. Roll up jellyroll style and secure with a toothpick.
2. Using half the butter, butter an ovenproof casserole dish large enough to contain the four rolled chicken breasts.
3. Dredge rolled chicken in flour mixture, shaking off excess, then in egg wash, allowing excess to drip off. Roll in coconut mixture, coating completely.
4. Place breaded chicken roll seam side down in buttered casserole dish. Dot with butter.
5. Bake in a preheated 400° oven for 20 minutes.
6. Remove casserole from oven. With needle-nosed pliers and a fork to hold chicken, remove toothpicks. Remove cooked chicken from casserole to heated plates with a spatula.

WALNUT CHEESE CHICKEN

A rich, beautiful stuffing, accented with a walnut breading.

2 whole chicken breasts, skinned, boned, halved, flattened,
   with fat removed
1/2 cup (4-ounces) softened cream cheese
2 cloves garlic, minced
1 tablespoon chopped fresh basil or 1/2 teaspoon dried basil
1 tablespoon finely chopped green onion (scallions)
1 teaspoon grated Parmesan cheese
Toothpicks, wooden
1 tablespoon olive oil
1/2 cup flour for dredging
2 eggs, beaten with 1 tablespoon milk in a small bowl
1/2 cup breading crumbs, page 75
1/2 cup finely chopped walnuts
1 tablespoon butter
Dash balsamic vinegar

PREPARATION
1. Mix cream cheese, garlic, basil, green onions, and Parmesan cheese with
    a fork in a mixing bowl.

ASSEMBLY
1. On a flat surface place chicken breast skin side up, spoon and spread
    cheese stuffing equally on each chicken breast. Roll up jellyroll style and
    secure with a toothpick.
2. Oil an ovenproof casserole dish large enough to contain the four
    rolled chicken breasts.
3. Place flour in a dish. Mix crumbs with walnuts and place in a dish.
4. Dredge rolled chicken in flour, shaking off excess, then in egg
    wash, allowing excess to drip off. Roll in walnut-crumb breading,
    coating completely.

Walnut-cheese chicken continued-

5. Place breaded chicken roll, seam side down in oiled casserole
   Dot with butter.
6. Bake in a preheated 400° oven for 20 minutes.
7. Remove casserole from oven. With needle-nosed pliers and a fork
   to hold chicken, remove toothpicks. Remove cooked chicken from
   casserole to heated plates with a spatula. Drizzle a little balsamic
   vinegar on and around chicken.

*When you roll chicken in flour and in egg mixture, do it with two
forks. I find it is not so messy. Then roll in crumb mixture.*

Helpful Hint

*Danger from infused olive oil–Oils infused with garlic or herbs can
be contaminated with the bacterium that causes botulism. It cannot be identified
by smell, sight, or taste. Bacteria originates on the garlic and can readily
grow in oil stored at room temperature. Buy only commercially prepared infused
oil that contains phosphoric or citric acid. Store the bottle in the refrigerator
after you open it. You can infuse oil yourself, just make sure you follow
professional directions.*

*"Cooking is a creation. As a creation, it is a personalized view of the
way we like to express our feelings. It is how we share our sense of art,
our knowledge, and our taste with other people. Food, after all, is not
merely a product. It is necessary to our sustenance. Food is the support
of live and is the center of the way we live when we take a moment to sit
down are share life, share conversation, and share joy. That is the joy
of cooking, which is a cliché, and yet is it the ultimate way we really
fulfill ourselves and those around us. When people come to us and reach
out to us, we must reach out with a very personalized and individual
way of expressing our beliefs."*
Piero Selvaggio

=========WEDDING STYLE ROLLED CHICKEN

This chicken dish was always a favorite for weddings and special functions in the restaurant.

2 whole chicken breasts, skinned, boned, halved, flattened thin,
  with fat removed
4 slices ham, trimmed to same size as chicken breast
4 slices Provolone cheese, trimmed to same size as chicken breast
1/2 teaspoon fresh or dried rosemary, chopped
Toothpicks, wooden
2 tablespoons butter
1/2 cup flour
2 eggs, beaten with 1 tablespoon milk in a small bowl
1 cup breading crumbs, page 75
1 cup chicken gravy (available at markets; prepared according to
  directions on label)
1 teaspoon Marsala wine (optional)
1/2 cup frozen peas, thawed
1/4 cup chopped fresh parsley

ASSEMBLY

1. On a flat surface place chicken breasts skin side up; place ham, cheese, and rosemary on each chicken breast. Roll up jellyroll style and secure with a toothpick.
2. Using half the butter, butter an ovenproof casserole dish large enough to contain the four rolled chicken breasts.
3. Place flour in a dish. Place crumbs in a dish.
4. Dredge rolled chicken in flour, shaking off excess, then in egg wash, allowing excess to drip off. Roll in crumbs, coating completely.
5. Place breaded chicken roll seam side down in buttered casserole dish. Dot with butter.
6. Bake in a preheated 400° oven for 20 minutes.

Wedding style rolled chicken continued-

7. While chicken is cooking, heat a saucepan over medium heat,
   add chicken gravy, Marsala wine, and peas, stirring
   occasionally. Keep warm.
8. Remove casserole from oven. With needle nose-pliers and a fork
   to hold down chicken, remove toothpicks. Remove cooked chicken
   from casserole to heated plates with a spatula. Spoon sauce on and
   around rolled chicken. Garnish with chopped parsley.

Helpful Hint

*If something runs over in the oven and you have a fire, shut off
the oven, then put the fire out with salt, or baking soda. Do not use water.*
*I was conducting a class at the Learning Connection in Boston.
We were cooking Scallops Casino with a convection oven. The bacon flew
off the scallops, landed on the bottom of the oven, and started to smoke. The
fire alarms went off and within minutes we had four firemen in the class.*
*This was not a good way to make friends and influence the Boston fire
department.*

"Ingredients to a cook is like dresses and jewelry to a woman."
Yuan Xical

231

ROLLED GOUDA CHICKEN

Gouda cheese is Holland's most famous cheese; it's yellow interior is dotted with little holes. It has a mild, creamy, nut like flavor. It is made from cow's milk, aged from a few weeks to over a year.

2 whole chicken breasts, skinned, boned, halved, flattened rather
   thin, with fat removed
4 pieces Gouda cheese, cut into 1/2-inch by 1/2-inch cube
1/4 cup chopped fresh parsley
Toothpicks, wooden
2 tablespoons butter
1/2 cup flour
2 eggs, beaten with 1 tablespoon milk in a small bowl
1 cup breading crumbs, page 75

ASSEMBLY

1. On a flat surface place chicken breast skin side up, place cheese and parsley in middle of each breast. Roll up jellyroll style and secure with a toothpick.
2. Using half the butter, butter an ovenproof casserole dish large enough to contain the four rolled chicken breasts.
3. Place flour in a dish. Place crumbs in a dish.
4. Dredge rolled chicken in flour, shaking off excess, then in egg wash, allowing excess to drip off. Roll in crumbs, coating completely.
5. Place breaded chicken roll, seam side down, in buttered casserole dish. Dot with butter.
6. Bake in a preheated 400° oven for 20 minutes.
7. Remove casserole from oven. With needle-nosed pliers and a fork to hold chicken, remove toothpicks. Remove cooked chicken from casserole to heated plates with a spatula.

Helpful Hint

To clean a crusted cookie sheet that does not fit into your sink, wet a paper towel with warm water and a little dish soap, place it flat on the cookie sheet. Allow it to sit for a little while. You will find it a lot easier to clean

One of my greatest pleasures when the temperature drops below freezing is cooking dinner in my fireplace. I usually start the fire an hour or so before my guests arrive. During cocktails and hors d'oeuvres, I let the fire die down. I have this wonderful three-level grate that fits in my fireplace; I can choose how close to place the grate to the fire.

There are so many great foods that can be cooked on the grill: veal, lamb, pork, steaks, chicken, shrimp, swordfish, salmon and soft vegetables such as zucchini, eggplant and onions.

It's important to marinate the food. It improves the flavor and oils the food so that it doesn't stick to the grill. You can make good marinades by using oil, balsamic vinegar, soy sauce, garlic and herbs of your choosing.

When cooking meats, except for pork and chicken, cook the meat rare. Then place the entrée in an ovenproof casserole and keep it in a warm oven or on the side of the fire to rest while eating your first course. When ready to serve, place the entrée on a plate and spoon any juices from the bottom of the casserole on and around the entrée.

It's a novelty for my guests to watch me cook on the fire. It becomes a great social event. Set a table near the fireplace if you can. And after cooking, put another log on the fire.

CHICKEN BREAST
BAKED
IN PUFF PASTRY

================CHICKEN IN PUFF PASTRY

All recipes are for two in this chapter.

============Hints and suggestions

RECIPES: Chicken and seafood recipes are for two servings, unless otherwise specified. Double or triple the ingredients for more servings.

PREPARING AHEAD: If you prepare recipes ahead of time, take them out of the refrigerator 30 minutes before cooking time.

REMOVE SKIN FROM CHICKEN: To remove skin from fresh chicken, use a paper towel to hold the chicken skin, pull the skin while holding down the chicken and the skin should come right off.

FLATTEN CHICKEN: You can flatten trimmed chicken breasts between two pieces of wax paper or plastic wrap with the bottom of a sauté pan or a meat mallet, available in kitchen stores.

BREADING CRUMBS ON CHICKEN: If the boneless breasts of chicken are dry, moisten the chicken with a little milk and the crumbs will stick to the chicken.

INSULATED COOKIE SHEET: When baking puff pastry, often the bottom will burn before the top browns. Use an insulated cookie sheet. It has an air space between the layers.

PASTRY SHELLS: In recipes using puff pastry, roll an extra shell. Decorating with the extra pastry allows you to create designs that compliment the dish.

In the early 1970s, just after the restaurant opened, my cousin Donald, a priest who worked in the academic field, was free that summer. He asked me if he could work in the restaurant as a waiter. It would provide him with a little extra money and a change of pace.

We had both worked in a small restaurant during our high school days. On his first day of work, we assigned him to Lorraine for training. She took him under her wing and we did not tell anyone, even Lorraine, that he was a priest. This was to protect his privacy and to not make the staff and customers uncomfortable.

Father Donald was about 30 years old, very good-looking, and he fit in very well with the staff, especially Lorraine. Her devil horns of seduction were working full time when she worked with him. She was recently divorced. Her husband, a service man at Quonset, had run off with another woman and left her to fend for herself and her young son.

In jest one evening, she said to him "Will you marry me"? Donald replied, "Sure, I will marry you any day you want." This comedy of words went on all summer.

On Donald's last night before going back to teach, he came in for dinner dressed in his clerics. We assigned Lorraine to his table. As she approached the table with the relish tray in one hand and the water pitcher in the other, she looked at her customers and saw Donald dressed as a priest. She almost dropped the water pitcher in his lap. Her expression was worth a million dollars. Father Donald looked at her in a quiet, shy way and said. "I told you I would marry you anytime you wanted to."

We all had a chuckle for a long time over this story.

One thing we tried to do when possible was promote from within our own ranks. If we had a good dishwasher or salad person and we needed a line cook or bus person, he or she got promoted. It was always such a pleasure to see a dishwasher get a bussing position.

The transition from dishwasher to bus person was an amazing thing to watch. The first night they came in with their new shoes, new black trousers, white shirt and bow tie. From the kitchen to the dining room is quite a challenge for a young person. The biggest challenge is carrying those big trays with cooked food, then bringing the trays of dirty dishes back into the kitchen. We held our breath many times watching those shaky trays.

We had promoted a nice young man named Ricky. During a really busy evening while on my way to the walk-in, I went around the corner and there was Ricky hiding. I said to him in rather a loud voice, "What are you in charge of?" He looked at me with a sad look and said, "Silence." I smiled and said, "Get back to work."

Ricky eventually became a waiter and a bartender. It was so gratifying to see so many young people grow up with us. Working in a restaurant prepares students for future work and education.

My own career started in high school working in a restaurant after school. I always knew I wanted to own a restaurant, so it was easy for me to decide on a career. My dream of owning my own restaurant came true, but sometimes getting through every day was a nightmare. That's just the way of the restaurant industry. It is a business where you need to prove yourself with every meal you serve.

Choosing the right career can be a very stressful experience for most young students. Working, teaching and guiding young people is a training ground for our common future.

I am proud of the thousands of young people who have worked for us and with us. Later in life, they have come back to the restaurant to visit– as friends, diners, doctors, chefs, executives, mothers and fathers. We fervently hope that their time spent in the restaurant helped make a difference in their lives.

APPLE, HAM AND CHEESE CHICKEN

Cooking in puff pastry is a little more work, but the presentation and wonderful flavors are worth the effort.

2 whole chicken breasts, skinned, boned, halved, flattened,
   with fat removed
1/2 cup breading crumbs, page 75
2 tablespoons olive oil
Flour for rolling puff pastry and dusting casserole
2 Pepperidge Farm patty shells, thawed (puff pastry sheets
   can be used also)
2 slices ham
2 slices Swiss cheese
1 apple, peeled, cored and quartered
Dash nutmeg
1/4 cup finely chopped fresh parsley
1 teaspoon butter
Water for sealing pastry
1 egg beaten with 1 teaspoon milk in a small bowl

PREPARATION
1. Place crumbs in a flat dish and press chicken into crumbs, coating completely.
2. Heat 1 tablespoon olive oil over medium heat in a skillet; sauté breaded chicken breasts on both sides until just cooked. Cool.
3. On a floured board roll thawed puff pastry shells into 8-inch rounds. Place the pastry between plastic wrap. Keep in refrigerator until ready to use.

ASSEMBLY
1. Thinly oil and flour an insulated cookie sheet or an ovenproof casserole dish.

Apple, ham and cheese chicken continued-

2. On a flat surface, lay out pastry on plastic wrap. Place cooked chicken breast in the middle of pastry, top with slice of ham, other chicken breast, slice of Swiss cheese, half apple, dash of nutmeg, and dot with butter.
3. Wrap chicken like a package, seal seams with water. Spread egg wash on crust with fingers or pastry brush. Place puff pastry package on prepared cookie sheet.
4. Bake on middle rack on a preheated 400° oven for 20 minutes.
5. Remove cooked chicken package from cookie sheet to heated plates with a spatula.

If baking in a convection oven cut cooking time about 5 minutes, or until crust turns a nice brown color.

Helpful Hint

If you have a sunny spot in your yard, on your deck or in your house, you can plant your own herb garden. You can cultivate fresh herbs in pots or in a small garden in your yard. The flavor of fresh herbs can make your meals outstanding.

"I hear and I forget.
I see and I remember.
I do and I understand."
Chinese Proverb

=ASPARAGUS AND PEPPER CHICKEN IN A CRUST

Asparagus can be blanched in a microwave; place asparagus in an ovenproof dish with a cover with 2 teaspoons water. Cook on high heat for about 4 minutes. Chill asparagus in cold water to stop it from cooking.

2 whole chicken breasts, skinned, boned, halved, flattened,
   with fat removed
2 Pepperidge Farm patty shells thawed, (puff pastry sheets can
   be used also)
1/2 cup breading crumbs, page 75
2 tablespoons olive oil
Flour for rolling puff pastry and dusting casserole
8 fresh asparagus spears, trimmed, blanched al dente
1 large red bell pepper (or jar of roasted peppers)
1/4 teaspoon dried basil or 2 tablespoons fresh chopped basil
4 slices American cheese
Water for sealing pastry
1 egg beaten with 1 teaspoon milk in a small bowl

PREPARATION
1. Place crumbs in a flat dish and press chicken into crumbs, coating completely.
2. Heat 1 tablespoon olive oil over medium heat in a skillet; sauté breaded chicken breasts on both sides until just cooked. Cool
3. On a floured board roll thawed puff pastry shells into 8-inch rounds. Place between sheets of plastic wrap. Keep in refrigerator until ready to use.
4. Heat broiler. Cut red pepper in four, remove seeds, and trim cores.
5. Cook the peppers, skin side up under a broiler until skin blisters; peel off skins. Cool.

Asparagus and pepper chicken in a crust continued-

ASSEMBLY
1. Thinly oil and flour an insulated cookie sheet or ovenproof casserole dish.
2. On a flat surface, lay out pastry on plastic wrap. Place cooked chicken breast in middle of pastry, top with 4 asparagus spears, trimmed so that they fit on chicken the long way. Top with other chicken breast, red pepper, basil, and 2 slices American cheese.
3. Wrap chicken like a package; seal seams with water.
4. Spread egg mixture on crust with fingers or pastry brush. Place puff pastry package on prepared cookie sheet.
5. Bake on middle rack in a preheated 400° oven for 20 minutes.
6. Remove cooked chicken package from casserole to heated plates with a spatula.

If baking in a convection oven cut cooking time down about 5 minutes, or until crust turns a nice brown color.

Store asparagus in the refrigerator, in a dish, standing upright, in about 1 inch of water, cover with a plastic bag.

"Give me books, French wine, fruit, fine weather and a little music out doors, played by somebody I do not know."

John Keats

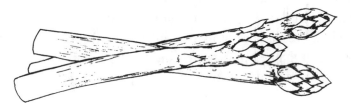

CHICKEN WELLINGTON

Chicken Wellington was one of our signature dishes at the restaurant. We first tried this dish on a Sunday afternoon as a special. I had made Beef Wellington many times, and decided to try the Wellington with chicken. I had prepared and rolled enough pastry for about 40 orders; in that afternoon, we sold about 90 orders. What a crazy time trying to roll and prepare this dish, in between every thing else that was going on. We eventually put it on the menu and it became a favorite for weddings, special dinners, and a great menu item.

2 whole chicken breasts skinned, boned, halved, flattened,
  with fat removed
2 Pepperidge Farm patty shells thawed (puff pastry sheets
  can be used also)
1/2 cup breading crumbs, page 75
2 tablespoons olive oil
1 small can of pâté or fresh pâté from a specialty market
Water for sealing pastry
2 medium mushroom caps
1/4 cup finely chopped fresh parsley
Flour for rolling puff pastry and dusting casserole
1 egg beaten with 1 teaspoon milk in a small bowl

PREPARATION

1. Place crumbs in a flat dish and press chicken into crumbs
  coating completely.
2. Heat 1 tablespoon olive oil over medium heat in a skillet;
  sauté breaded chicken breasts on both sides until cooked. Cool.
3. On a floured board, roll thawed puff pastry shells into 8-inch
  rounds. Place between sheets of plastic wrap. Keep in refrigerator
  until ready to use.

ASSEMBLY

1. Thinly oil and flour an insulated cookie sheet or ovenproof casserole.
2. On a flat surface, lay out pastry on plastic wrap. Top pastry with
  one cooked chicken breast, top with slice of pate. Top with other
  cooked chicken breast. Add more pâté, parsley, and mushroom cap.
  Do this with each portion.

Chicken Wellington continued-

3. Wrap chicken like a package, seal seams with water.
   Spread egg mixture on crust with fingers or a pastry brush. Place
   the puff pastry package on the prepared cookie sheet.
4. Bake on middle rack in a preheated 400° oven for 20 minutes
5. Remove cooked chicken package from casserole to heated
   plates with a spatula.

*If baking in a convection oven cut cooking time down about
5 minutes, or until crust turns a nice brown color.*

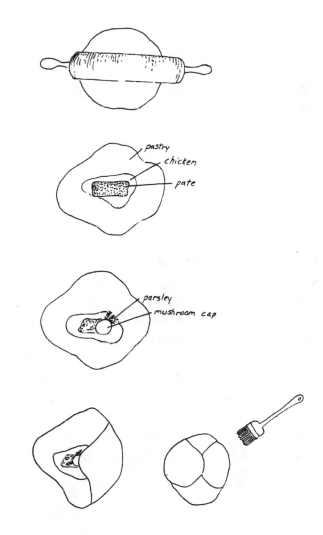

===CHICKEN WITH PORTABELLA, SPINACH AND ONIONS IN PASTRY

This dish seems like a lot of work, but it is not that bad. Do each step ahead, then bake just before dinner.

2 whole chicken breasts, skinned, boned, halved, flattened,
    with fat removed
1/2 cup breading crumbs, page 75
4 tablespoons olive oil
Flour for rolling pastry and dusting casserole
2 Pepperidge Farm patty shells, thawed (puff pastry sheets
    can be used also)
1 tablespoon butter
1 medium onion, peeled and thinly sliced
1 tablespoon dry sherry
2 medium portabella mushrooms, stems removed, wiped clean
1 tablespoon butter
2 cloves garlic, minced
2 cups tightly packed, trimmed, fresh spinach
2 ounces blue cheese or Gorgonzola cheeze
Water for sealing pastry
1 egg beaten with 1 teaspoon milk in a small bowl

PREPARATION
1. Place crumbs in a flat dish and press chicken into crumbs,
   coating completely.
2. Heat 1 tablespoon olive oil over medium heat in a skillet;
   sauté breaded chicken on both sides until just cooked. Cool.
3. In the same sauté pan that the chicken was cooked in, melt
   1 tablespoon butter and add onions; sauté slowly for about
   20 minutes or until onions are soft and brown. Add sherry and
   cook until all liquid is evaporated. Cool. Put cooled onions
   in a strainer and drain. Set aside.
4. Heat same sauté pan, add 2 tablespoons olive oil; sauté
   the portabella on both sides until slightly softened. Cool.

Chicken with portabella, spinach and onions in pastry continued-

5. In the same sauté pan that the portabellas were cooked in melt 1 tablespoon butter over medium heat. Sauté garlic for just a minute, stir in spinach, and cook until wilted. Cool.
6. On a floured board roll thawed puff pastry shells into 8-inch rounds. Place between sheets of plastic wrap. Keep in refrigerator until ready to use.

ASSEMBLY
1. Thinly oil and flour an insulated cookie sheet or an ovenproof casserole dish.
2. On a flat surface, lay out pastry on plastic wrap. Place 1 cooked chicken breast in the middle of pastry. Top evenly with cooked onion and portabella mushroom. Top with other cooked chicken breast, top with spinach and blue cheese.
3. Wrap chicken like a package. Seal seams with water. Do this with each portion.
4. Spread egg wash on pastry with your fingers or pastry brush. Place the puff pastry package on prepared cookie sheet.
5. Bake on middle rack in a preheated 400° oven for 20 minutes.
6. Remove cooked chicken package from cookie sheet to heated plates with a spatula.

If baking in a convection oven cut cooking time about 5 minutes, or until crust is nice and brown.

"I didn't have paprika so I used another spice.
I didn't have potatoes so I substituted rice.
I didn't have tomato sauce so I used tomato paste;
(A whole can, not a half can: I don't believe in waste.)
A friend gave me this recipe and said "you just can't beat it.
There must be something wrong with her, I can't even eat it!"
Unknown

FENNEL CHICKEN

Fennel is cultivated throughout the Mediterranean and in the Americas. It has a bulbous, broad base that can be eaten raw or cooked. The greens of this plant can be used like dill, for delicate flavors, or as a garnish.

2 whole chicken breasts, skinned, boned, halved, flattened,
    with fat removed
2 tablespoons olive oil
1/2 cup breading crumbs, page 75
1 tablespoon butter
1 (1/4-cup) medium onion, peeled and sliced thin
1 fennel bulb, washed, trimmed and sliced thin
1/2 red bell pepper, sliced thin, cored and seeded
1 teaspoon balsamic vinegar
Flour for rolling pastry and dusting casserole
2 Pepperidge Farm patty shells, thawed, (puff pastry sheets can be
    used also)
2 slices American cheese
1/4 cup finely chopped fresh parsley
Water for sealing pastry
1 egg beaten with 1 teaspoon milk in a small bowl

PREPARATION

1. Place crumbs in a flat dish and press chicken into crumbs, coating completely.
2. Heat 1 tablespoon olive oil over medium heat in a skillet; sauté breaded chicken breasts on both sides until cooked. Cool.
3. In the same sauté pan, heat 1-tablespoon butter over medium heat; sauté onion, sliced fennel, and red bell pepper until soft, about 4 minutes. Stir in balsamic vinegar. Cool.
4. On a floured board, roll thawed puff pastry shells into 8-inch rounds. Place between sheets of plastic wrap. Keep in refrigerator until ready to use.

Fennel chicken continued-

ASSEMBLY
1. Oil and flour an insulated cookie sheet or ovenproof casserole dish.
2. On a flat surface, lay out pastry on plastic wrap. Place cooked chicken in middle of puff pastry. Spoon fennel stuffing evenly on each chicken breast. Top with other cooked chicken breast. Top each portion with one slice American cheese and chopped parsley.
3. Wrap chicken like a package; seal seams with water.
    Spread egg mixture on crust with fingers or pastry brush.
4. Place puff pastry package on prepared cookie sheet.
5. Bake on middle shelf of a preheated 400° oven for 20 minutes.
6. Remove cooked chicken package from cookie sheet with a spatula. Serve on heated plates.

If baking in a convection oven cut cooking time down about 5 minutes, or until crust turns a nice brown color.

====HOT PEPPER JELLY CHICKEN IN A CRUST

Jalapeño chilies are named after the city Jalapa, the capital of Veracruz, Mexico. Of all the chili peppers, this variation seems to be the most popular because they are easily seeded. They can be stuffed with cheese, fish, or meat. Many restaurants offer them as appetizers.

2 whole chicken breasts, skinned, boned, halved, and flattened, with fat removed
1/2 cup milk
3/4 cup crushed cornflake cereal for breading
2 tablespoons olive oil
Flour for rolling puff pastry and dusting casserole
2 Pepperidge Farm patty shells, thawed (puff pastry sheets can be used also)
3/4 cup (6-ounces) cream cheese, room temperature
1/2 cup jalapeño jelly (available in super market)
1/4 cup chopped green onions (scallions)
1/4 cup finely chopped fresh parsley
1/4 (2-ounces) cup shredded cheddar cheese
Water for sealing puff pastry
1 egg beaten with 1 teaspoon milk in a small bowl

PREPARATION

1. Place 1/2 cup milk in a small mixing bowl. Add chicken breasts. Put crushed corn flakes in a flat dish and press chicken into crumbs, coating completely.
2. Heat 1 tablespoon olive oil over medium heat in a skillet; sauté breaded chicken breasts on both sides until cooked. Cool.
3. On a floured board, roll thawed puff pastry shells into 8-inch rounds.
4. Place between sheets of plastic wrap. Keep in refrigerator until ready to use.
5. Mix cream cheese with a fork in a mixing bowl to soften, stir in jalapeño jelly, chopped green onions, chopped parsley, and shredded cheddar.

Hot pepper jelly chicken in a crust continued-

ASSEMBLY
1. Oil and flour an insulated cookie sheet or ovenproof casserole.
2. On a flat surface, lay out pastry on plastic wrap, and place one breast in middle of pastry. Spoon and spread 1/4 of the cream cheese mixture on chicken breast, top with other chicken breast and the other 1/4 of the cream cheese mixture. Do this with both portions.
    Wrap chicken like a package, seal seams with water.
3. Spread egg mixture on crust with fingers or pastry brush.
4. Place puff pastry package on prepared cookie sheet.
5. Bake on middle shelf of a preheated 400° oven for 20 minutes.
6. Remove chicken package from casserole with a spatula.

If baking in a convection oven cut cooking time down about 5 minutes, or until crust turns a nice brown color.

"A wonderful culinary experience is savored over and over long after the meal is finished".
                    Author

=====*SPINACH AND THREE CHEESE CHICKEN*

Spinach and three cheeses in puff pastry is certainly an appetizing dish when entertaining. The preparation can be done ahead of time; the package refrigerated and baked just before dinner. If you cannot find smoked mozzarella use the regular mozzarella.

2 whole chicken breasts, skinned, boned, halved, flattened,
   with fat removed
1/2 cup breading crumbs, page 75
3 tablespoons olive oil
1 small onion, chopped
2 cloves garlic, chopped
1 pound spinach, cleaned stems removed and chopped coarsely
1/4 cup grated Parmesan cheese
1/4 cup shredded smoked mozzarella
1/4 cup ricotta cheese
1/4 cup finely chopped fresh parsley
1 tablespoon plain fresh or dried bread crumbs
Flour for rolling puff pastry and dusting casserole
2 Pepperidge Farm patty shells, thawed (puff pastry sheets can
   be used also)
Water for sealing pastry
1 egg beaten with 1 teaspoon milk in a small bowl

PREPARATION

1. Place crumbs in a flat dish and press chicken into crumbs,
    coating completely.
2. Heat 1 tablespoon olive oil over medium heat in a skillet;
    sauté breaded chicken breast on both sides until cooked. Cool.
3. In the same sauté pan heat 1 tablespoon olive oil over medium heat;
    sauté chopped onion and garlic, until onion turns yellow. Stir in
    chopped spinach and cook, while stirring until spinach is wilted. Cool.
4. Into cooled spinach stir in Parmesan cheese, shredded smoked
    mozzarella, ricotta cheese, chopped parsley, and plain bread crumbs.
5. On a floured board, roll thawed puff pastry shells into 8-inch
    rounds. Place between sheets of plastic wrap. Keep in refrigerator
    until ready to use.

Spinach and three cheese chicken continued-

ASSEMBLY
1. Thinly oil and flour an insulated cookie sheet or ovenproof casserole dish.
2. On a flat surface, lay out pastry on plastic wrap. In the middle of pastry place one cooked chicken breast. Spoon spinach-cheese stuffing evenly on each chicken breast. Top with other chicken breast.
   Do this with each portion.
3. Wrap chicken like a package, sealing seam with water.
4. Spread egg wash on crust with fingers or a pastry brush. Place puff pastry package on prepared cookie sheet.
5. Bake on middle rack in a preheated 400° oven for 20 minutes.
6. Remove cooked chicken package from cookie sheet to heated plates with a spatula.

If baking in a convection oven cut cooking time down about 5 minutes, or until crust turns a nice brown color.

Helpful Hint
Wooden spoons make the best stirrers when sautéing. They do not get hot, and will not scratch nonstick coatings. To prevent new spoons from absorbing food smells soak them in cider vinegar overnight.

"Life is simply a matter of concentration; you are what you set out to be. You are a composite of the things you say, the books you read, the thoughts you think, the company you keep and the things you desire to become."

B.C. Forbes

============WATERCRESS CHEESE CHICKEN

*Watercress is a member of the mustard family; it needs cool clean
running water to grow, and is found in and around brooks and streams.
It has a slight bitter and peppery taste. When I think of watercress,
I think of the ladies luncheons of old with their fancy dresses and big hats.*

2 whole chicken breasts, skinned, boned, halved, flattened,
   with fat removed
2 Pepperidge Farm patty shells thawed (puff pastry sheets can be
   used also)
1/2 cup breading crumbs, page 75
2 tablespoons olive oil
Flour for rolling puff pastry and dusting casserole
1/2 cup (4-ounces) cream cheese, room temperature
1/2 cup chopped watercress, trimmed of stems
2 cloves garlic, finely chopped
2 large mushroom caps, without stems, cleaned
1/4 cup finely chopped fresh parsley
Water for sealing pastry
1 egg beaten with 1 teaspoon milk in a small bowl

PREPARATION
1. Place crumbs in a flat dish and press chicken into crumbs,
   coating completely.
2. Heat 1 tablespoon olive oil over medium heat in a skillet;
   sauté breaded chicken breasts on both sides until cooked. Cool.
3. On a floured board roll thawed puff pastry shells into 8-inch
   rounds. Place between sheets of plastic wrap. Keep in refrigerator
   until ready to use.
4. Mix cream cheese with a fork until softened in a mixing bowl;
   stir in chopped watercress and chopped garlic.

Watercress cheese chicken continued-

ASSEMBLY
1. Thinly oil and flour an insulated cookie sheet or ovenproof casserole.
2. On a flat surface, lay out pastry on plastic wrap. Place cooked chicken breast in middle of pastry, spoon and spread watercress stuffing on chicken. Top with other chicken breast, mushroom cap and chopped parsley. Do this with each portion.
3. Wrap chicken like a package; seal seams with water. Spread egg mixture on crust with fingers or pastry brush. Place puff pastry package on prepared cookie sheet.
4. Bake on middle rack in a preheated 400° oven for 20 minutes.
5. Remove cooked chicken package from casserole to heated plates with a spatula.

If baking in a convection oven cut cooking time down about 5 minutes, or until crust turns a nice brown color.

"Appreciation is a wonderful thing; it makes what is excellent in others belong to us as well."
Voltaire

==========TOMATO CHEESE CHICKEN PIZZA

*Puff pastry is a rich, delicate, multilayered French pastry.
It is difficult to make. I find it much easier to purchase it frozen
in the grocery store.*

1 whole chicken breast, skinned, boned, flattened,
   with fat removed
2 Pepperidge farm patty shells, thawed (puff pastry sheets
   can be used also)
Flour for rolling pastry and dusting cookie sheet
1/2 cup breading crumbs, page 75
1 tablespoon olive oil
1 cup tomato sauce (marinara)
1/4 cup chopped fresh basil or 1/4 teaspoon dried basil
1 tablespoon grated Parmesan cheese
2 slices provolone cheese
1/4 cup finely chopped fresh parsley

PREPARATION
1. On a floured board, roll thawed puff pastry shells into 8-inch
   rounds. Place between sheets of plastic wrap. Keep in
   refrigerator until ready to use.

ASSEMBLY
1. Thinly oil and flour a cookie sheet.
2. Place crumbs in a flat dish and press chicken into crumbs,
   coating completely
2. Place rolled puff pastry on cookie sheet; place a chicken breast
   in the center of the puff pastry, crimp pastry around chicken,
   higher than chicken, like a little wall.
3. Spoon and spread tomato sauce evenly on chicken, top with
   basil, Parmesan cheese, provolone cheese, and parsley.
4. Bake in a preheated 400° oven for 20 minutes.
5. Remove cooked chicken pizza from cookie sheet with a large
   spatula.
      *For variety top with any of the pizza toppings,
   a great dish that turns on the kids.*

SEAFOOD SHELLFISH

EPD '90

=====PURCHASING SEAFOOD AND SHELLFISH

Buy the fish last when shopping. Therefore, when you have your cart filled with everything else you need, buy the fish. Make sure the fish counter passes the smell test before you buy anything. Check to see if the fish is stored on ice and price tags should not be sticking out of the fish. When the counter passes all your tests, it's the fish's turn for inspection. Make sure the fish looks firm and request to smell your fish of choice when the store employee takes it out of the case to weigh it. They will look at you like you have two heads, but it is better to do this, than to have to return or throw out the fish when you get home. If the seafood does not meet your standards, select another choice of seafood. If you are planning on scallops and they are not right, change your menu to another choice. After purchasing the seafood, I always ask the clerk to give a small plastic bag of ice. While bagging at the cash register, I put the seafood in the bag with the ice, especially on warm days. If it is easier for you, have a small cooler in your car with ice packs, especially fish and chicken. Store the fish in a bowl on ice in the coldest section your refrigerator.

Seafood is wonderful when it is fresh and cooked properly. Be careful of raw shellfish and fish. Dangerous bacteria can be hiding in raw seafood. If you use frozen fish, thaw it out in the refrigerator not on the counter. You should plan to have seafood that is in the freezer for dinner take it out a day ahead in order to thaw it in the refrigerator.

When you purchase lobsters, store them dry in the bag they came in, keep them the refrigerator. (Do not store them in fresh water.)

Nutrition experts recommend at least two servings of seafood a week. Follow the basic rules in seafood safety and you will enjoy many wonderful seafood meals. In this cookbook, there are many wonderful seafood and shellfish ideas for that memorable meal.

1/2 pound saltine crackers
1/2 pound Ritz crackers
1/4 cup grated Parmesan cheese
1 teaspoon paprika
1/3 cup clarified butter
1/4 cup sherry wine
1/4 cup chopped green onions (scallions)

PREPARATION
1. Add crackers in a food processor using medium shredder disk or steel blade.
2. Add Parmesan cheese and paprika to crackers. Mix with steel blade in food processor, add clarified butter and sherry wine. Pulse by turning machine on and off until blended, add chopped scallions and mix one second. Mixture should be moist but not wet. If too moist add a few more crackers, if to dry add more butter and wine.
3. This tasty topping can be stored in a tight container in the refrigerator for a month.

CLARIFIED BUTTER
Clarified butter loses about one fourth of its original volume.

1. Melt butter in a saucepan. Remove from heat, and allow butter to rest for a few minutes.
2. Spoon the clarified butter from the top and discard milk part. Strain clarified butter (The milk part can be used in mashed potatoes or vegctables).
3. Or refrigerate and remove solid butter on top and discard milk part. Store covered in refrigerator.

One of the nice things about operating a first-class restaurant is being part of our customers' special occasions. While I was working in the kitchen one morning, a young man walked in the back door and asked if he could make a reservation. He wanted to come in at 7:30, because he was going to ask his girlfriend to marry him that evening and wondered if I could do him a couple of favors.

He wanted special flowers at the table and champagne waiting at the table when they were seated. But the important thing was he wanted us to take the engagement ring and freeze it in an ice cube that would be put into her champagne glass.

That evening, the champagne was served and she was given the glass with the special ice cube. As they toasted, she noticed the ice cube and could see something in the ice but she was not sure what it was. As the ice melted, he said, "Will you marry me?" We tried to maintain their privacy from a distance as we watched. The ice melted; she carefully drank her champagne; and then he placed the cold ring on her finger. They married and for many years celebrated their wedding anniversary dinner with us.

We also had a special way to keep track of customers' wedding anniversaries and birthdays. Frank would write their names in the reservation book if he noticed any of those special celebrations that evening. When the new reservation book came in for the New Year, we would enter the special occasion notations on the appropriate days. When a couple came in the following year, he could say "Happy Anniversary" or "Happy Birthday." It would blow their minds that he could remember their special day. Our sneaky system worked very well.

One of the busiest and most stressful times in a restaurant is the time between Thanksgiving and New Year's Day. The day after Thanksgiving, the fall decorations come down, and we put up the Christmas decorations. I love the fall decorations because they made the restaurant so cheerful, with the pumpkins, leaves and bright fall colors. Christmas time is another story: Lights, glitter, poinsettias and Christmas Party time.

In one of the dining rooms, there was a beautiful hand-crafted bay window. I always spent a bit of time on this window since it was the focal point of the room. I bought a large double poinsettia that practically filled the window to give it a festive look.

One evening, a couple of weeks into the Christmas season, I was making the rounds of the restaurant before closing. I went into the room with the bay window and noticed the large poinsettia was gone.

"What happened to the poinsettia?" I asked a busboy who was setting a table nearby. He looked at me in a puzzled way and then told me that a lady who was having dinner with her friends asked him to put the poinsettia in her car. She said her friends had given her the poinsettia as a Christmas gift.

"She was so nice that I helped her put the poinsettia in her car and she tipped me two dollars," he said. I thought to myself, "These ladies probably were having a good time enjoying Christmas cheer and challenged one of them to steal the poinsettia as a joke." Well the joke was on me, because she got the poinsettia and I ended with an empty window.

I found out later that the busboy had walked through the dining rooms, past waiters, waitresses, the host and the coatroom person, out to the parking lot with that poinsettia in his hands. No one questioned what he was doing. I guess if you are bold, you can get away with almost anything.

STRIPED BASS
BLUE FISH

STRIPED BASS AND BLUEFISH

All recipes are written for two in this chapter.

Hints and Suggestions

SKIN SIDE DOWN: The smoother side with a darker color is usually the skin side. If you have any doubts about what side is the skin side, ask the clerk when you purchase the fish.

SKINNING FISH: To skin fish, use a long sharp knife, grasp skin tightly, and move knife forward, keeping it tight against the skin to cut the fish away. (An easier way is to ask the clerk to do it for you.)

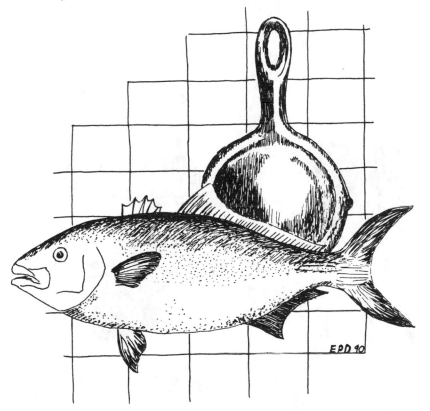

I received a phone call one day from WGBH, a PBS station in
Boston. They were looking for a wine cellar in which to stage an introduction
for a program on California wines and we had the cellar they wanted.

The wine cellar at the Red Rooster is a classic with an old stone
foundation. We chose a Sunday afternoon for the filming. I thought they
would send a couple of technicians and one camera. I was ever so wrong;
two large trucks with much equipment and people arrived to make it happen.
What really surprised me was that the segment was to be hosted by
Peter Graves of "Mission Impossible" fame.

Equipment and wires went through the dining room near the wine
cellar. Our customers started to come in for dinner and wondered what
was going on. The host explained what was going on and then asked if
they wanted a quiet area or if they wanted to be in the middle of the
filming. Almost everyone wanted to see the action.

After filming in the wine cellar, Peter Graves came into the
dining room and visited with everyone. Dinner at the Rooster that day
was more than just dinner. It was theater. I watched the television listings
each week, waiting for that program to air. It finally did, and the introduction
that took all afternoon to film lasted all of 45 seconds.

===============BLOCK ISLAND STRIPED BASS

It was always nice when a local fisherman stopped by the back door of the restaurant with his daily catch. I would always be especially pleased when the catch included a nice 20 pound striped bass.

1 pound striped bass fillets, skinned, checked for bones, cut into
  two servings
1/2 cup whole egg mayonnaise
1/2 cup sour cream
1/4 cup chopped green onions, (scallions)
1/4 cup finely chopped fresh parsley
1 teaspoon lemon juice
1/4 cup seafood crumbs, page 257
1/2 cup water or fish stock

PREPARATION
1. Mix mayonnaise, sour cream, chopped green onions, chopped parsley, lemon juice, and seafood crumbs in a mixing bowl.

ASSEMBLY
1. Select an ovenproof casserole dish just large enough to contain the fish.
2. Place skinned fish in casserole skin side down; add water or fish stock, spoon mayonnaise topping evenly on fish.
3. Bake fish in a preheated 400° oven for 20 minutes.
4. Remove fish to heated plates with a spatula. Spoon a little of the juice around fish.

Note. In the directions, the fish is placed in the casserole skin side down. The skin is removed first, then put in casserole that side down. The top of the fish is the side the topping is spread.

Helpful Hint
When shopping for pots and pans, always look for a thick, heavy bottom so that the heat will be evenly distributed. Pick up the pan and see how heavy it feels. Your investment in good pans will pay off for years.

=========LETTUCE WRAPPED STRIPED BASS

Atlantic striped bass is anadromous, meaning that it migrates from saltwater to spawn in fresh water. It can range in size from 2 to 70 pounds. I love to prepare and cook this wonderful sport fish. The flesh is firm and can be prepared in a variety of ways including broiling, grilling, poaching, and steaming.

1 pound striped bass fillets skinned, checked for bones, cut into
   two servings
2 large iceberg lettuce leaves
Saucepan of boiling water
1/4 teaspoon salt
Dash of white pepper
4 tablespoons butter
1/2 cup chopped green onions, (scallions)
1/2 cup white wine
1/2 cup fish stock of clam juice
1 tablespoon flour
1/2 cup heavy cream

PREPARATION
1. One at a time dip lettuce leaves in boiling water for 30 seconds, Remove to a bowl of cold water to stop cooking. Drain and pat dry on paper towels.
2. Season the bass fillets with salt and pepper. Melt 1 tablespoon of butter over medium heat in a skillet. Sauté the fish for 1 1/2 minutes on each side. Cool.

ASSEMBLY
1. With 1 teaspoon butter, butter a casserole dish just large enough to contain the fish package side by side. Spread green onions evenly over the bottom of the casserole.

Lettuce wrapped striped bass continued–

2. Use a flat surface and spread lettuce leaf flat. Place one piece of fish in the center of the lettuce leaf. Fold in the sides and then the top, wrapping the fish in the lettuce. Do this with both pieces of fish. Place the two lettuce packets seam side down in the baking dish. Pour in the wine and fish stock. Cover with a piece of parchment paper or aluminum foil.
3. Bake the casserole in a preheated 400° oven for 20 minutes.
4. With a slotted spoon, transfer the packets to a warm dish. Cover with aluminum foil to keep warm. Transfer the poaching liquid to a saucepan. Boil over high heat until the liquid is reduced in half.
5. While the liquid is reducing, melt 1 1/2 tablespoons of butter in a small saucepan, stir in flour and cook for 1 minute, or until flour and butter become a paste. Gradually add poaching liquid and cream. Whisk over medium low heat, stirring, until heated through and slightly thickened, do not allow to boil.
6. Place the lettuce-wrapped fish on heated plates and spoon sauce on and around fish packets.

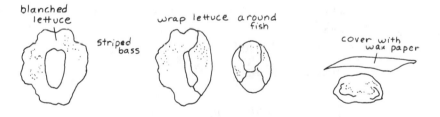

"A room without books is like a body without a soul."
Cicero

LEMON STRIPED BASS WITH PESTO

Prepared pesto is available in the refrigerated section of most supermarkets. Pesto is an uncooked sauce made from fresh basil, garlic, pine nuts, Parmesan cheese, and olive oil. The ingredients can be crushed with a mortar and pestle or processed in a food processor. Pesto should be stored in the refrigerator.

1 pound striped bass filets, skinned, checked for bones, cut into
   two servings.
1/2 cup water or fish stock
1/4 cup pesto
1/4 cup seafood crumbs, page 257
1 small onion sliced thin
6 thin slices lemon, seeds and rind removed
1/4 cup finely chopped fresh parsley
1 teaspoon butter

ASSEMBLY

1. Select an ovenproof casserole dish just large enough to contain
    the fish side by side.
2. Place skinned fish, skin side down in casserole. Add water; spread pesto
    evenly on fish; top pesto with crumbs, sliced onion, sliced lemon
    and chopped parsley. Dot with butter.
3. Bake fish in a preheated 400° oven for 20 minutes or until fish
    flakes easily with a fork.
4. Remove fish from casserole to heated plates with a spatula.

    Spoon a little of the juice around fish.

"Cooking is at once child's play and adult joy.
And cooking done with care is an act of love."
Craig Clairborne

BLUEFISH PERNOD

*Bluefish is found along the Atlantic and Gulf coasts; it has a
fine-textured flesh and can be silver gray in color. Remove the dark
oily strip that runs down the center of the filet to prevent the
flesh from absorbing a strong fishy flavor. Bluefish ranges from
3 to 10 pounds and should be used within a day of being caught.*

1 pound bluefish fillets skinned, checked for bones, cut into
  two servings.
1 small onion peeled, cut in half and sliced thin
Pinch thyme
Pinch pepper
1 red bell pepper, cored, seeded and cut into 1/4 inch strips
1/4 cup Pernod liquor
1/4 cup water or fish stock

ASSEMBLY

1. Select an ovenproof casserole just large enough to contain the
    fish.
2. Place skinned bluefish in casserole, skin side down; top with onion,
    thyme, pepper and top decoratively with red pepper strips.
3. Mix Pernod with water and spoon over prepared bluefish.
4. Bake in a preheated 400° oven, on middle shelf, for 20 minutes.
5. Remove the fish from casserole to heated plates with a spatula;
    spoon juices on and around fish.

Pernod is a yellowish licorice-flavored liqueur from France.

Anisette can be substituted in place of Pernod.

Helpful Hint
*If you need to use a ladder on grass or soft earth, set the legs inside
coffee cans so that they won't sink in while you're on the ladder.*

*"Cookery is my one vanity and I am a slave to any guests
who praises my culinary art."*
Marjorie Kinnan Rawlings

BLUEFISH WITH APPLES

"The blues are running" is a term used in Narraganset Bay, Rhode Island, by fisherman when the bluefish arrive in our waters. They come to this area all at once and, for the fisherman, it's great. They give a good fight and are fun to catch and eat.

1 pound bluefish fillets, skinned, checked for bones, cut into
    two servings
1/4 cup minced onion
2 baking apples, peeled, cored and chopped fine
1 teaspoon lemon juice
2 tablespoons chopped fresh dill or 1 teaspoon dried dill
1 tablespoon Dijon-style mustard
2 tablespoons whole egg mayonnaise
2 tablespoons seafood crumbs page 257
1/4 cup chopped parsley
1 teaspoon butter
1/4 cup water or fish stock

PREPARATION
1. Mix onion, apples, lemon juice, dill, mustard, mayonnaise, crumbs, and parsley in a mixing bowl.

ASSEMBLY
1. Butter an ovenproof casserole dish just large enough to contain bluefish side by side. Place skinned fish, skin side down, add water and spread apple topping evenly on fish.
2. Bake in a preheated 400° oven for 20 minutes.
3. Remove fish from casserole to heated plates with a spatula. Spoon some remaining topping and juice around bluefish.

"Parsley the jewel of herbs, both in the pot and on the plate."
Albert Stockli

Helpful Hint
When cutting flowers from your garden, try to cut them only in the late evening or early morning. Carry a bucket of water with you, after you cut the flowers, immediately submerge the stems in water.

BLUEFISH WITH SESAME

Sesame seeds have a nutty, sweet flavor that makes them versatile in many styles of cooking and baking.

1 pound bluefish fillets, skinned, checked for bones, cut into
   two servings
2 tablespoons butter
1/2 teaspoon grated lemon peel (zest), save juice from lemon
1 tablespoon peeled minced fresh ginger
1/4 teaspoon Oriental sesame oil
1 teaspoon Dijon-style mustard
1/2 teaspoon soy sauce
Dash cayenne
1/4 cup chopped green onions (scallions)
2 tablespoons sesame seeds

PREPARATION
1. Over medium heat, in a medium skillet, melt 2 tablespoons
   butter, stir in grated lemon peel and minced ginger and cook for
   a minute. Stir in lemon juice, sesame oil, mustard, soy sauce,
   cayenne, and green onions. Cool.

ASSEMBLY
1. Select an ovenproof casserole dish just large enough to contain
   the bluefish side by side. Place skinned fish skin side down; spoon
   sauce on and around fish. Spread sesame seeds evenly on bluefish.
2. Bake in a preheated 400° oven for 20 minutes.
3. Remove fish from casserole with a spatula to heated plates.
   Spoon sauce on and around fish.

Helpful Hint
If you are painting indoors, and wish to eliminate the toxic paint smell, stir six drops of pure vanilla extract into a gallon of latex paint. Open the windows to get rid of the toxic fumes. The vanilla neutralizes the paint smell.

ORANGE-FENNEL BLUEFISH

The marriage of these aromatic flavors brings out distinct
flavors to spark up Bluefish or any dark fleshed fish.

1 pound bluefish fillets skinned, checked for bones, cut into
  two servings
1 1/2 teaspoons olive oil
1 1/2 tablespoons lime juice
1 small red onion, halved and sliced thin
1 orange, peeled, sliced and quartered (remove seeds)
1 large fennel bulb, sliced thin
1/2 cup fennel greens, chopped
1 teaspoon butter
1/4 cup water

PREPARATION

1. Mix olive oil, lime juice, onion, orange, fennel bulb, and fennel greens
   in a mixing bowl, coating vegetables with olive oil.

ASSEMBLY

1. Butter an ovenproof casserole dish just large enough to contain
   the bluefish side by side. Place skinned fish skin side down; add water,
   and spread fennel topping evenly on fish.
2. Bake in a preheated 400° oven for 20 minutes.
3. Remove fish from casserole to heated plates with a spatula.
   Spoon remaining topping and juice around bluefish.

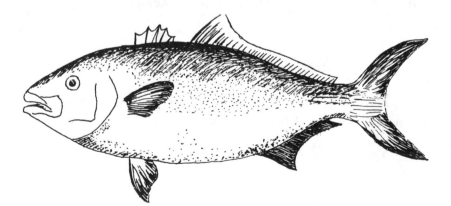

YOGURT BAKED BLUEFISH

Yogurt, a dairy product that is the result of milk that has fermented and coagulated because it's been invaded by friendly bacteria, has been used for centuries for its health benefits.

1 pound bluefish fillets, skinned, checked for bones, cut into
  two servings
1/2 cup plain yogurt
1 teaspoon soy sauce
1/4 teaspoon grated fresh ginger
1/2 teaspoon Dijon-style mustard
1/4 cup finely chopped fresh parsley
1/4 cup chopped green onions (scallions)
1 teaspoon butter
1/4 cup water or fish stock

PREPARATION
1. Mix yogurt, soy sauce, ginger, mustard, parsley, and green onions in a mixing bowl.

ASSEMBLY
1. Butter an ovenproof casserole dish just large enough to contain the fish side by side. Place skinned fish, skin side down, add water, and spread yogurt topping evenly on bluefish.
2. Bake in a preheated 400° oven for 20 minutes.
3. Remove the fish from casserole to heated plates with a spatula, spoon a little of remaining juices around bluefish.

"The time to stop talking is when the other person nods his head affirmatively but says nothing."
Henry S. Haskins

271

COD (SCROD)

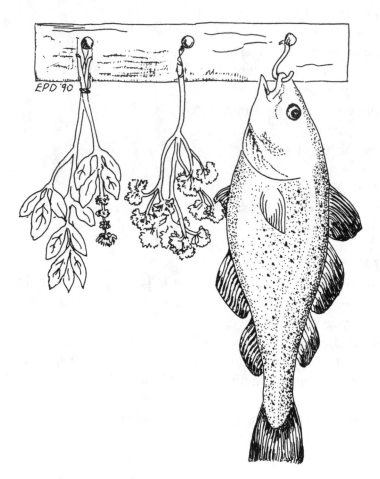

EPD '90

All recipes are written for two in this chapter.

================*Hints and Suggestions*

SKIN SIDE DOWN: The smoother side with a darker color is usually the skin side. If you have any doubts about what side is the skin side, ask the clerk when you purchase the fish.

SKINNING FISH: To skin fish, use a long sharp knife, grasp skin tightly, and move knife forward, keeping it tight against the skin to cut the fish away. (An easier way is to ask the clerk to do it for you.)

THE SAILOR AND THE WAITRESS

In the early 1960s, North Kingstown, Rhode Island, was a busy place. The Navy was here at Quonset Point and between Navy personnel and civilian personnel, the local restaurants were very busy. We fed at least 1,000 people a day at the Chick-n-Pick restaurant.

One evening just about closing time a lone sailor was sitting at the counter, sipping coffee. My sister Terry was the waitress, and this sailor began to make amorous advances toward her. She replied that she was happily married and was not interested. He continued his quest, and she again told him she was not interested.

During the conversation, she was emptying the coffee urn. He said to her, "You — waitresses are all the same." Something clicked in her after that word and before he knew what was happening, he was wearing the gallon of coffee she had in her hand. I ran out to see what the commotion was and there was this sailor in his whites covered in coffee from head to toe. He was burning and she was crying. We had to call the Shore Patrol to make sure he got to the base hospital.

The next day I tried to find out if he was OK but I was not able to get any information. That evening was unusually quiet at the restaurant and I soon found out that the Shore Patrol had put the restaurant off limits as a dangerous place for Navy personnel.

I went to Quonset and spoke to the officer in charge and explained the situation and he lifted the ban and put us back on limits. A few nights later the sailor came back in the restaurant and apologized to my sister. She shook his hand and went back to business as usual.

=================BROILED COD (SCROD)

*Cod (Scrod), one of the most popular saltwater fish, can range
from 1 1/2 pounds to 100 pounds. I always like using the 10 to
15 pounders. Cod comes from the North Atlantic and the
North Pacific. Cod, a versatile fish, lends itself to baking,
poaching, braising, broiling, and frying.*

1 pound cod scrod skinned, checked for bones, cut into two servings
2 tablespoons butter
Juice of a half lemon
1/8 teaspoon paprika
1/2 cup fish stock (clam juice can be used)
Lemon wedges

PREPARATION
1. Melt butter in a small saucepan. Stir in lemon juice and
    paprika.

ASSEMBLY
1. Select an ovenproof casserole dish large enough to contain
    the fish in one layer.
2. Place skinned fish in casserole dish skin side down, add fish stock,
    then brush with butter mixture, leaving excess in casserole.
3. Preheat broiler; broil fish 3 inches from heat for about 6 or 8
    minutes, depending on the thickness of the fish.
4. Remove cooked fish from casserole dish to heated plates with
    a spatula. Spoon a spoonful of the liquid from the bottom of the pan
    on the fish, and garnish with lemon wedges.

*"Food's like street theater–immediate and temporary.
Only difference, thankfully, is that food is every day."*
Betty Fussell

=BLUE CHEESE AND PEPPERCORN COD (SCROD)

Green peppercorn, is a soft, under ripe pepper berry that is usually preserved in brine. They have a flavor that is less pungent than the pepper berry in other forms. They are available in jars and small cans. Once opened, peppercorns should be refrigerated.

1 pound cod scrod, skinned, checked for bones, cut into two servings
1/4 pound blue cheese (Gorgonzola can be used)
2 tablespoons green peppercorns
1/4 cup finely chopped fresh parsley
1/4 cup seafood crumbs, page 257 (or seasoned bread crumbs)
1 cup milk
Dash paprika

PREPARATION
1. Crumble blue cheese with a fork in a mixing bowl. Mix in peppercorns, chopped parsley, and crumbs.

ASSEMBLY
1. Select an ovenproof casserole dish large enough to contain the fish side by side.
2. Place skinned fish in casserole dish skin side down, add milk; spread blue cheese mixture evenly on fish. Sprinkle with paprika.
3. Bake the fish in a preheated 400° oven for 20 minutes.
4. Remove cooked fish from casserole to heated plates with a spatula. Spoon some topping and juices around fish.

Helpful Hint

Cut orange in half, scoop out the pulp; slice the bottom of orange to keep it from rocking. Fill with sherbet for an in-between course, appetizer, or dessert.

CAJUN PECAN COD (SCROD)

Living in the North all my life, when I heard the word Cajun it brought to my mind some sort of music. That was until I visited New Orleans for a culinary conference a few years ago and met Chef Paul Prudhomme. I watched him do a cooking demonstration on Cajun cooking. He heated a large black frying pan until it was very hot and sautéed chicken and fish that were covered with his spices. His style of cooking is still on many menus today. Instead of sautéing, I top the fish with a spicy topping then bake it. In place of cod, use any white fish.

1 pound cod scrod, skinned, checked for bones, cut into two servings
2 tablespoons olive oil
2 teaspoons lemon juice
1/3 cup finely chopped pecans
2 tablespoons grated Parmesan cheese
1 tablespoon dry or fresh plain bread crumbs
1/2 teaspoon thyme
1 tablespoon Cajun seasoning (available in most markets)
2 tablespoons finely chopped fresh parsley
1/2 cup water or fish stock (clam juice can be used)

PREPARATION
1. Mix olive oil, lemon juice, chopped pecans, Parmesan cheese, bread crumbs, thyme, Cajun seasoning, and chopped parsley in a mixing bowl.

ASSEMBLY
1. Select an ovenproof casserole large enough to contain the cod side by side.
2. Place skinned cod skin side down in casserole, add water or fish stock, and spoon the Cajun topping evenly on fish.
3. Bake in a preheated 400° oven for 20 minutes.
4. Remove cooked cod from casserole dish to heated plates with a spatula. Spoon some of the remaining sauce around fish.

CRUMBED COD (SCROD)

This simple recipe highlights the delicate flavor of the Cod Scrod.

1 pound cod scrod, skinned, checked for bones, cut into two servings
1/2 cup wine for fish stock (clam juice can be used)
2 teaspoons fresh lemon juice
1/2 cup seafood crumbs, page 257
Dash paprika
1 teaspoon butter

ASSEMBLY

1. Select an ovenproof casserole dish large enough to contain the cod side by side.
2. Place skinned cod in casserole dish, skin side down. Add wine or fish stock. Top cod with lemon juice, spread crumbs on cod evenly, sprinkle with paprika and dot with butter.
3. Bake in a preheated 400° oven for 20 minutes
4. Remove cooked cod from casserole dish to heated plates with a spatula.

Helpful Hint

You, the host or the hostess, are the best icebreaker at your dinner party. Welcome your guests with enthusiasm and introduce them to all your other guests. The host should start the conversation and make all the guests feel at home.

"All those photographs of great chefs picking out their own tomatoes at quaint little markets are staged. In reality, everything is delivered."

Thomas McNamee

==========CRISPY OVEN BAKED COD (SCROD)

A great way to enjoy the natural flavors of cod scrod. Serve with oven roasted potato wedges.

1 pound center cut cod scrod, skinned, checked for bones, cut into two servings
1 large egg
1 teaspoon whole grain mustard
1/2 teaspoon dried dill
1/4 teaspoon ground red pepper (cayenne)
1/2 cup seasoned dry bread crumbs
1/2 cup yellow corn meal
2 tablespoons olive oil
Lemon wedges
Tartar sauce

PREPARATION
1. Mix egg and whole grain mustard in a small mixing bowl.
2. Mix dill, cayenne, bread crumbs, and corn meal in a mixing bowl.

ASSEMBLY
1. Using 1 tablespoon olive oil, oil casserole dish just
   large enough to contain the fish side by side.
2. Dip fish in egg with a fork, then roll in crumbs, coating
   completely. Place in casserole dish. Drizzle with remaining olive oil.
3. Bake in a preheated 400° oven for 20 minutes.
4. Remove cooked fish from casserole to heated plates
   with a spatula. Garnish with lemon wedges and tartar sauce.

Tartar Sauce is a mixture of mayonnaise, green relish, and chopped capers.

"The test of good manners is to be patient with bad ones."
Gabirol

================COD (SCROD) BAKED WITH A MACADAMIA CRUST

The macadamia tree, native to Australia, named for John McAdam, a chemist who cultivated it, was first grown for ornamental purposes. In the 1880's the macadamia tree journeyed to Hawaii, then to California. Hawaii is now the world's largest macadamia exporter.

1 pound cod scrod, skinned, checked for bones, cut into two servings
1/4 cup fresh lemon juice
2 tablespoons olive oil
1 tablespoon grated onion
1/4 cup chopped fresh parsley
1/2 teaspoon Worcestershire sauce
1/2 cup crushed cornflake crumbs
1/2 cup finely chopped macadamia nuts
1 tablespoon butter

PREPARATION

1. In a small mixing bowl mix, lemon juice, oil, onion, parsley, and Worcestershire.
2. Place fish in a dish large enough to contain it. Spoon lemon juice mixture over fish. Place in refrigerator 30 minutes, turning occasionally.
3. Mix cornflake crumbs and macadamia nuts in a dish.

ASSEMBLY

1. Use 1 teaspoon butter, to butter an ovenproof casserole dish large enough to contain the fish side by side.
2. Press skinned fish into crumbs, covering completely. Place in buttered casserole dish, skin side down. Dot with remaining butter.
3. Bake the fish in a preheated 400° oven for 20 minutes.
4. Remove cooked fish from casserole to heated plates with a spatula.

"Simple pleasures...are the last refuge of the complex."
Oscar Wilde

======COD (SCROD) BAKED WITH VEGETABLES

A wonderful way to enjoy beautifully roasted vegetables and fish.

1 pound cod scrod skinned, checked for bones, cut into two servings
1 tablespoon butter
1 cup sliced mushrooms
1 cup onions, sliced thin
1/2 cup grated carrot
1/2 cup chopped parsley
1/cup chopped green onions (scallions)
1/2 cup white wine or fish stock (clam juice can be used)
1/2 cup seafood crumbs, page 257

ASSEMBLY

1. With half the butter, butter an ovenproof casserole large enough to contain the fish side by side.
2. Add sliced mushrooms, sliced onions, grated carrot, chopped parsley, and chopped scallions in the bottom of the casserole. Place skinned fish skin side down on vegetables. Add wine. Top fish with crumbs, and dot with remaining butter.
3. Bake in a preheated 400° oven for 20 minutes.
4. Remove cooked fish from casserole dish to heated plates with a spatula. Spoon vegetables and liquid on and around fish.

<u>Helpful Hint</u>

The most frustrating experience is removing the price and bar code from glassware and dishes when you purchase them. What I do is place the glassware or dishes in a warm oven (not hot oven) for a couple of minutes, until they are warm. It is amazing how easy the tag peels off.

"The discovery of a new dish does more for human happiness than the discovery of a new star."
        Brillat-Savarin

COD (SCROD) BILL

A vibrant topping that excites the taste buds.

1 pound cod scrod, skinned, checked for bones, cut into two servings
2 tablespoons butter
1 small onion, chopped
1/2 cup red bell pepper chopped, (halved, cored, seeds removed)
1/2 cup chopped green onions (scallions)
1 cup fresh or dried breadcrumbs
1/4 cup chopped fresh parsley
1/2 teaspoon dry mustard
1/2 cup shredded cheddar cheese
1/2 cup white wine or fish stock (clam juice can be used)

PREPARATION

1. Melt 1 tablespoon butter in a medium skillet over medium heat; sauté onion, until yellow. Stir in green onions and chopped peppers; cook for one minute. Remove from heat. Stir in breadcrumbs, chopped parsley, dry mustard, and cheddar cheese. Cool.

ASSEMBLY

1. Butter an ovenproof casserole dish large enough to contain the fish side by side.
2. Place skinned fish in casserole dish, skin side down. Add wine or fish stock. Spread topping on fish evenly.
3. Bake in a preheated 400° oven for 20 minutes.
4. Remove cooked fish from casserole dish to heated plates with a spatula. Spoon any remaining topping and juices on and around fish.

Dry mustard is a finely ground mustard seed; mixed with a little water it becomes a very pungent paste, and can be used in sauces and salad dressings.

*"Success is not so much what you are,
but rather what you appear to be."*
Anonymous

COD (SCROD) EN PAPILLOTE

This dish can be prepared in puff pastry as well.

1 pound cod scrod, skinned, checked for bones, cut into two servings
1 tablespoon butter
1 cup mushrooms, sliced
1/4 cup chopped green onions (scallions)
1 red bell pepper, cored, seeded, and sliced
1 teaspoon lemon juice
1 teaspoon Dijon-style mustard
6 stalks asparagus, trimmed
2 slices American cheese
2 pieces parchment paper 12x12 (aluminum foil can be used)

PREPARATION

1. Melt butter over medium heat in a medium skillet; stir in mushrooms, scallions, and red pepper, sauté until mushrooms are wilted. Stir in lemon juice. Cool.

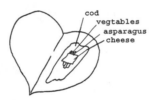

ASSEMBLY

1. Cut 2 large heart shaped pieces of cooking parchment or foil, and place one fish on each piece of parchment, putting it toward the fold so that you can fold a layer of the paper on the top. Spread the fish with mustard, top mustard with sautéed vegetables. Top vegetables with 3 pieces of asparagus and top with slice of American cheese. Crimp the edges. You have a tightly closed package.
2. Preheat oven to 400° and place each parchment package on a cookie sheet, cook for 20 minutes or until parchment is puffed.
3. Serve in parchment on heated plates and cut open with a sharp knife, being careful of the steam when opening package.

Parchment paper is available in most supermarkets.

"Experience is a good teacher, but she sends in terrific bills."
Minna Antrim

================COD (SCROD) HORSERADISH

The mayonnaise and horseradish ends up as a crust on the scrod.

1 pound cod scrod, skinned, checked for bones, cut into two servings
1/4 cup sour cream
1/4 cup whole egg mayonnaise
1 tablespoon prepared white horseradish
1 teaspoon dried dill or 1 tablespoon chopped fresh dill
1/4 cup seafood crumbs, page 257
1 tablespoon butter

PREPARATION
1. Thoroughly mix sour cream, mayonnaise, horseradish, dill, and crumbs in a mixing bowl.

ASSEMBLY
1. Butter an ovenproof casserole dish just large enough to contain fish in one layer.
2. Place skinned fish skin side down in buttered casserole dish. Spread mayonnaise topping evenly on fish.
3. Bake in a preheated 400° oven for 20 minutes.
4. Remove cooked fish from casserole dish to heated plates with a spatula. Spoon any remaining topping from casserole dish around fish.

Mayonnaise is a thick, creamy dressing that is an emulsion of vegetable oil, egg yolks, lemon juice, and seasonings.

Helpful Hint
Here are some tried and true mood enhancers while entertaining. Play some background music that is not loud enough to disrupt, but just nice to hear. Light some candles, lower the lighting, and arrange fresh flowers that are low enough so that you can see the guest on the other side of the table. Set a beautiful table and the most important thing "be relaxed hosts."

"You always pass failure on the way to success."
Mickey Rooney

===============COD (SCROD) ITALIAN STYLE

Fresh basil has a pungent flavor that some describe as a cross between cloves and licorice. A key herb in the Mediterranean kitchen, it has become increasingly popular in the American cuisine. Basil grows easily in the garden, in pots, and during the winter in a sunny window.

1 pound cod scrod, skinned, checked for bones, cut into two servings
1/4 cup water or fish stock (clam juice can be used)
1/4 cup seafood crumbs, page 257
1 cup marinara sauce
1 teaspoon dried basil (or 1/4 cup chopped fresh basil)
1 teaspoon grated Parmesan cheese
2 slices provolone cheese
1/4 cup chopped fresh parsley

ASSEMBLY
1. Select an ovenproof casserole dish large enough to contain the fish side by side.
2. Place skinned fish in casserole skin side down. Add water or fish stock. Spoon seafood crumbs evenly on cod. Spoon marinara sauce evenly on top of crumbs, top with basil, sprinkle with Parmesan cheese; top with provolone cheese and chopped parsley.
3. Bake fish in a preheated 400° oven for 20 minutes.
4. Remove cooked fish from casserole to heated plates with a spatula. Spoon remaining sauce around fish.

Helpful Hint
Keep a dinner party journal; include dates, guest lists, menus, wines, and the purpose of the dinner party. That way you will not repeat the same menu for future dinners. Note any problems or anything interesting that happened during that evening.

"The trouble with eating Italian food is that five or six days later you're hungry again."
P. J. O'Rourke

COD (SCROD) MEXICAN STYLE

Mexican style scrod can capture many taste buds. Cheese,
tomatoes, and the peppers make this dish special.

1 pound cod scrod, skinned, checked for bones, cut into two servings
1/2 cup canned chopped tomatoes, (or fresh tomatoes, seeds and
    skins removed)
1/2 green bell pepper, cored, seeded, and chopped
1/2 red bell sweet pepper, cored, seeded, and chopped
1/4 cup chopped green onions (scallions)
1/2 cup shredded cheddar cheese
1/4 cup seafood crumbs, page 257
Dash ground red pepper (cayenne)
1/2 cup white wine or fish stock (clam juice can be used)

PREPARATION
1. Mix tomatoes, peppers, green onions, cheddar cheese, crumbs, and
    cayenne in a mixing bowl.

ASSEMBLY
1. Select an ovenproof casserole dish large enough to contain
    the fish side by side.
2. Place the fish in casserole dish skin side down, add wine or fish
    stock. Spread tomato topping evenly on fish.
3. Bake in a preheated 400° oven for 20 minutes.
4. Remove cooked fish from casserole dish to heated plates with a
    spatula. Spoon remaining topping around fish.

"Food is our common ground, a universal experience."
James Beard

========================COD (SCROD) THERESE

This dish, is named after my sister Terry who worked for 30 years in my kitchens. She cooked this dish many times in the restaurant. Here are a few variations that can be added to the mayonnaise mixture; 1 teaspoon of mustard, 1 teaspoon chopped sun-dried tomatoes, 1 teaspoon of chutney, 1 teaspoon minced dried apricots, or 1/4 cup minced red sweet peppers.

1 pound cod scrod, skinned, checked for bones, cut into two servings
1/2 cup mayonnaise
1/4 cup sour cream
1/2 teaspoon dried dill
1/4 cup chopped green onions (scallions)
1/4 cup finely chopped fresh parsley
1/2 cup water or fish stock (clam juice can be used)
1/4 cup seafood crumbs page 257

PREPARATION
1. Mix mayonnaise, sour cream, dill, chopped green onion, and parsley in a mixing bowl.

ASSEMBLY
1. Select an ovenproof casserole dish large enough to contain the cod side by side.
2. Place skinned cod in casserole dish, skin side down. Add water or fish stock and spoon crumbs evenly on cod; spread mayonnaise topping evenly on top of crumbs.
3. Bake the fish in a preheated 400° oven for 20 minutes.
4. Remove cooked fish from casserole to heated plates with a spatula.

Helpful Hint
If someone is drinking tea at the table, use a small dish as a receptacle for the dipped, wet teabag.

"Nothing great was every achieved without enthusiasm."
Ralph Waldo Emerson

====COD (SCROD) WITH A PISTACHIO CRUST

Pistachio nuts have a delicate, mild flavor that is great for just eating or for flavoring dishes. Domestic pistachio nuts are cultivated in California. They are either dyed red or blanched white. When you shell the pistachios, use only the nuts that are partly open.

1 pound cod scrod, skinned, checked for bones, cut into two servings
1/4 cup unsalted shelled pistachios
1/2 cup plain fresh or dried bread crumbs
1 tablespoon grated Parmesan cheese
2 tablespoons melted butter
1 tablespoon Dijon-style mustard

PREPARATION
1. Chop the pistachios into medium-fine pieces.
2. Mix pistachios, bread crumbs, Parmesan cheese and
   1 tablespoon melted butter in a mixing bowl with a fork
   until crumbs are evenly moistened.

ASSEMBLY
1. Butter an ovenproof casserole large enough to contain the fish
   side by side.
2. Place fish in casserole skin side down; spread mustard on top of each
   cod fillet. Spoon and spread crumbs evenly on cod fillets.
3. Bake in a preheated 400° oven for 20 minutes.
4. Remove cooked fish from casserole to heated plates with
   a spatula. Enjoy the wonderful aroma.

Helpful Hint
When you need ground nuts, try using your hand-held cheese grater.

"There is no such thing as a great talent without great will-power."
Honore de Balzac

=======COD (SCROD) WITH A CARAWAY CRUST

Caraway seeds have a nutty, delicate anise flavor. They are used extensively in German, Austrian, and Hungarian cuisine.

1 pound cod scrod, skinned, checked for bones, cut into two servings
1/2 cup fresh rye bread crumbs (can be made in food processor)
1 tablespoon Dijon-style mustard
1 teaspoon caraway seeds, finely ground
1 tablespoon chopped fresh parsley
1/4 cup whole egg mayonnaise
1 tablespoon butter

PREPARATION
1. Mix bread crumbs, mustard, caraway seeds, parsley and mayonnaise in a mixing bowl.

ASSEMBLY
1. Butter an ovenproof casserole dish just large enough to contain cod in one layer.
2. Place skinned cod, skin side down in buttered casserole dish. Spoon and spread the caraway topping evenly on the cod.
3. Bake in a preheated 400° oven for 20 minutes.
4. Remove cooked fish from casserole dish to heated plates with a spatula. Spoon any remaining topping from casserole dish around fish.

Helpful Hint
When planning a dinner party, go through a mental "dress rehearsal." Think of every detail from the start to the finish. Think of every dish, napkin, table setting, food, cooking equipment, cocktails, wine, etc. Make a list, shop early for the non-perishables and stay cool. Cook what you do best and enjoy a nice evening with your guests.

*"It is the sauce that distinguishes a good chef. The **saucier** is a soloist in the orchestra of a great kitchen."*
Fernand Point

===COD (SCROD) WITH APPLES AND TOMATO

The aroma from this dish will make your kitchen smell wonderful.

1 pound cod scrod, skinned, checked for bones, cut into two servings
1 tablespoon olive oil
1/2 cup chopped onion
2 cloves garlic, chopped
1 teaspoon curry powder
1 whole clove
1 tablespoon lemon juice
1 green apple, peeled, cored, and chopped
1/2 cup canned diced tomato, (or fresh tomato, skinned and
    seeds removed)
1/2 cup chopped fresh parsley
1/4 cup white wine or fish stock (clam juice can be used)
1/2 cup seafood crumbs, page 257
1 tablespoon butter

PREPARATION
1. Heat olive oil over medium heat in a medium skillet; sauté
   onion and garlic until onion turns yellow. Stir in curry and
   cook for 30 seconds (to develop flavor), then add clove,
   chopped apples, lemon juice, diced tomato, and chopped parsley.
   Cook while stirring for about 5 minutes. Remove clove. Cool.

ASSEMBLY
1. Select an ovenproof casserole dish large enough to contain
   the cod side by side.
2. Place skinned cod skin side down in casserole; add white wine or fish
   stock, and spoon apple topping evenly on cod filets. Top with crumbs
   and dot with butter.
3. Bake in a preheated 400° oven for 20 minutes.
4. Remove cooked cod from casserole dish to heated plates with a
   spatula. Spoon some remaining sauce around fish.

"Everything you see I owe to spaghetti."
Sophia Loren

=======COD (SCROD) WITH CRAB STUFFING

*The word **scrod** comes from the fisherman of old. When the boats came in from a long fishing trip the best fish was on top. Locals called the top fish scrod. Scrod could be haddock, pollock, hake, or cod.*

1 pound cod scrod, skinned, checked for bones, cut into two servings
1/2 cup seafood crumbs, page 257
1/4 cup whole egg mayonnaise
1 (6-ounce) can crabmeat (check for small bones); fresh crabmeat can
   be used as well.
1 teaspoon lemon juice
1/4 cup shredded cheddar cheese
1/4 cup white wine
1/4 cup water or fish stock (clam juice can be used)

PREPARATION
1. Mix crumbs, mayonnaise, crabmeat, lemon juice, and cheddar
   in a mixing bowl.

ASSEMBLY
1. Select an ovenproof casserole dish large enough to contain
   the cod.
2. Place skinned cod in casserole dish, skin side down; add wine and
   fish stock. Spoon and spread crab topping evenly on fish.
3. Bake in a preheated 400° oven for 20 minutes.
4. Remove cooked cod from casserole dish to heated plates with a
   spatula. Spoon some of the juices around cod.

"Without bread,
without wine,
love is nothing."
French Proverb

===COD (SCROD) WITH OLIVES AND TOMATO

The olive branch has long been a symbol of peace. The silvery-leafed olive tree has been considered sacred as far back as the 17ᵗʰ century B.C.. The olive is a small, oily fruit that contains a pit. It is grown for its oil and fruit in subtropical zones.

1 pound cod scrod skinned, checked for bones, cut into two servings
1/2 cup finely chopped onion (scallions)
2 cloves garlic, minced
1 cup diced canned tomato (or diced fresh tomato; seeds and skin removed)
1/4 cup sliced black olives, (pitted)
1/2 cup red bell pepper, cored, seeded and sliced thin
1 tablespoon fresh lemon juice
1/2 cup seafood crumbs, page 257
1/2 cup white wine or water
1 tablespoon butter

PREPARATION
1. Mix chopped onion, minced garlic, diced tomato, sliced olives, sliced red pepper, lemon juice, and crumbs in a mixing bowl.

ASSEMBLY
1. Select an ovenproof casserole dish large enough to contain the cod side by side.
2. Place skinned cod in casserole dish, skin side down. Add water or wine. Spoon tomato topping evenly on cod; dot with butter.
3. Bake fish in a preheated 400° oven for 20 minutes
4. Remove cooked fish from casserole to heated plates with a spatula. Spoon some of the remaining juices and tomato on and around fish.

"Men that can have communication in nothing else can sympathetically eat together, can still rise into some glow of brotherhood over food and wine."
Thomas Carlyle

==============COD (SCROD) WITH PEANUTS

*Peanuts are widely grown throughout the United States;
about half the national crop is used to make peanut butter.
The peanut is actually a legume and not a nut. After flowering,
the plant bends down to earth and buries its pods in the ground.
It is estimated that Americans eat enough peanut butter each
year to cover the floor of the Grand Canyon. One acre of peanuts
can yield more than 30,000 peanut butter sandwiches.*

1 pound cod scrod, skinned, checked for bones, cut into two servings
1/2 cup peanut butter (smooth or chunky)
1 egg
1/4 cup milk
1/4 teaspoon curry powder
1/4 cup chopped fresh parsley
1/4 cup chopped fresh green onions (scallions)
1/2 cup water or fish stock
1/4 cup chopped unsalted peanuts

PREPARATION
1. Mix peanut butter, egg, milk, curry powder, chopped parsley,
   and chopped green onions in a mixing bowl.

ASSEMBLY
1. Select an ovenproof casserole dish large enough to
   contain the cod side by side.
2. Place skinned cod in casserole, skin side down. Add water.
   Spoon peanut butter topping evenly on fish. Sprinkle
   with chopped peanuts.
3. Bake fish in a preheated 400° oven for 20 minutes.
4. Remove cooked cod from casserole to heated plates with a
   spatula. Spoon some of the remaining juices around fish.

*"If people let government decide what foods they eat and what
medicines they take, their bodies will soon be in as sorry a state
as are the souls of those who live under tyranny."*
Thomas Jefferson

293

=====COD (SCROD) WITH SUMMER TOMATOES

Native tomatoes in season are the best for flavor and texture. There is nothing compared to the aroma you get when you pick a fresh tomato from your garden.

1 pound cod scrod, skinned, checked for bones, cut into two serving
1/2 cup water or fish stock, (clam juice can be used)
1/2 cup seafood crumbs, page 257
1/4 cup chopped fresh parsley
2 ripe tomatoes sliced
1 tablespoon grated Parmesan cheese
1 teaspoon butter

ASSEMBLY

1. Select an ovenproof casserole dish large enough to contain the cod side by side.
2. Place skinned cod in casserole dish, skin side down and add water. Top cod evenly with crumbs and parsley, top with sliced tomatoes and grated Parmesan cheese; dot with butter.
3. Bake in a preheated 400° oven for 20 minutes.
4. Remove cooked cod from casserole to heated plates with a spatula.

Helpful Hint

When inviting guests to your home for dinner, it is important to ask them if they have any food allergies or restrictions. It eliminates their embarrassment at the dinner table if you have cooked something they cannot eat.

"Part of the secret of success in life is to eat what you like and let the food fight it out inside."
Mark Twain

COD (SCROD) WITH TOMATO AND SPINACH GREEK STYLE

Enjoy a combination of flavors that include mint. It is a symbol of hospitality. Greek mythology claims that mint was once the nymph Mentha. She angered Pluto's wife Persephone, who turned her into this aromatic herb. There are over 30 species of mint.

1 pound cod scrod, skinned, checked for bones, cut into two servings
1 tablespoon olive oil
1/2 cup finely chopped onion
2 garlic cloves, minced
1/2 cup chopped green onion (scallion)
1/4 cup finely chopped celery
1 carrot, peeled, and sliced thin
1/2 pound fresh spinach, stems removed and chopped coarsely
1/4 cup chopped fresh parsley
1/2 cup canned crushed tomato
1/4 teaspoon dried mint (or 5 fresh leaves chopped)

PREPARATION

1. Heat olive oil in a medium-size skillet; sauté chopped onion and minced garlic until onion turns yellow. Stir in green onions, chopped celery, sliced carrots, chopped spinach, tomatoes, and mint. Simmer for 10 minutes. Cool.

ASSEMBLY

1. Select an ovenproof casserole dish large enough to contain the cod side by side.
2. Place skinned cod in casserole skin side down. Spoon tomato mixture on and around fish. Loosely cover casserole with aluminum foil.
3. Bake in a preheated 400° oven for 20 minutes.
4. Remove cooked cod from casserole dish to heated plates with a spatula. Spoon the tomato mixture and juices on and around fish.

"If you're given champagne at lunch, there's a catch somewhere."
Lord Lyons

=======FETA AND VEGETABLE COD (SCROD)

The aroma and flavors from this dish will certainly excite the taste buds.

1 pound cod scrod, skinned, checked for bones, cut into two servings
1 tablespoon olive oil
1/2 cup chopped onion
1/2 cup thinly sliced green bell pepper (cored, seeded)
1 garlic clove, minced
1/2 cup sliced mushrooms
1 cup canned diced tomato (or diced fresh tomato, seeds and skin removed)
1/4 teaspoon dried oregano
1/4 cup chopped fresh parsley
Pinch red pepper flakes
1/2 cup fish stock or water (canned clam juice can be used)
1/2 cup crumbled Feta cheese

PREPARATION
1. Heat olive oil over medium heat in a skillet; sauté onions for a minute, then stir in minced garlic, mushrooms, and sliced peppers. Cook for about 1 minute. Stir in diced tomato, oregano, parsley, and pepper flakes. Simmer for about 5 minutes over medium heat, stirring occasionally. Cool.

ASSEMBLY
1. Select an ovenproof casserole dish large enough to contain the cod side by side.
2. Place skinned cod in casserole, skin side down. Add the fish stock.
3. Spread tomato sauce on and around cod and top with Feta cheese.
4. Bake cod in a preheated 400° oven for 20 minutes.
5. Remove cooked cod from casserole to heated plates with a spatula. Spoon the tomato sauce on and around cod.

"Wine makes a symphony of a good meal."
Fernande Garvin

PARMESAN COD (SCROD)

*The flavors of Parmesan cheese, sour cream, Tabasco, and
the mild flavor of paprika are rewarding. Paprika, is a powder
made by grinding aromatic sweet pepper pods; the pods are
quite tough, so several grindings are necessary to produce
the proper texture.*

1 pound cod scrod, skinned, checked for bones, cut into two servings
Dash Tabasco
1/4 teaspoon paprika
2 tablespoons grated Parmesan cheese
1/4 cup chopped fresh parsley
1/2 cup sour cream
1/4 cup seafood crumbs, page 257
2 teaspoons butter

PREPARATION
1. Mix Tabasco, paprika, grated cheese, chopped parsley,
    sour cream, and crumbs.

ASSEMBLY
1. With 1 teaspoon butter, butter an ovenproof casserole dish large
    enough to contain the cod side by side.
2. Place skinned cod in casserole skin, side down. Spread Parmesan
    topping evenly on cod; and dot with butter.
3. Bake the cod in a preheated 400° oven for 20 minutes.
4. Remove cooked cod from casserole to heated plates with a
    spatula. Spoon any remaining topping on and around cod.

Helpful Hint
*If you need a larger table after you've used your leaf extensions,
go to the lumberyard and have a rectangular piece of plywood cut
at least half again as long as your table. Place a protective cloth
over your table, and put the plywood on top. Place a layer of cloth
on top of the plywood as a cushion.*

TOMATO FETA COD (SCROD)

Feta cheese is a classic Greek cheese made of sheep or goat milk. It is cured and stored in its own salty whey brine (whey is the watery liquid that separates from the solid cheese). Feta, is often referred to as pickled cheese.

1 pound cod scrod, skinned, checked for bones, cut into two servings
1/4 cup olive oil
1/4 cup white wine
1/4 cup chopped fresh parsley
1 garlic clove, minced
1/4 cup fresh chopped basil or 1/4 teaspoon dried basil
1/4 cup chopped green onions (scallions)
6 slices fresh tomatoes
1/4 cup seafood crumbs, page 257
1/4 cup crumbled Feta cheese

PREPARATION
1. Mix olive oil, wine, parsley, minced garlic, basil, and chopped green onions in a mixing bowl.

ASSEMBLY
1. Select an ovenproof casserole dish large enough to contain the cod side by side.
2. Place skinned cod in casserole skin side down. Top cod with sliced tomatoes. Spoon olive oil sauce on tomatoes, top with crumbs and Feta cheese.
3. Bake cod in a preheated 400° oven for 20 minutes
4. Remove cooked cod from casserole to heated plates with a spatula. Spoon some remaining juices on and around fish.

"Give a man a fish and he will eat for a day. Teach a man to fish and he will eat for the rest of his life."
Chinese proverb

One day a fellow restaurateur, Rose Farina, called to say that she wanted to make reservations for lunch. She was hosting Liberace since he was performing at the local Warwick Musical Theater. We arranged a private room so he would not be bothered.

He walked in wearing jeans and a sweatshirt, no rings and very low key. They had lunch and then I went to meet him. He was very nice and asked if there were any antique shops in the area. He left with the addresses of the shops, and I was pleased to have met him and shaken his hand.

About three hours later, I received three phone calls thanking me for sending him to their shops. He had bought out all the merchandise in those shops. At the time, he owned an antique shop in Las Vegas and was stocking it.

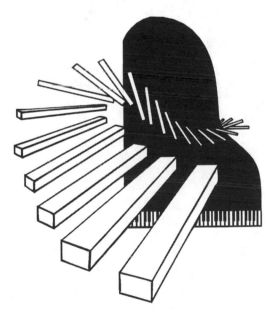

HALIBUT

===============*Hints and Suggestions*

SKIN SIDE DOWN: The smoother side with a darker color is usually the skin side. If you have any doubts about what side is the skin side, ask the clerk when you purchase the fish.

SKINNING FISH: To skin fish, use a long sharp knife, grasp skin tightly, and move knife forward, keeping it tight against the skin to cut the fish away. (An easier way is to ask the clerk to do it for you.)

PARCHMENT PAPER: Parchment paper is available in any good cooking store or market. If you cannot find it, aluminum foil works as well.

THE DISHWASHER AND THE LOBSTERS

The dishwashing staff at a restaurant is usually made up of kids 16 years old and older, and it's usually their first job. Many times we hired dishwashers who were friends of employees, and, for the most part, that worked out well.

But this one time we hired a dishwasher without an inside recommendation. He seemed to fit in just fine, or so I thought, until one night I saw him leaving the restaurant carrying a bag. I asked him what he had in the bag and he kind of shrugged his shoulders. So I asked him to open the bag, and to my surprise it was full of lobsters.

"What are you doing with those lobsters?" I asked and he replied, "I guess I finally got caught!" Naturally I had to discharge him.

The next day his mother called and asked why I fired her son. I told her and she said, "You should give him his job back, and next time he takes things just take it out of his pay."

I think she was just afraid that she would never taste lobsters again!

ITALIAN STYLE HALIBUT

Beautiful halibut is baked with the hearty flavors of red peppers,
garlic, marinara sauce, and provolone cheese. Marinara sauce can be
your own family favorite or you can use the many selections
(all ready made) from the supermarket.

1 pound halibut fillets, skinned, boned, cut into two servings
1 tablespoon olive oil
1/2 cup chopped onion
1/2 cup chopped red bell pepper, cored and seeded
1/2 cup chopped green onions (scallions)
2 garlic cloves, minced
1/4 cup chopped fresh parsley
1/4 teaspoon dried basil
1 cup marinara sauce
1/4 cup seafood crumbs, page 257
4 thin slices provolone cheese
1/2 cup white wine or fish stock (clam juice can be used)

PREPARATION
1. Heat olive oil over medium heat in a medium skillet; sauté
   chopped onion and cook for just a minute. Stir in chopped pepper,
   green onions, garlic, parsley, and basil; sauté while stirring
   for 2 minutes. Stir in marinara sauce and simmer for about 5 minutes.
   Stir in crumbs. Cool.

ASSEMBLY
1. Select an ovenproof casserole dish large enough to contain
   the halibut.
2. Place skinned halibut in casserole dish, skin side down.
   Add white wine or fish stock. Spread the sauce evenly on the fish.
   Top with provolone cheese.
3. Bake in a preheated 400° oven for 20 minutes.
4. Remove cooked halibut from casserole dish to heated plates
   with a spatula. Spoon the sauce on and around halibut.

GARDEN STYLE HALIBUT

A pleasing one-dish meal and all the vegetables are included.

1 pound halibut fillets, skinned, boned, cut into two servings
1/2 red bell pepper, cored, seeded and sliced thin
1/4 cup chopped fresh parsley
1/2 cup diced fresh tomato, skin and seeds removed
   (or diced canned tomato)
1 small onion, peeled cut in half and sliced
1 small zucchini, sliced thin
1/4 teaspoon tarragon
1/2 cup sliced mushrooms
1/2 cup white wine
1/4 cup seafood crumbs, page 257
1 teaspoon butter

PREPARATION
1. Mix sliced red pepper, parsley, tomato, onion, zucchini, tarragon, sliced mushrooms, and wine in a mixing bowl.

ASSEMBLY
1. Select an ovenproof casserole dish large enough to hold the halibut and vegetables.
2. Place the skinned halibut in the casserole, dish skin side down, spread crumbs evenly on fish. Spoon vegetables around halibut, dot with butter.
3. Bake in a preheated 400° oven for 20 minutes.
4. Remove cooked halibut from casserole dish to heated plates with a spatula. Spoon vegetables and sauce on and around halibut.

"Wherever I sit is the head to the table."
Henry Louis Mencken

HALIBUT FLORENTINE

A rewarding recipe that accents delicate flavors.

1 pound halibut fillets, skinned, boned, cut into two servings
1 teaspoon butter
1/4 cup chopped onion
1/2 pound fresh spinach, trimmed, washed, and rough chopped
Dash nutmeg
1/4 cup seafood crumbs, page 257
1/2 cup white wine or fish stock, (clam juice can be used)
4 thin slices Monterey Jack cheese

PREPARATION
1. Melt butter in a skillet over medium heat; sauté onion until golden.
    Stir in spinach and nutmeg, sauté until spinach is wilted,
    then stir in crumbs. Cool.

ASSEMBLY
1. Select an ovenproof casserole dish large enough to contain
    the halibut.
2. Place the skinned halibut in casserole dish, skin side down
    and add wine. Spread spinach evenly on halibut, top spinach
    with Monterey jack cheese.
3. Bake in a preheated 400° oven for 20 minutes.
4. Remove cooked halibut from casserole dish to heated plates
    with a spatula. Spoon some remaining juices on and around fish.

Helpful Hint
*In busy households where the microwave sees a lot of use,
splattering of food in the microwave can be messy. Scrubbing
sometimes can be difficult and can damage the interior surfaces.
Place a microwave safe bowl of water in the microwave and heat
it on high heat for 10 minutes or a little longer, depending on the
dried food. The steam loosens the dried particles and they can be
wiped off with a paper towel.*

=HALIBUT OVEN POACHED IN LETTUCE LEAVES

*Halibut are abundant in the northern Atlantic and Pacific waters.
A large member of the flatfish family, it can weigh up to 1000 pounds.
Most halibut caught are 50 to 100 pounds. I love cooking halibut;
the flesh is white, firm, and mild flavored. Halibut is a great inspiration
for a chef's creativity.*

1 pound halibut fillets, skinned, boned, cut into two servings
2 Iceberg lettuce leaves, large enough to wrap fish
   (blanched and ribs removed)
1 leek, white part only, washed and cut in crosswise slices
1 carrot, peeled, cut in thin angled slices
4 mushrooms, sliced
2 teaspoons sour cream
1/2 teaspoon dried dill or
1 teaspoon chopped fresh dill
1 cup white wine or fish
   stock (clam juice can be used)
2 teaspoons butter

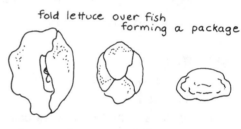

ASSEMBLY

1. Spread blanched lettuce leaves on work surface and arrange each
   serving of fish in the middle of each lettuce leaf. Top each halibut
   fillet, top with leeks, carrots, mushrooms, sour cream, and dill.
   Fold each lettuce leaf over, enclosing halibut completely.
2. Select a covered ovenproof casserole dish large enough
   to contain the two lettuce packages.
3. Place lettuce packages in casserole. Add white wine, dot with
   butter, and cover casserole.
4. Bake in a preheated 400° oven for 20 minutes, or simmer in a
   covered skillet on top of range on medium heat for 15 minutes.
5. Remove halibut packages from casserole dish to heated plates with
   a spatula. Spoon sauce on and around fish.

*To blanch lettuce: dip lettuce in boiling water for 30 seconds;
then plunge into cold water to stop cooking. Drain and pat dry.
Trim large ribs from cored end of lettuce.*

=============HALIBUT WITH FRESH FENNEL

*Halibut fillets are boneless. I liked to use fillets because the
dinner never had to worry about bones. Halibut steaks
have the small center bone. Halibut steaks are great grilled.*

1 pound halibut fillets, skinned, boned, cut into two servings
1 tablespoon butter
1/2 cup sliced onion
1 fennel bulb, white part sliced thin (washed)
1/2 cup white wine or fish stock (clam juice can be used)
1 cup canned diced tomato, drained or fresh tomato, peeled, and diced
   diced, peeled and seeded
1 garlic clove, minced
1/4 teaspoon dried thyme
1/4 cup chopped fresh parsley
1/2 cup half-and-half cream or evaporated milk

PREPARATION
1. Melt butter over medium heat in a skillet; sauté onion until soft.
   Stir in sliced fennel and sauté while stirring for a minute.
   Add wine and cook for about 10 minutes until the fennel is tender.
   Stir in chopped tomatoes, garlic, thyme, parsley, and cream. Cool.

ASSEMBLY
1. Select an ovenproof casserole dish just large enough to
   contain the halibut.
2. Place skinned halibut in casserole dish, skin side down;
   spoon fennel sauce on and around halibut.
3. Bake in a preheated 400° oven for 20 minutes.
4. Remove cooked halibut from casserole dish to heated plates
   with a spatula. Spoon fennel and sauce on and around halibut.

Fennel bulbs are usually available in most markets.

"Dinning is and always was a great artistic opportunity."
Frank Lloyd Wright

======HALIBUT WITH LEEKS IN PARCHMENT

Aluminum foil can be used instead of parchment paper.

1 pound halibut fillets, skinned, boned, cut into two servings
1 tablespoon olive oil
2 slender leeks, white part only, washed and cut into
   match stick size strips (julienne)
1 medium red bell pepper, cored and seeded, and cut into thin slices
6 mushrooms, sliced thin
1/4 teaspoon tamari or soy sauce
1 teaspoon minced fresh thyme or 1/4 teaspoon dried
2 sheets of parchment about 12 inches by 12 inches or
   aluminum foil

PREPARATION

1. Heat olive oil in a medium skillet, add leeks and pepper strips.
   Sauté for about 2 minutes or until vegetables are soft; add
   sliced mushrooms, cook for another minute. Stir in soy sauce
   and thyme. Cool.

ASSEMBLY

1. Fold each parchment in half. Starting at the bottom, cut out
   and around to make a half-heart shape. Open each sheet and place
   one piece of halibut against the fold. Divide the leek mixture
   with a little of its liquid and place on the fish.
   Fold the parchment starting at the point and continue to fold.
   Then crimp the edges to seal into loose packets.
2. Place packets on a cookie sheet and bake in a preheated 400°
   oven for 20 minutes.
3. Transfer packets to heated plates and, with a knife, slit open.
   Be careful of the steam.
   Parchment paper is available in most supermarkets.

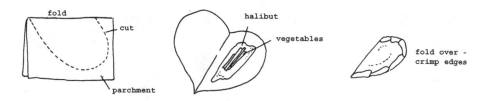

The most challenging and busiest day of the year at a restaurant is usually Mother's Day. Getting through the day is difficult enough without a major disaster. Mother's Day is especially interesting because the clientele is large tables of families, including children, parents and grandparents. Therefore, the menu must satisfy everyone.

One Mother's Day, things were going well until about 5 in the afternoon when a little girl went to the bathroom and flushed her doll down the toilet. The doll got caught in the sewage pipe and blocked up the pipes in all of the rest rooms. We had to close down both rest rooms. We were lucky that the kitchen was on another pipe so that we were able to keep cooking.

However, closing down rest rooms on such a day was a disaster. We had a bathroom in the office on the second floor, and Frank, the host that day, had to take reservations for customers to use the restroom on the second floor. He not only had a constant line at the door of people waiting for their dinner reservations, but also had to keep the line in order for the bathroom.

We finally finished Mother's Day and we had to get Roto-Rooter to clean out the sewage pipe. We lost the rest rooms for the day and the little girl lost her doll. It's just incredible what one little thing can do to disrupt an entire restaurant.

LOBSTER

All recipes are for two in this chapter.

============*Hints and Suggestions*

STORING LOBSTERS: Lobster is at its very best when cooked live.
Do not store them in fresh water. They will keep overnight in a bag in
the refrigerator. Lobsters should be killed just before cooking.

TOMALLEY: The soft, pale green material in the body is called the
tomalley, When cooked, tomalley has a rich, slightly sweet taste and is
wonderful when added to a stuffing. It functions as the lobster's liver,
protecting it against pollutants, so tomalley should not be eaten regularly,
but occasionally.

ROE: The roe comes from female lobsters. A female lobster's eggs are
dark green when raw and turn red when thoroughly cooked, at which
point they are known as "coral." Coral has a mild flavor and is often
used as a coloring agent in lobster bisque and stuffings.

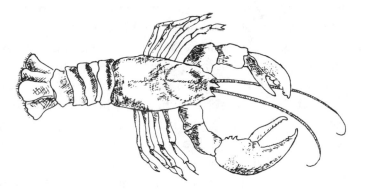

=ENJOYING DINNER WITH TWO GREAT LADIES

Christine Hennessey, a well-known ballet dancer who came from Rhode Island, was the sister of Frank Hennessey, my partner at the Red Rooster Tavern. After Christine retired from being prima ballerina at the Winnipeg Ballet Company in Canada, she came back to Rhode Island to open a ballet school. She had worked with Agnes deMille in several projects and Miss de Mille was invited to Rhode Island College to see their production of *Oklahoma*.

Christine asked me if I would escort Miss deMille at dinner and the performance. She had suffered a stroke and had a tough time getting around, so of course I said yes. It was such a pleasure sitting next to such a wonderful lady at dinner and then at the theater. The college actors worked so hard to show her a great production. She enjoyed the performance and afterwards was invited to a cast reception honoring her. I was so proud to be her escort that evening.

◇◇◇◇◇◇

I have been a member of the International Association of Culinary Professionals for 11 years. Every year we have a conference in a different city. To see Julia Child being a part of the conference is a shock at first, but she is everywhere. Seeing her becomes a special part of the conference.

In the year 2000, we had the conference here in Rhode Island, chaired by Nancy Barr, a good friend of Julia's. Julia and the mayor of Providence announced the site two years before the actual event. So for two years, we, the host committee, had many meetings to organize this monumental task.

To make it interesting, we held meetings in different places. I hosted one meeting and had a cookout. Susan Sampson from Sakonnet Vineyards hosted another meeting. Julia was at that meeting. She had come down from Cambridge for the day. Nancy Barr invited a few of us to go to Back Eddy, a restaurant in Westport, Massachusetts, owned by Chris Schlesinger.

Chris's restaurant, the East Coast Grill in Cambridge, Massachusetts, is a restaurant that Julia enjoys. When we arrived, Julia needed a little help walking into the restaurant. I just happened to be next to her and took her arm as we walked in through a full restaurant to our table. The restaurant quieted down to a whisper as she walked through. What a presence that lady has, and I was proud to be walking with her. I felt ten feet tall. It was a great culinary evening since Chris sent out many samples of his fine cuisine. I have since sat at Julia's table four times and the feeling has always been special.

=========================STEAMED LOBSTERS

Unless you are a purist about eating a whole lobster, most restaurants will take the lobster apart for you. You can do this as well at home. On a cutting board, place the lobster (be prepared for the juice to flow out of the lobster) then remove the claws and tail. With a large knife split the tail into two pieces, then take the claws and, with the back of the knife, crack them open. Stand the head part on the plate and surround it with tail and claws. The lobster is easier to eat and less messy. Use your hands, a nutcracker, and a small fork to remove all the meat.

2 lobsters, 1 1/4 to 1 1/2 pounds each
2 cups water
1 teaspoon sea salt
1/4 pound melted butter
Lemon wedges

ASSEMBLY

1. Select a pot with a tight-sealing lid, large enough to hold the two lobsters.
2. Add water and salt to the pot and bring to a boil. Place live lobsters in the pot (be careful of the steam) and cover.
3. Cook lobsters about 12 minutes. Add 5 minutes for each additional 1/2 pound of lobster.
4. Remove cover (be careful as the steam will be hot); remove lobsters to heated plates.
5. Serve with melted butter and lemon wedges.
6. Serve with individual nutcrackers and a bowl for the shells.

====CHILLED LOBSTER IN A HALF OF MELON

Crabmeat or chopped cooked shrimp can be used instead of lobster; this is great for a summer lunch or dinner.

1 large ripe melon, cantaloupe, honeydew, or any melon
1 apple peeled, cored, and sliced thin
1/4 cup chopped pecans (optional)
1/4 cup mayonnaise
1/4 cup sour cream
1/4 cup chopped green onions (scallions)
3/4 pound fresh cooked lobster meat, cut into bite-size pieces

PREPARATION
1. Using a small paring knife, flute the melon in half, or just cut in half. Remove seeds and take a slice off the bottom to keep flat. Keep refrigerated until ready to use.
2. Mix sliced apple, pecans, mayonnaise, sour cream, and chopped green onions in a mixing bowl; stir in lobster. Keep in refrigerator until ready to use.

ASSEMBLY
1. Spoon chilled lobster mixture into melon halves. Garnish plate with cherry tomatoes, lettuce, and lemon wedges.

Cook the lobsters the same as steamed lobsters (page 313).

Cool and remove meat from shells.

"No act of kindness, no matter how small, is ever wasted."
AESOP

SUMMER LOBSTER SALAD

Lobster is considered the king of the crustacean family. In many restaurants dining on a lobster dinner is the ultimate dinner. On Mothers Day and New Years Eve, we served more lobsters than on any other day of the year. The most popular variety in the country is the Maine Lobster. We are very lucky here in Rhode Island; these lobsters are available in our local waters.

1 pound fresh cooked lobster meat, cut up into bite-size pieces
1/4 cup mayonnaise
1/4 cup sour cream
Dash white pepper
1/4 cup chopped fresh parsley
1/4 cup chopped green onions, (scallions)
1/4 cup finely chopped celery
1/4 teaspoon dried or fresh dill
Garnish for plate, lettuce and cherry tomatoes

ASSEMBLY

1. Mix mayonnaise, sour cream, pepper, parsley, green onion, celery, and dill in a mixing bowl; stir in lobster
   Store in refrigerator until ready to use.
2. Spoon lobster salad on garnished plates.

To prepare lobster meat, cook lobsters the same as steamed lobsters (page 313). Cool and remove meat from shells.

"The torch of love is lit in the kitchen."
French Proverb

=LOBSTER RED ROOSTER FISHERMAN STYLE

We served many thousand Red Rooster style fisherman lobsters at the restaurant. The words in this recipe are many, but it is not that hard to do. The lobsters can be prepared ahead and stored in the refrigerator. Remove lobsters from refrigerator 1/2 hour before baking.

2 live lobsters, 1 1/2 to 2 pounds each
1/2 pound scallops
2 large shrimp peeled, deveined, and tails off
2 1/2 cups seafood crumbs, page 257
1 cup melted butter
2 1/2 cups water
1 teaspoon sea salt or regular salt

PREPARATION

1. On a cookie sheet with sides to contain the liquid in lobsters, place the lobsters on their back and kill the lobsters with a sharp knife just where the tail starts.
   Cut the lobsters down the center, between the claws. Remove claws, keeping elastic band on until you have removed the claws, then remove elastic. With your fingers carefully split the lobster open, being careful not 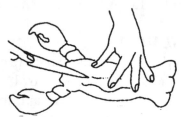 break the back. Remove sack near the head and discard. Leave the roe and tamale if you wish. Put prepared lobster in refrigerator until ready to stuff.
2. Cook the claws in one cup of water for 10 minutes in a covered pan. Cool claws in cold water. Use a nutcracker to remove all cooked meat from claws. Remove small bone in claw meat.

claws
removed

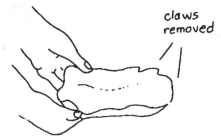

Lobster Red Rooster Fisherman style continued-

ASSEMBLY
1. Select an ovenproof pan (such as a lasagna pan) large enough to contain the lobsters.
2. Place lobsters in pan, add scallops in tail part, add cooked lobster claw meat in middle, and place raw shrimp in head section.
3. Press seafood crumbs on top of seafood. Spoon 1/2 cup melted butter on crumbs and add 1 1/2 cups water and salt to pan.
4. Cover with aluminum foil and press around edges to seal casserole pan.
5. Bake lobster in a preheated 425° oven for 30 minutes. Remove aluminum foil carefully from pan, being careful of the steam. Return pan to oven for about 5 minutes.
6. Remove lobsters to a large heated plate with a spatula in the front of the lobster and hold the tail with a towel.
7. Serve with remaining melted butter and lemon wedges.

The largest lobster caught on record was trapped off Nova Scotia, Canada, on February 11, 1977, it weighed 44 pounds 6 ounces and was three feet six inches long from the end of the tail fan to the tip of the large claw. The lobster was sold to a New York restaurant.

"When you teach your son, you teach your son's son."
The Talmud

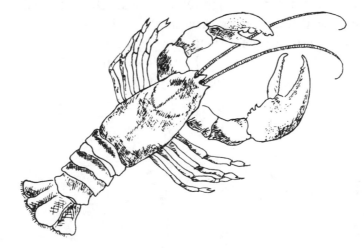

317

=================LOBSTER THERMIDOR

Lobsters should be cooked close to the day of purchase. Do not put them in fresh water. They will keep overnight in a bag in the refrigerator. Lobsters must be cooked live or killed before cooking. It is believed that Napoleon's chef created this dish.

2 lobsters, 1 1/2 to 2 pounds
1 tablespoon butter
1/2 cup sliced mushrooms
1/2 cup chopped green onions (scallions)
1 (10-ounce) can lobster bisque or shrimp bisque
1/4 cup milk
1 teaspoon Dijon-style mustard
6 small mushroom caps
1/2 red bell pepper, cored, seeded, and sliced in eight slices
2 teaspoons grated Parmesan cheese
Paprika
1 cup water

PREPARATION
1. Steam lobster (see page 313). Cool lobster in cold water.
2. Remove claws, put lobster on its back and cut with a sharp knife from top to bottom. With your fingers, carefully split the lobster open, do not break the back. Remove sack near the head and discard. Remove meat from tail with a small fork; remove roe and tamale. Carefully wash inside of shell.
3. Crack claws with a nutcracker and remove meat. Discard small bone inside claw. Cut all lobster meat into bite size pieces. Keep lobster meat in refrigerator until ready to use.
4. Melt 1 teaspoon butter on medium heat in a skillet; sauté sliced mushrooms and green onions until mushrooms are wilted. Cool

Lobster Thermidor continued-

ASSEMBLY

1. Mix lobster bisque, mustard, and milk in a mixing bowl.
   Stir in cooled mushrooms and lobster meat.
2. Select an ovenproof pan (such as a lasagna pan) large enough to
   contain the lobsters.
3. Place lobster in pan. Spoon lobster mixture into lobster shells
   evenly. Alternate the mushroom caps and sliced pepper on top
   of the lobster. Sprinkle with Parmesan cheese, dot with
   remaining butter and color with paprika. Add 1 cup of water to pan.
4. Bake lobster in a preheated 400° oven for 15 to 20 minutes or
   until heated through.
5. Remove to heated plates with a large spatula in the front of
   lobster and hold the tail with a towel.

Garnish with greens, lemon halves, and cherry tomatoes.

"When two men in business always agree,
one of them is unnecessary."
William Wrigley, Jr.

SALMON

All recipes are written for two in this chapter.

Salmon Continued-

================*Hints and Suggestions*
SKIN SIDE DOWN: The smoother side with a darker color is usually the skin side. If you have any doubts about what side is the skin side, ask the clerk when you purchase the fish.
SKINNING FISH: To skin fish, use a long sharp knife, grasp skin tightly, and move knife forward, keeping it tight against the skin to cut the fish away. (An easier way is to ask the clerk to do it for you.)
REMOVING BONES: Salmon have small needle-size bones; which you can feel with you fingers. Use needle-nose pliers, or tweezers to remove bones.

APPLE SALMON IN PUFF PASTRY

American cheese is great in puff pastry recipes because it melts into a sauce.

1 pound salmon fillets, skinned, boned, cut into two servings
Oil for cookie sheet
Flour for rolling pastry and dusting cookie sheet
2 Pepperidge Farm patty shells, thawed (or puff pastry sheets)
1 tablespoon apple jelly
1/2 apple, peeled, cored, and cut into 6 slices
1/2 teaspoon dried dill or 2 teaspoons chopped fresh dill
1/4 cup chopped green onions (scallions)
2 slices American cheese
Water for sealing pastry
1 egg beaten with 1 teaspoon milk in a small bowl

PREPARATION
1. On a floured pastry board, roll puff pastry into two 8-inch rounds. Keep puff pastry in plastic wrap in the refrigerator until ready to use.

ASSEMBLY
1. Oil and flour an insulated cookie sheet, or regular cookie sheet.
2. Spread pastry on a flat surface on plastic wrap.
3. In the center of each pastry, place a salmon fillet, spread on apple jelly, top with sliced apple, dill, green onions, and American cheese. Fold the pastry toward the center over the salmon, and wrap like a package, sealing seams with water.
4. Place pastry packages on prepared cookie sheet. Brush with egg wash.
5. Bake in a preheated 400° oven, on middle shelf, for 20 minutes.
6. Remove pastry packages from cookie sheet to heated plates with a spatula.

When using a convection oven, cut cooking time down 5 minutes.

APRICOT-HORSERADISH SALMON

Apricots have been cultivated in China for over 4,000 years.
California produces about 90 percent of the American crop.
The apricot is a relative of the peach.

1 pound salmon fillets, skinned, boned, cut into two servings
1/2 cup fresh bread crumbs
1/4 cup apricot jam
2 teaspoons prepared white horseradish
1/4 cup apple cider or apple juice
1 tablespoon butter

PREPARATION

1. Mix bread crumbs, apricot jam, horseradish, and cider in a
   mixing bowl.

ASSEMBLY

1. Butter an ovenproof casserole large enough to contain the
   skinned salmon, place salmon skin side down. Spread the
   apricot-horseradish topping evenly on salmon.
2. Bake in a preheated 400°oven for 20 minutes.
3. Remove salmon from casserole dish to heated plates with
   a spatula. Spoon any remaining topping and juices around salmon.

=======================BROILED SALMON

When cooking salmon fillets on an outside grill, use a fish rack.
It helps keep the soft salmon from breaking up.

1 pound salmon fillets, skinned, boned, cut into two servings

MARINADE:
1/4 cup olive oil
Juice of half lemon
1/4 cup chopped parsley
1/4 teaspoon dried dill
Pinch white pepper

2 tablespoons butter
1 teaspoon mashed anchovy fillets
1/4 cup chopped fresh parsley
Lemon wedges

PREPARATION
1. Place the salmon fillets in a casserole dish just large enough
   to contain them. Mix marinade in a small bowl, spoon on salmon
   and refrigerate. Take out 1/2 hour before cooking.
2. Cream butter and mashed anchovy in a small bowl.

ASSEMBLY
1. Heat broiler, place salmon on broiler or char-grill, about
   four inches from heat source. Cook about 3 minutes on each
   side, basting with marinade.
2. Spread anchovy butter on bottom of heated plate. Place broiled
   fillets on top of anchovy butter.
   Garnish with parsley and lemon wedges.

If you do not like using the anchovy, leave it out. Add a little
dill and lemon juice to the butter.

> *"Reading mean borrowing."*
> *Georg Christoph Lichtenberg*

=============CINNAMON-APRICOT SALMON

Apricots are grown throughout the world. The kernels of the apricot pits are used in confections and to flavor liqueurs. Apricot kernels are poisonous until roasted.

1 pound salmon fillets, skinned, boned, cut into two servings
1 teaspoon low-sodium soy sauce
1/2 teaspoon minced fresh ginger (peeled)
1/4 teaspoon ground cinnamon
1/2 cup apricot jam or jelly
1/4 cup chopped green onions (scallions)
1 teaspoon white vinegar
1/4 cup water
1 teaspoon butter

PREPARATION
1. Mix soy sauce, ginger, cinnamon, apricot, green onions, vinegar, and water in a mixing bowl.

ASSEMBLY
1. Select an ovenproof casserole large enough to contain the salmon; place skinned salmon, skin side down in casserole. Spoon apricot sauce on and around salmon, dot with butter.
2. Bake in a preheated 400° oven for 20 minutes.
3. Remove cooked salmon from casserole dish to heated plates with a spatula. Spoon some remaining sauce on and around salmon.

"The most important tool in the kitchen is my tasting spoon."
Paul Sale

═══════════════════════════CURRIED SALMON

Pacific salmon is abundant and extremely flavorful; its high fat and soft-textured flesh are a chef's dream. Most salmon come from the Alaskan waters. Fresh salmon is the canvas for some of the world's most famous dishes; its uses are never ending. We often used farm-raised salmon from Maine, which is always available and fresh.

1 pound salmon fillets, skinned, boned, cut into two servings
1/4 cup whole egg mayonnaise
1/4 cup sour cream
1/4 cup chopped green onions (scallions)
1/2 teaspoon curry powder
1/4 cup seafood crumbs, page 257
1/4 cup chopped fresh parsley
1/2 cup water

PREPARATION
1. Mix mayonnaise, sour cream, green onions, curry powder, crumbs, and parsley in a mixing bowl.

ASSEMBLY
1. Select an ovenproof casserole dish large enough to contain the salmon. Place skinned salmon skin side down. Spread curry topping evenly on salmon and add water to casserole.
2. Bake in a preheated 400° oven for 20 minutes.
3. Remove salmon from casserole dish to heated plates with a spatula.

"Necessity never made a good bargain."
Benjamin Franklin

COULIBIAC OF SALMON

Do not let the name Coulibiac scare you. This recipe is a little work, but worth it. It can be prepared earlier in the day. Take out of the refrigerator 1/2 hour before cooking.

1 pound salmon fillets, skinned, boned, cut into two servings
1 1/4 cup fish stock, chicken stock, or water
1/2 cup rice
2 Pepperidge Farm patty shells, thawed (you can use sheets as well)
Flour for rolling pastry and dusting cookie sheet
1 tablespoon butter
1/4 cup finely chopped onion
1/2 teaspoon dill or 1 teaspoon chopped fresh dill
Pinch dried oregano
Pinch dried basil
1/4 cup chopped green onions (scallions)
2 eggs, hard-cooked, shelled and sliced
1/4 cup sour cream
1/4 cup chopped fresh parsley
Water for sealing pastry
1 egg beaten with 1 teaspoon milk in a small bowl

PREPARATION

1. Place fish stock and rice in a small saucepan with a cover; bring to a boil. Cover pan, turn heat on low and cook for 25 minutes. Set aside.
2. On a floured pastry board, roll puff pastry into two 8-inch rounds. Place in plastic wrap, store in refrigerator.
3. Melt butter over medium heat in a skillet; sauté onion until golden. Stir in rice, oregano, basil, and chopped green onions. Cool.

ASSEMBLY

1. Butter and flour an insulated cookie sheet or regular cookie sheet.

Coulibiac of salmon continued-

2. Spread pastry on a flat surface. Spoon the rice in the center of
   the pastry, top with sliced egg, top with salmon fillets, sour
   cream, and chopped parsley.
3. Fold the pastry toward the center over the filling. Seal seams
   with water.
4. Place pastry on cookie sheet. Brush with egg wash.
5. Bake in a preheated 400° oven, on middle shelf, for 20 minutes.
   (If using a convection oven cut cooking time 5 minutes.)
6. Remove the salmon package from cookie sheet to heated plates with
   a spatula.

   *Hard-cooked eggs: To cook eggs in their shells, place a single
   layer of them in a saucepan; fill with water to 1 inch above top
   of eggs. Cover and bring to a boil, then remove from heat and
   allow to stand covered for 15 minutes. Drain off hot water and
   immediately cool with running cold water until cold.*

"I couldn't wait for success...so I went ahead without it."
Jonathan Winters

GREEN PEPPERCORN SALMON

Green peppercorns are the soft under ripe berries that are usually preserved in brine. They are sold in small cans or jars; available in specialty stores.

1 pound salmon fillets, skinned, boned, cut into two servings
2 tablespoons drained green peppercorns
1/4 cup whole egg mayonnaise
1/4 cup sour cream, or crème fraiche
1 teaspoon chopped fresh dill or 1/2 teaspoon of dried dill
1/4 cup chopped green onions (scallions)
1/4 cup seafood crumbs page, 257
1/2 cup water

PREPARATION
1. Mix gently green peppercorns, mayonnaise, sour cream, dill, green onions, and crumbs in a mixing bowl.

ASSEMBLY
1. Select an ovenproof casserole dish large enough to contain the salmon. Place skinned salmon skin side down and spread peppercorn topping evenly on salmon. Add water to casserole.
2. Bake in a preheated 400° oven for 20 minutes
3. Remove salmon from casserole dish to heated plates with a spatula. Spoon some remaining topping around salmon.

Crème fraiche has the thickness of sour cream. It can be purchased in some stores or can be made at home. Combine 1 cup heavy cream and 2 tablespoons buttermilk in a glass container. Cover and let stand at room temperature for about 15 hours. Stir well and refrigerate, covered; can be stored up to 10 days in refrigerator.

"A professional is someone who can do his best work when he doesn't feel like it."
Alfred Alistair Cooke

HOISIN-SESAME SALMON

*Hoisin sauce is a brownish-red sweet and smooth condiment.
It is referred to as "Chinese ketchup" in Chinese cooking. What makes
hoisin so appealing in many dishes is the near-perfect balance among the
sweet, sour, and salty elements. Tasting them all at once excites all the
taste buds. The chili paste gives this dish a little kick. If you do not need
the kick, leave it out.*

1 pound salmon fillets, skinned, boned, cut into two servings
2 tablespoons hoisin sauce
2 tablespoons soy sauce
3 drops Asian sesame oil
1/4 teaspoon chili paste or hot sauce (optional)
1 tablespoon sesame seeds
1/4 cup water

PREPARATION
1. Mix hoisin sauce, soy sauce, sesame oil, and chili paste in a
   small mixing bowl.

ASSEMBLY
1. Place the salmon fillets in a casserole dish just large enough to
   contain salmon filets. Place skinned salmon fillets skin side down. Spoon
   hoisin mixture on salmon fillets, some will run off but that's ok.
   Sprinkle with sesame seeds. Add water to casserole.
2. Bake in a 400° oven for 20 minutes.
3. Remove cooked salmon from casserole dish to heated plates
   with a spatula. Spoon some remaining sauce on and around the
   salmon.

"To escape criticism—do nothing, say nothing, be nothing."
Elbert Hobbard

=====================LEMON-THYME SALMON

Thyme is a member of the mint family, a perennial herb, native to southern Europe and the Mediterranean. It is a basic herb in French cooking.

1 pound salmon fillets, skinned, boned, cut into two servings
1/4 cup chopped fresh parsley
1 tablespoon grated Parmesan cheese
1 teaspoon chopped fresh thyme or 1/2 teaspoon dried
1 teaspoon grated lemon peel (zest)
2 cloves garlic, minced
1 cup fresh white bread crumbs (can be made in food processor)
2 tablespoons softened butter

PREPARATION
1. Mix parsley, Parmesan cheese, thyme, lemon peel, garlic, bread crumbs, and 1 tablespoon of the softened butter in a mixing bowl.

ASSEMBLY
1. Butter an ovenproof casserole dish just large enough to contain salmon in one layer.
2. Place skinned salmon, skin side down in casserole, spread the lemon-thyme topping evenly on the salmon.
3. Bake in a preheated 400° oven for twenty minutes.
4. Remove cooked salmon from casserole dish to heated plates with a spatula. Spoon remaining topping around salmon.

Helpful Hint

If you live in an area with well water and the inside of your dishwasher is stained, add one cup of orange concentrate TANG in your dishwasher. Run the dishwasher on the wash cycle without soap. I find this works wonderfully; it works well if you have city water as well. If the stain is very bad, it may take more than one cycle in the dishwasher.

"Doubt grows with knowledge."
Johann Wolfgang von Goethe

MEDITERRANEAN SALMON

A robust flavor for the delicate salmon, serve with simple starch and vegetables.

1 pound salmon fillets, skinned, boned, cut into two servings
1/4 cup chopped, drained, oil-packed sun-dried tomatoes
1/4 cup chopped pitted brine-cured black olives
1/4 cup chopped pitted green olives
2 garlic cloves, minced
3/4 teaspoon chopped fresh rosemary
3/4 teaspoon chopped fresh thyme
2 teaspoons whole grain mustard
1/2 cup fresh bread crumbs (or Japanese panko crumbs if available)
1/4 cup chopped fresh parsley
1 tablespoon butter, softened

PREPARATION
1. Mix sun-dried tomatoes, black and green olives, minced garlic, rosemary, thyme, mustard, bread crumbs, and parsley in a mixing bowl.

ASSEMBLY
1. Butter an ovenproof casserole dish large enough to contain the salmon; place skinned salmon, skin side down, spread olive topping evenly on salmon.
2. Bake in a preheated 400° oven for 20 minutes.
3. Remove salmon from casserole dish to heated plates with a spatula. Spoon remaining olive topping around salmon.

Panko are Japanese bread crumbs, used for coating fried foods. They're coarser than normal bread crumbs. Panko is available in Asian markets, specialty markets and seafood markets.

"You can never plan the future by the past."
Edmund Burke

NAPA VALLEY SALMON

There are hundreds of different honeys throughout the world, most of them are named after the flower. Store honey in a tightly sealed container in a cool dry place. If the cover on the honey is stuck and hard to open, run hot water on the cover and it should open with no problem.

1 pound salmon fillets, skinned, boned, cut into two servings
1/2 teaspoon dry ground mustard
1 1/2 teaspoons honey
1/2 teaspoon thyme
1 (10-ounce) package of fresh spinach, trimmed, cleaned, and
   roughly chopped
1 clove garlic, minced
1 teaspoon olive oil
1/2 cup Red California seedless grapes, cut in half
1/4 cup dry red wine

PREPARATION

1. Whisk ground mustard, honey, and thyme in a mixing bowl. Add salmon to the bowl coating salmon completely with honey mixture.
2. Mix spinach, garlic, and olive oil in a mixing bowl. (Make sure spinach is coated with oil).

ASSEMBLY

1. Select an ovenproof casserole dish large enough to contain the salmon. Spread the spinach in bottom of casserole dish; place skinned salmon on spinach, skin side down, spoon all remaining honey mixture on salmon. Add grapes and red wine to casserole.
2. Bake in a preheated 400° oven for 20 minutes.
3. Remove cooked salmon from casserole dish to heated plates with a spatula. Spoon spinach, sauce, and grapes around the salmon.

ONION-CILANTRO SALMON

Cilantro is widely used in Asian, Caribbean, and Latin American cooking. Cilantro is the leaves and stems of the Coriander plant. It is available in most supermarkets.

1 pound salmon fillets, skinned, boned, cut into two servings
1/2 cup chopped red onion (white onion can be used)
1/4 cup chopped cilantro (fresh parsley can be used)
2 tablespoons fresh or dried white bread crumbs
Dash ground red pepper (cayenne)
1/2 teaspoon soy sauce
1/4 cup olive oil
1 tablespoon butter

PREPARATION
1. Mix onion, cilantro, bread crumbs, cayenne, soy sauce, and olive oil in a mixing bowl.

ASSEMBLY
1. Butter an ovenproof casserole dish just large enough to contain salmon in one layer.
2. Place skinned salmon, skin side down in casserole; spread onion mixture evenly on salmon.
3. Bake in a preheated 400° oven for 20 minutes.
4. Remove cooked salmon from casserole dish to heated plates with a spatula. Spoon any remaining topping around salmon.

"Expectation has a lot to do with satisfaction.
It's easy to expect too much and walk away disappointed."
Meridith Ford, Providence Journal Restaurant Critic

RED FLANNEL SALMON

Fresh beets and horseradish give this salmon dish a peppy taste.

1 pound salmon fillets, skinned, boned, cut into two servings
1 tablespoon butter
1/4 cup finely chopped onion
1/2 cup grated raw fresh beets, peeled, stemmed (use plastic gloves
    to keep fingers from turning red)
1 teaspoon minced fresh thyme or (1/2 teaspoon dried thyme)
1/2 cup fresh bread crumbs or panko (Japanese bread crumbs)
1 tablespoon prepared white horseradish
1/2 cup water

PREPARATION

1. Melt butter over medium heat in a skillet; sauté onions until golden.
   Stir in grated beets, sauté while stirring for about 4 minutes,
   or until beets are soft. Remove from heat; stir in thyme,
   bread crumbs, and horseradish. Cool.

ASSEMBLY

1. Select an ovenproof casserole dish large enough to contain the
   salmon. Place skinned salmon skin side down; spread the beet
   topping evenly on salmon. Add water to bottom of casserole.
2. Bake in a preheated 400° oven for 20 minutes.
3. Remove salmon from casserole to heated plates and spoon
   remaining topping and juices on and around salmon.

*Panko (Japanese bread crumbs) are available in Asian markets
and in the Asian food section of some supermarkets.*

*"Sometimes, dramatic results can be achieved when you
seize control of a table of diners and give them far more than
they ever dreamed."*
                      Charlie Trotter

ROASTED HONEY SALMON

A little sweet from the honey, a little tart from the mustard, a little pungent from the garlic, this salmon has a robust taste.

1 pound salmon fillets, skinned, boned, cut into two servings
4 garlic cloves, minced
1/4 cup Dijon-style mustard
1/4 cup honey
2 tablespoons chopped fresh dill, or 1 tablespoon dried dill
1/2 cup olive oil

PREPARATION
1. Mix garlic, mustard, honey, dill, and olive oil in a mixing bowl.

ASSEMBLY
1. Select an ovenproof casserole large enough to contain the salmon. Place skinned salmon skin side up; spoon honey mixture on salmon and marinate in refrigerator for about 2 hours. Turn salmon over after one hour. Take out of refrigerator 20 minutes before cooking.
2. Bake in a preheated 400° oven for 20 minutes, basting with juices after ten minutes.
3. Remove salmon from casserole to heated plates and spoon some of the juices on and around salmon.

" Don't choose to be right, choose to be happy!"
Annamous

337

ROLLED STUFFED SALMON

The presentation of this salmon is so beautiful. Accent it with fresh asparagus.

1 pound salmon fillets, thick center cut, skinned, boned, cut into
    two servings
1 teaspoon butter
1/4 cup minced onion
1/4 cup chopped mushrooms
1/4 cup diced red bell peppers, cored and seeded
1/4 cup crab meat canned or fresh
4 ounces scallops or shrimp chopped coarsely
1/4 cup fresh or dried plain bread crumbs
1 tablespoon mayonnaise
1 teaspoon butter
2 tablespoons seafood crumbs, page 257
1 (10 3/4-ounce) can cream of shrimp or lobster bisque soup
1/2 cup milk
1 tablespoon chopped fresh basil of 1/2 teaspoon dried basil

PREPARATION

1. Place skinned salmon on flat cutting board skin side down. Butterfly the
   salmon. With a sharp knife beginning in the center cut salmon
   in half, stopping before you reach the end. Do this on each side.
   Open the salmon and you should have the salmon double size.
   Store in refrigerator until ready to use.
2. Melt butter in a skillet; and sauté onions until golden.
   Stir in mushrooms and peppers and sauté for a few minutes.
   Remove from heat and cool. Stir in crabmeat, scallops,
   bread crumbs, and mayonnaise; mix thoroughly.

Rolled stuffed salmon continued-

ASSEMBLY
1. Butter an ovenproof casserole large enough to contain the rolled salmon.
2. On a flat surface place salmon skin side up; spread stuffing evenly on each salmon fillet. Start with one end and roll salmon like a jelly roll. Secure with a toothpick. Place rolled stuffed salmon in buttered casserole dish. Top with seafood crumbs.
3. Bake in a preheated 400° oven for 20 minutes.
4. While salmon is cooking, mix cream of shrimp soup, milk and basil in a sauce pan. Heat while stirring, and keep warm.
5. Remove cooked salmon with a large spatula to heated plates. Remove toothpick, spoon 2 tablespoons of sauce on and around salmon. Use extra sauce later for a cup of soup.

SALMON IN PUFF PASTRY

This is a beautiful presentation when entertaining.

1 pound salmon fillets, skinned, boned, cut into two servings
Flour for rolling pastry and dusting cookie sheet
2 Pepperidge Farm patty shells, thawed (or puff pastry sheets)
1/2 teaspoon dried dill, or 2 teaspoons chopped fresh dill
1/4 cup chopped green onions (scallions)
2 slices American cheese
Water for sealing pastry
1 egg and 1 teaspoon milk, beaten together

PREPARATION

1. On a floured pastry board, roll puff pastry into two 8-inch rounds. Store rolled puff pastry in plastic wrap and keep in refrigerator.

ASSEMBLY

1. Butter and flour an insulated cookie sheet or regular cookie sheet.
2. Spread pastry on a flat surface.
3. In the center of each rolled pastry place a salmon fillet, top with dill, green onions and top with American cheese.
   Fold the pastry toward the center over the salmon, and wrap like a package, sealing seams with water.
4. Place pastry packages on prepared cookie sheet. Brush with egg mixture.
5. Bake in a preheated 400° oven on, middle shelf for 20 minutes.
6. Remove pastry packages from cookie sheet to heated plates with a spatula.
   If you are using a convection oven cut cooking time down 5 minutes.

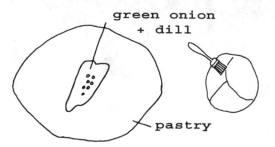

green onion + dill

pastry

decorate

=====SALMON POACHED IN LETTUCE LEAVES

Small bones can be removed from salmon filets with needle nose pliers or tweezers. A small bone remover tool is available in specialty stores.

1 pound salmon fillets, skinned, boned, cut into two servings
Iceberg lettuce leaves large enough to wrap fish in
  (blanched, and ribs removed)
1/2 cup minced onion
1/4 cup white vinegar
1/4 cup white wine
2 teaspoons butter
1/4 cup half-and-half cream or evaporated milk
1 teaspoon lime juice
1/2 cup fish stock or white wine
1/2 teaspoon dried dill or 2 teaspoons chopped fresh dill
1/4 cup chopped green onions (scallions)
1/4 cup seafood crumbs, page 257

PREPARATION
1. Cook onions, vinegar, and white wine in a sauce pan and
    bring to a boil until all liquid evaporates. (Caution, be careful not
    to scorch.) Remove from heat. Stir in 1 teaspoon butter, cream, lime
    juice, and fish stock.

ASSEMBLY
1. Select a covered ovenproof casserole just large enough
    to contain the salmon packages.
2. Spread the blanched lettuce leaves on a work surface and place
    salmon in the middle. Top with dill and chopped green onion.
    Fold lettuce leaves over, enclosing salmon completely.
3. Place salmon packages seam side down in casserole dish. Top
    with crumbs, spoon prepared sauce around salmon, dot with butter.
4. Bake covered casserole in a preheated 400° oven for 20 minutes.
5. Remove salmon packages from casserole to heated plates with a
    spatula; spoon sauce on and around salmon.
    *To blanch lettuce, place lettuce leaves in boiling water for 30
    seconds. Plunge in cold water to stop cooking, Drain and pat dry.*

=SALMON WITH A DILLED MUSTARD TOPPING

*Dill, thought by the Romans to be a good luck symbol,
has been used for thousands of years.*

1 pound salmon fillets, skinned, boned, cut into two servings
1/2 cup whole egg mayonnaise
1 teaspoon whole grain mustard
1 tablespoon finely chopped fresh dill or 1 teaspoon dried dill
1/2 teaspoon brown sugar
1/2 teaspoon fresh lime juice
1/2 cup water

PREPARATION
1. Mix mayonnaise, mustard, dill, brown sugar, and lime juice
   in a mixing bowl.

ASSEMBLY
1. Select an ovenproof casserole dish large enough to contain the
   salmon. Place skinned salmon, skin side down, and spread the
   dill mixture evenly on salmon and add water to casserole.
2. Bake in a preheated 400° oven, on bottom shelf, for 20 minutes.
3. Remove salmon from casserole dish to heated plates with spatula.

*We all heard this so many times from our mothers as we stood
looking in the refrigerator with the door open.*
"Are you warming the food or are you cooling the room?"

=====SALMON WITH A HORSERADISH CRUST, ORANGE VODKA SAUCE

This salmon dish is beautiful in taste and color. We served this dish very often at the restaurant.

1 pound salmon fillets, skinned, boned, cut into two servings
1 cup fresh or dried plain bread crumbs
1 teaspoon grated fresh horseradish
1/4 cup melted butter
2 tablespoons chopped fresh parsley
1/4 teaspoon ground thyme
1 cup water
1 cup orange juice
2 tablespoons vodka
1/4 cup chopped green onions (scallions)
2 teaspoons cornstarch

PREPARATION
1. Mix bread crumbs, horseradish, melted butter chopped parsley, and thyme in a mixing bowl.

ASSEMBLY
1. Select an ovenproof casserole large enough to contain the salmon. Place skinned salmon, skin side down, and spread the horseradish mixture evenly on each fillet, patting it into the salmon. Add 3/4 cup water to casserole.
2. Bake in a preheated 400° oven for 20 minutes.
3. While salmon is cooking, put orange juice, vodka, and green onions into a small saucepan. Bring to a low boil. In the meantime, mix remaining 1/4 cup water and cornstarch together in a small cup or bowl. While stirring, add cornstarch mixture to hot orange juice in small amounts making a smooth sauce. (You do not have to use all the cornstarch mixture.) Keep warm.
4. Remove cooked salmon from casserole dish to heated plates with a spatula. Spoon orange sauce on and around salmon.

SALMON WITH GREEN LENTILS

There are several varieties of lentils; cooking time may vary. Check the package for cooking times. Do not add salt when cooking lentils, it toughens them. This is a wonderful way to serve salmon, and it becomes a complete meal.

1 pound salmon fillets, skinned, boned, cut into two servings
1/2 cup green lentils, washed, small stones removed
    (brown lentils can be used also)
1 small carrot, diced
1 small turnip, diced (purple top)
1 small celery stalk, diced
1 small onion, chopped
1 garlic clove, minced
1/4 teaspoon ground thyme
1 bay leaf
Water for cooking lentils
2 tablespoons butter
1/4 cup seafood crumbs, page 257
1/4 cup chopped fresh parsley

PREPARATION

1. Combine lentils, carrots, turnips, celery, onion, garlic, thyme, and bay leaf in a saucepan, add water to cover. Bring to a boil, cover, and simmer until lentils are tender, add extra water if needed (about 25 minutes). Drain lentil mixture reserving 1/2 cup of cooking liquid. Return lentil mixture to sauce pan. Stir in 1 teaspoon butter and 1/2 cup of cooking liquid. Remove bay leaf. Keep warm. (While lentils are cooking you can also bake the salmon.) Lentils can be cooked ahead and reheated.

ASSEMBLY

1. Butter an ovenproof casserole dish just large enough to contain salmon fillets, place skinned salmon, skin side down, in casserole.
Spread crumbs evenly on salmon, dot with butter.
2. Bake in a preheated 400° oven for 20 minutes.
3. Remove salmon from casserole dish to heated plates with a spatula, spoon warm lentils around salmon and garnish with chopped parsley.

=======SALMON WITH RED WINE AND GRAPES

Atlantic salmon supplies have diminished greatly over the years because of pollution. Canada supplies most of the Atlantic salmon presently. Maine is supplying an increasing volume of aqua cultured salmon. Farmed salmon are raised in salt water, their flesh does not have the same rich flavor and texture as their wild relations, but are very good to cook and eat.

1 pound salmon fillets, skinned, boned, cut into two servings
1 1/2 teaspoons cornstarch
1/4 cup water
1 1/2 cups dry red wine
2 tablespoons fresh lemon juice
1/4 cup chopped green onions (scallions)
1/4 cup seafood crumbs, page 257
1 cup white seedless grapes
1 teaspoon butter

PREPARATION
1. Mix cornstarch and water in a small bowl making a smooth paste. Heat wine, lemon juice, and scallions in a saucepan; bring to a light boil. Add cornstarch mixture a little at a time while stirring until slightly thickened. Cool.

ASSEMBLY
1. Select an ovenproof casserole large enough to hold the salmon and grapes.
2. Place skinned salmon in casserole skin side down, top with crumbs, and add grapes. Spoon sauce on and around fish, dot with butter.
3. Bake in a preheated 400° oven for 20 minutes.
4. Remove salmon from casserole with a spatula. Spoon grapes and sauce on and around salmon.

"You can't wait for inspiration.
You have to go after it with a club."

Jack London

SALMON STUFFED WITH MASCARPONE-SPINACH

A wonderful combination of fresh spinach, cream cheese and Mascarpone makes this salmon dish one of my favorites. The salmon for this dish should be the thick end of the fish.

1 pound salmon fillets, skinned, boned, cut into two servings
3 ounces of fresh spinach leaves, trimmed, washed and finely
   chopped
1/4 cup (2-ounces) cream cheese room temperature
1/4 cup (2-ounces) Mascarpone cheese room temperature
Pinch nutmeg
3/4 cup fresh or dried plain bread crumbs
2 tablespoons melted butter
1 tablespoon grated Parmesan cheese
1 tablespoon olive oil

PREPARATION

1. Mix spinach, cream cheese, Mascarpone cheese, and nutmeg in a mixing bowl with a fork.
2. Mix bread crumbs, melted butter, and Parmesan cheese in a mixing bowl with a fork until evenly moistened.

ASSEMBLY

1. On a cutting board, place skinned salmon skin side down. Slice down the center of each salmon fillet, forming a pocket for the spinach stuffing. Do not cut through the salmon.
2. Oil an ovenproof casserole large enough to contain the salmon, place sliced salmon skin side down.
   Spoon the spinach stuffing down the center of each salmon fillet.
   Top stuffed salmon evenly with prepared bread crumbs.
3. Bake in a preheated 400° oven for 20 minutes.
4. Remove salmon carefully to heated plates with a spatula.

*"When life handed me a lemon, not only did I make lemonade,
I also wrote the recipe and then sold that recipe!"
JoAnna Lund, author, Healthy Exchanges Cookbook*

SALMON WITH SUN-DRIED TOMATO AND WHITE BEANS

This salmon dish is all you need for dinner.

1 pound salmon fillets, skinned, boned, cut into two servings
1/4 cup sun-dried tomatoes (packed in olive oil)
1/2 cup fresh or dried plain bread crumbs
1/4 teaspoon chopped fresh thyme
2 tablespoons chopped fresh parsley
1 teaspoon soft butter
1 tablespoon olive oil
1/4 cup chopped onion
1/4 cup finely diced peeled carrot
1/4 cup diced red bell pepper, stemmed and seeded
1 (15 1/2-ounce) can of small white beans, or cooked dried beans
1/4 cup chopped canned tomatoes
1 tablespoon balsamic vinegar
1/4 cup water

PREPARATION
1. Place sun-dried tomatoes in the bowl of a food processor fitted with a metal blade and puree. Add the bread crumbs, thyme, parsley, and butter; puree until incorporated.
2. Heat the oil in a medium sauté pan over medium heat; add onion, carrot, and diced pepper, and sauté until vegetables are softened. Stir in beans, tomatoes, and balsamic vinegar, and cook until beans are hot, and keep warm on low heat.

ASSEMBLY
1. Select an ovenproof casserole dish just large enough to contain the salmon in one layer.
2. Place skinned salmon, skin side down, in casserole, spread sun-dried tomato topping evenly on salmon and add water to casserole.
3. Bake salmon in a preheated 400° oven for 20 minutes.
4. Remove cooked salmon from casserole dish to heated plates with a spatula; spoon beans around salmon.

================================SALMON WELLINGTON

A pleasing presentation and wonderful to eat.

1 pound salmon fillets, skinned, boned, cut into two servings
2 Pepperidge Farm patty shells, thawed
Flour for rolling pastry and dusting cookie sheet
2 teaspoons butter
1 small onion, finely chopped
3/4 cup chopped fresh spinach, stems removed, washed
2 tablespoons chopped fresh tarragon or 1/2 teaspoon dried
2 tablespoons sour cream
1 egg beaten with 1 teaspoon milk in a bowl

PREPARATION

1. On a floured pastry board, roll puff pastry into two 8-inch rounds. Wrap in plastic wrap and refrigerate.
2. Melt 1 teaspoon butter over medium heat in a skillet; sauté onions until golden. Stir in spinach and cook until wilted; remove from heat and cool for a few minutes. Stir in tarragon and sour cream. Cool.

ASSEMBLY

1. Butter and flour a cookie sheet. (Insulated if you have one.)
2. On a flat surface lay out pastry, and place a salmon fillet in center. Spread spinach stuffing evenly on each salmon fillet. With fingers or a pastry brush, moisten pastry around salmon with a little of egg wash. Wrap pastry around salmon like a package and seal the seams. Brush the egg wash on the outside of pastry package.
3. Put salmon package on buttered and floured cookie sheet.
4. Bake on middle shelf of a preheated 400° oven for 20 minutes.
5. Remove salmon package from cookie sheet with a spatula. Serve on heated plates.

"A wise man knows everything; a shrewd one, everybody."
Anonymous

=================SUGAR-GLAZED SALMON

This dish can be a little tricky, but it is worth the effort.
It is amazing there is no sweetness from the sugar.

1 pound salmon fillets, skinned, boned, cut into two servings
1/2 cup sugar (Use a bit more sugar if needed.)
1 teaspoon butter
1/4 cup minced onion
1/4 cup chopped green onions (scallions)
1 teaspoon soy sauce
1/2 cup sour cream

PREPARATION
1. Place sugar in a flat plate. Heat a nonstick skillet with a metal handle
   over medium heat. Dip salmon in sugar on both sides. Place skinned
   salmon in hot skillet skin side up until sugar caramelizes.
   (Watch this carefully it takes only one minute to burn.)
   Turn salmon over and glaze other side.
2. Place skillet in a preheated 400° oven for 10-15 minutes. Salmon should
   be skin side down. (Make sure your skillet has no plastic handles.
   If so bake, in an ovenproof pan).

ASSEMBLY
1. Remove cooked salmon from pan and place on heated plate,
   return skillet to burner, add butter, onion, and green onion.
   Sauté for a minute, add soy sauce and sour cream. Stir until blended,
   and remove from heat; do not overcook or sauce will separate.
   Spoon sauce on and around salmon.

"Some books are to be tasted, others to be swallowed,
and some few to be chewed and digested."
Francis Bacon

=============SPAGHETTI-SQUASH SALMON

Spaghetti squash is such a surprise as it turns into spaghetti after cooking.

1 pound salmon fillets, skinned, boned, cut into two servings
1/2 teaspoon Oriental five-spice powder
1 teaspoon grated orange peel (zest)
1 tablespoon brown sugar
1 tablespoon butter
1/4 cup chopped green onions (scallions)
2 cups cooked spaghetti squash
2 teaspoons Dijon-style mustard

PREPARATION
1. Cook spaghetti squash (directions on next page).
2. Mix five-spice powder, orange peel, and 2 tablespoons brown sugar in a mixing bowl.
3. Mix cooked and cooled spaghetti squash with 1 tablespoon of the brown sugar mixture in a mixing bowl. (Save remaining brown sugar mixture for later).

ASSEMBLY
1. Butter (1-teaspoon) an ovenproof casserole dish large enough to contain the salmon fillets and the squash.
2. Spread squash mixture evenly on bottom of buttered casserole dish. Place skinned salmon fillets, skin side down, on squash, spread mustard evenly on salmon, sprinkle with remaining brown sugar mixture, dot with butter.
3. Bake in a 400° oven for 20 minutes.
4. Remove salmon from casserole dish to heated plates with a spatula, spoon squash and juices around salmon.

Spaghetti-squash salmon continued-

COOKING SPAGHETTI SQUASH:

Preheat oven to 400°. Cut squash lengthwise and remove seeds. Place squash, cut side down in a casserole dish large enough to contain the squash. Add water to casserole to a depth of about 1/2 inch. Bake for 45 minutes, until tender when pierced with a fork; remove squash from casserole with a spatula and cool.
Scrape inside of squash with a fork to remove spaghetti like strands.
To Microwave:
Prepare the squash the same as above; casserole dish must be glass with a cover. Microwave on high for 15 minutes, or until squash is tender and can be pierced with a fork.

==STUFFED SALMON FILLET IN PUFF PASTRY

Although this recipe seems like a lot of work, most of it can be done ahead of time. The entire salmon package can be prepared ahead and stored in the refrigerator until ready to use. Take salmon package out of the refrigerator 1/2 hour before baking. Sauce can be made ahead and reheated. Salmon mousseline stuffing is light and tasty.

1 pound salmon fillets, skinned, boned, cut into three servings
Flour for rolling pastry and dusting cookie sheet
2 Pepperidge Farm patty shells, thawed (or puff pastry sheets)
1/4 cup heavy cream, chilled
1 large egg white, chilled
1 teaspoon dried dill
1 teaspoon butter
1/4 cup minced onion
1 cup chopped fresh mushrooms
1/2 teaspoon tarragon
1 teaspoon butter
1 egg beaten with 1 teaspoon milk in a small bowl
1 (10 3/4-ounce) can cream of shrimp soup
1 tablespoon chopped fresh basil or 1/4 teaspoon dried basil
1/2 cup milk

PREPARATION
1. On a floured pastry board, roll puff pastry into two 8-inch rounds. Keep rolled puff pastry in plastic wrap in the refrigerator until ready to assemble.
2. To make salmon mousseline, puree one piece of salmon in a chilled food processor until salmon forms a smooth paste. Add the cream, egg white, and dill and process until the ingredients are incorporated. Store in refrigerator until ready to use.

Stuffed salmon fillet in puff pastry continued-

3. Heat a skillet, add butter and sauté onions until translucent. Add
   mushrooms and cook until liquid is released and evaporated.
   Remove from heat and cool.

ASSEMBLY
1. Butter and flour an insulated cookie sheet or regular cookie
   sheet.
2. Spread rolled pastry on a flat surface.
3. In the center of pastry, place a salmon fillet; spread salmon mousseline
   evenly on each salmon fillet, and spoon mushrooms evenly on top of
   mousseline. Fold the pastry toward the center over the salmon,
   and wrap like a package. Seal the seams with egg wash.
4. Place the pastry packages on prepared cookie sheet. Brush with egg
   wash.
5. Bake in a preheated 400° oven, on middle shelf, for 20 minutes.
6. While salmon is cooking, heat, while stirring, cream of shrimp
   soup, basil, and milk in a small sauce pan. Keep warm.
7. Remove pastry packages from cookie sheet to heated plates
   with a spatula. Spoon about three tablespoons of sauce around
   each salmon package.

   (There will be extra sauce left over; enjoy a cup of soup).

Helpful Hint
*That troublesome knob on furniture that is always loose can
be repaired; unscrew the knob and coat the screw with clear
fingernail polish. Reattach the knob and let the polish harden.*

*"Some people like to paint pictures, or do gardening, or build a
boat in the basement. Other people get a tremendous pleasure out
of the kitchen, because cooking is just as creative and imaginative
an activity as drawing, or wood carvings, or music."*
Julia Child

SUN-DRIED TOMATO SALMON

Sun-dried tomatoes are available in small jars packed in oil in the grocery store. Sun-dried tomatoes are available dry-packed as well. Either style can be used in this recipe. If you use the oil packed, drain oil before chopping.

1 pound salmon fillets, skinned, boned, cut into two servings
1 1/2 tablespoons chopped sun-dried tomatoes
1/4 cup whole egg mayonnaise
1/4 cup sour cream
1/4 cup chopped green onions (scallions)
1/4 cup seafood crumbs, page 257
1/2 cup water

PREPARATION
1. Mix sun-dried tomatoes, mayonnaise, sour cream, green onions, and crumbs in a mixing bowl.

ASSEMBLY
1. Select an ovenproof casserole dish large enough to contain the salmon. Place skinned salmon, skin side down. Spread the sun-dried tomato topping evenly on salmon and add water to casserole.
2. Bake in a preheated 400° oven for 20 minutes.
3. Remove salmon from casserole dish to heated plates with a spatula. Spoon some remaining topping around salmon.

Helpful Hint
Keep baking soda handy by putting it in a grated cheese shaker. I keep it near my sink, ready to remove odors, food stains from counters and dishes.

"When we decode a cookbook, everyone of us is a practicing chemist, cooking is really the oldest, most basic application of physical and chemical forces to natural materials."
Arthur E. Grosser

==================*TORTILLA CRUSTED SALMON*

I like to serve a half portion of the baked tortilla crusted salmon with greens as a lunch or first course. I served this dish at the South County Museum in Rhode Island for its' annual summer dinner in the Museum. It's fun serving dinner in the middle of all the artifacts. You would not use the salsa with the greens. Use a light dressing on the greens.

1 pound salmon fillets, skinned, boned, cut into two servings
1 small bag of corn tortilla chips
1 tablespoon olive oil
1 egg beaten with 1 teaspoon milk in a small bowl
1 teaspoon butter
1/4 cup prepared salsa (mild, medium, or hot)

PREPARATION
1. Crush tortilla chips by hand; then place them in a blender or food processor and process until mixture is ground fine.

ASSEMBLY
1. Oil an ovenproof casserole just large enough to contain the salmon.
2. Place crumbs in a dish.
3. Place salmon in egg wash, and then roll in tortilla crumbs until completely coated. Place breaded skinned salmon in oiled casserole dish, skin side down, and dot with butter.
4. Bake in a preheated 400° oven for 20 minutes or until salmon is firm to the touch.
5. While salmon is cooking heat salsa on medium heat in a small saucepan.
6. Remove cooked salmon from casserole with a spatula to heated plates and spoon warm salsa around salmon.

*"It's difficult to think anything but pleasant thoughts
while eating a homegrown tomato."*
Lewis Gizzard

SCALLOPS

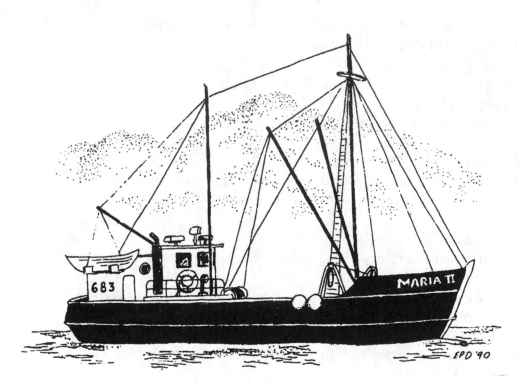

All recipes are for two in this chapter.

==================*Hints and Suggestions*

STORING SCALLOPS: The two best-known species of scallops in America are the large sea scallops and the smaller bay scallops. Bay scallops are generally considered to be the most desirable and are usually more expensive and more difficult to get. Sea scallops are larger and have a small muscle on the side of the scallop that should be removed.

I always store scallops in a bowl and cover the scallops with milk when I place them in the refrigerator. The reason I do this is that most of the time the scallops are covered with fine sand, and the milk removes most of the sand. When you take the scallops out of the milk, do it carefully, with a slotted spoon. You will see the sand in the bottom of the bowl. Place the scallops on paper towels if you need them to be dry before cooking.

I also find that the milk gives the scallops a sweet taste, especially if the scallops have been previously frozen. Do not be afraid to ask the clerk to smell the scallops before purchasing them. Fresh scallops should have a nice sweet smell. If they smell strong, purchase something else.

HONEY-MUSTARD SCALLOPS

Whole grain mustard is available in most markets, do not use hot dog mustard.

1 pound scallops (if small leave whole, if large cut each one in half)
2 garlic cloves, minced
1 tablespoon butter
1/2 cup whole grain mustard (stone ground mustard)
1/4 cup chopped fresh parsley
1/4 cup white wine or fish stock (clam juice can be used)
1/4 cup seafood crumbs, page 257
1 teaspoon butter

PREPRATION
1. Mix garlic, honey, mustard, parsley, and scallops in a mixing bowl.

ASSEMBLY
1. Spoon scallops into two individual casseroles.
   Add white wine, top with crumbs and dot with butter.
2. Bake in a preheated 400° oven for 15 minutes, or until scallops
   are firm. Do not overcook. Serve in casserole dishes.
   I like to place the casseroles on cookie sheets to bake. They are easier
   to take out of the oven, and it reduces spill over in the oven.

Serve scallops in the individual casseroles on a dinner plate.

"Burgundy makes you think of silly things,
Bordeaux makes you talk of them and
Champagne makes you do them."
Brillat-Savarin

SALT POND SCALLOPS

Salt Pond Scallops, are available in Rhode Island from September to December. These scallops are tender, delicious, and cherished by chefs, they are so delicate, you only need to cook them for just a few minutes. They are expensive and hard to get. I named this dish for Salt Pond Scallops because they are so great, but any scallops can be used in this dish.

1 pound scallops (if small leave whole, if large cut each one in half)
1/2 cup seafood crumbs, page 257
1/4 cup onion, minced
2 cloves garlic, minced
1/4 teaspoon tarragon
1/4 cup chopped fresh parsley
1 tablespoon softened butter
1/4 cup chopped green onion (scallions)
1/4 cup white wine or fish stock, (clam juice can be used)

PREPARATION
1. Mix crumbs, minced onion, minced garlic, tarragon, chopped parsley, softened butter, and chopped green onion in a mixing bowl.

ASSEMBLY
1. Select two individual casserole dishes, add scallops and wine, spread topping evenly on scallops.
2. Bake casseroles in a preheated 400° oven for 15 minutes, or until scallops are firm; do not over cook. Serve in casserole dishes.

"Cook-books have always intrigued and seduced me. When I was still a dilettante in the kitchen they held my attention, even the dull ones, from cover to cover, the way crime and murder stories did."
Gertrude Stein

SCALLOPS AND SPINACH

Frozen scallops are available year round. I find frozen scallops are better to use out of season.

1 pound scallops (if small leave whole, if large cut each one in half)
1 tablespoon butter
1/4 cup chopped onion
1/2 pound fresh spinach, cleaned and stems removed, roughly chopped
1 teaspoon grated Parmesan cheese
Dash nutmeg
4 slices American cheese
1/4 cup seafood crumbs, page 257

PREPARATION

1. Melt 1 teaspoon of butter in a skillet; sauté onions for just a minute, stir in spinach, Parmesan cheese, and nutmeg. Sauté until spinach is wilted. Cool.

ASSEMBLY

1. Select two ovenproof individual casserole dishes.
2. Spread spinach evenly on bottom of casserole dishes, top with scallops, American cheese, crumbs, and dot with butter.
3. Bake casseroles on cookie sheet in a preheated 400° oven for 15 minutes or until scallops are firm; serve in casserole dishes.

Serve scallops in casserole dishes on plates. Serve starch and vegetables in side dishes.

"To give life to beauty, the painter uses a whole range of coulours, musicians of sounds, the cook of tastes–and it is indeed remarkable that there are seven coulours, seven musical notes and seven tastes."
                                    Lucien Tendret

SCALLOPS AU GRATIN

Gratin is a casserole that is topped with cheese, crumbs, and butter, then baked in the oven, or browned under the broiler.

1 pound scallops (if small leave whole, if large cut each one in half)
1 1/2 tablespoons butter
1/4 cup onion, chopped
1 1/2 tablespoons flour
1 cup milk
Dash nutmeg
2 slices American cheese
1/4 cup seafood crumbs, page 257
2 teaspoons grated Parmesan cheese

PREPARATION

1. Melt 1 tablespoon butter over medium heat in a saucepan; sauté onion until golden, add flour and stir while cooking for 1 minute; add milk and a dash of nutmeg. Cook while stirring until thickened. Cool.

ASSEMBLY

1. Add scallops to cooled sauce. Spoon scallop mixture into two individual ovenproof casserole dishes. Top scallops with sliced American cheese, crumbs, Parmesan cheese, and dot with remaining butter.
2. Bake casseroles on a cookie sheet, in a preheated 400° oven for 15 minutes, or until scallops are firm. Do not overcook. Serve in casserole dishes.

Scallops perish quickly out of the water,
they are usually sold shucked.

"Happy and successful cooking doesn't rely only on know-how;
it comes from the heart, makes great demands on the palate
and needs enthusiasm and a deep love of food to bring it to life."
Georges Blanc

SCALLOPS BAKED NATURAL

A simple way to enjoy the wonderful natural flavor of scallops, the scallop is so delicate to taste.

1 pound scallops (if small leave whole, if large cut each one in half)
2 teaspoons butter
1 cup seafood crumbs, page 257
1/2 cup half-and-half cream or evaporated milk
Dash paprika

ASSEMBLY

1. Butter 2 individual casseroles with half the butter; with half the crumbs spoon a layer on the bottom of each casserole. Top with scallops, add cream, and cover with remaining crumbs. Dot with butter and paprika.
2. Bake casserole in preheated 400° oven for 15 minutes or until scallops are firm. Be careful not to overcook. Serve in casserole dishes.

Helpful Hint

Forget the crystal, make a squash vase. Select an unblemished butternut squash that is not too ripe. Try to find one that will stand upright. If you can't, use a knife to cut a thin slice off the bottom to even it out. Cut off the top of the squash about 2 inches below the stem. Use your knife to remove the flesh to reach the seed filled interior. With a small spoon or melon baller, hollow out the squash, removing seeds, membranes and any excess flesh. Leave about 3/4-inch thickness of flesh around the entire shell. Now your vase is ready for flowers. Fill it with water and place it on a saucer to protect the surface of your table. Create a flower arrangement using fall colors.

"Nothing sharpens sight like envy."
Thomas Fuller

The color and aroma of this dish will perk up all the senses.

1 pound scallops (if small leave whole, if large cut each one in half)
1 small onion, halved and thinly sliced
1 small sweet red bell pepper, cored, seeded and sliced thin
1 small green bell pepper, cored, seeded and sliced thin
1/4 cup chopped green onions (scallions)
1/4 cup chopped fresh parsley
2 tablespoons olive oil
1/4 teaspoon fennel seeds
1/4 teaspoon dried basil or 2 tablespoons chopped fresh basil
1/4 cup white wine or fish stock (clam juice can be used)
1/4 cup seafood crumbs, page 257
2 slices smoked bacon, cut in half

PREPARATION
1. Mix sliced onion, red and green peppers, green onions, parsley, olive oil, fennel, and basil in a mixing bowl.

ASSEMBLY
1. Select two individual ovenproof casseroles. Add scallops, wine, and top with crumbs. Spread prepared vegetables on top of crumbs evenly; top with bacon slices.
2. Bake in a preheated 400° oven for 15 minutes, or until scallops are firm. Serve in casserole dishes.

When using large scallops, make sure to remove the little muscle on the side of the scallop, which can be a little chewy.

"No one who cooks, cooks alone. Even at her most solitary, a cook in the kitchen is surrounded by generations of cooks past, the advice and menus of cooks present, the wisdom of cookbook writers."
Laurie Colwin

SCALLOPS TURNOVER

This scallop dish a bit of work but it is worth it. Make it earlier in the day and bake at dinner time.

2 Pepperidge Farm patty shells, thawed
Flour for rolling pastry and dusting cookie sheet

FILLING:
2 teaspoons butter
1 clove garlic, chopped
1/4 cup fresh sliced mushrooms
1 tablespoon flour
2 tablespoons dry sherry
1 tablespoon half-and-half cream
1/2 pound scallops (if small leave whole, if large cut each one in half)
1/4 cup toasted sliced almonds
1/4 cup shredded Gruyere cheese or grated Parmesan cheese
2 tablespoons sour cream
1/4 cup frozen peas, thawed
1/4 cup chopped green onions (scallions)
1/2 teaspoon dried tarragon or 2 teaspoons fresh chopped tarragon
Dash ground red pepper (cayenne)

1 egg beaten with 1 teaspoon milk in a small bowl

PREPARATION

1. On a floured pastry board, roll puff pastry into two 8-inch rounds. Place pastry rounds between plastic wrap and keep in refrigerator.
2. To make filling: Melt 1 teaspoon butter in a skillet over medium heat, add garlic and mushrooms; sauté until mushrooms are wilted. Add flour and stir until flour cooks in with the mushrooms. Stir in dry sherry and cream, stir and make a smooth sauce. Remove from heat and cool. Stir in scallops, toasted almonds, cheese, sour cream, peas, green onions, tarragon, and dash cayenne.

Scallop turnover continued-

ASSEMBLY

1. Butter and flour an insulated cookie sheet or regular cookie sheet.
2. Place rolled pastry on a flat surface.
   Spoon the scallop mixture in the center of the pastry.
   Moisten the edges with egg wash and
   fold like a turnover and crimp with a fork to seal.
   Place turnovers on floured cookie sheet and brush egg wash on pastry. (Can be prepared ahead and refrigerated at this point).
1. Bake in a preheated 400° oven, on middle shelf,
   for 15 to 20 minutes or until pastry is golden.
2. Remove pastry from cookie sheet to heated plates with a spatula.

To toast almonds, place almonds in a pie plate and bake until light golden brown. Watch carefully, they will burn quickly.

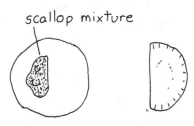

scallop mixture

"A host is like a general: it takes a mishap to reveal his genius."
Horace

================================TARRAGON SCALLOPS

The entire scallop including the roe, is edible; the roe is enjoyed mostly by Europeans. In the United States, we usually eat the adductor muscle that hinges the two shells.

Tarragon, a plant indigenous to Siberia, South Russia and West Asia, was unknown in Europe. It became a cooking ingredient in Italian, French, and English cooking during the late medieval period. The classic béarnaise sauce is tarragon's best-known use.

1 pound scallops (if small leave whole, if large cut each one in half)
1 cup half-and-half cream
1/2 teaspoon dried tarragon or 2 tablespoons fresh chopped tarragon
1/4 cup chopped green onions (scallions)
1/4 cup seafood crumbs, page 257
2 teaspoons butter

ASSEMBLY
1. Select two small individual ovenproof casseroles.
2. Mix scallops, cream, tarragon, and green onions in a small bowl, spoon into casserole, top with crumbs, and dot with butter.
3. Bake casseroles on cookie sheet in a preheated 400° oven for 15 minutes, or until scallops are firm. Do not overcook.
4. Serve in casserole dishes.

Serve in individual casseroles on a dinner plate, serve starch and vegetables on individual dishes.

"The pleasures of the table belong to all ages, to all conditions, to all countries and to every day."
Brillat-Savarin

=SCALLOPS BAKED WITH TOMATO AND PEAS

Store scallops in milk in the refrigerator. The milk draws out the frozen taste and provides a fresh caught flavor; it also helps remove some of the sand sometimes found in scallops.

1 pound scallops (if small leave whole, if large cup each one in half)
1/4 cup frozen green peas, thawed
8 cherry tomatoes
1/4 cup white wine or fish stock (clam juice can be used)
1/4 teaspoon dried basil or 2 tablespoons chopped fresh basil
1/4 cup seafood crumbs, page 257
1/4 cup chopped fresh parsley
2 teaspoons butter

ASSEMBLY
1. Place scallops into two individual casserole dishes; add peas, cherry tomatoes, wine, and basil. Top with crumbs, chopped parsley and dot with butter.
2. Bake on a cookie sheet in a preheated 400° oven for 15 minutes, or until scallops are firm. Be careful not to overcook, serve in casserole dishes.

"Some men see things as they are and say "Why?"
I dream things that never were and say "Why not?"
George Bernard Shaw

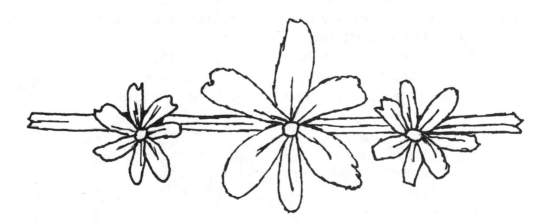

YOGURT FENNEL SCALLOPS

Scallops are classified into two broad groups: Bay scallops, with meat about 1/2-inch in diameter, are sweeter, more succulent and more expensive than the larger, more widely available sea scallops, whose meat averages 1 1/2-inches in diameter.

This is a great way to oven-fry scallops.

1 pound scallops (if small leave whole, if large cut each one in half)
1/2 cup plain yogurt
1/2 cup fine, dry, plain bread crumbs
1/4 cup grated Parmesan cheese
1/4 teaspoon ground fennel
1 garlic clove, minced
Dash ground red pepper (cayenne)
1/2 teaspoon paprika
1 tablespoon olive oil
Lemon wedges

PREPARATION
1. Place scallops in a bowl; stir in yogurt and mix well. Store in refrigerator for at least one hour.
2. Mix bread crumbs, Parmesan cheese, fennel, minced garlic, paprika, and cayenne in a mixing bowl.

ASSEMBLY
1. Oil a cookie sheet.
2. Drain scallops; a few at a time place scallops in bread crumb mixture and coat completely. Shake off excess and place on oiled cookie sheet, leaving a little room between scallops.
3. Bake in a preheated 400° oven for about 8 minutes. (The scallops will not be dark brown, but a pale color when done.)
4. Remove scallops to heated plates with a spatula. Serve at once. Garnish with lemon wedges.

Ground fennel is not always available in markets. I use a coffee grinder that is used only for spices to grind up fennel seeds.

Every evening after all the dinners were cooked, I would go out to the dining room to say hello and good-bye to guests.

One evening outside the men's room there was a man in a wheelchair, waiting for help. I asked him if he needed to go to the men's room and he nodded yes. I then realized he could not speak. I attempted to help him up and found that he had limited mobility.

After an attempt or two he was on his feet. I went around him and placed my hands under his arms and we shuffled through the men's room door and passed the sink to the urinal. He just stood there, and I said, "Is there anything further I can do for you, sir?" He pointed to the stall. I then said, "You need to use the other facility?" He nodded yes. I turned him around trying to back him into the stall, but he stood and would not make any attempt to undo his belt and sit down.

He then pointed to the roll of toilet paper. I said to myself, "What does he need the paper for, if he has not sat down?" He kept pointing to the roll and I said to him, "Do you want toilet paper? " He nodded yes, and I then reached down and unrolled some of the toilet paper and handed it to him. He proceeded to blow his nose, and I then realized his mission for visiting the men's room.

We hobbled out of the men's room, and I returned him to the wheelchair. He went to the bar with my help, and I helped him sit on a barstool, where he had an after-dinner drink with the pretty young lady who had brought him out for the evening.

SHRIMP

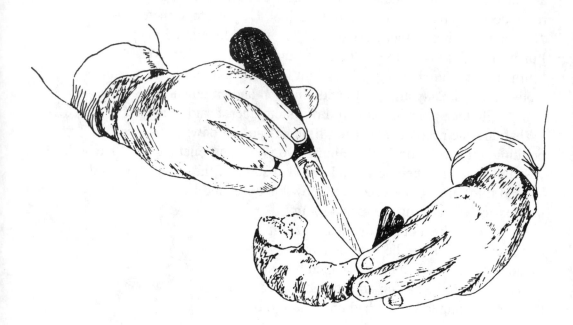

All recipes are for two in this chapter.

============*Hints and Suggestions*

SIZE OF SHRIMP: I use U-10 or U-12 shrimp in most recipes. The letter "U" means <u>under</u> 10 or 12 shrimp to a pound. The number means the count of shrimp in each pound. That is why the smaller the number; the larger the shrimp.

=========================*CRUNCHY SHRIMP*

Living in a small town has many advantages, for example knowing everyone at the post office. I mail many cookbooks; one day the lady at the counter said to me. "I cooked a shrimp recipe from your cookbook last night." I replied, "that's great did you enjoy it?" She replied. "My husband thought it was too crunchy". I thought for a minute and replied. "Did you peel the shrimp?" She said. "Oh I guess I missed that line in the recipe."
We both had a laugh about the crunchy shrimp.

CHUTNEY SHRIMP WELLINGTON

Smaller shrimp can be substituted in this dish.

The early Greeks and Romans used cultivated mushrooms in a wide variety of dishes. The cultivated mushroom is available in most supermarkets today. To clean mushrooms wipe them with a damp towel; do not soak them in water.

6 U-10 or U-12 shrimp, shelled, deveined, tails removed and cut in three
2 Pepperidge Farm patty shells, thawed
Flour for rolling pastry, and dusting cookie sheet
2 teaspoons butter
1/4 cup chopped onions
1/4 cup sliced mushrooms
1/4 cup chopped green onions (scallions)
2 teaspoons mango chutney
1/4 teaspoon curry powder
1/4 cup chopped fresh parsley
1 hard cooked egg, chopped
1 egg beaten with 1 teaspoon milk in a small bowl

PREPARATION

1. On a floured board, roll puff pastry into two 8-inch rounds. Store puff pastry between plastic wrap and keep in refrigerator.
2. Melt 1 teaspoon butter over medium heat in a skillet; sauté onion for just a minute, stir in shrimp, mushrooms, and green onions, cook until shrimp turn pink. Cool.
3. Mix shrimp mixture, chutney, curry, parsley, and chopped egg in a mixing bowl.

Chutney Shrimp Wellington continued-

ASSEMBLY
1. Butter and flour an insulated cookie sheet or regular cookie sheet.
2. Place rolled pastry on a flat surface. Into the center of each pastry, spoon equal amount of shrimp mixture.
   Moisten edges with egg wash; wrap pastry around shrimp. Place pastry package on floured cookie sheet; brush egg wash on pastry.
3. Bake in a preheated 400° oven on middle shelf for 20 minutes or until golden brown.
4. Remove pastry to heated plates with a spatula.

Parchment paper, can be used instead of buttering and flouring the cookie sheet

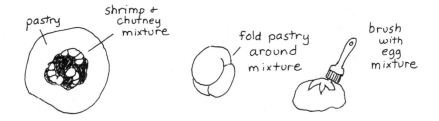

"Too much of a good thing can be wonderful."
May West

*Cajun seasoning might include garlic, onion, chilies, pepper,
mustard and celery. There are many Cajun-seasoning blends
on the market today, all with their own distinct characteristics.
Most are boldly flavored, representing Cajun cooking.*

Shrimp are marketed according to size (number per pound).

8 U-12 uncooked shrimp, shelled, deveined and tails intact
1/2 cup olive oil
1 1/2 tablespoons Cajun seasoning
1/4 cup chopped green onions (scallions)
1 tablespoon honey
1 tablespoon soy sauce

ASSEMBLY

1. Select an ovenproof casserole just large enough to hold the shrimp. Add all ingredients to casserole dish and mix to coat. Refrigerate for at least 1 hour, stirring occasionally.
2. Bake in a preheated 400° oven for about 15 minutes, stirring occasionally. This dish is great with pasta or rice.

*"The primary requisite for writing well about food
is a good appetite."*

A. J. Liebling

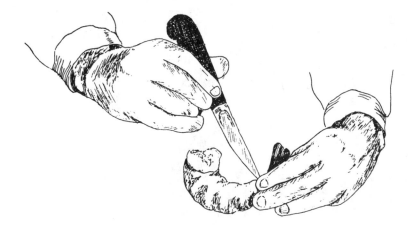

These are also great served as passed appetizers.

8 uncooked U-10 or U-12 shrimp, shelled, deveined and tails
  removed
2 egg whites
1/2 teaspoon curry powder
1 tablespoon butter
1 cup unsweetened shredded coconut
2 tablespoons Chinese hoisin sauce

PREPARATION
1. Whisk egg whites and curry powder in a small mixing bowl.

ASSEMBLY
1. Butter an ovenproof casserole dish large enough to contain the
   shrimp.
2. Place the coconut in a flat dish. Dip shrimp in egg
   whites, then roll shrimp evenly in coconut. Place shrimp on
   buttered ovenproof pan.
3. Bake in a preheated 400° oven for 15 minutes, until
   shrimp are firm.
4. Spread hoisin sauce evenly on dinner plates and place shrimp on
   top of hoisin sauce.

Helpful Hint

*One of the most versatile items in the kitchen is a muffin pan. It
can be used as a serving tray for cold drinks–the cups don't slide.
The muffin pan is also great that summer cookout to hold condiments
such as ketchup, mustard, mayonnaise, and relish. It also makes
great large ice cubes for punch.*

"Life is to short to drink the house wine."
Helen Thomas

================HOMESTEAD STYLE SHRIMP

My version of a tasty shrimp dish, I have enjoyed at a local restaurant.

8 uncooked U-10 or U-12 shrimp, shelled, deveined and tails removed
1 tablespoon butter softened
2 cloves garlic, minced
1/4 cup chopped fresh parsley
1/4 cup chopped green onions (scallions)
2 tablespoons plain dry or fresh bread crumbs
1 tablespoon olive oil
2 slices Swiss or Gruyere cheese

PREPARATION

1. Mix butter, garlic, parsley, green onions, and bread crumbs
   in a mixing bowl.

ASSEMBLY

1. Select and oil two small individual casserole dishes.
2. Place 4 shrimp in each casserole dish; top shrimp with crumb topping
   and cheese.
3. Bake in a preheated 400° oven for 15 to 20 minutes.
4. Serve shrimp in casserole dishes on a dinner plate.
   Serve starch and vegetables on side dishes.

HELPFUL HINT

*Vinegar is the one of the best cleaners for washing a deck. One
quart of vinegar to three quarts of water. Spray the deck (about a 5-by 5
area at a time) with this solution. Wait a few minutes and brush with
a short bristle brush that will not dig into the wood. Then rinse with
water. A cloudy day is best for cleaning, because the deck needs to
stay wet so the surface can be cleaned thoroughly. You can also put this
solution in a power washer. Deck should be very dry before applying
waterproofing.*

"Tastes are made, not born."
Mark Twain

OVEN-FRIED SHRIMP

Crunchy shrimp with a dynamic sauce.

8 jumbo shrimp (U10 or U12) peeled, deveined and tails removed
1 teaspoon grated orange peel (zest)
1/4 teaspoon dried crushed pepper
1/2 cup fresh orange juice
1 tablespoon olive oil
1/4 cup fine dry bread crumbs
1/4 cup fine crushed corn flakes
1 egg beaten with 1 teaspoon milk in a bowl

1/2 cup orange marmalade
1/2 teaspoon prepared white horseradish
1 teaspoons soy sauce

PREPARATION
1. Mix grated orange peel, crushed pepper, orange juice, and shrimp
   in a mixing bowl. Marinate for 1/2 hour in refrigerator.

ASSEMBLY
1. Oil an ovenproof baking sheet. Mix bread crumbs and cornflake
   crumbs in a small bowl. Remove shrimp from marinade; dip in egg,
   then in crumbs, coating completely one at a time, and place on
   baking sheet.
2. Bake in a preheated 400° oven for 15 minutes.
3. While shrimp are baking, heat orange marmalade, horseradish, and
   soy sauce in a saucepan over medium low heat, stirring occasionally.
   Do not allow to boil. Keep warm.
4. Remove shrimp from baking sheet to heated plates, spoon sauce
   around shrimp.

Rice is a natural with this dish.

*"The most indispensable ingredient of all good home cooking:
love for those you are cooking for."*
> Sophia Loren

The flavors in this shrimp dish are delicate and peppy.

8 uncooked U-10 or U-12 shrimp, shelled, deveined, tails removed
2 garlic cloves, minced
1/4 pound butter softened
1 tablespoon medium-dry sherry
1/4 cup chopped fresh parsley
1/4 cup chopped green onions (scallions)
1/4 cup finely chopped sweet red bell pepper, cored, and seeded
1/4 cup fine dry bread crumbs
1/4 cup sliced almonds
1 tablespoon olive oil

PREPARATION
1. Mix garlic, butter, sherry, parsley, green onions, pepper, and bread crumbs.

ASSEMBLY
1. Oil an ovenproof casserole dish just large enough to
   contain the shrimp in a single layer (or individual casserole dishes).
2. Place shrimp in casserole dish; top shrimp evenly with crumb topping
   and sprinkle with almonds.
3. Bake in a preheated 400° oven for 15 minutes, or until shrimp are
   firm to the touch.
4. Remove shrimp with spoon to heated plates, or serve in individual
   casserole dishes. Spoon any remaining juices on shrimp.

Helpful Hint
Simple scissor sharpening: Just use them to cut fine-grated sandpaper.
About half a dozen cuts will sharpen most scissors.

"Life is like an onion.
You peel it off one layer at a time;
and sometimes you weep."
Carl Sandburg

=============SHRIMP BAKED WITH SPINACH

Fresh spinach and nutmeg are a great complement to this shrimp dish.

8 uncooked U-12 shrimp shelled, deveined, tails removed
2 1/2 tablespoons butter
1/4 cup chopped onion
8 ounces fresh spinach, washed, trimmed, and roughly chopped
1 tablespoon flour
1 cup milk
1/4 cup chopped fresh parsley
Dash nutmeg
1/4 cup chopped green onions (scallions)
1/4 cup seafood crumbs, page 257
1 tablespoon grated Parmesan cheese

PREPARATION

1. Melt 1 tablespoon butter over medium heat in a skillet;
   sauté onion until yellow, then stir in spinach and cook until wilted.
   Cool.
2. Melt 1 tablespoon butter in a saucepan. Stir in flour and make
   a smooth paste. Gradually add milk and continue stirring until
   sauce thickens. Remove from heat; stir in parsley, nutmeg, and
   green onions. Cool.

ASSEMBLY

1. Butter two individual casseroles and place a layer of spinach
   evenly in the bottom of each one. Place 4 shrimp on top of spinach,
   and spoon sauce on and around shrimp, top with crumbs and
   Parmesan cheese.
2. Bake casseroles on a cookie sheet in a preheated 400° oven
   for 15 minutes. Serve in casseroles.

*Place casseroles on serving plates; use side dishes for starch
and vegetables.*

SHRIMP IN SPICY COCONUT MILK

Garlic, chili pepper, curry, and coconut milk are distinct in this shrimp dish.

8 uncooked U-10 or U-12 shrimp, shelled, deveined, tails removed
1 tablespoon olive oil
1/2 cup finely chopped onion
2 cloves garlic, minced
1 tablespoon fresh ginger, peeled and minced
1/2 small green chili pepper, such as Serrano or jalapeno
    thinly sliced into rings, remove seeds
1/2 cup flour
1/2 teaspoon curry powder
1 cup coconut milk
Cooked rice

PREPARATION
1. Heat oil in a skillet over medium heat; sauté onion and garlic for just a minute, then stir in ginger and pepper. Cook for just a minute.

ASSEMBLY
1. Mix flour and curry in a small mixing bowl.
2. Select an ovenproof casserole just large enough to contain the shrimp. Spoon the onion mixture on bottom. Dip shrimp in flour, coating completely. Shake off excess flour, place floured shrimp on top of onion, and add coconut milk.
3. Bake in a preheated 400° oven for 15 minutes
4. Place the hot rice on plates and spoon shrimp and sauce on and around rice.

This dish can be also served with pasta.

"Food is meant to tempt as well as nourish,
and everything that lives in the water is seductive."
Jean-Paul Aron

==SHRIMP WITH BALSAMIC, GARLIC, HERBS

Balsamic vinegar is new to the American cuisine;
the Italians have enjoyed its wonderful flavor for many years.

8 uncooked U-10 or U-12 shrimp shelled, deveined and tails removed.
1/4 cup olive oil
1/4 cup vermouth or white wine
1 teaspoon lemon juice
1/4 cup chopped fresh parsley
2 garlic cloves, finely chopped
1 teaspoon dried oregano or dried or fresh basil
1/4 cup balsamic vinegar

PREPARATION
1. Mix olive oil, vermouth, lemon juice, parsley, garlic, oregano, and balsamic vinegar in a mixing bowl.

ASSEMBLY
1. Select an ovenproof casserole dish just large enough to contain the shrimp in a single layer (or individual casserole dishes). Place shrimp in casserole; spoon balsamic vinegar marinade over shrimp. Marinate for 1 hour in the refrigerator.
2. Bake shrimp with marinade in a preheated 400° oven for 15 minutes, basting once or twice, until shrimp is firm to the touch.
3. Remove shrimp with spoon to heated plates, or serve in individual casserole dishes. Spoon juices on and around shrimp.

The U number is the amount of shrimp in a pound.

"To be a successful cook you must be exposed to many flavors and ideas, but you should keep your own style and agenda."
Author

SHRIMP WITH PROSCIUTTO

This Italian style shrimp is wonderful served with pasta.

8 uncooked U-10 of U-12 shrimp, shelled, deveined and tails removed
1/4 olive oil
2 cloves garlic, minced
1/4 pound Prosciutto, cut in fine julienne
1/4 cup red wine
1/4 cup tomato paste
1/2 teaspoon dry powdered mustard
1/2 teaspoon dried oregano
1/4 cup chopped fresh parsley
Dash ground red pepper (cayenne)
2 slices Provolone cheese

PREPARATION

1. Heat the oil over medium heat in a saucepan; sauté garlic while
   stirring for a minute, stir in Prosciutto and cook for a minute.
   Stir in red wine, tomato paste, dry mustard, oregano, parsley, and
   cayenne. Allow the mixture cook for about 2 minutes. Cool.

ASSEMBLY

1. Select two individual casseroles. (If you are serving pasta, you can
   use one casserole.) Place 4 shrimp flat in casserole and spoon sauce
   on shrimp, top with Provolone cheese.
2. Bake casseroles on a cookie sheet in a preheated 400° oven
   for 15 to 20 minutes. Serve in casseroles or spoon on pasta.

*"Tomatoes and oregano make it Italian, wine and tarragon
make it French. Sour cream makes it Russian; lemon and
cinnamon make it Greek. Soy sauce makes it Chinese;
garlic makes it good."*
　　　　　　　　Alice May Brock

STUFFED SHRIMP

Baked stuffed shrimp, a classic shrimp dish that is served in many of Rhode Island's traditional restaurants. We served many of these shrimp at the Red Rooster and the Pump House Restaurants.

8 U-10 or U-12 uncooked shrimp, shelled, deveined and tails intact
1/2 cup water
1/4 cup melted butter
Lemon wedges
STUFFING:
1 cup seafood crumbs, page 257
2 tablespoons melted butter
1 (10-ounce) can, (or fresh crabmeat), drained, check for bones.
2 tablespoons white wine
1 teaspoon lemon juice
2 tablespoons chopped green onions, green part only (scallions)
1 tablespoon mayonnaise

PREPARATION

1. Mix all the ingredients for stuffing. Keep in refrigerator until ready to use.
2. Using a sharp knife, slice the underside of the shrimp, being careful not to go all the way through, remove vein.

ASSEMBLY

1. In the palm of hand compress 1 tablespoon of stuffing, then press into shrimp.
2. Place stuffed shrimp in a ovenproof pie plate, or individual casserole, add water.
3. Bake in a preheated 400° oven for 15 minutes. Shrimp will turn white and firm when done.
4. Remove shrimp to heated plates, or serve in casserole dishes. Serve with side of melted butter and lemon wedges.

This stuffing is great for stuffed mushrooms and stuffing fish.
Any left over stuffing can be refrigerated or frozen for future use.

============FLYING FRIENDS DURING DINNER

When we bought the Pump House Restaurant in the early 1980s, we knew that many surprises were in store for us: learning the quirks of a new building, staff who are strangers, a new menu and two restaurants to keep track of. The Pump House is a wonderful stone building, built in 1888 as a steam-engine-powered water pumping station for the town of South Kingstown, RI.

The building has a large stone chimney and we did not know it housed a colony of bats. One Saturday evening during dinner two bats decided to make their debut. A restaurant can get away with having flies, mosquitoes, bees and lots of other things, but bats flying around the dining room are something else.

"Is that a bat?" asked one customer. "I don't know!" replied a waiter. Well, it did not take long for everyone to realize they really were bats. Everyone left the dining room. Then Bob, our partner-manager, gathered the staff, got out brooms and eventually got rid of the bats. The guests reluctantly came back into the dining room to finish their evening with us, and eventually everyone had a good laugh about the bats. Later, we were able to get someone from town to remove the entire colony from the chimney.

In the 1960's and early 1970's, Quonset Naval Base and Davisville Seabee Base were bustling with great activity. The restaurant was just a half-mile from the bases. During that period, we hired many Navy wives. One day this pretty lady named Nora came in for a job, and she had a very strong Italian accent. As we interviewed her, we decided that she should be part of our team. She had a wonderful charm and European flair, something we thought the restaurant could use. She soon became one of our most popular waitresses and one of our very good friends.

The base closed in the late 1970's; the Navy left and so did all of our Navy wives. Nora stayed in touch, she and her family still remain our good friends.

On the way to a friends wedding, going through Providence on the freeway, she said to me "Normand, in all the time I have known you, why have you not taken me there?" She was looking at our beautiful State House. I said, "Nora, the State House is only open during the day." On the way back from the wedding, the State House was beautifully lit and she mentioned it again. "I want to go there, is it a good restaurant?" she then said, "that building is a steak house right?" I explained to her the building was the "State House', the seat of the government in Rhode Island. It was really funny, because in all the time she lived in Rhode Island she thought the State House was a steak house.

SOLE
FLOUNDER

clean, crisp,
well balanced white wine

EPD '90

386

All recipes are for two in this chapter.

==================*Hints and Suggestions*

FISH SIZE: In all the sole dishes, I suggest 3 to 4-ounce fillets, because I find this size is best to work with, but you may use whatever is available.

SKIN SIDE DOWN: The smoother side with a darker color is usually the skin side. If you have any doubts about what side is the skin side, ask the clerk when you purchase the fish.

SOLE: When you purchase sole, here in the States it is actually flounder, unless the fish is imported from Europe.

ASPARAGUS-CHEESE SOLE

Asparagus is grown in sandy soil so thorough washing is necessary to ensure the tips are not gritty. If the asparagus stems are tough, remove outer layer with a vegetable peeler. The more mature the plant the larger the stem. I like to use the pencil size asparagus when available.

4 3 to 4-ounce pieces of sole or flounder
8 fresh asparagus spears trimmed and blanched
1/4 cup white wine or fish stock (clam juice can be used)
4 slices Monterey Jack cheese or American cheese
1/2 teaspoon dried dill or 1 teaspoon fresh chopped dill
1/4 cup seafood crumbs, page 257
1 tablespoon butter

ASSEMBLY

1. Select an ovenproof casserole large enough to contain the fish.
2. Roll fish, skin side up around two asparagus spears, trimmed to same size as fish. Place rolled fish, seam side down, in casserole dish and add wine. Top with cheese, dill, crumbs, and dot with butter.
3. Bake in a preheated 400° oven for 20 minutes
4. Remove fish with spatula to heated plates. Spoon some remaining juices on and around fish.

To blanch asparagus, place it in boiling water for 3 minutes. Cool immediately in ice water.

"The Romans had a saying when they wanted something done quickly. "Do it," they said, "in less time that it takes to cook asparagus."

Alexander Dumas

==================================CRAB STUFFED SOLE

*This stuffing can be used for any type of fish. Chopped shrimp
can be used instead of crabmeat.*

4   3 to 4-ounce pieces of sole or flounder
1/4 cup white wine or fish stock (clam juice can be used)
4 thin slices Monterey Jack cheese or American cheese
Dash paprika
2 teaspoons butter

STUFFING:
1 cup seafood crumbs, page 257
1 tablespoon mayonnaise
1/2 cup crabmeat (canned or fresh) check for bones
1 tablespoon white wine
1 teaspoon lemon juice
1/4 cup chopped green onions (scallions)

PREPARATION
1. Mix all the ingredients in a mixing bowl for stuffing.

ASSEMBLY
1. Select an oven proof casserole dish large enough to contain
    the rolled sole.
2. On a flat surface place sole, skin side up; spread the stuffing evenly
    on each sole fillet. Roll the sole like a jellyroll and place in casserole
    dish, seam side down.
3. Add fish stock to casserole, place cheese on top of each rolled
    stuffed sole, top with paprika and dot with butter.
4. Bake in a preheated 400° oven for 20 minutes.
5. Remove rolled sole to heated plates with a spatula. Spoon some
    remaining juices on and around sole.

"All good cooks learn something new every day."
Julia Child

GARDEN POACHED SOLE

A wonderful one-dish meal that includes vegetables and fish.

    Nutmeg was one of the spices that Columbus was looking for when he sailed from Spain to the West Indies. Nutmeg was extremely popular throughout most of the world. The hard, egg-shaped nutmeg seed can be grated with a nutmeg grater, as you need it. As you grate it, the aroma will perk up your senses. It is funny that Connecticut is called the nutmeg state. That came about in early times when peddlers carved wooden replicas of whole nutmeg and fooled housewives into buying them.

4   3 to 4-ounce pieces of sole or flounder
1 small carrot peeled, and cut like matchsticks (julienne)
1 small zucchini cut like matchsticks (julienne)
1 small onion, sliced thin
4 asparagus spears, trimmed
4 cherry tomatoes
1/2 cup white wine or fish stock, (clam juice will work fine)
1/4 cup seafood crumbs, page 257
Dash nutmeg

PREPARATION
1. Select a covered ovenproof casserole dish large enough to contain the sole and vegetables. Roll fish skin side in and place in casserole.
2. Add all the prepared vegetables and wine; top with crumbs and nutmeg.
3. Bake covered in a preheated 400° oven for 20 minutes.
4. Remove fish to heated plates with a spatula. Spoon vegetables on and around fish.

Helpful Hint
    Spices should never be stored near a range. The heat tends to cause a loss of flavor, potency, and color. All spices should be stored in a cool dry location.

"Americans, more than any other culture on earth, are cookbook cooks."
                John Thorne

*Horseradish should be used within four weeks of opening,
otherwise it starts to lose its hotness and starts to turn bitter.*

4   3 to 4-ounce pieces of sole or flounder folded in half
1 medium onion, cut in half and sliced thin
1/2 cup white wine or fish stock, (clam juice can be used)
1/4 cup seafood crumbs, page 257
1 (11-ounce) can cream of shrimp soup
1 teaspoon grated white horseradish
1/4 cup chopped fresh parsley
1/4 cup milk
Dash nutmeg

ASSEMBLY

1. Select an ovenproof casserole dish large enough to contain
    the four sole fillets.
2. Spread the onions evenly on the bottom of the casserole,
    add fish fillets, wine and top with crumbs.
3. Mix shrimp soup, horseradish, chopped parsley, milk, and nutmeg
    in a mixing bowl.
4. Bake casserole in a preheated 400° oven for 15 minutes.
    Take out of oven and spoon horseradish sauce on and around fish.
    Return casserole to oven and cook 5 minutes more, or until
    heated through.
5. Remove sole to heated plates with a spatula. Spoon onions
    and sauce on and around fish.

*The sauce in this dish is a little bold; I suggest rice and
simple vegetables.*

*"When you find a waiter who is a waiter and not an
actor, musician or poet, you've found a jewel."*
André Soltner

POACHED SOLE AND SALMON WITH VEGETABLES

This dish is a one-pot meal. Serve with nice crusty bread.

4   3 to 4-ounce pieces of sole or flounder
4 large spinach leaves without stems
1/2 pound of salmon fillets, boned, skinned and cut in four even pieces
1/2 teaspoon dried dill or 1 teaspoon chopped fresh dill
1 cup fish broth or clam juice
1/4 cup seafood crumbs, page 257
1 teaspoon butter

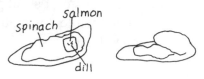

JULIENNE THESE VEGETABLES:
1 medium carrot, peeled
1 trimmed leek, white part only (washed)
1 small zucchini
1/2 red bell sweet pepper, cored and seeded
1/2 yellow or green bell pepper, cored and seeded
   (To julienne vegetables, cut into pieces about the size of
   match sticks. Vegetables can be prepared ahead and stored covered
   in refrigerator).

ASSEMBLY
1. On a flat surface place sole fillets skin side up, press spinach
   leaf into fish, top with salmon and sprinkle with dill.
   Roll sole so that salmon is in center.
2. Select an ovenproof casserole dish with a cover. Place fish
   in casserole seam side down, place julienne vegetables on and around
   fish. Add fish broth, top with crumbs and dot with butter.
3. Bake covered casserole in a preheated 400° oven for 20 minutes.
4. Remove fish from casserole with a large spoon to heated plates
   and spoon vegetables and juice on and around fish.

> *"Wine makes every meal an occasion,*
> *every table more elegant, every day more civilized."*
> *André Simon*

POACHED SOLE WITH GRAPES

Grapes have been consumed in many ways for as long as man can remember. There are thousands of grape varieties, each with its own particular use and charm. Because most supermarket grapes have been sprayed with insecticide, grapes should be thoroughly washed.

4   3 to 4-ounce pieces of sole or flounder
1/4 cup finely chopped onion
1/2 pound seedless white grapes
1/4 cup seafood crumbs, page 257
Dash nutmeg
1 tablespoon butter
1/2 cup white wine or fish stock (clam juice can be used)

ASSEMBLY

1. Select a covered ovenproof casserole just large enough to contain fish.
2. Roll fish skin side in and place in casserole seam side down. Place chopped onion and white grapes around fish. Top fish with crumbs and nutmeg, dot with butter and add wine.
3. Bake covered in a preheated 400° oven for 20 minutes.
4. Remove fish with spatula to warm plates, spoon grapes and liquid on and around fish.

"A wine drinker, being at table, was offered grapes at dessert.
"Thank you," he said, pushing the dish away from him,
"but I am not in the habit of taking my wine in pills."
Brillat-Savarin

ROLLED STUFFED SOLE

Instead of crab you can use chopped shrimp or lobster.

4 3 to 4-ounce pieces of sole or flounder
2 eggs, beaten in a small bowl
1 cup plain bread crumbs, dried or fresh
2 teaspoons butter
1 cup sliced fresh mushrooms

STUFFING:
1/4 cup (2-ounces) cream cheese, room temperature
1/2 cup crab meat (canned or fresh), check for bones
2 ounces Roquefort cheese or Blue cheese, room temperature
1/2 teaspoon lemon juice
1/2 teaspoon Pernod or Anisette (optional)
1/4 cup chopped fresh parsley
1/4 cup chopped green onions (scallions)
Dash hot pepper sauce (Tabasco)
Dash Worcestershire sauce
1 tablespoon plain bread crumbs

PREPARATION
1. Mix stuffing ingredients in a mixing bowl. Refrigerate at
   least 20 minutes to firm up.

ASSEMBLY
1. On a flat surface place fish skin side up, spread 1/4 of filling
   evenly on each fish fillet. Roll fish like a jellyroll.
2. Butter with 1 teaspoon butter an ovenproof casserole dish large
   enough to contain the rolled fish.
3. Place crumbs in a flat dish. Dip each rolled fish fillet carefully in
   beaten egg, then roll in crumbs. Place in buttered casserole dish,
   seam side down and not touching each other.
4. Bake in a preheated 400° oven for 20 minutes.
5. While fish is cooking, heat a skillet; add 1 teaspoon of butter
   and mushrooms; sauté until mushrooms are wilted. Keep warm.
6. Remove fish to heated plates with a spatula and spoon sliced
   mushrooms on and around fish.

====SOLE BAKED WITH A MUSTARD TOPPING

Whole grain mustard can be stone ground mustard. The mustard plant belongs to the same family as broccoli, and Brussels sprouts. Through the centuries, mustard has been used for culinary as well as medicinal purposes.

4   3 to 4-ounce pieces of sole or flounder
1/2 cup whole egg mayonnaise
1/2 tablespoon whole grain mustard
1/4 cup chopped green onions (scallions)
1/4 cup water or white wine
1/4 cup seafood crumbs, page 257

PREPARATION
1. Mix mayonnaise, mustard, and green onions in a small bowl.

ASSEMBLY
1. Fold sole in half. Place fish in an ovenproof casserole dish large enough to contain the fish. Add water.
2. Spoon crumbs evenly on fish. Spoon mustard mixture evenly on fish.
3. Bake in a preheated 400° oven for 20 minutes.
4. Remove fish from casserole dish to heated plates with a spatula.

Low fat or diet mayonnaise will not work as well in this recipe. Use whole egg mayonnaise, such as Hellmann's.

"I am so helplessly addicted (to mustard) that I cannot manage to slip on an apron unless I know it is within easy reach."
Bert Greene

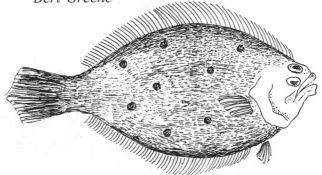

SOLE BAKED WITH ALMONDS

Almond is the kernel of the fruit of the almond tree, grown in California and warmer countries. Almonds are available blanched, whole, sliced, chopped, smoked, and in paste. Toasting and baking almonds intensifies their flavor and adds crunch to any dish.

4   3 to 4-ounce pieces of sole or flounder
1/2 cup seafood crumbs, page 257
1/2 cup sliced almonds
1/4 cup chopped fresh parsley
1 tablespoon butter
1/2 cup white wine or fish stock (clam juice can be used)
Lemon wedges

ASSEMBLY

1. In an ovenproof casserole dish large enough to contain the fish, lay fish skin side down. Top evenly with crumbs, almonds, and chopped parsley. Dot with butter and add wine.
2. Bake in a preheated 400° oven for 15 minutes.
3. Remove fish with a spatula to heated plates. Garnish with lemon wedges.

> *"The smell of almonds toasting in a metal pan...is the most agreeable incense I know....I am decidedly addicted to the perfume of these nuts."*
>   Bert Greene

=======SOLE BAKED WITH BANNANAS AND GRAPEFRUIT JUICE

I put this dish on the menu in the restaurant because of the shock value and wonderful flavor of the combinations. The sweetness of the banana, the tartness of the grapefruit and the taste and smell of the curry.

4   3 to 4-ounce pieces of sole or flounder
2 ripe bananas peeled, and cut in half
1 cup grapefruit juice, unsweetened
1/4 cup seafood crumbs, page 257
1/4 teaspoon curry powder
1/4 cup sliced almonds
1 tablespoon butter

ASSEMBLY
1. Select an ovenproof casserole large enough to hold the sole.
2. Roll sole skin side up around a half of banana and place in casserole dish. Add grapefruit juice, top with crumbs, curry and almonds. Dot with butter.
3. Bake in a preheated 400° oven for 20 minutes.
4. Remove fish with a spatula to heated plates; spoon remaining juices on and around fish.

Curry powder is widely used in Indian cooking. Curry powder is actually a blend of about 20 spices, herbs, and seeds. Every one in India has their own variation and blend of what they think curry should taste like

"A cook is creative, marrying ingredients in the way a poet marries words."
                    Roger Vergé

==SOLE IN PASTRY WITH A SCALLOP MOUSSE

Mousse is a French term meaning "froth" or "foam."
Mousses are rich and are usually made from meat, fish, shellfish,
cheese, and vegetables. Beaten egg whites and cream make this
dish light and delicate.

4   3 to 4-ounce pieces of sole or flounder
2 Pepperidge Farm patty shells, thawed, cut in two
Flour for rolling pastry and for dusting baking sheet
Oil for baking sheet
1 egg beaten with 1 teaspoon milk in a small bowl
1 (10-ounce) can cream of shrimp soup
1/2 cup milk

MOUSSE:
1/4 pound scallops
1/4 teaspoon salt
Dash paprika
Dash white pepper
1/8 cup chopped green onion (scallions)
Dash nutmeg
1 egg white
1/2 cup heavy cream

PREPARATION

1. On a floured board roll pastry, making 4 rounds about 5 inches
   in diameter. Wrap rolled pastry in plastic wrap and place
   in refrigerator.
2. To make mousse:
   Chill steel blade and work bowl of a food processor (or blender) in the
   refrigerator for about 20 minutes. In the cold bowl of the processor,
   add scallops, salt, paprika, pepper, green onion, nutmeg, egg white,
   and cream. Pulse processor for a minute; use a spatula to scrape side
   of processor, making sure all is blended; process until mixture is thick.
   Store in refrigerator covered with plastic wrap until ready to use.

Sole in pastry with a scallop mousse continued-

ASSEMBLY
1. Oil and flour a baking sheet (insulated if possible).
2. Place sole fillets on a flat surface, skin side up.
   Spread mousse mixture evenly on each piece of sole. Roll like a
   jellyroll. Position rolled sole in the center of rolled pastry. Wrap pastry
   around rolled fish, seal seams egg wash. Brush egg mixture on puff
   pastry and place on floured cookie sheet.
3. Bake in a preheated 400° oven on middle shelf for 20 minutes.
4. While fish is cooking, heat cream of shrimp soup and milk in a saucepan,
   stirring occasionally. Keep warm.
5. Spoon some sauce on bottom of heated plate. Remove sole packages
   with a spatula and place on sauce. Serve extra sauce on side.
   Serve two portions for dinner. Serve one portion as an appetizer.

*If sauce is a little too thick, add more milk. A little sherry can
be added to the sauce.*

*"If you accept a dinner invitation you have the moral
obligation to be amusing."*
The Duchess of Windsor

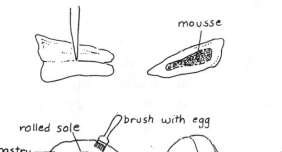

====SOLE BAKED WITH TOMATO AND CHEESE

This dish is wonderful with native tomatoes and fresh basil.
The total dishes around the world in which tomato is the main
ingredient must amount to thousands. Tomato ketchup is America's
'national condiment', it's the first thing kids go for when eating in a
restaurant or at home.

4 3 to 4-ounce pieces of sole or flounder
1 teaspoon butter
1 cup seasoned bread crumbs
8 slices fresh tomato
1/2 teaspoon dried basil or fresh chopped basil
4 slices provolone cheese
1/4 cup chopped fresh parsley
1 teaspoon olive oil

ASSEMBLY

1. Butter an ovenproof casserole dish large enough to contain the fish.
2. Place crumbs in a flat plate and press fish into crumbs. Place
   breaded fish in prepared casserole. Top each sole fillet with 2 tomato
   slices, sprinkle with basil, top with slice of provolone cheese, chopped
   parsley, and drizzle with olive oil.
3. Bake in a preheated 400° oven for 20 minutes.
4. Remove fish from casserole to heated plates with a spatula.

Helpful Hint

If you are using frozen seafood, thaw it in the refrigerator in
a bowl of milk. The milk will add moisture and sweeten up the
seafood.

"Imagination is more important than knowledge."
Albert Einstein

==SOLE STUFFED WITH SHRIMP MOUSSELINE

This dish was very popular at the restaurant. The shrimp mousseline is very light and airy.

4   3 to 4-ounce pieces of sole or flounder cut in half lengthwise
1/2 cup seafood crumbs, page 257
1 teaspoon butter
1/2 cup white wine or fish stock

MOUSSELINE:
1/2 pound fresh shrimp, raw, shelled,
   deveined, tails removed
1 egg white
1/2 cup heavy cream
1/2 teaspoon dried dill
  or 1 teaspoon chopped fresh dill
Sprig fresh parsley
Dash white pepper

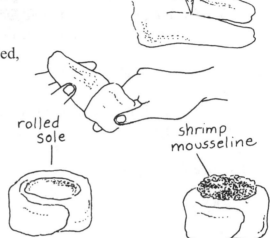

PREPARATION

1. To make mousseline:
   Chill steel blade and work bowl of a food processor (or blender)
   in the refrigerator for about 20 minutes. In the cold bowl of processor,
   add shrimp, egg white, heavy cream, dill, parsley, and white pepper.
   Turn on processor for a minute and turn off. Use a spatula to scrape
   side of processor making sure all is blended. Mixture will be thick.
   Store in refrigerator covered with plastic wrap until ready to use.

ASSEMBLY

1. Select an ovenproof casserole dish large enough to contain the
   eight rolled sole.
2. Roll sole around finger and place in casserole dish side by side.
   Spoon mousse mixture in middle of each roll making sure that the sole
   stays round. Top with crumbs, dot with butter and add wine to casserole.
3. Bake in a preheated 400° oven for 20 minutes.
4. Remove rolled fish from casserole to heated plates very carefully
   with a spatula; spoon wine juices on and around fish

SOLE TIMBALE WITH OYSTERS

Satirist Jonathan Swift wrote in the 18th century, "He was a bold man that first ate an oyster." Oysters have been a culinary favorite for thousands of years. If you try to open oysters yourself, be very careful; find the correct oyster knife, then make sure to hold the oyster with a towel to protect yourself from the knife slipping and hurting you. We served oysters on the half-shell at the restaurant. When a party of four ordered oysters on the half shell, it meant opening 24 oysters in a short period of time. I have had many slips with the knife. Special gloves are available for opening oysters. It is easier to get the oysters opened at the fish market, or buy a pint.

4   3 to 4-ounce pieces of sole or flounder cut in half lengthwise
1/2 pint fresh oysters
1/2 cup white wine of fish stock (clam juice can be used)
4 slices American cheese, cut in half
Dash nutmeg
1/4 cup chopped fresh parsley
1/4 cup seafood crumbs, page 257
2 teaspoons butter

ASSEMBLY
1. Select an ovenproof casserole dish large enough to contain the 8 fish rounds.
2. Roll sole around a finger to make a round. Place each fish round in casserole, in each fish round spoon oysters. Add wine, top with piece of American cheese, nutmeg, parsley, crumbs, and dot with butter.
3. Bake in a preheated 400° oven for 20 minutes
4. Remove rolled fish to heated plates with a spatula. Spoon some remaining juices on and around fish.

rolled
sole

oysters

SOLE TURNOVER WITH SCALLOPS AND SPINACH

Choose spinach leaves that are crisp and dark. Store in refrigerator until ready to use. Wash thoroughly.

4 3 to 4-ounce pieces of sole or flounder
2 teaspoons butter
1/4 cup finely chopped onion
1/2 pound fresh spinach, trimmed, washed and chopped
1/4 pound fresh scallops (small or chopped coarsely)
1 teaspoon dried dill or 1 tablespoon fresh chopped dill
1/2 cup water or white wine
4 thin slices Monterey Jack cheese
1/4 cup seafood crumbs, page 257

PREPARATION
1. Melt 1 teaspoon butter in a skillet over medium heat; sauté chopped onion until golden. Lower heat; stir in spinach until spinach wilts. Cool.
2. Add scallops and dill to cooled spinach mixture. Keep cold until ready to use.

ASSEMBLY
1. Select a casserole dish just large enough to contain the sole.
2. Place sole, skin side up, on a flat surface; spoon scallop mixture in middle of sole fillet; fold sole and press around to hold stuffing inside of fish. Place sole in casserole; add water, top sole with cheese, crumbs, and dot with remaining butter.
3. Bake in a preheated 400° oven for 20 minutes.
4. Remove sole from casserole dish to heated plates with a spatula.

"All cooks, like all great artists, must have an audience worth cooking for."
André Simon

SOLE WELLINGTON

Pepperidge Farm patty shells or Puff Pastry sheets, can be found in the freezer department in any supermarket.

4 3 to 4-ounce pieces of sole or flounder
2 Pepperidge Farm patty shells, cut in two, thawed
Flour for rolling pastry, and dusting cookie sheet
1 1/2 tablespoons butter
1/2 cup chopped green onions (scallions)
1/4 cup chopped mushrooms
1/4 cup chopped fresh parsley
1/2 teaspoon dried dill or 1 teaspoon chopped fresh dill
3/4 cup small shrimp or chopped shrimp
2 slices American cheese
1 egg beaten with 1 teaspoon milk in a mixing bowl

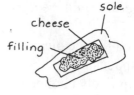

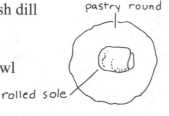

PREPARATION
1. On a floured board roll pastry, making four rounds about five inches in diameter. Wrap rolled pastry in plastic wrap and place in refrigerator.
2. Melt 1 tablespoon butter in a skillet; sauté green onions, mushrooms, and parsley, until mushrooms soften.
   Add shrimp and cook for a minute, until shrimp firms up. Cool

ASSEMBLY
1. Butter and flour a cookie sheet (preferably the insulated type)
2. On a flat surface lay out fish skin side up. Place 1/2 slice cheese on each fish fillet, then spread with 1/4 of the filling on each fish, roll fish around filling like a jellyroll.
3. Place rolled puff pastry on a flat surface. In the center of each pastry place a rolled sole, seam side down. Wrap pastry around fish like a small package, moisten seams with egg wash. Place on floured cookie sheet and brush pastry with egg wash.
4. Bake in a preheated 400° oven on middle shelf for 20 minutes.
5. Remove fish package from cookie sheet with a spatula.
   Serve two portions for dinner. Serve one portion as an appetizer.

=========SOLE WITH APPLES EN PAPILLOTE

Parchment paper can be purchased in most markets or specialty stores.

4 3 to 4-ounce pieces of sole or flounder
1 teaspoon butter
1/4 cup sliced mushrooms
1/4 cup chopped green onion (scallions)
1 large clove garlic, minced
1 teaspoon lemon juice
1/4 teaspoon dried tarragon
1 medium-size tart apple, peeled, cored and coarsely chopped
1/4 cup chopped fresh parsley
2 tablespoons sour cream or plain yogurt
2 pieces of parchment 12 x 12 inch (or aluminum foil)

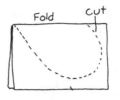

PREPARATION

1. Melt butter in a skillet over medium heat; sauté mushrooms, green onions, and garlic until mushrooms wilt. Off heat, stir in lemon juice, tarragon, apple, sour cream, and parsley. Cool.

ASSEMBLY

1. Fold each parchment sheet in half, and starting at the bottom, cut out and make a half-heart shape. Open each sheet and place one piece of sole in the middle. Spread apple mixture evenly on each sole fillet, place another sole fillet on top of apple mixture. Fold the parchment starting at the point and continue to fold, then crimp the edges to seal.
2. Place parchment packets on a cookie sheet and bake in a preheated 400° oven for 20 minutes.
3. Transfer the packets to heated plates with a spatula; with a knife cut open. (Be careful of the steam). Serve in paper if you wish.

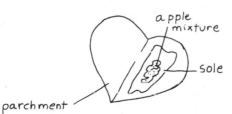

405

SOLE WITH APPLES

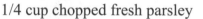

Calvados is a dry apple brandy made in Calvados, the Normandy region of northern France.

4 3 to 4-ounce pieces of sole or flounder
2 apples, peeled, cored, and sliced
1/4 cup seafood crumbs, page 257
Dash nutmeg
1 tablespoon butter
1/4 cup Calvados, cider or apple juice
2 tablespoons water
1/4 cup light cream or half-and-half
1/4 cup chopped fresh parsley

ASSEMBLY

1. Select an ovenproof casserole dish with a cover.
2. Fold sole in half and place in casserole, top with sliced apples, crumbs, nutmeg, dot with butter, and spoon Calvados on fish and add water.
3. Bake covered casserole in a preheated 400° oven for 15 minutes. Remove cover; add cream and chopped parsley. Return to oven uncovered for about 5 minutes, just enough time to heat cream.
4. Remove fish with spatula to heated plates and spoon apples and juices on and around fish.

> *"The secret of staying young is to live honestly, eat slowly, and lie about your age."*
> Lucille Ball

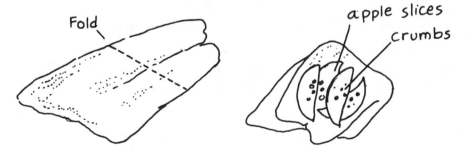

=====================SOLE WITH LETTUCE

Lettuce is grown throughout the world, and because it peaks at different times of the year, there is always an abundance of this salad favorite. Running cold water in the cavity after removing the core should clean lettuce. Invert the head and let the water drain out.

4 3 to 4-ounce pieces of sole or flounder
1/2 head lettuce, trimmed, cored and sliced like
    cole slaw
1/2 cup white wine or fish stock (clam juice can be used)
4 slices American cheese
Dash nutmeg
1/4 cup chopped fresh parsley
1/4 cup seafood crumbs, page 257
Dash paprika
1/4 cup white wine or clam juice
1 tablespoon butter

ASSEMBLY

1. Select an ovenproof casserole dish with a cover. Place sliced lettuce evenly on bottom, fold fish skin side in and place on lettuce. Top fish with American cheese, chopped parsley, nutmeg, crumbs, paprika, wine, and dot with butter.
2. Bake in covered casserole dish in a preheated 400° oven for 20 minutes.
3. Remove fish from casserole with a spatula to heated plates, spoon lettuce and juices around sole.

"Lettuce is like conversation: it must be kept fresh and crisp, and so sparkling that you scarcely notice the bitter in it."
Charles Dudley Warner

SOLE WITH SPINACH AND PERNOD

Pernod is a licorice-flavored liquor made in France. Other flavored liquors that can be substituted in this recipe, include Anisette, Sambuca or Amaretto.

4 3 to 4-ounce pieces of sole or flounder
2 teaspoons butter
1/4 cup onion, chopped fine
1/2 pound fresh spinach, trimmed, washed, and rough chopped
1/4 teaspoon ground fennel
Dash cayenne
1 tablespoon Pernod
1/4 cup seafood crumbs, page 257
1/4 cup white wine or water

PREPARATION

1. Melt 1 teaspoon of butter in a skillet over medium heat; sauté chopped onion until golden, stir in spinach, fennel, cayenne, Pernod, and half of the crumbs. Sauté just a minute until spinach is wilted. Cool.

ASSEMBLY

1. Select an ovenproof casserole dish just large enough to contain the fish. Place fish, skin side up, on a flat surface; spoon spinach mixture in the middle of each fish fillet, fold fish and press around to hold stuffing inside. Place fish in casserole; add wine, top with remaining crumbs and dot with butter.
2. Bake in a preheated 400° oven for 20 minutes.
3. Remove fish from casserole dish to heated plates with a spatula. Spoon some remaining juices around fish.

"It isn't so much what's on the table that matters, as what's on the chairs."
              W. S. Gilbert

===================TOMATO-RICOTTA SOLE

*Ricotta is wonderful to cook with; it stays firm and mixes well.
This dish is wonderful in the late summer and fall when native
tomatoes are at their best.*

4 3 to 4-ounce pieces of sole or flounder
1 tablespoon butter
1 garlic clove, minced
1/4 cup chopped green onions (scallions)
1/4 cup chopped onions
Pinch thyme
1/3 cup (3-ounces) ricotta cheese
1 egg beaten in a small bowl
1/4 cup chopped fresh parsley
4 (1/4-inch) thick fresh tomato slices
1/4 cup seafood crumbs, page 257
1/2 cup (4-ounces) grated mozzarella cheese
1/2 cup white wine or fish stock (clam juice can be used)

PREPARATION
1. Melt 1 teaspoon butter in a skillet over medium heat; sauté
    garlic, green onions, and onions, until softened, about 3 minutes. Cool.
2. Thoroughly mix cooled onion mixture, thyme, ricotta cheese, beaten egg,
    and parsley in a mixing bowl. Keep in refrigerator until ready to use.

ASSEMBLY
1. Butter an ovenproof casserole that will contain 2 pieces of sole,
    and in it place 2 pieces sole, skin side up. Spread 1/2 of ricotta mixture
    on each sole fillet, top with other sole fillet skin side down, pressing
    around to enclose filling. Top each portion with two slices of tomato,
    crumbs and mozzarella cheese; add wine to casserole.
2. Bake casserole in a preheated 400° oven for 20 minutes.
3. Remove fish from casserole to heated plates with a spatula. Spoon
    some juices from casserole on and around fish.

TUNA
SWORDFISH

All recipes are for two in this chapter.

TUNA
SWORDFISH

A restaurant is a great place for young people to get their first job and over the years we had many wonderful ones on our staff.

But sometimes, young people will be, well, young people. In the 1970s, a local policeman called to tell me that unusual traffic was happening in our restaurant parking lot after business hours. That evening I hid my car after work and waited in the shadows.

Sure enough, about eight cars of youths arrived. I owned the building next door to the restaurant and watched them all go into the cellar through the bulkhead door.

The cellar had only one window and that was under a porch. I got on my stomach and pushed myself under the porch to see what was going on. They were all sitting in a circle, smoking funny tobacco. I left them to their fun and decided to take care of the situation the next night.

The next night when they were in the cellar, I locked the bulkhead door from the outside, and then watched the reaction through the window. One of the smokers decided to leave but found he could not get out. He motioned to the others that the door was stuck. They all tried to get out but couldn't. I watched them panic for about a half hour and then decided to take the lock off the door.

When someone is stuck like this, the tendency is to keep trying the door. Someone tried the door one last time and opened it. I was outside the door waiting for them. When they saw me, a look of panic hit them. "Did you all learn something tonight?" I asked. They all said, "Yes." "Do not smoke on my property again," I told them.

I ended up losing two nights' sleep, but I had kept us out of the newspapers with a potentially embarrassing story.

SPICY BAKED TUNA STEAK

Bluefin tuna that weigh up to 1000 pounds have been caught off the Rhode Island coast.

1 pound tuna steaks, skinned, cut into two servings
1 tablespoon olive oil
1 small onion, chopped
1 small green bell pepper, cored, seeded, and chopped
1 stalk celery, chopped
1 garlic clove, minced
1/4 cup chopped fresh parsley
1/4 teaspoon oregano or basil
1/2 cup crushed tomato (canned)
1/4 cup red wine or water
1/4 cup seafood crumbs, page 257

PREPARATION
1. Heat olive oil in a skillet on medium heat; sauté onion, pepper, celery, and garlic until vegetables are soft; stir in parsley, oregano, tomato, and wine. Cook for about three minutes. Cool.

ASSEMBLY
1. Select an ovenproof casserole dish just large enough to contain tuna, spread crumbs on tuna; spoon tomato mixture on and around tuna.
2. Bake casserole in a preheated 400° oven for 20 minutes.
3. Remove tuna from casserole to heated plates with a spatula, spoon sauce on and around tuna.

The sauce from this dish is excellent with pasta.

"If six cooks followed the same recipe,
the finished dish would vary six times."
Theodora Fitzgibbon

TUNA MEDITERRANEAN

Tuna, a member of the mackerel family, is caught in temperate oceans throughout the world. Tuna is the most popular fish in the world for canning. The deep red color of fresh tuna is so beautiful.

1 pound tuna steaks, skinned, cut into two servings
1/4 cup olive oil
1/4 cup fresh tomato, skinned, seeds removed and chopped
   or canned chopped tomato
1 small onion, chopped
2 garlic cloves, chopped fine
1 teaspoon capers
1/4 cup chopped fresh parsley
1/4 cup white wine

PREPARATION
1. Mix olive oil, tomatoes, onions, garlic, capers, and parsley in a mixing bowl.

ASSEMBLY
1. Select an ovenproof casserole dish just large enough to contain the tuna. Place tuna in casserole dish, add tomato topping and marinate the tuna in the refrigerator for at least 2 hours. Turn the tuna in the marinade a few times.
2. Remove casserole from refrigerator 30 minutes before ready to cook. Add white wine.
3. Bake casserole with marinade and wine in a preheated 400° oven for 20 minutes.
4. Remove tuna from casserole to heated plates with a spatula; spoon tomato mixture on and around tuna.

The caper is a flower bud from a bush native to the Mediterranean and parts of Asia; the buds are picked, dried in the sun and pickled in vinegar brine.

"Salt is born of the purest parents: the sun and the sea."
Pythagoras

===============*BAKED SAFFRON SWORDFISH*

Saffron, the yellow-orange stigmas from a small purple crocus, is the world's most expensive spice. Each flower provides only three stigmas, which must be carefully hand picked and dried. It takes 14,000 stigmas for each ounce of saffron. A little of this spice goes a long way.

1 pound swordfish, cut into two servings
1 tablespoon butter (olive oil can be used as well)
1 garlic clove, minced
1/4 cup chopped onion
1/4 cup chopped fresh parsley
1 pinch saffron
1/4 teaspoon bitters
1/4 cup plain fresh or dried bread crumbs
1/4 cup white wine
1/4 cup milk

PREPARATION
1. Melt 1 teaspoon butter in a skillet over medium heat; sauté garlic, onion, parsley, saffron, and bitters until vegetables are soft. Stir in bread crumbs and wine. Cool.

ASSEMBLY
1. Select an ovenproof casserole dish just large enough to contain the swordfish. Place swordfish in casserole, add milk and spread saffron topping evenly on swordfish, dot with remaining butter.
2. Bake in a preheated 400° oven for 20 minutes.
3. Remove swordfish from casserole to heated plates with a spatula, spoon some remaining sauce from casserole around swordfish.

Bitters are available in most grocery stores and liquor stores. They are made from the distillation of aromatic herbs, barks, roots, and plants. Bitters come in a small bottle, and used as a digestive aid, appetite stimulant, and in alcoholic drinks.

"Bread always falls on its buttered side."
English proverb

MONTAUK SWORDFISH

Montauk Point is the most southern point of Long Island, NY. Swordfish are caught in the late summer in these warm waters and the waters off Block Island. The fishing village of Galilee, Rhode Island, is where all the fishing boats arrive with their catch. Sometimes the captain of a boat would call me and say, "I've got a good one for you." By this, he meant a harpooned swordfish. I would meet him and buy the whole swordfish. I would bring it to the restaurant in my truck, carry it into the kitchen, and place it on the bench and butcher it into portions. I always liked to use swordfish that weighed about 125 pounds or so, because each quarter when sliced was a perfect portion.

1 pound swordfish, cut into two servings
1/4 cup sour cream
1/4 cup whole egg mayonnaise
1 teaspoon whole grain mustard or any good mustard
1 teaspoon lemon juice
1/4 cup chopped green onions (scallions)
1/2 cup milk
1/4 cup seafood crumbs, page 257

PREPARATION
1. Mix sour cream, mayonnaise, mustard, lemon juice, and green onions in a mixing bowl.

ASSEMBLY
1. Select an ovenproof casserole just large enough to contain swordfish. Place swordfish in casserole, add milk, top with crumbs and spread the mayonnaise topping evenly on the crumbs.
2. Bake in a preheated 400° oven for 20 minutes.
3. Remove swordfish from casserole to heated plates with a spatula.

"A recipe is only a theme, which an intelligent cook can play each time with a variation."
Madame Benoit

============== *PESTO-CHEESE SWORDFISH*

The topping melts into a light sauce as it cooks.

*Pesto is a wonderful thick sauce that does not require cooking.
Originated in Genoa, Italy, the sauce includes pine nut kernels, grated
Parmesan cheese, salt, fresh basil, and olive oil. In Italy, the sauce is
classically prepared, by using a mortar and pestle. Here in the States
we usually use a food processor. Pesto is available in most grocery stores.*

1 pound swordfish, cut into two servings
1 tablespoon pesto
3 ounces cream cheese, softened
1/4 cup fresh or dried plain bread crumbs
1/4 cup grated Parmesan cheese
1/2 cup milk

PREPARATION

1. Mix pesto and cream cheese in a mixing bowl, stir in bread crumbs and
   Parmesan cheese.

ASSEMBLY

1. Select an ovenproof casserole just large enough to contain the
   swordfish. Place swordfish in casserole, add milk and spread the
   pesto-cheese topping evenly on swordfish.
2. Bake swordfish in a preheated 400° oven for 20 minutes.
3. Rcmove swordfish from casserole to heated plates with a
   spatula. Spoon remaining juices around swordfish.

"Dinner for me is always a celebration."
Author

SPANISH STYLE SWORDFISH

This swordfish dish with its rich sauce is great with pasta.

1 pound swordfish, cut into two servings
1 tablespoon olive oil
1/4 cup chopped onion
1/4 cup thinly sliced red bell pepper, cored, and seeded
1/4 cup thinly sliced green bell pepper, cored, and seeded
1 clove garlic, minced
1 cup crushed tomatoes (canned)
1/4 teaspoon oregano
1/4 teaspoon chili powder
1/4 cup chopped fresh parsley
1/2 teaspoon lemon juice
1/4 cup seafood crumbs, page 257

PREPARATION
1. Heat olive oil in a skillet over medium heat; sauté onions, red and green peppers, and garlic. Sauté for a couple of minutes; stir in tomatoes, oregano, chili powder, parsley, and lemon juice. Simmer for about 20 minutes. Cool.

ASSEMBLY
1. Select an ovenproof casserole large enough to contain the swordfish. Place swordfish in casserole; spread crumbs evenly on swordfish and spoon tomato mixture on and around swordfish.
2. Bake swordfish in a preheated 400° oven for 20 minutes.
3. Remove swordfish to heated plates with a spatula. Spoon sauce on and around swordfish.

Chili powder is a seasoning mixture of dried chilies, oregano, garlic, cumin, coriander, and cloves.

"The honest flavor of fresh garlic is something I can never have enough of."
James Beard

====SWORDFISH BAKED WITH POTATO CHIPS

Potato chips were first served in Saratoga Springs, New York, in the mid-19th century. Potato chips are now an all-American favorite. They are available in many flavors and sizes.

1 pound swordfish, cut into two servings
1/2 cup milk
1/4 cup seafood crumbs, page 257
1/2 cup crushed potato chips
Dash paprika
Dash thyme
1 teaspoon butter
Lemon wedges

ASSEMBLY

1. Select an ovenproof casserole dish just large enough to contain the swordfish. Place swordfish in casserole, add milk, spread crumbs evenly on swordfish, top with potato chips spreading evenly, and sprinkle with paprika, thyme, and dot with butter.
2. Bake swordfish in a preheated 400° oven for 20 minutes.
3. Remove swordfish from casserole to heated plates with a spatula. Garnish with lemon wedges.

> *"Part of the secret of success in life is to eat what you like."*
> Mark Twain

SWORDFISH WITH BITTERS

Bitters are made from the distillation of barks, roots, herbs, and plants. Bitters are used in cocktails, aperitifs, food, and also as a digestive aid. Bitters have a bittersweet taste.

1 pound swordfish, cut into two servings
1 tablespoon butter, softened
1 tablespoon flour
1/4 teaspoon Angostura bitters
1/4 cup chopped red bell pepper, cored, and seeded
1/4 cup chopped onion
1/4 cup chopped green onion (scallions)
1/2 cup milk

PREPARATION
1. Mix butter, flour, and bitters in a mixing bowl into a paste; stir in peppers, onions, and green onions.

ASSEMBLY
1. Select an ovenproof casserole just large enough to contain the swordfish. Place swordfish in casserole, add milk, spread the bitters topping evenly on swordfish.
2. Bake swordfish in a preheated 400° oven for 20 minutes.
3. Remove swordfish from casserole to heated plates with a spatula.

<u>Helpful Hint</u>
Use an envelope to fill a salt or pepper mill. Snip the corner off an envelope to make a fast, disposable funnel.

"Tempting things often seem better when they are shared. Good food is good enough alone, but it takes on eminence when there a is host, or hostess–preferably both–with undiluted love for the act of hospitality, and guests to match."
Evan Jones

SWORDFISH WITH CRUMBS

Most swordfish is available in steaks and chunks. Because it is so firm, swordfish can be prepared in almost any manner including sautéing, grilling, baking, and broiling.

1 pound swordfish, cut into two servings
1/2 cup milk
1/2 cup seafood crumbs, page 257
2 teaspoons butter
Lemon wedges

ASSEMBLY

1. Select an ovenproof casserole dish just large enough to contain the swordfish.
2. Place swordfish in casserole and add milk. Spread crumbs evenly on swordfish; dot with butter.
3. Bake swordfish in a preheated 400° oven for 20 minutes.
4. Remove swordfish from casserole to heated plates with a spatula. Serve with lemon wedges.

Helpful Hint

Music sets the tone for a dinner party. It is a pleasant backdrop during cocktails and pleasant for the guests to hear when they arrive. Once the guests are seated for dinner, the music should be lowered and conversation should take over.

"The best host is not he who spends the most money to entertain his guests, but he who takes the most intelligent interest in their welfare and makes sure that they will have a good time, something to drink, something that is both good and new, if possible."
André Simon

===*SWORDFISH WITH GARDEN VEGETABLES*

Swordfish is a large sport and food fish found in the warmer waters throughout the world. Swordfish averages between 80 to 200 pounds. Some can weigh up to 1000 pounds or more. Swordfish is one of the most popular eating fishes in the United States; harpooned swordfish is the freshest and best tasting.

1 pound swordfish, cut into two servings
1 small carrot, peeled, cut like matchsticks (julienne)
1/2 small red bell pepper, cored, seeded, and sliced thin
1/2 small green bell pepper, cored, seeded, and sliced thin
1 small onion, cut in half and sliced thin
1 small zucchini, cut like matchsticks (julienne)
1/4 cup chopped fresh parsley
1/4 teaspoon fennel seeds
1/4 teaspoon dried basil or 1 tablespoon chopped fresh basil
1 1/2 tablespoons olive oil
1/2 cup water or white wine
1/4 seafood crumbs, page 257
2 slices bacon, cut in half (optional)

PREPARATION
1. Mix carrots, peppers, onions, zucchini, parsley, fennel, basil, and olive oil in a mixing bowl.

ASSEMBLY
1. Select an ovenproof casserole dish just large enough to contain swordfish, add water to casserole, spread crumbs on swordfish, spread vegetable topping evenly on swordfish, top with slices of bacon.
2. Bake casserole in a preheated 400° oven for 20 minutes.
3. Remove swordfish from casserole to heated plates with a spatula. Spoon remaining vegetables on and around swordfish.

"When our souls are happy, they talk about food."
Charles Simic

============WATERCRESS BAKED SWORDFISH

Watercress with swordfish may sound strange, but it will surprise you with the peppery flavor.

1 pound swordfish, cut into two servings
1/2 cup finely chopped watercress with large stems removed
1/4 cup plain yogurt or sour cream
1/4 cup whole egg mayonnaise
1 garlic clove, minced
1/4 cup plain dried or fresh bread crumbs
1/2 cup milk

PREPARATION
1. Mix watercress, yogurt, mayonnaise, garlic, and bread crumbs in a mixing bowl.

ASSEMBLY
1. Select an ovenproof casserole just large enough to contain swordfish. Place swordfish in casserole, add milk and spread watercress topping evenly on swordfish.
2. Bake in a preheated 400° oven for 20 minutes.
3. Remove swordfish from casserole to heated plates with a spatula. Spoon a little of remaining sauce from casserole around swordfish.

"Cookery is naturally the most ancient of the arts,
as of all the arts it is the most important."
George Ellwanger

In the 1960's, I had the pleasure of hiring a young Korean boy. When he applied for the job, he could not speak English except for a few words: "I want to work" and "I am hungry."

His father was American and his mother was Korean. Duan came to the States when he was about 16. He worked for us with great gusto. He wanted to learn and was very talented.

One day I said to Duan, "Go downstairs and get a package of Jello." After a time he came up and said, "No such thing, boss." I said, "Duan I know there is Jello down there." I went downstairs with him to get the Jello and I noticed the commercial package read "gelatin." He was right: "no such thing, boss." We sometimes call things something different than what they really are.

Duan worked for me through college and graduated from the Rhode School of Design. During high school, he completed many paintings, and he had a wonderful show at the high school. He painted three for me, and I have them in my home. He became a great line cook and a good friend. He is now an architect.

Operating a restaurant near a Naval installation was always interesting. Every night the sailors hit the roads, and sometimes things got wild. Everyone was usually in a festive mood, especially the sailors who had just come back from the Antarctic. It was not unusual for a scuffle to break out, especially if two sailors had their eye on the same lady. I usually had to run out of the kitchen and try to get them apart. Sometimes it was easy, and sometimes I took my life in my hands.

We had a wonderful elderly lady named Ellen who worked as our dishwasher. One evening a fight started up, and Ellen said to me, " I'll take care of this one!" "You can't do it– they will kill you!" I said. "No one hits an old lady!" she replied. Well, to my amazement, she was right. She went up to those two men and broke up the fight. In a couple of minutes, they had their arms around each other and her as well. So from then on Ellen successfully broke up any confrontations in the restaurant.

POTATOES
VEGETABLES

======*POTATOES AND VEGETABLES*

Potatoes and Vegetables Continued-

===============*Hints and Suggestions*

WASHING VEGETABLES: If you sprinkle salt or vinegar into
the water when you are washing vegetables and greens,
it will draw out insects and sand.

=======TWO VARIATIONS OF ACORN SQUASH

Acorn squash is an oval-shaped dark green winter squash.

Serves 2

APPLESAUCE ROASTED ACORN SQUASH

1 acorn squash, cut in half
1 tablespoon butter
3 tablespoons applesauce
1/8 teaspoon cinnamon or apple pie spice

ASSEMBLY
1. Select an ovenproof casserole dish just large enough to contain the two squash halves; place squash in casserole dish cut side up, add butter.
2. Bake in a preheated 400° oven for 45 minutes, covered, loosely with aluminum foil.
3. Mix applesauce with cinnamon. When squash is cooked, spoon applesauce into squash; return to oven for about 10 minutes to heat applesauce.
4. Remove from casserole with a spatula to plates.

===

MAPLE ROASTED ACORN SQUASH

1 acorn squash, cut in half
2 tablespoons maple syrup or brown sugar
1 tablespoon soft butter
1/8 teaspoon cinnamon

ASSEMBLY
1. Mix maple syrup, soft butter, and cinnamon in a mixing bowl.
2. Select and ovenproof casserole dish just large enough to contain the two squash halves; place squash in casserole cut side up, spoon maple mixture into squash, spreading around.
3. Bake in a preheated 400° oven for 45 minutes, covered loosely with aluminum foil.
4. Remove from casserole with a spatula to plates.
   Cut a slice off the bottom of each squash half to keep it from rocking.

ROASTED ASPARAGUS

Asparagus is a world class vegetable served in restaurants and homes. It should be stored in the refrigerator standing upright in a container with about one inch of water. Cover the asparagus with a plastic bag.

Asparagus is so wonderful to serve; it adds color, tastes so good, and lends itself to many culinary variations. If the asparagus stems are tough, remove the outer layer with a vegetable peeler before cooking.

Serves 2

1 bunch asparagus, trimmed and peeled
1 tablespoon olive oil
1 drop or two sesame oil
1 teaspoon soy sauce
1/2 teaspoon balsamic vinegar
1 teaspoon sesame seeds (optional)

ASSEMBLY

1. Place asparagus in an ovenproof casserole dish. Mix olive oil, sesame oil, soy sauce, and balsamic vinegar in a mixing bowl. Spoon the sauce on asparagus coating the asparagus. Sprinkle with sesame seeds.
2. Bake in a preheated 400° oven for about 10 minutes, or until asparagus is a little soft to the touch. Serve on a side plate and spoon sauce from pan on and around asparagus.

> *"The air pulses with the warm smell of lilac, but as we pass each door, the lilac dominance is subdued by heady wafts of asparagus cooking."*
> *Jane Grigson*

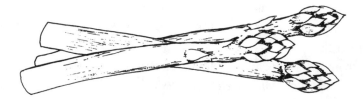

===========QUICK WAY TO COOK ASPARAGUS AND BROCCOLI

If you are cooking a larger amount, adjust cooking time. These recipes are for two or four persons.

ASPARAGUS

Trim asparagus and place in an ovenproof glass casserole with a glass cover. Asparagus can be crowded. Add 1 tablespoon water and 1 tablespoon butter; microwave on high for 4 minutes. Asparagus will be bright green and cooked perfectly, if the asparagus are large, cook for another 1/2 minute.

BROCCOLI

Trim broccoli to bite size pieces (florets) and place in an ovenproof glass casserole with a glass cover. Broccoli can be crowded. Add 1 tablespoon water and 1 tablespoon butter. Microwave on high for 4 minutes. Broccoli will be bright green and cooked perfectly.

Helpful Hint

Wash your vegetables in a water and vinegar bath to kill the bacteria I always wash my greens in a light vinegar and water bath, then spin dry the greens. Do not use this procedure on fruit like strawberries and raspberries they have little pores that absorb some of the vinegar and could affect the taste. Wash your hands after handling fruit and vegetables.

"Broccoli is one of the most amazing pharmaceutical packages in nature's food pharmacy."
Jean Carper

==================ROASTED VEGETABLES

*Roasted vegetables are fantastic; the flavors remain in the
vegetables and absorb the soy and spices as they roast. While
the vegetables are roasting, stir them on occasion.
I did not include root vegetables such as carrots in this recipe, because
they require longer roasting time unless they are blanched ahead.*

Serves 4

1 medium onion, cut in half and sliced
1 small red bell pepper, halved, cored, seeded, and sliced
1 small green bell pepper, halved, cored, seeded, and sliced
1 leek, trimmed, washed, and sliced
1 small zucchini, sliced
1 small summer squash, sliced
4 mushrooms, cleaned and sliced
1/2 cup olive oil
1 teaspoon dried basil or 1/4 cup chopped fresh basil
1/8 teaspoon fennel seeds
1 teaspoon soy sauce

PREPARATION
1. Mix onion, peppers, leeks, zucchini, squash, mushrooms, olive oil,
    basil, fennel seeds, and soy sauce in a mixing bowl. Mix well to coat
    vegetables with olive oil and spices.

ASSEMBLY
1. Select an ovenproof casserole large enough to contain the
    vegetables without crowding them. Add vegetables to casserole.
2. Bake in a preheated 400° oven for about 30 to 40 minutes, stirring
    on occasion until vegetables are cooked but firm.

"How do they taste? They taste like more."
H. L. Mencken

432

===========BAKED BUTTERNUT SQUASH FLUFF

Butternut squash is a large winter squash that looks pear-shaped. The color of the smooth outer shell is a light yellow to tan; the flesh is sweet and orange. When peeling butternut squash use disposable gloves because the pulp of the butternut stains your hands and is difficult to remove.

We served this vegetable, autumn through winter. I love this recipe because the Cream of Wheat keeps the squash from watering.

Serves 4

1 medium butternut squash, peeled, seeded, and cut into chunks
Water
2 tablespoons butter
1 tablespoon brown sugar or maple syrup
1/8 teaspoon cinnamon
2 tablespoons uncooked Cream of Wheat cereal

PREPARATION
1. Place squash in a saucepan, add water to cover squash, bring to a boil and cook until squash is cooked. Drain, and mash squash with butter, brown sugar, cinnamon, and Cream of Wheat. Can be prepared ahead.

ASSEMBLY
1. Select an ovenproof casserole dish just large enough to contain the squash mixture. Spoon the squash mixture into casserole.
2. Bake in a preheated 400° oven for 20 minutes.
3. Serve as a side dish with your favorite dinner.

<u>Helpful Hint</u>
When a guest has an accident and breaks one of your most prized possessions, be sensitive to the guest's embarrassment. Clean it up and do not make a fuss; be nonchalant and make light of it. Do not let it affect the mood of the dinner.
Then scream to yourself later.

OVEN BAKED BEANS

Beans are the seeded pods of various legumes. They are among the oldest food known, dating back at least 4000 years. Beans are rich in protein, calcium, phosphorus and iron. They are easily grown and stored, making them a staple throughout the world wherever animal protein is scarce.

Serves 4

1 tablespoon butter
1/2 cup chopped onion
1 garlic clove, minced
2 (16-ounce) cans of small white beans
1/2 cup ketchup
1 tablespoon brown sugar
1 1/4 teaspoon mustard
1 teaspoon barbecue sauce
1 teaspoon maple syrup

PREPARATION
1. Melt butter in a medium skillet over medium heat; sauté onions and garlic for about 2 minutes. Off heat, stir in beans, ketchup, brown sugar, mustard, barbecue sauce, and maple syrup.

ASSEMBLY
1. Place beans in an ovenproof casserole large enough to contain the beans.
2. Bake in a preheated 400° oven for 20 minutes.
3. Serve beans in a side dish.

"Boston runs to brains as well as to beans and brown bread."
William Brann

=======*OVEN BAKED SWEET POTATO NANCY*

Sweet Potato is native to tropical areas of the Americas; it is a large edible root that belongs to the morning glory family.

Serves 4

4 sweet potatoes, cut in half lengthwise, then cut each half in 3
  wedges lengthwise way. Each potato should have six wedges.
3 egg whites
1/2 teaspoon salt
1 teaspoon five-spice powder
1/4 teaspoon white pepper
1/2 teaspoon salt
Non stick cooking spray or parchment paper

PREPARATION
1. Lightly beat egg whites in a mixing bowl with a whisk; stir in salt,
    five-spice powder, and pepper.

ASSEMBLY
1. Select a baking sheet. Lightly coat with a non stick cooking
    spray, or use a sheet of parchment paper.
2. Working in batches, toss potatoes in egg white mixture and
    place skin side down on the baking sheet. Do this with all the potatoes.
3. Bake in a preheated 400° oven for about 25 minutes.
4. Remove potatoes from baking sheet with a spatula to dinner plates.

Five-spice powder is available in most supermarkets or in an oriental market. The five spices are fennel seeds, star anise, ginger, cloves and cinnamon

"Just give me a potato, any kind of potato, and I'm happy."
Dolly Parton

CARROT AND TURNIP FLUFF

We served these vegetables in autumn and every Thanksgiving in the restaurant, cooking them in batches throughout the day. Carrots are very popular and turnips are marginal; mashing them together softens the strong turnip taste, and the butter and honey gives them a little sweetness. Cream of Wheat mashed with the vegetables gives them a lighter fluffy consistency.

Serves 4

1 medium turnip, peeled, cut in quarters
4 carrots, peeled, cut in slices
Water
2 tablespoons butter
1 tablespoon honey
2 tablespoons uncooked Cream of Wheat cereal

PREPARATION

1. Select a saucepan large enough to contain the turnips and carrots, add water to cover, bring to a boil and cook until vegetables are soft. Drain vegetables and mash, with butter, honey, and Cream of Wheat.

ASSEMBLY

1. Select an ovenproof casserole dish just large enough to contain the turnip and carrot. Spoon the turnip and carrot into casserole. (Can be prepared ahead and baked just before dinner.)
2. Bake in a preheated 400° oven for 20 minutes.
3. Serve with your favorite entrée.

"To own a bit of ground, to scratch it with a hoe, to plant seeds, and watch the renewal of life–this is the commonest delight of the race, the most satisfactory thing a man can do."
Charles Warner

Carrots are favorites in many kitchens; this recipe sweetens and glazes the carrots. Other vegetables can be substituted, such as diced turnips or diced butternut squash. If you sauté green beans or asparagus, use soy sauce instead of honey.

Serves 4

1 1/2 cups carrots, peeled and sliced
1 tablespoon butter
1 teaspoon honey
1/8 teaspoon five spice powder (allspice can be used also)
1 tablespoon water

ASSEMBLY

1. Heat a nonstick skillet with a cover over medium heat and
    melt butter until slightly bubbly. Add carrots, honey and five-spice powder;
    sauté while stirring on high heat for just a minute. Add water, (carefully,
    it may sputter a little) cover pan and turn heat to low. Do not remove
    cover for 10 minutes and carrots should be cooked.
    Serve with your favorite entrée.

Five-spice powder is available in most markets, also available in oriental markets.

HELPFUL HINT

When a recipe calls for honey, molasses, corn syrup or maple syrup, coat the measuring cup or spoon with nonstick cooking spray. The sticky liquid slides out of the cup or spoon with ease.

*"Knowledge can be communicated
but not wisdom."*
  Herman Hesse

===FOUR VARIATIONS OF ROASTED CARROTS

Carrots have been cultivated and eaten for thousands of years, renowned for their health-giving properties and high vitamin A content. They are available year-round, making them a highly popular vegetable. They are eaten either raw or cooked.

Serves 4
To blanch (par cook) carrots:
1 pound carrots
Water

Peel and slice carrots into one-inch slices. Place carrots in a small sauce pan, cover with water, bring to a low boil and cook until carrots are tender, about 15 minutes. Drain and cool. (Or steam carrots)
Prepared carrots in these recipes are roasted just before dinner.

CRISPY CARROTS
Blanched carrots
1/4 cup butter, melted
1/2 cup crushed corn
1 tablespoon olive oil

ASSEMBLY
1. Dip cooked carrots in melted butter; then roll in crumbs. Place on oiled cookie sheet.
2. Bake in a preheated 400° oven for 15 minutes.

==

ORANGE ROASTED CARROTS
Blanched carrots
1 tablespoon butter
1/4 cup chopped parsley
2 tablespoons orange juice
1 tablespoon brown sugar

ASSEMBLY
1. Butter an ovenproof casserole dish just large enough to contain the carrots. Mix carrots, butter, parsley, orange juice and brown sugar in a mixing bowl. Spoon carrots into buttered casserole dish.
2. Bake in a preheated 400° oven for 20 minutes

Roasted carrots continued-

FIVE SPICE ROASTED CARROTS
Blanched carrots
1 tablespoon butter
1/2 teaspoon five spice powder (allspice can also be used)
1 tablespoon honey
1/4 cup chopped green onions (scallions)

ASSEMBLY
1. Butter an ovenproof casserole just large enough to contain the carrots. Mix cooked carrots, five-spice powder, honey, and green onions in a mixing bowl. Spoon carrots into buttered casserole dish.
2. Bake in a preheated 400° oven for 20 minutes.
    Five-spice powder is available in most markets.

===

DILL LEMON CARROTS
Blanched carrots
1 tablespoon butter
1/2 teaspoon grated lemon peel (zest)
1/2 teaspoon dried dill or 1 teaspoon chopped fresh dill
1 tablespoon honey

ASSEMBLY
1. Butter an ovenproof casserole just large enough to contain the carrots. Mix cooked carrots, grated lemon rind, dill, and honey in a mixing bowl. Spoon carrots into buttered casserole dish.
2. Bake in a preheated 400° oven for 20 minutes.

> *"No matter what time of the day the carrot is picked, the temperature will be the same: warm at the skin from its earthly bed but chill as the night wind at the heart, a taste sensation unequaled by any other fresh-dug thing in the universe."*
> *Bert Greene*

DILLED BEETS

Beets add a beautiful color to the plate. Just before cooking, wash fresh beets gently so as not to pierce the thin skin! Do not peel or trim their stems until after cooking.

Serves 4 to 6

1 1/2 pounds fresh beets or 2 (15-ounce) cans sliced beets
3/4 cup sour cream
1/2 cup beet juice
1/2 teaspoon dried dill or 1 teaspoon chopped fresh dill
1/4 cup chopped green onions (scallions)

PREPARATION

1. Place beets in a saucepan and cover with water, bring to a low boil and cook until tender, about 40 minutes, depending on the size of the beets. Drain (reserve 1/2 cup beet juice) and allow them cool a little; cut off both ends, then hold them under cold, running water and slip off their skins. Slice beets or dice them. The beets may stain your hands, if you wish use disposable gloves. If you use canned beets drain and reserve 1/2 cup of the beet liquid.

ASSEMBLY

1. Mix beet and all the above ingredients in a saucepan. Heat mixture over medium heat stirring occasionally, until heated through.
2. Spoon heated beets onto dinner plates and enjoy the beautiful color.

*"The beet is the most intense of vegetables...
Beets are deadly serious."*
Tom Robbins

===================================HARVARD BEETS LINDA

Each evening, the staff was offered all the leftover vegetables to take home. One evening, a waitress took some Harvard beets. She put the covered container on the floor of her car, underneath her feet.

The road in front of the restaurant had a traffic light, and when the light was green, she started to leave the driveway, but a car ran the red light and struck her car on the side. The container of beets opened and went up her dress.

When the rescue squad arrived, she was rather stunned and the front of her dress was all red. They thought she was really hurt and brought her to the hospital. As they started to remove her dress to find out what was wrong, all the little beets started to fall out. It was one of the most unusual cases the hospital had ever seen, and though she was not hurt, that story went around the restaurant and the hospital for some time.

Harvard Beets
Serves 4 to 6
1 1/2 pounds fresh beets or 2 (15-ounce) cans sliced beets
1/2 cup sugar
1 1/2 teaspoons cornstarch
1/4 cup cider vinegar
3/4 cup beet juice
1 teaspoon butter

PREPARATION
1. Place beets in a saucepan and cover with water, bring to a low boil and cook until tender, about 40 minutes, depending on the size of the beets. Drain (reserve 3/4 cup beet juice) and allow them cool a little; cut off both ends, then hold them under cold, running water and slip off their skins. Slice beets or dice them. The beets may stain your hands, if you wish use disposable gloves. If you use canned beets drain and reserve 3/4 cup of the beet liquid.

ASSEMBLY
1. Mix sugar and cornstarch in a saucepan; stir in vinegar and beet juice. Over medium heat, bring to a light boil to thicken. Add beets and butter, heat to another boil and serve.

═════════════FESTIVAL ROASTED POTATOES

*For many years, we had the pleasure of hosting a dinner for the performers of the Kingston Chamber Music Festival. Rudi Hempe, editor of the **Standard-Times**, a local newspaper, was president of the festival and one of the organizers for this event. The founder and artistic director of the festival is David Kim, a wonderfully talented violinist, who today is the concertmaster of the Philadelphia Orchestra. One year, we had the dinner in my home. The menu was poached pears with greens, filet mignon, stuffed native tomatoes, fresh asparagus, roasted potatoes and native blueberry mousse. The roasted potatoes seemed to be greatly enjoyed.*

Serves 4

Small red, Yukon gold, or any small potato, washed and cut into
a large dice (the amount or potatoes is up to you, depending on size)
1 red bell pepper, cored, sliced thin
1 large red onion, peeled, and rough chopped
Salt and pepper to taste
1 teaspoon fresh rosemary
1/2 cup olive oil to glaze potatoes
1 cup cornflake crumbs (available in supermarkets)

ASSEMBLY

1. Mix potatoes, peppers, onions, salt, pepper, rosemary, and olive oil in a mixing bowl. Place the cornflake crumbs in a mixing bowl, bread the oiled potatoes and vegetables a little at a time in the cornflake crumbs coating completely. (Use more crumbs if you need them).
2. Oil an ovenproof casserole dish (or cookie sheet). Spread potatoes evenly in dish.
3. Bake in a preheated 400° oven for about 50 minutes, turning potatoes occasionally, until they are soft and crispy.

Enjoy with your favorite violinist.

*"There is no species of human food that can be consumed
in a greater variety of modes than the potato."*
Sir John Sinclair

INDIVIDUAL POTATO TART

Potato tart can be a first course or a starch with dinner.

Serves 6
1 package Pepperidge Farm patty shells
Flour for rolling pastry
3 medium Yukon gold potatoes or baking potatoes
1 tablespoon olive oil
Salt and pepper to taste
Non-stick cooking spray or olive oil
1 egg beaten with 1 tablespoon milk in a small bowl

PREPARATION

1. On a lightly floured surface, roll out each puff pastry
   into a 6-inch round. Store in refrigerator between plastic
   wrap until ready to assemble.
2. Peel potatoes and slice into thin slices (use a mandoline if you
   have one). Place sliced potatoes in a mixing bowl with olive oil,
   salt and pepper and mix until all potatoes have a light coating of oil.

ASSEMBLY

1. Lightly oil 6 (1-cup) soufflé cups or 6 (1-cup) muffin tins.
   Place pastry in each cup and pat the pastry up the sides of the
   cup.
2. Arrange the potato slices in overlapping circles on the bottom
   of the tart until you reach 3/4 of the cup. Fold the pastry
   over the potatoes; brush the egg wash on pastry.
3. Bake in a preheated 400° oven for about 45 minutes or until
   potatoes are tender.
4. Remove from oven and with a fork or knife, lift potato tart
   out of cup.

   *For variations, add a little blue cheese or cheddar on top of
   potatoes or add Parmesan cheese with oil. Instead of individual tarts,
   make a large tart in a 10-inch spring form pan. Roll two 12-inch
   round crusts, one for the top and one for the bottom of pan. Use the
   above directions.*

CRISPY POTATO BALLS

The potato was cultivated by the ancient Incas thousands of years ago. It was not readily accepted in Europe, because it was thought to be poisonous. Sir Walter Raleigh was instrumental in changing the potato superstition when he planted them on property he owned in Ireland. The rest is history. Potatoes are most versatile in all kitchens and can be cooked in more ways than anyone can count.

Serves 4

1 cup mashed potatoes (can be leftover mashed potatoes)
1 cup finely chopped cooked ham
1/2 cup shredded cheddar
2 tablespoons whole egg mayonnaise
2 tablespoons chopped green onions (scallions)
1 egg, beaten
1/2 teaspoon mustard
2 tablespoons flour
1 cup cornflake crumbs (use extra if you need it)
1 teaspoon olive oil

ASSEMBLY

1. Mix mashed potato, ham, cheddar, mayonnaise, green onions, beaten egg, and mustard in a mixing bowl. Stir in enough flour to make a stiff mixture. Cool in refrigerator.
2. Shape in 1 1/2 inch balls, then roll in cornflakes and place on an oiled baking sheet. (Can be prepared ahead to this point and refrigerated)
3. Bake in a preheated 400° oven for 20 minutes. Serve hot.

"I thought opening a restaurant would be fun. If I had known how difficult it is, I probably wouldn't have done it."
Richard Perry–Café deLuxe & Salons

================================MASHED POTATO CAKES

Baked in muffin cups, these individual servings of mashed potatoes will make any dinner special. They can be prepared ahead and baked just before dinner.

Serves 8
2 pounds potatoes, peeled and cubed
1 tablespoon butter
1 tablespoon onion, finely chopped
2 cloves garlic, finely chopped
1 cup ricotta cheese
1 cup sour cream
1/2 teaspoon finely chopped rosemary
1 teaspoon salt
1/4 teaspoon white pepper
2 egg whites
cooking spray or olive oil
1/2 cup dry plain bread crumbs (or amount needed)

PREPARATION
1. Place potatoes in a sauce pan and cover with water; bring to a boil. Cover and cook for 20 minutes or until tender. Drain. Mash potatoes with butter, onion, and garlic; set aside.
2. Mix ricotta cheese, sour cream, rosemary, salt, and pepper in a mixing bowl until smooth.
3. Beat egg whites in a bowl with a whisk until frothy and then fold into ricotta mixture. Then mix ricotta mixture into potatoes until thoroughly mixed.

ASSEMBLY
1. Generously coat muffin cups with nonstick spray or olive oil; sprinkle muffins cups with bread crumbs, coating bottom and sides. Spoon potato mixture evenly into muffin cups; smooth the tops.
3. Bake in a preheated 400° oven for about 30 minutes or until sides are lightly browned. Remove from oven and allow to rest for about 15 minutes. Run a knife around sides of muffins, then invert onto a cookie sheet. Turn potato cakes over and serve.

-TEN VARIATIONS OF TWICE-BAKED POTATOES

Baked Stuffed Potatoes are great when entertaining; they can be prepared earlier in the day and refrigerated until ready to bake. Enjoy these variations.

*Preheat oven to 400°. Wash potatoes and spray with cooking spray, bake for 1 hour or until done. Cool to the touch. Cut a circle around top of potato; scoop out pulp and place in a bowl, set aside. Recipes are for **two** potatoes. All recipes can be prepared ahead.*

PARMESAN STUFFED POTATOES
Pulp from potatoes
1/4 cup plain yogurt or sour cream
1 tablespoon milk
1 tablespoon Parmesan cheese
1 tablespoon chopped green onion (scallions)
Dash garlic powder
Dash pepper
1/8 teaspoon paprika

ASSEMBLY
1. Mash all the above ingredients in a mixing bowl until light and fluffy. Spoon stuffing into potato shells and place on an ungreased pie plate.
2. Bake in a preheated 400° oven for 15 to 20 minutes or until completely heated.

"My idea of heaven is a great big baked potato and someone to share it with."
Oprah Winfrey

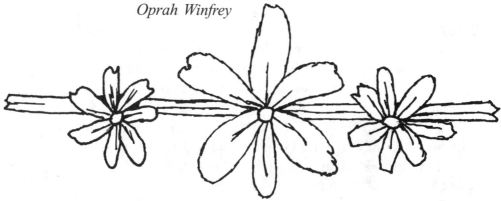

HAM STUFFED POTATOES
Pulp from potatoes
1/4 cup chopped ham
1 tablespoon chopped pimientos or chopped red bell pepper
1 tablespoon onion, minced
1/4 cup mayonnaise
1/4 cup shredded Swiss cheese
1/8 teaspoon paprika

ASSEMBLY
1. Mash all the above ingredients in a mixing bowl until light and fluffy. Spoon stuffing into potato shells and place on an ungreased pie plate.
2. Bake in a preheated 400° oven for 15 to 20 minutes or until completely heated.

****

BROCCOLI STUFFED POTATOES
Pulp from potatoes
1 tablespoon grated Parmesan cheese
1/4 cup shredded cheddar cheese
1/8 cup finely chopped ham
1 egg
1/4 cup broccoli, cut small and blanched firm

ASSEMBLY
1. Mash potato, Parmesan cheese, cheddar, ham, and egg in a mixing bowl until light and fluffy. Stir in broccoli and gently mix. Spoon stuffing into potato shells and place on an ungreased pie plate.
2. Bake in a preheated 400° oven for 15 to 20 minutes or until completely heated.

> *"Cookery is not chemistry. It is an art. It requires instinct and taste rather than exact measurements."*
> *Marcel Boulestin   (Author's note, except in baking.)*

Variations of twice-baked potatoes continued–

BLUE CHEESE STUFFED POTATOES
Pulp from potatoes
1/4 cup plain yogurt or sour cream
1/4 cup crumbled blue cheese
1 teaspoon grated onion
1/4 cup chopped green onions (scallions)

ASSEMBLY
1. Mash all the above ingredients in a mixing bowl until
   light and fluffy. Spoon stuffing into potato shells. Place
   on an ungreased pie plate.
2. Bake in a preheated 400° oven for 15 to 20 minutes or until
   completely heated.

****

BACON STUFFED POTATOES
Pulp from potatoes
1/4 cup sour cream
1/4 cup shredded cheddar cheese
2 tablespoons milk
1/4 cup chopped green onions (scallions)
2 slices bacon, cooked, drained, and chopped
Dash paprika

ASSEMBLY
1. Mash potatoes, sour cream, cheddar cheese, milk, and scallions
   in a mixing bowl until light and fluffy. Stir in bacon, spoon stuffing
   into potato shells and place on an ungreased pie plate.
2. Bake in a preheated 400° oven for 15 to 20 minutes or until
   completely heated.

"Tis the potato that's queen of the garden."
Irish proverb

Variations of twice-baked potatoes continued–

MEXICAN STUFFED POTATOES
Pulp from potatoes
1/4 cup sour cream
1/4 cup shredded cheddar cheese or Monterey Jack cheese
1/4 cup chopped green onion (scallions)
1/4 cup salsa, mild, medium, or hot (your choice)

ASSEMBLY
1. Mash potatoes, sour cream, Cheddar cheese and green onions in a mixing bowl until light and fluffy. Stir in salsa, spoon stuffing into potato shells, and place on an ungreased pie plate.
2. Bake in a preheated 400° oven for 15 to 20 minutes or until completely heated.

****

THREE CHEESE STUFFED POTATOES
Pulp from potatoes
1/4 cup cottage cheese (low fat can be used)
2 tablespoons grated Parmesan cheese
1/4 cup shredded mozzarella cheese
1/4 cup chopped green onions (scallions)
1/2 teaspoon dried dill or 1 tablespoon fresh dill

ASSEMBLY
1. Mash all the above ingredients until light and fluffy. Spoon stuffing into potato shells and place on an ungreased pie plate.
2. Bake in a preheated 400° oven for 15 to 20 minutes or until completely heated.

> *"Throughout my life, friends and fortune have come and gone, but I've always been able to count on a baked potato to see me through."*
> *Maggie Waldron*

Variations of twice-baked potatoes continued–

CRAB STUFFED POTATOES
Pulp from potatoes
1/4 cup sour cream
1 tablespoon minced green bell pepper
1/4 cup shredded cheddar cheese
1 tablespoon mayonnaise
1/2 cup caned crabmeat, drained and checked for small bones

ASSEMBLY
1. Mash potatoes, sour cream, pepper, cheddar cheese, and mayonnaise in a mixing bowl until light and fluffy.
    Stir in crabmeat, spoon stuffing into potato shells and place on an ungreased pie plate.
2. Bake in a preheated 400° oven for 15 to 20 minutes or until completely heated.

****

CREAM CHEESE STUFFED POTATO
Pulp from potatoes
4 ounces softened cream cheese
1/4 cup shredded carrots
1/4 cup shredded cheddar cheese
1/4 cup chopped green onions (scallions)
2 slices cooked bacon, chopped

ASSEMBLY
1. Mash all the ingredients above in a mixing bowl until light and fluffy. Spoon stuffing into potato shells and place on an ungreased pie plate.
2. Bake in a preheated 400° oven for 15 to 20 minutes or until completely heated.

"Potatoes are to food what sensible shoes are to fashion."
Linda Wells

Variations of twice-baked potatoes continued–

SPINACH STUFFED POTATOES
Pulp from potatoes
2 ounces softened cream cheese
1/4 cup shredded cheddar cheese
1 teaspoon finely chopped onion
1/4 cup frozen spinach, thawed, drained and squeezed dry

ASSEMBLY
1. Mash all the above ingredients in a mixing bowl until
    light and fluffy. Spoon stuffing into potato shells and place on an
    ungreased pie plate.
2. Bake in a preheated 400° oven for 15 to 20 minutes or until
    completely heated.

Helpful Hint
To clean pastry brushes that have egg or oil on them, put a few drops of dish detergent in heatproof cup with very hot water. Soak the brush for about 15 minutes, working it around to dislodge particles. Pour out dirty water and add clean hot water,
then rinse the brush several times.

"Excellent potatoes, smoking hot, and accompanied by melted butter of the first quality, would alone stamp merit on any dinner."
Thomas Walker

EASY BAKED RISOTTO

Risotto on a menu in a restaurant or in a home kitchen is a test of talent. To make it correctly takes a lot of timing, training, and expertise. This version is an easy way to be classic, but not completely traditional.

Serves 4

1 tablespoon butter
1/4 cup onion, chopped
1 garlic clove, minced
3/4 cup uncooked Arborio rice
1 3/4 cup chicken broth
2 tablespoons grated Parmesan cheese

ASSEMBLY

1. Melt butter in a medium ovenproof skillet with a cover over medium heat; sauté onions and garlic until tender.
2. Stir in rice and cook, stirring constantly, about 3-4 minutes. Add broth while stirring, raise heat and bring to a boil.
3. Cover and bake in a preheated 400° oven for about 20 minutes, or until liquid is absorbed. Remove skillet from oven, stir in Parmesan cheese. Serve immediately.

"In success, you deserve it; in defeat, you need it."
Winston Churchill

==============*CRUNCHY ZUCCHINI STICKS*

Two tasty variations that make zucchini special.

Serves 4

2 medium zucchini, washed, cut off ends, cut in fourths,
   then lengthwise in half to form sticks
1/2 cup wheat germ
1/4 cup finely chopped pecans, or almonds
1/4 cup grated Parmesan cheese
1/4 cup butter, melted

ASSEMBLY
1. Mix wheat germ, pecans and Parmesan cheese in a mixing bowl. Roll zucchini sticks in melted butter, lift with a fork, and bread buttered zucchini sticks in wheat germ mixture, coating evenly. Place on a cookie sheet, skin side down.
2. Bake in a preheated 400° oven for about 15 to 20 minutes.

****

================*STUFFED ZUCCHINI PARMESAN*

2 medium zucchini, washed, cut off ends
1/2 cup fresh bread crumbs
1/4 cup grated Parmesan cheese
2 tablespoons onion, minced
1 tablespoon chopped fresh parsley
1 egg, beaten in a small bowl
1 tablespoon butter

ASSEMBLY
1. Cut zucchini in half, lengthwise, and carefully remove seeds and some pulp from squash with a spoon. Chop removed pulps into small pieces and mix with crumbs, 2 tablespoons Parmesan cheese, onion, parsley, and beaten egg.
2. Spoon stuffing evenly in zucchini shells, dot with butter, sprinkle with remaining Parmesan cheese. Place stuffed squash on a cookie sheet.
3. Bake in a preheated 400° oven for 20 to 25 minutes until squash is cooked.

===OVEN BAKED SPINACH POLENTA SQUARES

Polenta can be prepared ahead. To reheat polenta squares, sauté
in a skillet with olive oil or reheat in the oven in an ovenproof
casserole with a little olive oil. Refrigerate extras for later.
Serves 8-10

4 tablespoons olive oil
1 tablespoon butter
1/2 cup chopped green onions (scallions)
1 teaspoon ground fennel or fennel seeds, slightly crushed
1/2 pound spinach, stems removed and finely chopped
2 cups ricotta cheese
2 cups whole milk
1 cup grated Parmesan cheese
1 1/2 cups yellow corn meal
1/2 teaspoon ground black pepper
1/2 teaspoon salt
Marinara sauce (optional)

PREPARATION
1. Heat 2 tablespoons olive oil and 1 tablespoon butter in a skillet
   over medium heat; Stir in green onions and fennel and cook until
   green onions soften, about 2 minutes. Stir in spinach and cook,
   stirring, until spinach is wilted. Remove from heat and set aside.
2. Whisk ricotta and milk in a large mixing bowl. Stir in Parmesan,
   corn meal, pepper, salt, and spinach mixture.

ASSEMBLY
1. Oil a 13x9x2 inch glass baking dish with 1 tablespoon olive oil.
2. Transfer spinach mixture to glass baking dish. Brush or spread 1
   tablespoon olive oil over top of polenta.
3. Bake in a preheated 375° oven for about 35 minutes, or
   until a little brown on edges and firm in center.
4. Remove from oven and allow to rest for about 10 minutes and
   cut in squares. Remove from casserole with a spatula.
5. Spoon a little warm marinara sauce on a plate and with a spatula,
   place a polenta square on sauce. Garnish with fresh basil or a
   spinach leaf. Polenta can be a first course or a side dish.

==================ROASTED POTATO WEDGES

This is a great way to make tasty potato wedges. You can peel the potato or leave the skins on. Substitute sweet potatoes for a change.
Serves 4

2 large baking potatoes cut into eight wedges
1/4 cup olive oil or vegetable oil
1/4 teaspoon garlic powder
1/4 cup grated Parmesan cheese
1/2 teaspoon paprika
1/2 cup seasoned dry bread crumbs

PREPARATION
1   Mix olive oil and garlic powder in a mixing bowl;
    stir in potato wedges coating potato with olive oil.
2. Mix Parmesan cheese, paprika, and bread crumbs
    in a mixing bowl.

ASSEMBLY
1. Line a baking sheet with aluminum foil, or oil a non-stick
    baking sheet.
2. One at a time, bread the oiled potato in the Parmesan cheese
    breading. Place on prepared baking sheet, skin side down.
3. Bake in a 400° oven for about 30 minutes or when easily
    pierced with a fork.

"I did toy with the idea of doing a cook-book....The recipes were to be the routine ones: how to make dry toast, instant coffee, hearts of lettuce and brownies. But as an added attraction, at no extra charge, my idea was to put a fried egg on the cover. I think a lot of people who hate literature but love fried eggs would buy if the price was right."
Groucho Marx

==================PERFECTLY COOKED RICE

I found this way to cook rice to be near perfect every time.
Rice goes with everything. For added flavor, substitute the water
with chicken broth, beef broth, consommé, or orange juice; add pecans,
chopped onions, sesame seeds, herbs or spices.

Yield: 3 cups rice

Melt 1 teaspoon butter in a 6 cup saucepan over medium high heat.
When butter is foaming, add 1 cup white long grain rice, and stir until rice
becomes translucent (just one minute). Add 2 1/2 cups of water and
bring to a boil. Lower the heat to the lowest setting on stove. Cook, covered,
for 25 minutes.
Do not open cover while cooking. Give the rice a stir and enjoy.

****

==========================ART AND DESIGN

We live in a wonderful age when art and design touch everything in
our lives.
Restaurants and home kitchens have drawn the attention of creative
designers. Wall-to-wall carpets and drab paneling no longer suffice. Designers
want to provide interesting spaces, comfort, atmosphere to compliment great
cooking and friendly encounters. Restaurants can provide stages where we can
act out who we are and who we want to be. People used to go out to dinner
because the food was good. Now they choose a restaurant because of its
seductive atmosphere and creative food.
Magazines and stores are featuring state-of-the-art home kitchens with commercial ranges and refrigerators. Fireplaces for cooking and wine storage
areas with wine refrigerators are in many home kitchens. Creative photography
is capturing the world of food and design in our magazines, television, and
even on the Internet.

"An epicure eats with his brain as well as his mouth."
Charles Lamb

SOUTH COUNTY JONNYCAKES

"Jonnycakes" were originally called, "journey cakes"; the small corn cakes were carried by travelers in their saddlebags. In South County Rhode Island, we have wonderful water-powered mills, Carpenter's Grist Mill built in 1703 by Samuel E. Perry. It is a working mill, in continuous operation since it was built. Water from Perry's Mill Pond supplies the power that turns the massive granite stones that cut and grind the kernels of whitecap flint corn to a fine meal. The mill is presently owned and operated by Bob and Diane Smith. I had the pleasure of attending one of their grindings. It was very neat to see the corn being ground, then to go home and make Jonnycakes with meal only one hour old. The Smiths are usually at all the country outdoor and indoor functions demonstrating the art of making their famous "Jonnycakes". Although, it is difficult to purchase the Rhode Island whitecap flint corn meal, I have found that store-bought corn meal works very well.

Serves 4 (10 to 12 Jonnycakes)
1 cup corn meal
1 tablespoon sugar
1/2 teaspoon salt
1 cup boiling water
3 or 4 tablespoons milk
Corn oil for griddle

PREPARATION
1. Combine cornmeal, sugar, and salt in a mixing bowl. Scald with boiling water and stir well. Thin immediately with milk to a mixture that will drop easily from a spoon. (Additional milk may be necessary, mixture should be consistency of thin mashed potato.)

ASSEMBLY
1. Heat a griddle or sauté pan over medium hot heat. Add oil and drop Johnnycake mixture by spoonful on griddle. Add more oil as you cook, do not allow griddle to get dry. Cook 5 to 6 minutes on each side or until a brown, crunchy crust is formed and inside is soft.
2. Place cooked Jonnycakes on warm plates and serve with butter and maple syrup. Can be used as a substitute for potatoes, or great for breakfast with sausage or bacon.

=================SWEET POTATO PANCAKES

White potatoes can be used instead of sweet potatoes;
when using white potatoes make sure to press potatoes in a strainer to remove
some of the moisture. You can also use a salad spinner to remove the moisture.

Serves 4 to 6
3 cups shredded, peeled, sweet potato
1/4 cup onion, minced
2 tablespoons chopped fresh green onions (scallions)
1 tablespoon lemon juice
1/4 cup chopped fresh parsley
1/4 teaspoon thyme
2 eggs, slightly beaten in a small bowl
2 tablespoons all purpose flour
1 teaspoon olive oil

PREPARATION
1. Thoroughly mix sweet potato, onion, green onion, lemon juice,
   parsley, thyme, eggs, and flour in a mixing bowl.

ASSEMBLY
1. Heat a 10-inch skillet or flat grill over medium heat; add oil,
   spoon about 2 tablespoons of potato batter onto hot skillet and
   flatten slightly.
   Cook about 5 minutes on each side. Heat an oven to 200° and
   place cooked pancakes on a cookie sheet to keep warm while
   cooking remaining pancakes.
      Pancakes can be prepared ahead and heated just before dinner.
      Serve a little sour cream with them if you wish.

   "Some people's food always tastes better than others, even if they
   are cooking the same dish at the same dinner...because one person
   has more life in them—more fire, more vitality, more guts—than others.
   A person without these things can never make food taste right, no
   matter what materials you give them...they have nothing in themselves
   to give. You have got to throw feelings into cooking."
                              Rosa Lewis

VEGETABLE STIR-FRY WITH RICE

Serve as a starch and vegetable or as a light meal.
You can sauté in chicken pieces or shrimp.

Serves 6

2 tablespoons vegetable oil or peanut oil
1 cup onions, chopped
1 cup thinly sliced celery
2 red bell peppers, cored, seeded, and sliced
2 green bell peppers, cored, seeded, and sliced
2 medium zucchini, cut in half and sliced into thin slices
2 carrots peeled and thinly sliced
1 cup sliced mushrooms
1/2 cup sliced green onion (scallions)
1 teaspoon five-spice powder (available in most grocery stores)
1 teaspoon hosin sauce
2 tablespoons soy sauce
3 cups cooked rice, page 456

ASSEMBLY

1. Heat oil in a heavy large skillet or wok; stir in onions and cook
   for just a minute, stir in celery and cook for just a minute, stir in
   peppers, zucchini, carrots and mushrooms.
   Sauté for a couple of minutes; add scallions, five-spice powder,
   hosin, and soy sauce. Cover and cook
   for about 3 minutes or until vegetables
   are tender. Stir in rice (over heat)
   and mix completely.

When a restaurant opened twenty-five years ago, all the menu needed was prime rib, steaks, baked stuffed shrimp and roasted stuffed chicken. Vegetables were frozen for the most part, and the potato of the day was usually baked or au gratin. Things have certainly changed. Most good restaurants today feature freshness, creativity and art in all of their food creations. We have many chefs who are stars on television and have written cookbooks that are designed for the home cook. The trend is that it's better to take some risks than to be bored. Home cooks become artists who design a dinner for taste, color, balance of ingredients, and putting a smile on your taste buds.

Supermarkets and food wholesalers show this awareness for good fresh food with displays that look like baskets of flowers set up to show off fruit and vegetables from around the world. A home cook creates a dinner for that special dinner party. A restaurant chef must reproduce his or her art consistently every single day.

==================THE CAKE AND THE JUDGE

We had booked a party for a Providence attorney that was to be a celebration for a man who had been named a judge. The attorney who booked the party arrived before his guests to give me a special cake for dessert. Indeed, it was special–it bore all the names of the guests, plus the crest of the judge. He told me he had been at the bakery for hours making sure this cake was perfect and it certainly was.

The cake was three-tiers high, so I took it and made room for it in the walk-in. The dinner was going well when Bill, their waiter, told me they were ready for the cake. I entered the walk-in and I almost died on the spot — a bag of potatoes had leaned on the cake and one side of it was gone. What could we do to make this cake presentable?

We took out whipped cream and tried to reconstruct the cake. I told Bill to present it quickly, than take it to the tray stand and start cutting it, but the host had other ideas. He had cleared a spot in the middle of the table so everyone could admire his special cake. Well, when Bill put the altered cake down, all hell broke loose. The host was not happy.

We served the cake, and the host was waiting for me after everyone in his party had left. I explained to him what we were going through in the kitchen, and just then, a bus boy went by us, holding a tray so high that it hit one of the ceiling beams. Wine and water spilled all over the man. I took a napkin and tried to help clean him up. The man finally left, not happy but OK.

I was so upset that I sent him a letter the next day apologizing and explaining what we went through in the kitchen trying to repair the cake. I finished by saying that his guests will always remember the night the bag of potatoes fell on his cake. He took my letter, copied it, and sent it to all the guests, and a negative was turned into a positive.

Now when we see each other, we always have a little laugh about that disastrous night.

DESSERTS

=================*AMARETTO BAKED PEACHES*

Amaretto is a liqueur made with the flavor of almonds, though it is often made with the kernels of apricot pits. The original liquor, Amaretto di Saronno, comes from Saronno, Italy. Many American distilleries are now producing amaretto. Peaches are so wonderful when they are in season and at their best.

Serves 4

4 large peaches, peeled, halved, and stoned (must be ripe)
1/2 cup Amaretti cookies, crushed fine, (macaroon cookies can be
    used as well) A food processor can be used.
2 egg whites
1 tablespoon ground almonds
1 tablespoon Amaretto liqueur
Pinch cinnamon
1 tablespoon soft butter

PREPARATION
1. Mix crushed cookies, egg whites, almonds, Amaretto liqueur, cinnamon,
    and 1 teaspoon of the butter in a mixing bowl. This mixture will not
    blend completely smooth.

ASSEMBLY
1. Butter an ovenproof casserole dish just large enough to contain
    the eight peach halves in one layer.
2. Spoon stuffing in each peach half.
3. Bake in a preheated 400° oven for 20 minutes.
4. Remove peaches from casserole to serving plates. Serve two halves
    to each person. Serve with vanilla ice cream or whipped cream.

*To remove skins from peaches, drop peaches in boiling water
for a minute (same way as removing skins from tomatoes) remove
peaches from boiling water and place in ice water, skins should
peel off easily*

============APPLE OR PEAR CRUMBLE

Apples are just about the country's number one snack food,
used in stuffing, pies, cakes, dinners and in more ways than I could ever
list. They last a long time if stored in the refrigerator.
Eating an apple is always satisfying.

Serves 4

6 baking apples, peeled, cored and sliced (ripe pears can be used)
1/4 cup flour, plus 2 tablespoons for later
3/4 cup light brown sugar plus 2 tablespoons for later
1/4 cup oatmeal
1 cup grated cheddar cheese
1/2 cup softened butter, plus 1 tablespoon for later
1/4 teaspoon cinnamon
1/4 teaspoon nutmeg
1/4 cup chopped walnuts or pecans

PREPARATION
1. Mix 1/4 cup flour, 3/4 cup brown sugar, oatmeal, cheddar cheese,
   1/2 cup softened butter, cinnamon, and nutmeg in a mixing bowl, Mix
   until mixture is in fine lumps, stir in walnuts and set aside.
2. Mix sliced apples, 2 tablespoons flour and 2 tablespoons brown sugar
   in a mixing bowl.

ASSEMBLY
1. Butter a medium-size ovenproof casserole dish; spread the apple
   mixture evenly in buttered casserole dish, spread the oatmeal mixture
   evenly on top of apples.
2. Bake in a preheated 400° oven for about 40 minutes or until
   crisp and brown.
3. Serve warm at a room temperature. Serve in individual dessert dishes,
   with vanilla ice cream or whipped cream.

"Why not" is a slogan for an interesting life."
Mason Cooley

APPLE BREAD PUDDING

Individual ovenproof dishes can be used in this recipe; cooking time would have to be adjusted. When the pudding is ready, it puffs up and the custard should be set.

Serves 6

5 baking apples, peeled, cored and sliced in large slices
2 tablespoons lemon juice
1/4 teaspoon nutmeg
1 loaf leftover bread, crust removed, sliced if needed (if bread is
   fresh, dry out in warm oven for a couple of minutes)
12 tablespoons (1 1/2-sticks) butter softened
4 tablespoons brown sugar
1 cup sliced almonds
1/4 cup cider, apple juice, or water
4 tablespoons sugar
4 eggs
1 1/4 cup milk
3/4 cup half-and-half cream

PREPARATION

1. Mix sliced apples, lemon juice, and nutmeg in a mixing bowl. (Lemon juice will keep the apples from discoloring.)
2. Melt 5 tablespoons butter in a skillet over medium heat, stir in four tablespoons brown sugar, and cook until brown sugar is bubbly; add almonds and cook for one minute; stir in cider and apples and cook for one minute. Cool.
3. Cream 6 tablespoons butter and 4 tablespoons of sugar in an electric mixer at medium high speed until light. Add the eggs one at a time, and beat until smooth. Go to low speed; slowly add the milk and cream. The batter can be a little lumpy.

Apple bread pudding continued–

ASSEMBLY
1. Butter a 9 x 12-inch ovenproof pan. Place a layer of bread on the bottom of the pan, then a layer of apples, then bread, then apples, ending up with bread. Pour the egg mixture evenly over the bread. Dust with a little sugar.
2. Bake in a preheated 350° oven for one hour. (or until custard is set)
3. Serve with sweetened mascarpone, whipped cream, or ice cream.

Mascarpone cheese comes from Italy's Lombardy region. Mascarpone is a buttery-rich cream cheese made from cow's milk. It can be blended with many flavors, but it's great on its own.

****
====*THE WAITRESS AND THE WEDDING CAKE*

Over the years, we hosted many weddings at the restaurant, and we became part of each family's day in trying to make every detail go as they wished. After the bride and groom cut the cake, we would bring it into the kitchen to cut and plate it and then serve it to the guests. As Lorraine, our senior waitress, was cutting the cake, she thought to herself, "This cake looks really good," and she couldn't resist tasting it.

While she was serving the cake to the guests, the bride's father asked her, "How's the cake taste?" She looked at him and wondered how he knew that she had tasted it. "Was it good?" he pursued. She replied "Yes."

Then he said, "Well, wipe the frosting off your chin." She was so embarrassed and wiped the frosting off her chin. They both laughed and she continued serving the cake.

==============*BAKED APPLES IN PUFF PASTRY*

*Apples can be prepared earlier in the day and stored in refrigerator.
Take out half hour before baking. When you sit down for your main course,
put the apples in the oven, they should be ready at dessert time.*

Serves 4

2 Pepperidge Farm patty shells, thawed, cut in two (puff pastry
   sheets can be used also)
Flour for rolling puff pastry and dusting cookie sheet
4 large baking apples, peeled and cored (Newton, Pippin, Rome
   or Granny Smith)
4 tablespoons softened butter, plus 1 teaspoon for cookie sheet
1/4 cup packed brown sugar
1 teaspoon ground cardamom
1/4 cup chopped pecans or walnuts
1 cup apple jelly
1 teaspoon lemon juice
2 tablespoons Calvados or apple brandy (optional)
1 egg beaten with 1 teaspoon milk in a small bowl

PREPARATION
1. On a floured board, roll thawed puff pastry shells about 5x5
   round. Wrap in plastic wrap and store in the refrigerator until ready
   to use. (You should end up with four rounds.)
2. Mix softened butter, brown sugar, cardamom, and pecans in a mixing
   bowl.
3. Heat over medium heat apple jelly, lemon juice, and Calvados in a
   saucepan, stir to a low boil. Remove from heat and keep for later.

Baked apple in puff pastry continued-

ASSEMBLY
1. Fill cored and peeled apples with pecan stuffing; place rolled
   puff pastry on a flat surface, place stuffed apple in the center of each
   rolled pastry, wet the pastry with a little egg wash, and wrap pastry
   around apple leaving a small opening on top.
2. Spread egg wash on crust with fingers or a pastry brush. Place on a
   buttered and floured cookie sheet, or cookie sheet covered with a piece
   of parchment paper.
3. Bake on middle rack in a preheated 400° oven for 25 minutes,
   or until apple starts to get bubbly and pastry is light brown.
4. Remove baked apples with spatula to individual plates and spoon the
   sauce around apples. Garnish with whipped cream if you wish.

*Parchment paper is a heavy, grease and moisture-resistant paper
with many culinary uses. Parchment paper is available in kitchen shops
and many supermarkets*

****
==========================*THE WEDDING CAKE*

Edna, our appetizer cook for many years, came in one Friday night
commenting "It took me all day to bake that damn wedding cake!"

After baking it at home, Edna had placed the cake in her bedroom on
the bed and told her daughter not to open the bedroom door because she didn't
want the dog to go in there. Well, for some reason, her daughter entered the
bedroom and accidentally left the door open.

At about 10 p.m. in the evening, I received a panicked telephone
call from Edna's daughter. She begged me to **PLEASE** give her mother
this message: ***"The dog ate the cake!"*** She told me she was afraid to talk
to her mother. Well, as expected Edna hit the roof. I told her we could bake
a new wedding cake after work if she wanted to. Well, she had no choice
since the wedding was the next morning, a Saturday. It took us until 3 a.m.
to bake a new wedding cake. The wedding went on as scheduled, and no
one knew the difference. Except the sick dog, the nervous daughter and
the tired cooks

================================BANANA CRISP

Sliced peeled peaches can be used instead of bananas.

Serves 4

4 ripe bananas, peeled and sliced
2 tablespoons water
1/4 cup brown sugar
1/4 teaspoon cinnamon
2 tablespoons dark rum (or 1 teaspoon of rum extract)
1/2 cup hazelnut or almond biscotti, crushed
2 teaspoons butter
Vanilla ice cream or vanilla frozen yogurt

PREPARATION
1. Mix water, brown sugar, cinnamon, and rum in a mixing bowl; stir in sliced bananas, coating bananas with liquid.

ASSEMBLY
1. Select four ovenproof individual custard dishes or small 1 1/2 cup gratin dishes; place dishes on a cookie sheet with sides. Spoon banana mixture evenly in each dish; press down to get all the bananas and juice in the dishes. Top with crushed biscotti, dot with butter.
2. Bake in a preheated 400° oven for about 15 minutes or until bubbly.
3. Remove from oven with a spatula onto serving plates and top with a scoop of ice cream; garnish with mint and a slice of banana.
   Brown sugar is white sugar combined with molasses, which gives it a soft texture.

<u>Helpful Hint</u>
Mustard bottles make a great garnishing tool. I like to reuse my plastic mustard squeeze bottles by washing them and filling them with sweet or savory sauces to garnish everything from desserts and appetizers to main courses.

================CARAMEL SLICED PEACHES

The peach is native to China where it was held in high esteem. Friends gave each other fresh peaches or peaches made of porcelain, to attest their affection. The flavor of a ripe fresh peach can stimulate all the senses. Make this dish when peaches are in season.

Serves 4

4 ripe peaches, peeled, pit removed, sliced
1/2 cup sugar
1 tablespoon water
1 cup half-and-half cream
1/4 teaspoon cinnamon
1 tablespoon chopped crystallized ginger (optional)
Pound cake
Vanilla ice cream or vanilla yogurt

ASSEMBLY

1. Place sugar in a heavy-based saucepan with 1 tablespoon water; slowly bring to a boil to dissolve the sugar, and then boil quickly so that the sugar caramelizes and turns a golden color. Take off heat, add cream and stir until cream is incorporated with caramel. (Be extremely careful when adding cream it will sputter and could burn you.) When caramel is a beautiful light brown color, stir in cinnamon, ginger and peaches. Return to heat and cook for one minute.
2. Slice pound cake and place on individual dessert dishes. Spoon peach topping evenly on each slice of pound cake. Place a scoop of ice cream on top of peaches. Garnish with crystallized ginger and sliced peach.

Peach topping can be prepared just before dinner. Store at room temperature.
Substituted pound cake with biscuits or any white cake without frosting or the peaches can be served just with ice cream.

"An apple is an excellent thing—until you have tried a peach!"
George Du Maurier

======CHOCOLATE-ALMOND PEAR IN PASTRY

Almond paste is made of blanched ground almonds, sugar, glycerin and sometimes almond extract. Once opened, almond paste should be wrapped tightly and refrigerated.

4 ripe pears
3 ounces almond paste (available in baking department of grocery store)
2 tablespoons sugar
3 tablespoons softened butter
1 egg
3/4 teaspoon ground ginger
1/4 teaspoon ground cinnamon
1/4 cup flour
2 ounces semisweet chocolate, melted
2 Pepperidge Farm patty shells, thawed and cut in two
Flour for rolling pastry
1 egg beaten with 1 teaspoon milk in a small bowl
1/2 cup Mascarpone cheese

PREPARATION

1. Peel the pears, leaving the stem intact. Carefully core the pear from the bottom with a melon baller or small spoon, taking care not to damage the sides. Cover pears with a damp cloth and set aside.
2. Mix almond paste and sugar in a mixing bowl with an electric mixer until mixture looks grainy, add butter a little at a time while continuing to beat. Add egg and beat until mixture is light, lump free and fluffy; add ginger, cinnamon, flour, and mix completely. Mix in melted chocolate. Refrigerate.
3. On a floured board, roll each thawed half puff pastry shell to about 5x5 round. Wrap in plastic wrap and store in refrigerator.

Chocolate-almond pear in pastry continued-

ASSEMBLY
1. Fill each pear cavity with chocolate mixture with spoon. Place rolled puff
   pastry on a flat surface, place stuffed pear in center of each pastry.
   Wet the inside of the pastry with a little egg wash and wrap around pear
   all the way to the stem.
2. Spread pastry with egg wash with your fingers or a pastry brush;
   place on cookie sheet covered with parchment paper. (If you do not have
   parchment paper, oil and flour the cookie sheet.) Store in refrigerator
   until ready to bake.
3. Bake in a 350° oven on middle shelf for about 30 minutes.
4. Spoon Mascarpone cheese evenly in the middle of dessert
   dishes. Remove stuffed pear from cookie sheet with a spatula
   and place on Mascarpone cheese. Serve with a spoon, knife and
   fork. Garnish with mint and fresh fruit.

Stuffed pears can be prepared earlier in the day.

*"Two of life's mysteries–how does the ship get into the bottle,
and how does the pear get into the bottle of **eau de vie**."*
Jane Grigson

Bing Cherries are large cherries that range in color from a garnet to almost black. I like to use the canned variety packed in water, but in the early summer when the fresh cherries are in all the markets use them. Cherries jubilee is a classic colorful dessert.

Serves 4

2 cups drained canned Bing (save juice) or dark fresh cherries,
　 pitted and stemmed
1 cup cherry juice (if you are using fresh cherries use water)
1/2 teaspoon cinnamon
Juice from 1/2 orange
Grated orange peel (zest) from half of orange
1 teaspoon cornstarch
1/4 cup cognac
1/4 cup cherry brandy
Vanilla ice cream

ASSEMBLY

1. Whisk cherry juice (or water), cinnamon, orange juice, orange peel, and cornstarch in a medium skillet over medium heat. Bring to a boil and allow it to bubble for 5 minutes, stirring occasionally. Stir in cherries and heat through; (if you are using fresh cherries cook for about 5 minutes) add the cherry brandy and cognac. Ignite carefully; cook until the flame goes out.
　 Spoon vanilla ice cream in individual dessert dishes, spoon the cherries on ice cream. Serve immediately before ice cream melts.

Helpful Hint

Protect the paint or wallpaper on the walls above your sink and stove by installing Plexiglas. I did that at the restaurant near the tray stands in the dinning rooms. Any food that splatters wipes off easily with a damp cloth.

"Everyone has something secret they like to eat."
M.F.K. Fisher

COCONUT CUSTARD PUDDING

The most delicate and enjoyable dessert after a nice dinner is custard.
Add 1 tablespoon of dark rum instead of vanilla for a different flavor.

Serves 6

1 tablespoon butter, softened
4 eggs
1 cup milk
1 (14-ounce) can sweetened condensed milk
1/2 teaspoon vanilla extract
1 cup sweetened flaked coconut
Hot water for water bath

ASSEMBLY

1. Butter 6 (3/4-cup) custard cups.
2. Gently whisk eggs, add milk, condensed milk, and vanilla in a mixing bowl.
3. Place custard cups in a 13x9x2-inch baking-dish. Spoon coconut evenly into each custard cup, fill each cup with custard.
4. Pour enough hot water into baking dish to come halfway up sides of filled cups.
5. Bake in a preheated 350° oven for 40 minutes, or until custard is set. Cool and place in refrigerator covered with plastic wrap until ready to use. Garnish with whipped cream and fresh berries.

"Probably one of the most
private things in the world
is an egg until it is broken."
M.F.K. Fisher

CRÈME CARAMEL

Custard that is baked in a caramel coated cup.

Serves 6
1 tablespoon butter
3/4 cup sugar
1 tablespoon water
6 eggs
3 cups half-and half-cream or milk
1 cup sugar
1 teaspoon vanilla
Hot water for water bath

PREPARATION

1. Butter 6 (3/4-ounce) custard cups.
2. Cook 3/4 cup sugar and water in a heavy saucepan over low heat, swirling pan occasionally, until sugar dissolves. Increase heat and boil without stirring until syrup turns a golden color. Quickly spoon the caramel evenly into the custard cups around the base of the cups. (Be very careful; caramel is very hot and can burn you.)
3. Gently whisk eggs, cream, sugar, and vanilla in a mixing bowl.

ASSEMBLY

1. Select a deep baking pan just large enough to contain the six cups; place cups in pan and fill with custard mixture.
2. Pour hot water in baking pan to about half way up the sides of the custard cups.
3. Bake in a preheated 350° oven for about 40 minutes or until custard is set.
4. Remove custard cups carefully from hot water and cool completely.
5. Cover with plastic wrap and chill in refrigerator for a few hours or overnight.
6. To serve, run a knife around custard, take your serving plate and place on top of custard dish up side down and turn over. In a moment, the custard should drop and the caramel will flow around custard. *Garnish with whipped cream, fresh fruit or enjoy it just as it is.*

This spicy, old-fashioned dessert brings flavors from the past. Before the modern home ovens, cooks of old cooked this pudding on the side of the fireplace slowly in iron pans. Boston suffered a sticky situation in the early 1900's when a 2 million-gallon storage tank of molasses collapsed and flooded the streets.

Serves 6 to 8

1 quart milk
1 cup yellow corn meal
1 cup molasses
3/4 teaspoon ground cinnamon
3/4 teaspoon ground ginger
1/2 teaspoon ground nutmeg
1/4 teaspoon salt
2 tablespoons butter
1 cup milk
Vanilla ice cream or whipped cream

PREPARATION
1. Heat (1-quart) milk over medium heat in a saucepan. When milk is hot, just before the boiling point, stir in corn meal, and cook over low heat, stirring constantly to prevent lumps. Off heat, stir in molasses, cinnamon, ginger, nutmeg, and salt.

ASSEMBLY
1. Butter a 1 1/2 quart baking dish. Pour the mixture into the pan.
2. Pour the remaining milk (1-cup) on top of pudding but do not stir in.
3. Bake in a 275° oven for 2 3/4 to 3 hours or until set.
4. Cool pudding to lukewarm, spoon into serving dishes and serve warm with ice cream or whipped cream.

Pudding can be prepared ahead and re-heated.

"The road up and the road down is one and the same."
Heraclitus

======COCONUT CRÈME CARAMEL WITH RUM

*A great dessert that can be made the day before your dinner party.
I enjoy the presentation, and sometimes I have my guests run the knife
around their own desserts and invert them. It is always a thrill to watch their
faces as the custard slowly drops onto the plate.*

Serves 6

1 tablespoon butter
3/4 cup sugar
1 tablespoon water
4 large eggs
1 (13-ounce) can unsweetened coconut milk
1/2 cup sweetened condensed milk
1/2 cup milk
1/4 teaspoon ground cinnamon
1 tablespoon vanilla extract
1 1/2 tablespoons dark rum liquor
Boiling water

PREPARATION
1. Butter 6 (3/4-ounce) custard cups.
2. Cook sugar and water in a heavy saucepan over low heat,
    swirling pan occasionally, until sugar dissolves. Increase
    heat and boil until syrup turns a golden color.
    Quickly spoon the caramel evenly into the custard cups around
    the base of the cups. (Be very careful; caramel is very hot and
    can burn you.)
3. Gently whisk eggs, coconut milk, condensed milk, milk,
    cinnamon, vanilla, and rum in a mixing bowl.

Coconut crème caramel with rum, continued-

ASSEMBLY

1. Select a deep baking pan just large enough to contain the six cups. Place cups in pan and fill each custard cup evenly with custard mixture.
2. Pour hot water in baking pan to about half way up the sides of the custard cups.
3. Bake in a preheated 350° oven for about 40 minutes or until custard is set.
4. Carefully remove baking pan from oven; allow to cool a little then remove cups from water to cool completely. When cups are completely cooled, cover in plastic wrap and store in refrigerator a few hours or overnight.
5. To serve, run a knife around custard, take your serving plate and place on top of custard dish upside down and turn over. In a moment, the custard should drop and the caramel will flow around custard. Garnish with whipped cream, fresh fruit, or enjoy just as it is.

Coconut milk is made by combining equal parts water and shredded fresh coconut meat and simmering until foamy. The mixture is strained through cheesecloth, squeezing as much of the liquid as possible.

"When we no longer have good cooking in the world, we will have no literature, no high and sharp intelligence, nor friendly gatherings, nor social harmony."

Marie-Antoine Carême

=====FIVE VARIATIONS OF FLAMED BANANAS

Preparing flamed desserts can be fun if you do it table side. Use a smaller side table to flame the dessert, not the dining room table, and be very careful.

Serves 4

BANANAS FOSTER

4 Bananas, peeled and sliced in one-inch chunks
1/2 stick of butter (1/8-pound)
1/4 cup brown sugar
1/2 teaspoon ground cinnamon
1/4 cup dark rum or brandy liquor
Vanilla ice cream or vanilla low fat frozen yogurt

ASSEMBLY

1. Heat butter and brown sugar in a skillet over medium heat, until sugar is dissolved and bubbly; stir in sliced bananas and cinnamon, sauté for a minute while stirring making sure bananas are coated with sugar mixture. Add rum and carefully ignite with a match, or if using a gas stove, tip pan carefully into the flame and the fumes will ignite. The liquor will burst into flames so be careful. Cook until the flame goes out. Spoon vanilla ice cream into individual small bowls, or custard dishes; spoon banana and sauce on vanilla ice cream.

Flamed bananas continued-

PRALINE BANANAS
4 Bananas, peeled and sliced in one-inch chunks
1/4 brown sugar
1 1/2 teaspoons cornstarch
1/2 cup evaporated skim milk
2 tablespoons chopped pecans
1 tablespoon butter
1 teaspoon vanilla extract
1/4 cup dark rum liquor
Vanilla ice cream or vanilla low fat frozen yogurt

ASSEMBLY
1. Combine brown sugar and cornstarch in a skillet;
    gradually whisk in milk, cook over medium heat, stirring constantly
    until mixture thickens slightly, stir in butter, pecans, vanilla, and bananas,
    stirring until butter melts. Add rum and carefully ignite with a match,
    or if using a gas stove, tip pan carefully into the flame and the fumes
    will ignite. The liquor will burst into flames so be careful. Cook until
    flame goes out. Spoon vanilla ice cream into individual small bowls
    or custard dishes. Spoon banana and sauce on vanilla ice cream.

BANANAS CACAO
4 Bananas peeled, and sliced in one-inch chunks
1/4 stick butter (1/8 pound)
1/4 cup brown sugar
1/2 large orange, grate peel (zest) and save juice
1/4 teaspoon cardamom
1/4 cup Crème de Cacao liqueur (dark rum can be used)
Vanilla ice cream or low fat frozen yogurt

ASSEMBLY
1. Heat butter and brown sugar in a skillet over medium heat until
    sugar is dissolved and bubbly; stir in orange peel, orange juice, and
    cardamom, cook for a minute; stir in bananas and heat through. Pour
    Crème de Cocoa over the bananas and ignite with a match, or if using
    a gas stove, tip pan carefully into the flame and the fumes will ignite.
    The liquor will burst into flames, so be careful. Spoon vanilla ice cream
    into individual small bowls, or custard dishes. Spoon bananas and
    sauce on vanilla ice cream.

Flamed bananas continued-

GRAND MARNIER-LIME BANANAS

4 bananas, peeled, and sliced in one-inch pieces
1/2 stick of butter
2 tablespoons brown sugar
1/2 cup orange juice
2 tablespoons grated orange peel (zest)
1 tablespoon lime juice
1/2 teaspoon vanilla extract
1/8 teaspoon cinnamon
1/4 cup Grand Marnier or Cointreau
Vanilla ice cream of low far frozen vanilla yogurt

ASSEMBLY
1. Heat butter and brown sugar in a skillet over medium heat
    until sugar is dissolved and bubbly; stir in orange
    juice, orange peel, lime juice, vanilla extract and cinnamon.
    Bring to a light boil, and then add bananas. Cook until bananas
    are heated. Pour Grand Marnier over bananas and ignite with
    a match, or if using gas stove tip pan carefully into the flame
    and the fumes will ignite. Carefully stir and remove from heat.
2. Spoon vanilla ice cream into individual small bowls, or custard
    dishes. Spoon bananas and sauce on ice cream.

Grand Marnier will not flame as much; it has only 40% alcohol.

Helpful Hint
*To distract those uninvited bees and wasps at your next cookout,
place a small amount of honey in a small dish. Place the dish away
from your guests and food. The bees and wasps, will be attracted to
the honey and leave you alone.*

Flamed bananas continued-

BANANAS COCONUT
4 Bananas, peeled and sliced in one-inch chunks
1/2 stick butter (1/8 pound)
2 tablespoons honey or brown sugar
2 tablespoons sliced almonds
1/4 cup grated coconut
1/4 cup Kahlúa liqueur or dark rum
Vanilla ice cream or vanilla low fat frozen yogurt

ASSEMBLY
1. Heat butter, honey, and almonds in a saucepan until bubbly; stir in
   coconut and bananas, cook until bananas are heated. Add Kahlúa and
   carefully ignite with a match. (Alcohol is only 53 proof it might not
   ignite much) If you are using a gas stove, tip pan carefully into the
   flame and the fumes will ignite. The liquor might burst into flames so
   be careful. Cook until flame goes out. Spoon vanilla ice cream into
   individual small bowls or custard dishes. Spoon banana and sauce
   on vanilla ice cream.

Helpful Hint
*In the summer fruit flies can be annoying, especially around
bananas and tomatoes. Drain some pickle juice from a jar of pickles
and place the juice in a glass on the counter near the area where the
flies are. In a few days, you will find the flies have drowned in the juice*

*"One of the goldenest of the golden rules in making up a menu....
is to pay special attention to the dessert course...nobody seems
able to resist a delicious dessert."*
Wolfgang Puck

===*GORGONZOLA-STUFFED PEARS IN PHYLLO*

Phyllo is tissue-thin layers of pastry dough used in various Greek and Near Eastern cooking; working with phyllo is tricky, you must work fast because it dries very quickly. When the pastry is cooked, it is light, crispy, and delicious.

Serves 4

4 ripe pears, peeled, and cored from bottom
1 cup sugar
1 cup white wine
1 cup water
1 tablespoon grated orange peel (zest)
1 teaspoon grated lemon peel (zest)
1 cinnamon stick, broken in half
4 cloves
1/2 cup (3-ounces) crumbled Gorgonzola cheese, softened
1/2 cup (4-ounces) cream cheese, softened
2 tablespoons honey
12 (8 x 8-inch sheets) of phyllo, covered with a damp towel
1/4 cup melted butter, room temperature
1 teaspoon ground cinnamon
Grand Marnier liqueur (optional)

PREPARATION

1. In a sauce pan (with a cover) just large enough to contain the pears, combine the sugar, wine, water, orange peel, lemon peel, cinnamon stick, and cloves. Add pears, turn over to remove air from pear, and then stand upright. Cover, bring to a boil and simmer for about 20 minutes or until tender when pear can be pierced with a knife. Remove pear with a slotted spoon from liquid and transfer to a dish to cool.
2. Mix Gorgonzola, cream cheese, and honey in a mixing bowl.

Gorgonzola-stuffed pears in phyllo continued-

ASSEMBLY
1. Spoon cheese stuffing into bottom of pears. Add cinnamon
   to melted butter.
2. On a work surface, arrange sheet of phyllo and brush with butter.
   Place another sheet on top of buttered sheet and butter, do this with one
   more sheet and butter. Do this 4 times for each pear. Wrap phyllo up and
   around pear to enclose it, twisting the top; brush with butter. Do this
   with the four pears, place pear packages on a cookie sheet.
3. Bake in middle shelf in a preheated 400° oven for 15 to 20 minutes.
4. Remove pears from cookie sheet to individual serving plates with a spatula.
   Spoon some Grand Marnier on plate if you wish.

This recipe can be prepared with puff pastry as well.

*Instead of the Gorgonzola stuffing for the pears, I also like to stuff
them with a mixture of 3/4 cup Mascarpone cheese and 1 tablespoon
fresh tarragon (1/2 teaspoon dried) use all the above procedures for
preparation.*

Helpful Hint
*When peeling pears and apples use a vegetable peeler, it takes half the
time and saves more fruit.*

"I am not young enough to know everything."
Oscar Wilde

================================MOCHA CARAMEL CUSTARD

Puddings and custards are such comfort foods, just as soups are. There is something soothing about custard, a nice way to end a wonderful dinner.

Serves 6

1 tablespoon butter
3/4 cup sugar
1 tablespoon water
6 eggs
1 tablespoon powdered chocolate-flavored drink mix
1 teaspoon instant coffee granules
1 cup half-and-half cream or milk
1 can (14-ounce) sweetened condensed milk
1 can (12-ounce) evaporated milk
1 teaspoon vanilla extract
Hot water for water bath

PREPARATION
1. Butter 6 (3/4-ounce) custard cups.
2. Cook 3/4 cup sugar and water in a heavy saucepan over low heat, swirling pan occasionally, until sugar dissolves; increase heat and boil without stirring until syrup turns a golden color. Quickly spoon the caramel evenly in the custard cups around the base of the cups. (Be careful; the caramel is very hot and can burn you.)
3. Gently whisk eggs, powered chocolate, coffee granules, cream, condensed milk, evaporated milk, and vanilla in a mixing bowl.

Mocha caramel custard continued-

ASSEMBLY

1. Select a deep baking pan just large enough to contain the six cups; place cups in pan and fill with custard mixture.
2. Pour hot water into baking pan to about half way up the sides of the custard cups.
3. Bake in a preheated 300° oven for about 40 minutes or until custard is set.
4. Remove custard dishes carefully from hot water and cool completely. Wrap in plastic wrap and chill covered in refrigerator for a few hours or overnight.
5. To serve, run a knife around custard. Take your serving plate and place on top of custard dish up side down and turn over. In a moment, the custard should drop and the caramel will flow around custard. Garnish with whipped cream, sprinkle of powdered chocolate and fresh mint.

Helpful Hint
When combining the liquid and eggs for custard, whisk gently. Vigorous whisking will create little air holes in the custard.

"Life is like a box of chocolates. You never know what you're going to get."
Grant Showley

MAPLE PECAN STUFFED PEARS

This tasty dessert will make the house smell wonderful. It can also be prepared with fresh peaches.
Cooking time for pears can vary depending on the ripeness of the pear.

Serves 6

6 large Anjou or Bosc pears, peeled and cut in half
2 teaspoons flour
1/3 cup brown sugar
1 1/2 tablespoons softened butter
1 cup finely chopped pecans
2 teaspoons Amaretto or Frangelico liqueur
1 1/2 cups apple juice
1/3 cup maple syrup
Vanilla ice cream or whipped cream

PREPARATION
1. Core and remove stem from each pear half. (Use a melon baller or small spoon.)
2. Mix flour and brown sugar in a mixing bowl. Stir in softened butter to a creamy consistency, then stir in Amaretto and pecans.

ASSEMBLY
1. Arrange pears, cut side up, in large glass baking dish.
2. Spoon the nut topping evenly into each pear cavity.
3. Pour apple juice around pears, drizzle pears with maple syrup.
4. Bake in a 375° oven for about 30 minutes, or until pears are tender when pierced with a sharp knife. Baste with juices while cooking.
5. Serve 2 stuffed pear halves with vanilla ice cream or whipped cream. Spoon juices on and around pear.

This dish can be prepared earlier and warmed just before dessert.

"The art of being wise is the art of knowing what to overlook."
William James

===================ORANGE POACHED PEARS

*Oranges have been associated with fertility, because this lush
evergreen tree can simultaneously produce flowers, fruit, and foliage.
Oranges are an excellent source of vitamin C and contain some vitamin A.*

Serves 4

4 ripe pears, peeled and cored from the bottom
2 cups orange juice
1/3 cup Grand Marnier liqueur
1 tablespoon grated orange peel (zest)
Water for poaching pears if needed
2 teaspoons cornstarch
3 tablespoons water
Orange peel strips for garnish (remove white part use just the orange peel)

PREPARATION
1. In a sauce pan (with a cover) just large enough to contain the
   pears, combine the orange juice, Grand Marnier, and orange peel. Add
   pears turn over to remove air from pear, and then stand upright.
   (Make sure the pears are covered with the liquid; if not, add a little water.)
   Cover, bring to a boil, then simmer for 20 minutes, or until tender
   when pierced with a knife. Use slotted spoon and transfer the cooked
   pears to a dish to cool.
2. Bring orange cooking liquid to a boil again and reduce to half.
   Mix cornstarch and water in a small bowl, then slowly stir into the
   orange juice. Cook over low heat, stirring constantly, until thickened. Cool.

ASSEMBLY
1. Place each poached pear in a dessert dish; spoon orange sauce on and
   around pear. Garnish with orange rind strips, whipped cream, and
   fresh berries. Serve with knife, fork, and spoon.

"The secret of business is to know something that nobody else knows."
Aristotle Onassis

===================================PANNA COTTA

*I was lucky to be part of a culinary tour of Tuscany recently. I especially enjoyed the delicate flavor of **panna cotta**. Panna cotta means cooked cream and usually served with fresh fruit sauces. Enjoy the two variations with five choices of sauces.*

Serves 6 or 8

1/4 cup cold water
4 teaspoons unflavored gelatin
4 cups heavy cream or whipping cream
1 tablespoon honey
1/4 teaspoon vanilla extract
3/4 cup sugar
1/4 teaspoon grated orange or lemon peel (zest)
1 tablespoon cream sherry
1 cup pine nuts (optional)
Nonstick cooking spray

PREPARATION
1. Pour 1/4 cup water in a small metal bowl; sprinkle gelatin over water and allow to soften (about 10 minutes). Place bowl over a saucepan of simmering water and heat until gelatin dissolves, and keep warm over water.
2. Combine cream, honey, vanilla, sugar, and orange peel in a saucepan; bring to a low boil, stirring until sugar is dissolved. Remove from heat and add sherry and gelatin, stir until well blended.

ASSEMBLY
1. Lightly coat with nonstick cooking spray 3/4 or 1 cup custard cups or teacups. Divide the pine nuts among the custard cups, saving a little for garnish. Ladle cream mixture into each cup, cool, and cover with plastic wrap and refrigerate overnight.
2. To serve, set cups in a small bowl of warm water to loosen panna cotta, about 1/2 minute. Run a small knife between panna cotta and cup, invert cups onto plates and the panna cotta should drop onto plates. Serve with sauce and garnish with remaining pine nuts.

===============*MASCARPONE PANNA COTTA*

A slightly heavier version of panna cotta, one spoonful of this
wonderful Italian dessert is a taste to savor long after dinner is over.

Serves 6 to 8

2 tablespoons water
2 tablespoons Grand Marnier liqueur or orange juice
4 teaspoons unflavored gelatin
1 cup (8-ounces) Mascarpone cheese
1 cup (8-ounces) sour cream
2/3 cup sugar
1 teaspoon vanilla extract
2 cups half-and-half cream
Nonstick cooking spray

PREPARATION
1. Pour water and Grand Marnier in a metal bowl; sprinkle
   gelatin over water, allow gelatin to soften (about 10 minutes).
   Place bowl over a saucepan of simmering water, heat
   until gelatin dissolves, and keep warm over water.
2. Whisk Mascarpone cheese, sour cream, sugar, vanilla,
   and cream in a mixing bowl until smooth; whisk in
   gelatin and mix completely.

ASSEMBLY
1. Lightly coat with nonstick cooking spray 3/4 or 1-cup molds
   or cups.
2. Pour panna cotta into prepared molds, cover with
   plastic wrap and refrigerate over night.
3. To serve, set cups in a small bowl of warm water to
   loosen panna cotta, about 1/2 minute. Run a small
   knife between panna cotta and cup, invert mold or cup onto plates.
   The panna cotta should drop onto plates. Serve with any of the five
   sauces and garnish with fresh fruit and mint.

Panna cotta continued-

FIVE SAUCES

STRAWBERRY SAUCE
1 (4-cups)pound fresh strawberries, stems removed, quartered
2 tablespoons cream sherry
1/4 teaspoon grated lemon peel (zest)
1/3 cup sugar
1/4 teaspoon vanilla extract

PREPARATION
1. Puree strawberries in a food processor and transfer to a
   saucepan over medium heat; add cream sherry, lemon peel, sugar,
   and vanilla. Simmer while stirring often until sauce is reduced to about 2
   cups. Cool. (Sauce can be made ahead and stored in refrigerator.)

==

FRESH CHERRY SAUCE
1 pound fresh cherries, pitted, stems removed
1/4 teaspoon grated lemon peel (zest)
1 tablespoon cream sherry
1/3 cup sugar
1/4 teaspoon vanilla extract
2 tablespoons Cherry Herring liqueur or any cherry liqueur

PREPARATION
1. Heat cherries, lemon peel, cream sherry, sugar, vanilla, and cherry
   liquor in a saucepan; bring to a light simmer, and cook until cherries
   are cooked (about 15 minutes).
2. Place a medium sieve over a bowl and sieve cherries,
   pressing with back of a soup spoon until all the pulp is sieved.
   Discard the skins that remain. Refrigerate sauce.

   Serve with panna cotta, ice cream and pound cake.

Five sauces continued-

BLUEBERRY SAUCE
1 pound blueberries, stems removed and picked over
2 tablespoons water
1/2 teaspoon ground cinnamon
1/4 teaspoon grated lemon peel (zest)
1/3 cup sugar
2 tablespoons cream sherry
1/4 teaspoon vanilla extract

PREPARATION
1. Heat blueberries, water, cinnamon, lemon peel, sugar,
   cream sherry, and vanilla extract in a sauce pan. Simmer while stirring
   often until blueberries are cooked and sauce is slightly thickened.
2. Place a medium sieve over a bowl and sieve the blueberry
   mixture, using the back of a spoon to press the pulp through the sieve.
   The skins should remain in sieve and discarded. Refrigerate sauce.
   Serve with panna cotta, ice cream and pound cake.
   ===

RASPBERRY MINT SAUCE
1 pound fresh raspberries, or blackberries, stems removed and
  picked over
1 tablespoon water
1 tablespoon chopped fresh mint
1/3 cup sugar
2 tablespoons cream sherry

PREPARATION
1. Heat raspberries, water, mint, sugar, and cream sherry in a saucepan to a
   low boil. Stir and cook until raspberries are cooked, and start to look
   like a sauce; it takes about 10 minutes for this to happen.
2. Place a sieve over a bowl and sieve raspberries, pressing with the back
   of a spoon until all the pulp is sieved. Discard remaining seeds and
   refrigerate sauce.
   Serve with panna cotta, ice cream and pound cake.

Five sauces continued-

This sauce must be made before you make the panna cotta.
The caramel must be put into the cups before panna cotta is put into
the cups. It is not necessary to spray the cups with this procedure.

CARAMEL SAUCE
1 cup sugar
2 tablespoon water

PREPARATION
1. Place 1 cup sugar in a heavy-bottomed small saucepan with
   2 tablespoon water. Slowly bring to a boil to dissolve sugar;
   then boil quickly so that the sugar caramelizes and turns a
   golden color. Quickly spoon the caramel evenly into the cups
   you are using for the panna cotta around the base of the cups.
   (Be careful; sugar is very hot and can burn you.)
2. Follow directions under assembly in the panna cotta recipe.
3. When the panna cotta is inverted on the plates the caramel
   will flow onto the plate.

> *"The only way to get rid of temptation is to yield to it."*
> *Oscar Wilde*
>
> *(Especially with this dessert)*

Peach Melba is a dessert created by the French chef A.Escoffier in the late 1800's for a popular Australian opera singer named "Dame Nellie Melba".

Serves 4

4 ripe peaches, peeled, pitted, and poached in a little sugar with
   water until slightly softened, about 10 minutes or depending on
   ripeness of peach. Remove from water with a slotted spoon and drain.
   (or use canned peach halves)
Melba sauce: See raspberry sauce, (leave out mint) page, 492
1/4 cup sliced almonds
Vanilla ice cream
Whipped cream

ASSEMBLY
1. In a dessert dish, add ice cream, top with 2 peach halves,
    almonds, Melba sauce, and whipped cream.

Decorate with fresh mint and serve with a cookie.

"A guest sees more in an hour than the host in a year."
Polish proverb

========================PINEAPPLE FOSTER

For a variation, place a slice of pound cake or sponge cake on a flat plate, spoon pineapple and juices on cake then top with a scoop of vanilla ice cream.

Serves 4-6

1 ripe pineapple, skinned, quartered, cored
   and cut into 1/2-inch slices
1/2 (1/8-pound) stick of butter
1/4 cup brown sugar
1/2 teaspoon ground cinnamon
1/4 cup dark rum liquor
Vanilla ice cream or vanilla frozen yogurt

ASSEMBLY
1. Heat butter and brown sugar in a skillet until sugar is dissolved and bubbly. Add sliced pineapple and cinnamon, sauté for a minute, carefully stirring to make sure all the pineapple slices are coated with the sugar. Add rum and carefully ignite with a match, or if using a gas stove, tip pan carefully into the flame and the fumes will ignite. The liquor will burst into flames so be careful. Remove from heat and wait for the flames to go out; spoon vanilla ice cream into individual small bowls, or custard cups. Spoon pineapple and sauce on vanilla ice cream. Serve immediately before ice cream melts.

*"Give me the luxuries of life and I will willingly
do without the necessities."*
Frank Lloyd Wright

Helpful Hint
When we made fruit pies at the restaurant we added 3 to 4 tablespoons of minute tapioca. Just mix it with sugar before adding to the fruit. It helped to keep the pies from watering.

The pineapple is native to Central and South America. Hawaii is now the fruit's leading producer.

For variation, you can add 1/2 cup grated coconut to the whipped cream. This dish can also be made with fresh strawberries, ripe peaches, or bananas.

Serves 6-8

1 ripe pineapple, skinned, quartered, cored
  and cut into 1/2-inch slices
6 tablespoons confectionery sugar (powdered sugar)
3 tablespoons Cointreau or Grand Marnier
3 tablespoons dark rum
1 cup heavy cream
2 tablespoons Kirsch
1 grated orange peel (zest)

ASSEMBLY

1. Add pineapple to a mixing bowl; stir in 4 tablespoons of confectionery sugar, Cointreau, and rum. Mix carefully and keep in refrigerator.
2. One hour before serving, whip the cream with remaining confectionery sugar. At the end of whipping add the Kirsch, and keep cold. Just before serving combine pineapple and whipped cream.
3. Spoon pineapple mixture into individual glass serving dishes or tall glasses. Garnish with grated orange peel, and fresh mint.

HELPFUL HINT

In working with a recipe that calls for a gelatin, it is important to remember that a few types of fruit contain proteases. Proteases are enzymes that break down the collagen in gelatin and do not allow it to set or "gel." These fruits include pineapple, kiwi, papaya, honeydew melon, fresh ginger, and bananas.

Canned pineapple is ok to use with gelatin.

=========POACHED PEARS WITH MASCARPONE

This dish can be prepared ahead. A beautiful presentation after a wonderful dinner.

Serves 4

4 ripe Bartlett or Bosc pears, peeled and cored from bottom
1 cup sugar
1 cup white wine
1 cup water
1 tablespoon grated orange peel (zest)
1 tablespoon grated lemon peel (zest)
1 cinnamon stick, broken in half
1 teaspoon vanilla extract
1/4 cup Mascarpone cheese
1/4 cup heavy cream
Chocolate sauce

PREPARATION
1. In a saucepan just large enough to contain the pears, combine the sugar, wine, water, orange peel, lemon peel, cinnamon stick, and vanilla; add pears, turning over to remove air from the pear, then stand upright. Cover, bring to a boil and simmer for about 20 minutes or until tender when pierced with a knife. Use a slotted spoon and transfer the pears to a dish to cool.
2. Strain the syrup to another saucepan. Boil on medium heat until syrup is reduced to half. Cool.

ASSEMBLY
1. Whisk 2 tablespoons of reduced syrup with mascarpone in a small bowl, chill.
2. Whip cream, stir in Mascarpone, and store in refrigerator until ready to use.
3. Spoon cream mixture into a pastry bag fitted with a plain tip. Pipe the cream mixture into pear centers. (Or spoon cream into the pear centers.) Place pear on flat dessert plates; pipe remaining Mascarpone around pear. Garnish with chocolate sauce and pear syrup. Serve with a knife, fork and spoon.

============PUMPKIN RUM CARAMEL CUSTARD

When making caramel use a heavy pan; it heats more evenly and reduces chances of burning. Using a lighter colored pan will allow you to see the color of the caramel.

Serves 6

3/4 cup sugar
1 tablespoons water
5 eggs
2 cups half-and-half cream
1 cup sugar
1 1/4 cups canned solid pack pumpkin
1/2 teaspoon ground cinnamon
1/4 teaspoon grated fresh nutmeg
1/8 teaspoon ground cloves
2 tablespoons dark rum or 1 teaspoon rum extract

PREPARATION
1. Select 6 (1-cup) custard cups.
2. Cook 2/3 cup sugar and water in a heavy saucepan over low heat, swirling pan occasionally, until sugar dissolves. Increase heat and boil without stirring until syrup turns a golden color. Quickly spoon the caramel evenly in the custard cups around the base of the cups. (Be careful, the caramel is very hot and can burn you.)
3. Gently whisk eggs, cream, and sugar in a mixing bowl; stir in pumpkin, cinnamon, nutmeg, cloves, and rum until blended.

ASSEMBLY
1. Select a deep baking pan just large enough to contain the six cups. Place cups in pan and fill with pumpkin mixture. Pour hot water in baking pan to about half way up the sides of the custard cups.
2. Bake in a preheated 350° oven for about 40 minutes or until custard is set.
3. Remove custard dishes carefully from hot water and cool completely; cover with plastic wrap.
4. Chill covered in refrigerator for a few hours or overnight
5. To serve, run a knife around custard. Take your serving plate and place on top of custard dish up side down and turn over. In a moment, the custard should drop and the caramel will flow around custard. Garnish with fresh berries and whipped cream.

═══════════════════════ROASTED MAPLE PEAR

Serve warm or at room temperature.
The combination of maple and fresh pears is wonderful.

Serves 6

6 firm-ripe Bosc pears with stems; cut a thin slice from bottom of
   pears to allow pears to stand upright
3 tablespoons butter
1 1/2 cups maple syrup
3 tablespoons sugar
1/4 cup Calvados, Apple Jack Brandy or Myers's rum
1 tablespoon lemon juice

ASSEMBLY

1. Butter with 1 tablespoon of the butter an ovenproof casserole
   large enough to contain the upright pears.
2. Put maple syrup in a mixing bowl, dip pears in syrup and
   coat completely. Sprinkle pears with sugar, coating completely, and
   place prepared pears upright in casserole dish.
3. Cut remaining butter in pieces and add to the remaining maple
   syrup. Stir in choice of liquor and lemon juice, and spoon around
   pears in casserole.
4. Bake in a preheated 350° oven, uncovered, and in the middle
   of the oven; bake for about 30 minutes or until tender when pierced
   with a knife.
5. Remove pears from oven carefully; the syrup will be hot.
   Remove pears from casserole with a slotted spoon or
   spatula to individual serving plates. Spoon some remaining
   sauce evenly around pears. Garnish with whipped cream.

Serve with a spoon, knife, and fork. Great with butter cookies.
When eating the pear remember the core is still inside the pear.

"I never eat when I can dine."
Maurice Chevalier

========SAUTÉED APPLES WITH APPLE JACK

Apples can be cooked just before dinner. Store at room temperature.

Serves 4

2 tablespoons butter
2 teaspoons brown sugar
1/2 teaspoon cinnamon
4 tart baking apples, peeled, cored, and sliced
1/4 cup seedless white raisins
1/4 cup pecan or walnut pieces
2 tablespoons Applejack or Calvados
1 pound cake
Vanilla ice cream or frozen vanilla yogurt

ASSEMBLY
1. Melt butter, brown sugar, and cinnamon in a skillet; cook until brown sugar bubbles. Stir in apples, raisins, and pecan pieces, and cook while stirring until apples are tender, about 10 minutes. Stir in Applejack and cook a couple of minutes. If you wish you can flame the apples. (Be careful when doing this.)
2. Slice pound cake and place on individual dessert dishes. (Instead of pound cake, biscuits or cooked patty shells can be a change.)
3. Spoon apples and sauce evenly on each slice of pound cake, top apples with a scoop of vanilla ice cream, and garnish with fresh mint.

Pound cake and Pepperidge Farm patty shells are available in any grocery store. Cooking instructions for the patty shells are on the package; shells can be cooked ahead and stored in a dry place.

Helpful Hint
Cleaning agents can leave a thin film on mirrors and pictures that have glass. In restaurants today smoking is not as much a problem as it was a few years ago. We had such a time to keep all the glass clean. We cleaned them with cleaning agents then took a cloth dampened with alcohol and finished the job. The glass was without streaks and bright.

================ *STRAWBERRIES ROMANOFF*

This dessert is at its best during summer strawberry season. It can be prepared ahead and stored in the refrigerator until ready to serve.

Serves 4

1 quart fresh ripe strawberries (set aside 4 perfect strawberries for
   garnish)
1/3 cup Grand Marnier or Cointreau
1 tablespoon grated orange peel (zest)
1 cup heavy cream
2 teaspoons powdered sugar
8 macaroon cookies

PREPARATION
1. Remove stems from strawberries, rinse well, and drain. Place on
   paper towels to dry.
2. Quarter strawberries and place them in a mixing bowl; stir in
   Grand Marnier, and orange peel; allow to seep (soak) for 1/2 hour.
3. Break up macaroon cookies into small pieces.
4. Whip cream and powered sugar until cream holds soft peaks;
    keep in refrigerator until ready to use.

ASSEMBLY
1. Stir whipped cream and macaroon cookies into strawberries,
   mixing carefully as to not crush the strawberries.
2. Spoon strawberry mixture into four dessert dishes, fan each
   saved strawberry and place on top of strawberries.

Macaroon cookies are made with ground almonds, sugar, and egg whites. Coconut, orange peel, or maraschino cherries can flavor the macaroons.

"A synonym is a word you use when you can't spell the other one."
Baltasar Gracian

========THREE VARIATIONS OF INDIVIDUAL FRUIT GALETTES

This is a wonderful way to serve a special fresh fruit dessert.

PINEAPPLE AND ALMOND PASTE GALETTES

Serves 6

1/2 cup almond paste (available in most supermarkets)
4 tablespoons softened butter
1/4 cup sugar
1 1/2 tablespoons dark rum
1 egg, room temperature
1 ripe pineapple, peeled and cored, cut in four
1 package Pepperidge Farm puff pastry sheets, thawed,
  each sheet cut in three at the seams
2 teaspoons sugar
Whipped cream or ice cream for garnish

PREPARATION
1. Thoroughly mix almond paste, butter and sugar in a mixing bowl;
   stir in rum and egg and mix into a smooth paste.
2. Slice pineapple quarters into 1/2-inch slices. Set aside.
3. Select an insulated cookie sheet and top with a piece of parchment
   paper. (Or butter and flour the cookie sheet.) Place each puff pastry
   rectangle on parchment paper. Fold edges of puff pastry about 1/8 inch
   to make a border on each side (like a little wall). Keep in refrigerator
   until ready to assemble.

ASSEMBLY
1. Into each puff pastry rectangle, spoon the almond paste, being careful
   to keep the paste inside the border. Top almond paste with pineapple
   slices in a row (to look neat), sprinkle pineapple with sugar.
2. Bake in a preheated 375° oven for about 20 minutes.
   Allow galettes to cool. Use a spatula to remove each galette to a
   serving plate, and garnish with whipped cream or vanilla ice cream

Variations of individual fruit galettes continued-

PEACH GALETTES

1/3 cup crushed Amaretti or almond biscotti
   (use a food processor)
3 ripe peaches, skin removed, quartered, pit removed, cut into
   1/4-inch slices.
1 package Pepperidge Farm puff pastry sheets, thawed,
   each sheet cut in three at the seams
1 tablespoon butter
2 tablespoons sugar
Whipped cream or vanilla ice cream for garnish

PREPARATION
1. Select an insulated cookie sheet, and top with a piece of parchment
   paper or (butter and flour cookie sheet). Place each puff pastry rectangle
   on parchment paper. Fold edges of puff pastry about 1/8 inch to make
   a border on each side (like a little wall). Store in refrigerator until
   ready to use.

ASSEMBLY
1. On each puff pastry rectangle, sprinkle the crushed Amaretti over
   the dough evenly inside the border.
2. Spread sliced peaches evenly inside the border, dot with butter
   and sprinkle with sugar.
3. Bake in a preheated 375° oven for 20 minutes.
   Allow galette to cool. Use a spatula to remove galette to a serving
   plate, and garnish with whipped cream or vanilla ice cream.
       Fresh plums are also great in this dish.

> *"The beginning is the most important part of the work."*
> *Plato*

Variations of individual fruit galettes continued-

APPLE GALETTES

3 Granny Smith apples, peeled, cored and diced (any baking apples)
1/2 cup seedless white raisins
1/2 cup chopped pecans
2 teaspoons ground cinnamon
1/4 cup brown sugar
2 tablespoons softened butter
1 tablespoon all-purpose flour
1 package Pepperidge Farm puff pastry sheets, thawed,
   each sheet cut in three at the seams
Whipped or vanilla ice cream

PREPARATION
1. Thoroughly mix diced apples, raisins, pecans, cinnamon,
   brown sugar, softened butter and flour in mixing bowl.
2. Select an insulated cookie sheet and top with a piece of parchment
   paper (or butter and flour a cookie sheet). Place each puff pastry
   rectangle on parchment paper.
   Fold edges of puff pastry about 1/8 inch to make a border on
   each side (like a little wall).

ASSEMBLY
1. Spoon the apple mixture carefully inside of each rectangle.
2. Bake in a preheated 375° oven for 20 minutes.
   Allow galettes to cool. Use a spatula to remove galette to a
   serving plate, and garnish with whipped cream or vanilla ice cream.

Helpful Hint
*When you are chopping nuts in a blender or food processor,
add a little sugar and the nuts shouldn't stick together.*

"We're drowning in information and starving for knowledge."
Rutherford D. Rogers

══════════════════════════════WALNUT PEAR IN PASTRY

Walnuts are the fruit of the walnut tree, grown in temperate zones throughout the world; they are delicious in a variety of sweet and savory dishes and in baked goods. Walnuts also make fragrant, flavorful oils.

Serves 4
4 ripe pears, peeled, and cored from bottom, try to save stem
1 tablespoon brown sugar
1 tablespoon butter, softened
1/2 cup walnuts, chopped fine
1/4 teaspoon ground cinnamon
2 Pepperidge Farm patty shells, thawed, and cut in two
Flour for rolling pastry and dusting cookie sheet
1 egg beaten with 1 teaspoon milk in a small bowl
Chocolate sauce for garnish
Whipped cream for garnish

PREPARATION
1. Mix brown sugar, butter, walnuts and cinnamon in a mixing bowl.
2. On a floured board, roll thawed half puff pastry shells to about 5x5 round. Wrap in plastic wrap and store in refrigerator.

ASSEMBLY
1. Fill pear cavity with walnut mixture. Place rolled puff pastry on a flat surface. Place stuffed pear in center of each pastry roll; wet the inside of pastry with a little egg wash, and wrap around pear all the way to the stem.
2. Spread egg wash on crust with fingers or a pastry brush; place on a cookie sheet covered with a parchment sheet. (If you do not have parchment, butter and flour the sheet.)
3. Bake in the middle rack in a preheated 400° oven for 25 minutes or until pastry is golden.
4. Remove pear from cookie sheet to individual serving plates with a spatula; garnish with chocolate sauce and whipped cream. Serve with a knife and fork.

"A conclusion is the place where you got tired of thinking."
Arthur McBride Block
"I finally finished writing the last recipe in this cookbook."
Author Normand J. Leclair

Every morning I have the pleasure of visiting a 98-year-old lady to make sure she is ok. We have coffee, read the newspaper, and talk. I have heard many stories about her life, career, and adventures. I could write a book on the stories I have listened to in the last few years. She taught school for many years and retired to help her son in his restaurant.

This is one of the stories she told me one morning.

Her son hosted a retirement party for her in his restaurant, when she retired from teaching. The party was a surprise, and without her knowing it the school administration had arranged a special phone call for her that evening. During the evening, she was told that she had a phone call. She answered the phone and the person on the other end said. "Hello Mrs. Greene, this is the president of the United States, and I want to wish you a great retirement!" (Mrs. Greene was a very popular as a teacher and was very active with 4-H.) Mrs. Greene replied to the president, "Yes, and I am Herbert Hoover" and hung up on him. She was told that she had hung up on the president. They tried to call the White House to apologize to the president but could not reach him.

ORDER FORM

TO ORDER EXTRA COPIES OF <u>CULINARY EXPRESSIONS</u>

To order on line:

Web Address: www.culinaryexpressionscookbook.com

Pay with a credit card thru PayPal

(A secure credit card payment site)

Price is $19.50 which includes postage and handling. Include your name and address.

To order by check:

Send a check to CULINARY EXPRESSIONS for $19.50 which includes postage and handling to:

Normand J. Leclair
Box 309
West Kingston, RI 02892

NAME_____

STREET_____

CITY_____STATE_____ZIP_____

If you wish to E-Mail me with any questions or suggestion:
NJL144@aol.com

Thank you,
Normand J. Leclair

INDEX

Index Continued-

Index Continued-

Chicken Breast Baked with Toppings Continued-

Chicken Baked with Toppings Continued-

======*CHICKEN BREAST BAKED WITH SAUCE, 158*
All recipes are for two in this chapter.

Chicken Baked with Sauce and Toppings Continued-

=== *ROLLED BAKED CHICKEN BREAST,* **217**
All recipes are for two in this chapter.

Index Continued-

Index Continued-

Index Continued-